ISHAI SAGI

SharePoint® 2013

HOW-TO

SAMS | 800 East 96th Street, Indianapolis, Indiana 46240 USA

SharePoint 2013 How-To

ISBN-13: 978-0-672-33447-4

ISBN-10: 0-672-33447-4

Library of Congress Cataloging-in-Publication Data: 2013937709

Printed in the United States of America

First Printing May 2013

Trademarks

Warning and Disclaimer

Bulk Sales

Sams Publishing offers excellent discounts on this book when ordered in quantity for bulk purchases or special sales. For more information, please contact

U.S. Corporate and Government Sales

1-800-382-3419

corpsales@pearsontechgroup.com

For sales outside of the U.S., please contact

International Sales

international@pearsoned.com

Editor-in-Chief

Greg Wiegand

Executive Editor

Neil Rowe

Development Editor

Mark Renfrow

Managing Editor

Sandra Schroeder

Project Editor

Seth Kerney

Copy Editor

Paula Lowell

Indexer

Lisa Stumpf

Proofreader

Kathy Ruiz

Technical Editor

J. Boyd Nolan

Publishing Coordinator

Cindy Teeters

Book Designer

Mark Shirar

Compositor

Jake McFarland

Contents at a Glance

Table of Contents

About the Author

Ishai Sagi is a Microsoft SharePoint expert who has been working on Microsoft SharePoint products since its initial release in 2001. Since then, Ishai has trained numerous end users, administrators, and developers in using Microsoft SharePoint and in developing solutions on the platform. Ishai is a regular speaker and an "ask the experts" panelist at Microsoft conferences around the world, including the United States, Australia, Europe, and Israel. Ishai is managing a SharePoint user group in Canberra, Australia—speaking about Microsoft SharePoint in free, open-to-the-public events every month. For his effort and contribution to the Microsoft SharePoint community, Ishai has received the Microsoft Most Valuable Professional award (MVP) in 2007 through 2013.

Ishai owns his own company, Extelligent Design (www.ExtelligentDesign.com), which is based in Australia and provides training, consulting, and custom development and sells products and solutions for Microsoft SharePoint. He is also the author of a SharePoint blog aimed at developers who want to develop code solutions for Microsoft SharePoint at www.sharepoint-tips.com.

Acknowledgments

Thanks as always goes first to Anja as well as to Chickpea and Sesame (who posed for the pictures in this book).

A very big thank you goes to the editors of this book: Neil Rowe, Mark Renfrow, Seth Kerney, and Paula Lowell, as they were so helpful and this book would have been very different if it weren't for their guiding hands and helpful comments. Thanks as well go to So Young Lee from Microsoft for her assistance in obtaining clarifications, and to the SharePoint team, who tried to help as much as they could–all much appreciated.

We Want to Hear from You!

As the reader of this book, you are our most important critic and commentator. We value your opinion and want to know what we're doing right, what we could do better, what areas you'd like to see us publish in, and any other words of wisdom you're willing to pass our way.

You can email or write us directly to let us know what you did or didn't like about this book—as well as what we can do to make our books stronger.

Please note that we cannot help you with technical problems related to the topic of this book.

When you write, please be sure to include this book's title and author as well as your name and phone or email address. We will carefully review your comments and share them with the author and editors who worked on the book.

Email: consumer@samspublishing.com

Mail: Sams Publishing
            ATTN: Reader Feedback
            800 East 96th Street
            Indianapolis, IN 46240 USA

Reader Services

Visit our website and register this book at informit.com/register for convenient access to any updates, downloads, or errata that might be available for this book.

Introduction

Overview of This Book

This book aims to be your companion as you learn how to use Microsoft SharePoint 2013. It lists common tasks that you are most likely to need to do when you use SharePoint as a working tool and shows how to accomplish these tasks in an easy, step-by-step manner.

This book is written for people who are unfamiliar with, or are unsure how to approach tasks in Microsoft SharePoint 2013. It also covers advanced tasks such as managing sites and security, editing and authoring pages, and using some of the more complex functionality available in Microsoft SharePoint 2013. However, this book is not intended to be an administration guide, a developer's handbook, or a complete and comprehensive user guide to everything you can do with Microsoft SharePoint. The end result of such a book would be a heavy, intimidating volume that might be harder to read through and learn from. Instead, this book focuses on assisting you with the basic tasks, covering the essentials and making sure you know where to go to do the most common day-to-day tasks that you encounter as a Microsoft SharePoint 2013 end user. Hopefully, this book will give you enough insight into the workings of SharePoint that you can continue learning more about the options and features available in SharePoint.

This book is written with the firm belief that to learn, you must do. You can use this book as a reference tool for finding out how to perform a certain task, or use it as a learning guide (if you have an environment) and perform the tasks outlined in this book one by one. Whatever method you chose, it is our hope that this book will be a helpful companion.

How to Benefit from This Book

This book is designed to be easy to read from cover to cover. It is divided into five parts to make looking up problems easier.

Part I, "Solutions for Readers," includes the most common and basic tasks that do not involve changing anything in SharePoint, but just viewing, browsing, and finding information. This part includes the following chapters:

- ▶ Chapter 1, "About Microsoft SharePoint 2013"
- ▶ Chapter 2, "Finding Your Way Around a SharePoint Site"
- ▶ Chapter 3, "Solutions Regarding Files, Documents, List Items, and Forms"
- ▶ Chapter 4, "Searching in SharePoint"
- ▶ Chapter 5, "Social Networking, Personal Sites, and Personal Details in SharePoint Server"

Part II, "Solutions for Authors and Content Managers," teaches you how to perform tasks that involve adding content to SharePoint or changing the way it looks. This part includes the following chapters:

- ▶ Chapter 6, "Creating and Managing Files, List Items, and Forms in SharePoint"
- ▶ Chapter 7, "Creating Lists and Document Libraries"
- ▶ Chapter 8, "Creating List Views"
- ▶ Chapter 9, "Authoring Pages"
- ▶ Chapter 10, "Managing Security"
- ▶ Chapter 11, "Workflows"

Part III, "Solutions for Site Managers," introduces advanced tasks involved in creating and customizing SharePoint sites. This part includes the following chapters:

- ▶ Chapter 12, "Creating Subsites"
- ▶ Chapter 13, "Customizing a SharePoint Site"
- ▶ Chapter 14, "Managing Site Security"

Part IV, "Solutions for Office365 Administrators," includes special tasks for Office 365 SharePoint environment and will guide you in creating an internet site or an intranet one on that platform. This part includes the following chapter:

- ▶ Chapter 15, "Managing an Office 365 SharePoint Site"

Finally, Part V, "Appendixes," provides shortcuts and links to help you find your way and achieve some tasks more quickly.

Ways to Continue Expanding Your Knowledge

This book does not claim to cover all that you can do with SharePoint. If you find yourself in need of more information, check out the built-in help system available in SharePoint itself. Almost every page in SharePoint has a help button that will open the help screen, enabling you to search for the topic you want help on. Additionally, you can find SharePoint manuals, training videos, and help articles from Microsoft on the Microsoft help site at http://tinyurl.com/SP2013Help.

If you cannot find what you want in the aforementioned site and help pages, plenty more help is available on the Internet from the SharePoint community, both in blogs and discussion forums. To find solutions to issues, try searching the Internet (using your search engine of choice). Many blogs and websites have information on how to achieve tasks in SharePoint.

If you have a question that you cannot find the answer for, try posting it on the Microsoft forums that are dedicated to such problems. You can find these forums at http://tinyurl.com/SP2013Forum.

Finally, if you need professional help, the author of this book can recommend trainers and consultants through his company at www.extelligentdesign.com.

CHAPTER 1

About Microsoft SharePoint 2013

IN THIS CHAPTER

What Is Microsoft SharePoint 2013?

SharePoint is a Microsoft platform that allows people to build websites. SharePoint 2013 is the fifth version of SharePoint from Microsoft, and it is also known as SharePoint 15 or Microsoft SharePoint Server 2013. It is very different from the versions that came before it.

SharePoint allows people to create websites with various types of content and for various types of purposes. Its many built-in features and components make it a comprehensive solution that can fit many needs.

One common use of SharePoint in organizations is to create sites that are used for team collaboration, as shown in Figure 1.1. These collaborative sites, also known as *team sites* or *group worksites*, enable team members to better work with one another. They can use the site to share documents, assign tasks, track team events on a shared web calendar, and much more. This use is known as a *team collaboration system*.

Many companies use SharePoint for their central document storage, replacing network folders. This use is known as an *electronic document management system*.

Another common use is as a corporate portal where the corporate employees can download forms, read corporate news, fill in surveys, and search for documents. This use is known as an *electronic content management system*, or an *intranet*. An example of how such a site would look like is shown in Figure 1.2.

Finally, some companies choose the SharePoint platform as the platform for their Internet site—where visitors from around the world can visit the company's website and read about its products, register for events, and do whatever it is the site has been configured to allow them to do. This use is known as a *web content management system*.

This variety of possible uses of SharePoint indicates the flexibility of the SharePoint platform. It is highly customizable—which means that one SharePoint site can look entirely different from another SharePoint site. This book shows mostly basic SharePoint sites (sites that have not been customized), and the sites that you will be using might look significantly different. Keeping that in mind is important when following the instructions in this book, because some of the things mentioned in this book and shown in the figures might differ from site to site.

The SharePoint platform is also known as SharePoint Foundation. This book uses *SPF* when referring to a SharePoint site that is built based on this platform.

The SharePoint product family has other products that can be added on top of SPF to enhance the sites in different ways. One of these products is called SharePoint Server, and even that has two versions—standard and enterprise—each adding more features. Often the term *SharePoint* is used to refer to either SPF or to the two extended versions of SharePoint Server—and this can be a bit confusing.

Because the SharePoint Server products are extensions of SPF, sites built using those products have all the capabilities of SPF sites, but with extra features. The following section explains some of the differences between SharePoint Server and SPF.

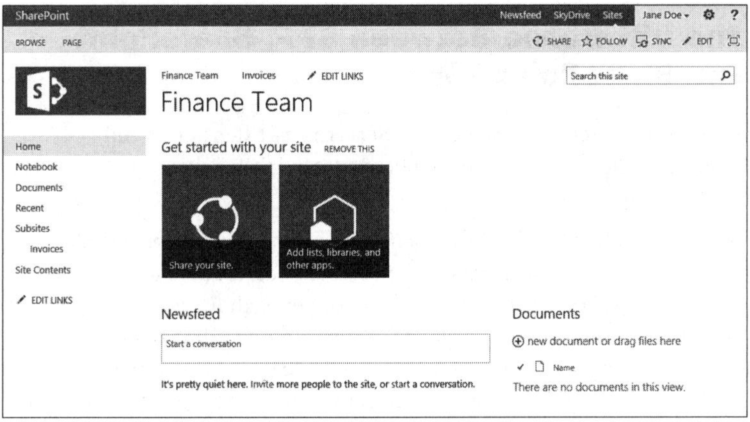

FIGURE 1.1　A standard SharePoint Team site.

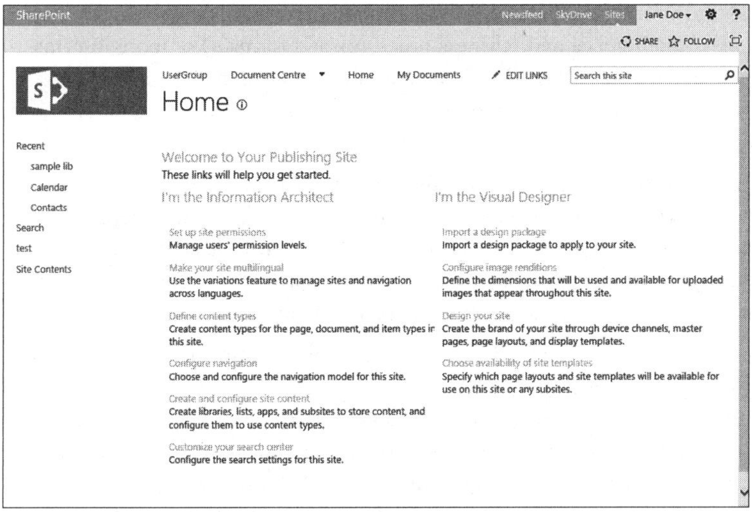

FIGURE 1.2　A customized SharePoint site, fit for an intranet.

SharePoint sites have many built-in features that make them useful, flexible, and customizable—such as security management, lists of information, document libraries (places to store and manage files and documents), views, alerts, and searches. This chapter covers all these and more.

Another member in the SharePoint family is the SharePoint offering that is part of the Microsoft service called "Office 365," referred to as SharePoint 365 in this book. This SharePoint option is available by registering with the Microsoft service, and it provides all the features of SPF along with some additional, optional features on some of the plans.

What Is the Difference Between SPF, SharePoint Server, and SharePoint 365?

As mentioned earlier in this chapter, SharePoint Server is an extension of SPF. SharePoint Server sites have features that are not available in SPF sites, and they enjoy all the features of SPF sites.

SPF sites work well for collaboration sites. Such a site gives groups of people the ability to upload and download documents, use discussion boards, assign tasks, share events, and use workflows. However, SPF does not have enough features to be a good platform for a corporate portal or for a corporate search solution. SharePoint Server offers extra features that upgrade SPF into a platform that can serve a corporation with enterprise searching (searching from one location across all the sites that that corporate has, and on documents and external systems that are stored in other locations, not just in SharePoint). It also has features for storing details about people and searching on them, and it enables employees to have their own personal sites where they can store documents (instead of on their machines). SharePoint Server has many more features related to business intelligence and business processes and forms. (For more information about personal sites, see "What Is a Personal Site?" later in this chapter and see Chapter 5, "Social Networking, Personal Sites, and Personal Details in SharePoint Server.")

Finally, SharePoint Server has a publishing feature that enables site managers to create publishing sites where they can easily author pages (as opposed to documents) and publish them using workflows. This is very important for large corporations that want to, for example, publish corporate news using an approval workflow or build an Internet site where every page must go through a special approval process.

SharePoint 365 is also based on SPF, but it offers optional features in addition, depending on the Office 365 plan you purchased. In some ways, these additional features, when added, increase the functionality of the SharePoint 365 site to be similar to the functionality of a SharePoint server site. This book does not detail the exact features offered in each plan, because those might change. This book treats SharePoint 365 as having the same features as SPF, except in Chapter 15, "Managing an Office 365 SharePoint Site," which details tasks that are unique to SharePoint 365.

How to Tell Whether a Site Is Based on SPF, SharePoint Server, or SharePoint on Office 365

You can't tell just by looking whether a site is hosted on a server that has SharePoint Server installed. Customizations that a company might have developed can cause an SPF site to look as if it has some extensions that come with SharePoint Server. On the other hand, customizations can cause a SharePoint Server site to look simpler; for example, it might remove the SharePoint Server–specific links that help identify a site as a SharePoint Server site.

However, you can look for one thing in most SharePoint sites to determine with a fair degree of certainty whether a site is SharePoint Server or SPF: You can look for the Newsfeed link under the Name dropdown at the top of the screen (see Figure 1.3). If you see that link, you are viewing a site that is running on a server with SharePoint Server, or an Office 365 site that has that feature. Not having the link does not necessarily mean that the site does not have SharePoint Server, however, because the administrator can choose to disable that functionality.

FIGURE 1.3   The Newsfeed link under the Name dropdown signifies that you are on a SharePoint Server or SharePoint in Office 365 site.

Additional differences between the two versions will become clear as you go through this book. Many topics in this book indicate that they are valid only in SharePoint Server, and you can always find whether they are available by trying to perform the task described.

A similar approach can help determine what features are available on your SharePoint 365 site. When a feature described in this book is missing, the most probable cause is that the feature is a part of a more advanced Office 365 plan, and you must upgrade your plan in order to use that feature. However, sometimes features that you should be able to use are not available for other reasons, so contacting your local Office 365 support or a Microsoft Office 365 Expert partner is always a good idea. One way to tell whether you are on an Office 365 site, though, is that it should say Office 365 on the top-left corner of the page (instead of SharePoint; refer to Figure 1.3). However, this is another area where the site's designer might have removed that text altogether, so not seeing it does not mean that you are not in an Office 365 environment.

What Is a Site?

The structure of SharePoint sites (sometimes referred to as *webs*) is very different from the structure of typical Internet sites that contain only pages. In SharePoint, a site can house more than just pages. It is a container that holds lists and libraries (discussed later in this chapter), and it can have other sites under it.

For example, a corporate portal might have a home site called SharePoint Intranet that contains information that people see when they browse to that site. That portal might also have a subsite called Human Resources that stores forms such as travel requests, expense claims, and other forms. The two sites are linked because the Human Resources site is under the SharePoint Intranet site. The two sites might share some attributes such as security (who is allowed to do what in the sites) and navigation (so that visitors to the sites can navigate between the sites), but they have separate content—for example, different pages, libraries, and lists. Figures 1.4 and 1.5 show examples of a site with subsites, and a site that is a subsite.

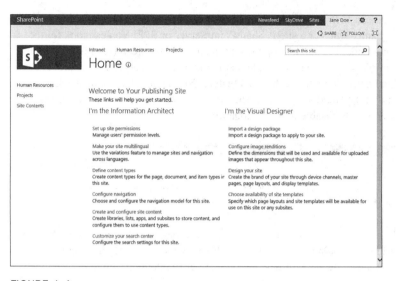

FIGURE 1.4 A site that has subsites. Human Resources and Projects are subsites of the SharePoint Intranet site.

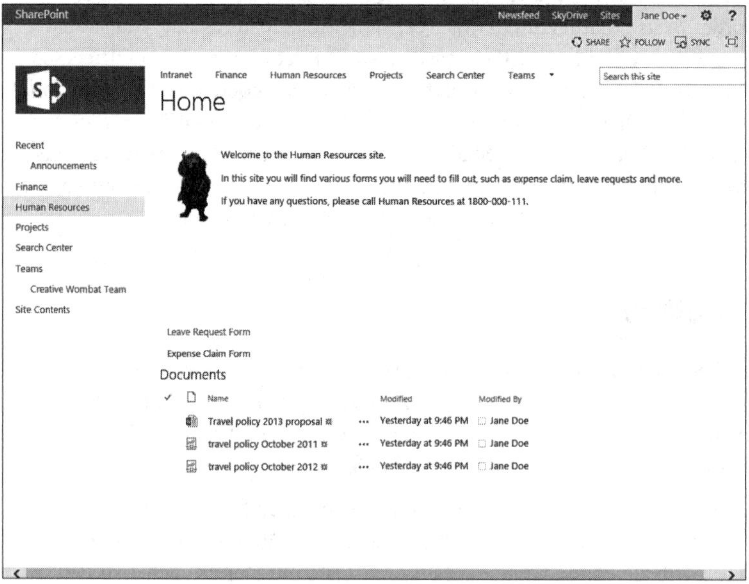

FIGURE 1.5 A site that is a subsite. The Human Resources site is under the SharePoint Intranet site.

Every SharePoint site is a member of a site collection. A site collection is, as the name implies, a collection of sites. Every site collection has a single site as its root site, and other sites can be built under the root site. A site collection has some attributes that are common to all the sites in that collection (for example, some search settings and a Recycle Bin for deleted items).

What Is a Personal Site?

A personal site is one that belongs to a specific user and is used to show user information that belongs, personally, to that user. The user can upload documents to a personal document library in the personal site, and only that user can see and manage these documents. This document library is easily accessible to the user using the SkyDrive link at the top of all SharePoint pages.

The personal site is also a place where users can manage their personal favorite items and comments that they have tagged throughout SharePoint or even outside SharePoint (see "What Is Tagging?" later in this chapter). The personal site has special pages with information that might be important to track. A user can track information by using newsfeeds that tell what colleagues are up to. In addition, users can run searches and stay up to date on those subjects. In addition, the personal site is usually the place from which users can modify their personal details in the corporate directory. An example of a basic personal site is shown in Figure 1.6.

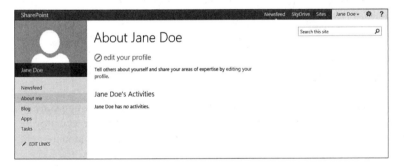

FIGURE 1.6   A personal site, showing the owner's information and links to the site's content.

A personal site usually has components that display information targeted specifically to that user. For example, it might have components that show the user's email, upcoming meetings from the person's calendar, a list of documents the user has recently worked on, and tasks assigned to the user.

NOTE   As mentioned earlier, personal sites are available only with SharePoint Server and some SharePoint 365 plans, but not with SPF.

For more in-depth information about the personal site and what you can do in it, see Chapter 5.

What Are SkyDrive and SkyDrive Pro?

With SharePoint 2013, Microsoft introduced a concept called *SkyDrive* into the SharePoint product, in addition to the Microsoft SkyDrive product that is available outside of SharePoint. As part of this concept, a SkyDrive link might appear on SharePoint pages' navigation, and when clicked, the user is by default redirected to the document library of the user's personal site. This document library serves as the user's personal, corporate SkyDrive (instead of being hosted by Microsoft, which is the original SkyDrive product). This library is also known as *SkyDrive Pro* (the two terms can get mixed up, where in some pages they are referred to as *SkyDrive*, and in some *SkyDrive Pro*).

The two terms also refer to client applications (installed on your computer)—one a free download from Microsoft called SkyDrive that is meant to synchronize your computer with your Microsoft SkyDrive (not SharePoint), and the other, SkyDrive Pro 2013, which comes as part of Microsoft Office 2013 and allows you to synchronize specific SharePoint document libraries and folders between SharePoint and your computer. This way, you can save a document to a specific folder on your computer, and it will be automatically uploaded to a specific folder in SharePoint, and vice versa.

For more in-depth information on how to synchronize a folder or a library with a folder on your computer, see Chapter 6, "Creating, Adding, and Editing Files, List Items, and Forms."

What Is a Ribbon?

As part of the Microsoft Office product family, SharePoint 2013 uses a design concept called a *ribbon* to display different menus and buttons, depending on what you are looking at. Knowing how to use the ribbon is important so you can move around in a site and perform actions in it.

This book covers many different actions available in different ribbons. Part II, "Solutions for Authors and Content Managers," explains how to author content, and Part III, "Solutions for Site Managers," explains how to manage websites. Although these tasks use the ribbon heavily, it is also important for readers who do not need to author information to be familiar with the ribbon concept to avoid getting lost. As you will see in Chapter 2, "Finding Your Way Around a SharePoint Site," and Chapter 3, "Solutions Regarding Files, Documents, List Items, and Forms," you use the ribbon to perform many types of navigational actions on documents and list items.

What Are Apps?

Apps are a new concept in SharePoint 2013. This all-encompassing term covers anything from site templates (different types of sites), list templates (different types of lists—for example, the Calendar list type is known as a Calendar app), web parts (see what is a web part later in this chapter), and custom solutions that developers can develop and deploy to a site. You can purchase apps and install them in your site, or you can just use the ones that came out of the box with SharePoint. Although this book sometimes refers to specific apps by different names (for example, Chapter 9, "Authoring Pages," refers to web parts as web parts instead of apps), the name *app* is appropriate to most kinds of templates or developer customizations.

What Is a List?

A SharePoint list is a container for information, similar to a simple database or spreadsheet. Using a list is the most common way to manage information in a SharePoint site.

In a list, data is gathered in rows, and each row is known as a *list item*. A list can have multiple columns—also known as *properties*, *fields*, or *metadata*. So a list item is a row with data in those columns.

For example, a list of contacts (as shown in Figure 1.7) may have the following columns:

- First Name
- Last Name
- Company
- Phone

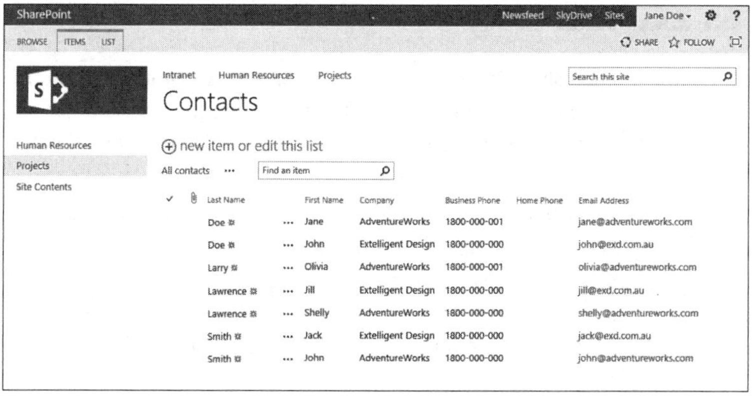

FIGURE 1.7   A contacts list, with sample data.

These columns may have the following list items:

- First Name: John
- Last Name: Doe
- Company: Extelligent Design
- Phone: 1800-000-000

Lists can be used in many cases. For example, you might use lists for links, tasks, discussions, announcements, or events. In SharePoint, users can create lists and columns. Lists can be used for almost anything that can be described by a group of columns.

The information in lists can be displayed on pages in a SharePoint site. For example, if the site manager wants to display a list of links on the site, that manager can add a web part (see "What Are Web Parts?" later in this chapter) that shows that list, as detailed in Chapter 9.

Different lists can have different security settings. List managers can define, for example, who is allowed to add items to a list, who is allowed to edit items, who is allowed to read the items, and so on. Similarly, each list item can have its own security settings, so different list items can be visible to different people. For example, an item that is a link to a restricted site can have security settings that prevent users who don't have access to that site from seeing it.

In some lists, you can attach files to list items—much like attachments in email. For example, in a contacts list, you could attach to each contact a picture and a resume, or in a list of tasks, you might attach documentation of what needs to be done to the task.

A list can hold different types of content, as explained later in this chapter, in the section "What Is a Content Type?"

For information on how to interact with lists, see Chapters 6 and 7, "Creating Lists and Document Libraries."

What Is an External List?

An external list is unlike other SharePoint lists. Strictly speaking, it is not a SharePoint list at all because it doesn't store information inside it. An external list is a view on external data—that is, data that is contained not within SharePoint but in external databases and systems.

When you add external lists to SharePoint sites, they are displayed in an interface that looks almost exactly like a regular SharePoint list. An external list also allows most of the same interactions with the items in the list that are offered with a regular SharePoint list. This book does not cover external lists, because they are an advanced feature of SharePoint 2013 that is created and configured by developers rather than used by end users.

What Is a Document Library?

A document library is a special instance of a list, in which every list item is a file. Files can be Microsoft Office documents, Adobe Acrobat documents (PDF files), or any other type of file that the system administrator allows. This book often refers to document libraries as simply *libraries*.

Most of the attributes of lists exist in document libraries. In fact, lists and documents libraries are similar in many ways. However, each item in a document library is a file, as shown in Figure 1.8. Therefore, when creating a new item in a document library, you need to either upload a file or create one. This process is explained in Chapter 6.

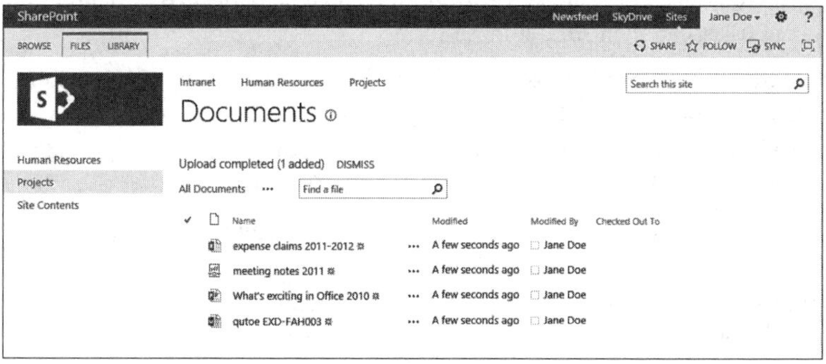

FIGURE 1.8   A sample document library with several types of documents.

Additionally, unlike in lists, in document libraries, each row can hold only one file. There isn't an option to attach more files to the row. Essentially, the file itself *is* the row.

Also, because a file can be downloaded, visitors to document libraries have different options available to them when browsing a document library than they have with lists.

Because document libraries and lists have so much in common, many instructions throughout this book apply to both. Where appropriate, the text makes clear that the instructions are for both. For example, the section "Add a Column to a List or Document Library" in Chapter 7 covers both document libraries and lists because the principle of how to create them is the same.

Several special document libraries templates are available in SharePoint. These templates are designed for specific types of content, but they are essentially document libraries. Some of these special cases are described later in this chapter.

What Is a Wiki Page Library?

A wiki page library is a special instance of a document library that is designed to store web pages that support the wiki syntax, allowing you to quickly create new pages or link to other pages in the library authoring the page. On those web pages, you can display different types of content—text, images, videos, and web parts. (For more information on web parts, see "What Are Web Parts?" later in this chapter.)

What Is a Form Library?

A form library is much like a document library, but it is supposed to host only Microsoft InfoPath forms. Microsoft InfoPath is electronic form-creation software that integrates with SharePoint. Forms created with InfoPath can be published to SharePoint form libraries, and users can then fill out these forms.

With SharePoint Server, you can load some InfoPath forms without having Microsoft InfoPath installed on your machine. In this case, the form opens in a browser, as a web form. If you have a program that can edit InfoPath forms, such as Microsoft InfoPath 2013 or Microsoft InfoPath Filler 2013, the form opens in that program.

If your company uses InfoPath for creating forms, you might want to learn how to read forms that are in form libraries, as explained in Chapter 3. You might also want to learn how to fill forms, as explained in Chapter 6. (This book does not cover creating Microsoft InfoPath forms.)

What Is an Asset Library?

An asset library is a special instance of a document library that is specially designed to store digital assets such as images, audio files, and videos.

This kind of library can be used as a repository for media files that will be used throughout the SharePoint environment—for example, corporate logos, training videos, and podcasts. Figure 1.9 shows an example of a site assets library with two images and a PowerPoint slide deck.

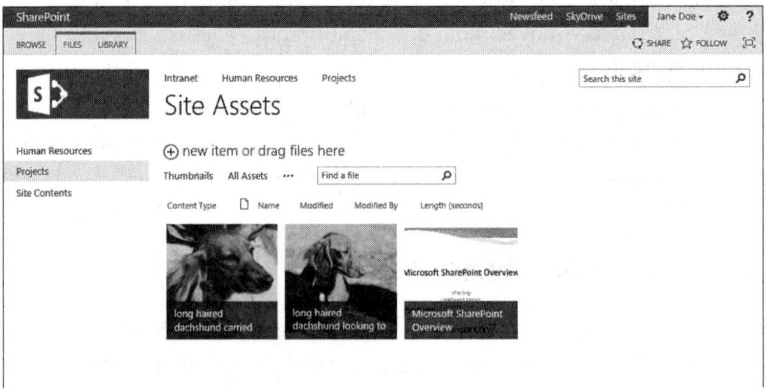

FIGURE 1.9   A sample asset library with a music file, a video file, and several stock photos to be added to pages in the site.

For more information on using the asset library as a repository for images and media files, see Chapter 9.

What Is a Picture Library?

A picture library is a special type of a document library that is dedicated to images. A picture library is useful for sharing photos with other people. For example, you can have a picture library as your stock photo repository, as shown in Figure 1.10. A picture library includes a special view that shows the images as thumbnails, as shown in Figure 1.10.

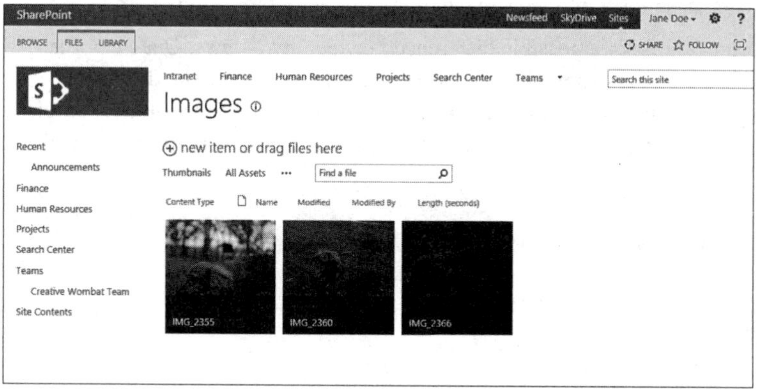

FIGURE 1.10 A picture library showing thumbnails of the pictures in it.

For more information about adding images to a picture library, see Chapter 6.

What Is a View?

Using views is a useful way for a list manager to create different ways to show the information in a list or library. Different views can show different columns and have different sorting and filtering, grouping, and styles.

In SharePoint, views can be either public or private:

- **Public**—The list's or library's managers create public views, and these views are available to anyone to use.

- **Private**—Users create private views. Only the user who created a private view can use that view. You may, for example, create a private view and customize it to show the information that you usually need to find the items or files that you usually work with.

Chapter 8, "Creating List Views," covers creating views in more details. Chapter 3 covers how to switch between views.

Several types of views are available in SharePoint. Most of the views that you will see are the standard tabular views that resemble printed worksheets—with column headers and values in rows, but no ability to edit the data directly. However, some special views styles show the information in the list in different ways. For example, the Datasheet view (also known as the Quick Edit view) allows directly editing the data, and a Calendar view shows items as part of a calendar.

A Calendar view shows the items in a list based on dates that are set on the items. Other views include the Gantt view and the Datasheet view. The Gantt view is similar to the Calendar view: It shows information based on dates in the list items' properties. The Datasheet view is a Microsoft Excel-like view that allows copying and pasting of data into the list or library, as well as editing multiple items using drag-and-drop. Chapter 8 covers these types of views in detail.

Let's look at an example of a possible difference between two views. One view for an announcement list might show the title of the announcement and the date that the announcement was changed (see Figure 1.11). A different view of the same list might show the body of the announcement and the date on which it will expire (see Figure 1.12).

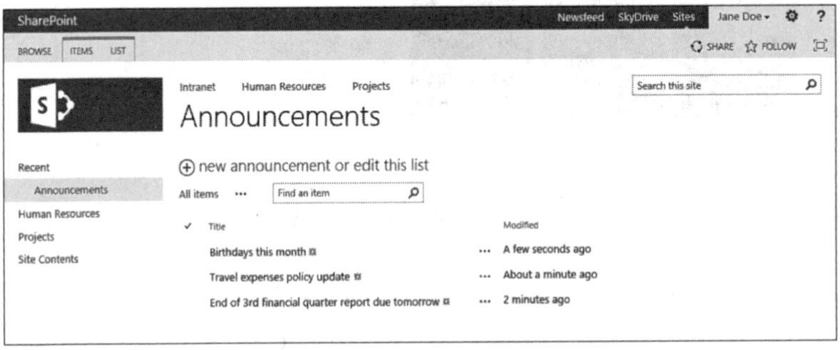

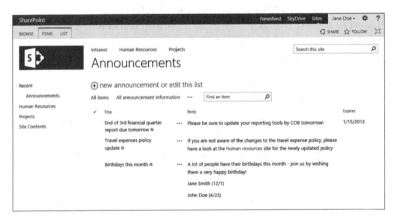

FIGURE 1.11 An announcement list in a view that shows the Title and Modified columns.

FIGURE 1.12 An announcement list in a view that shows the Title, Body, and Expires columns.

If you have multiple announcements, you can have different views sort the announcements in various ways. For example, one might sort by the title of the announcement, and the other might sort by the modification date. Figure 1.12 shows a view sorting the announcements by their creation date (with the one created first on top). Figure 1.13 shows a view that sorts on the title of the announcement.

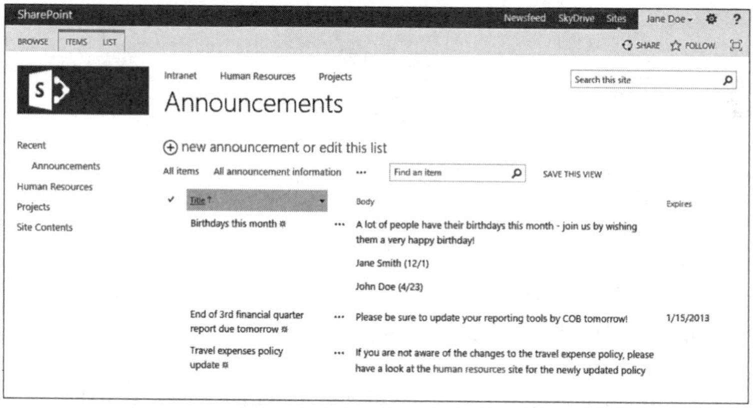

FIGURE 1.13   The announcement list in a view that sorts by the title.

Some views change the style in which the items are displayed. For example, Figure 1.14 shows the announcement list in boxed style.

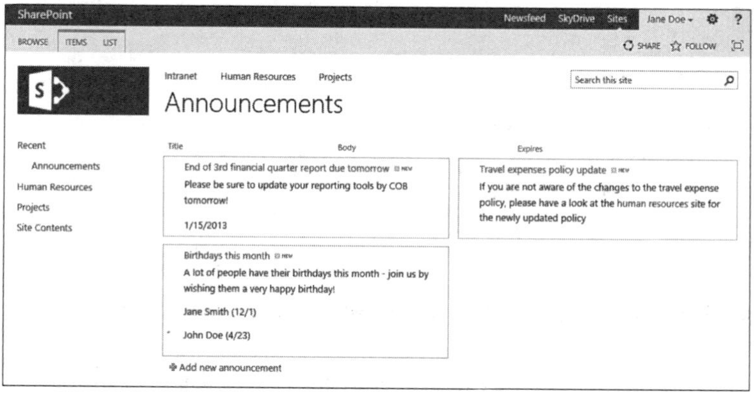

FIGURE 1.14   The announcement list shown with the boxed style.

An announcements list may have a filter applied to it to show only items that have not expired (refer to Figure 1.12). Other views can be configured not to have that filter. If you are viewing a list and the item you are looking for is not showing, consider the possibility that the current view is configured to filter that item.

Finally, some views might display the data grouped by one column. In such cases, you can view the groups and expand a group to see the items within the group. For example, in a contacts list, a view may be set up to group the contacts by their company name as shown in Figure 1.15. This way, you can expand the view for a specific company.

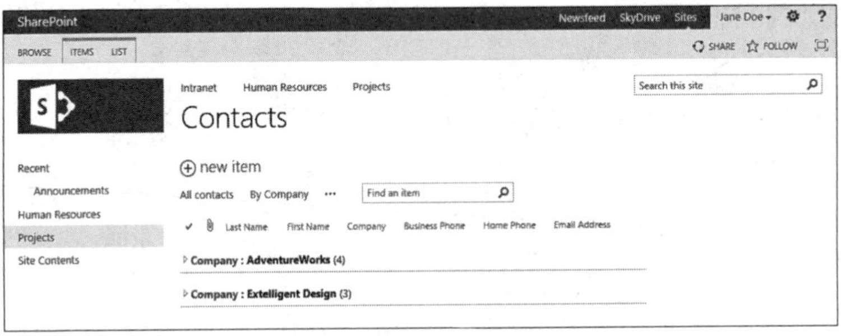

FIGURE 1.15   A contacts list, grouped by company.

To see the items in a group, you click the + sign next to the group name or on the group field's name that shows up as a link (in this example, the Company: link). The group expands, showing you the items that belong to that group (see Figure 1.16).

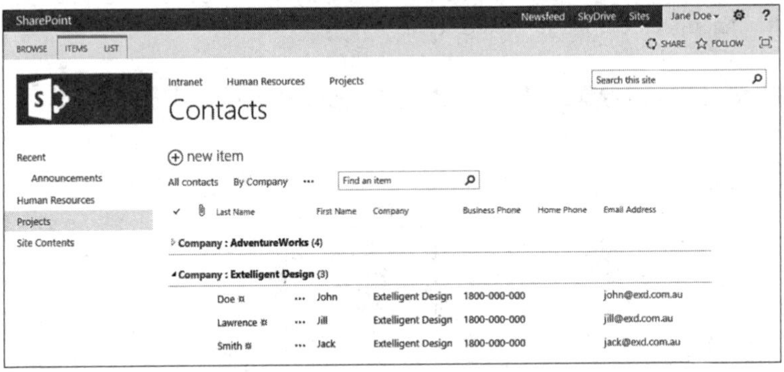

FIGURE 1.16   A contacts list, grouped by company, with Extelligent Design expanded.

SharePoint supports up to two grouping levels (for example, by country and then by company, as shown in Figure 1.17).

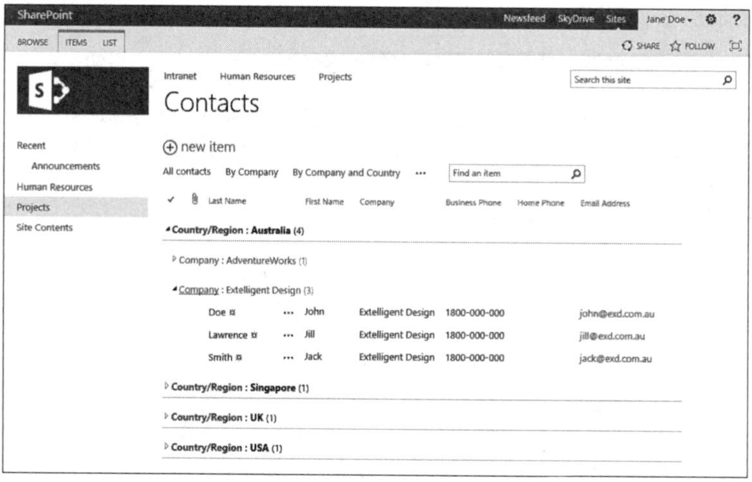

FIGURE 1.17   A contacts list, grouped by country and then by company, with Australia and Extelligent Design expanded.

As mentioned earlier, picture libraries have their own special views that show the pictures that are in the library as either thumbnails or filmstrips of the pictures.

Some views support paging. *Paging* is a common method in websites for showing large amounts of data without overloading the page. Using paging, the data in a list or library is split into pages, with each page showing only a certain number of the items. The user can navigate back and forth between the pages, using the paging buttons at the bottom of the page or the paging button in the Library ribbon or List ribbon (see Figures 1.18 and 1.19).

For example, say that you have a document library that contains 1,000 documents. Showing all the documents to the user at once might cause the page loading time to be quite slow, and a user might have difficulty finding a particular document. A more sensible approach would be to display the files in batches of 15 (for example), which makes it easier for the reader to see what information is available on the page. This is true even if you don't have thousands of documents! As your document library or list grows to have more and more files or rows, you will want to separate them into pages, as shown in Figures 1.18 and 1.19.

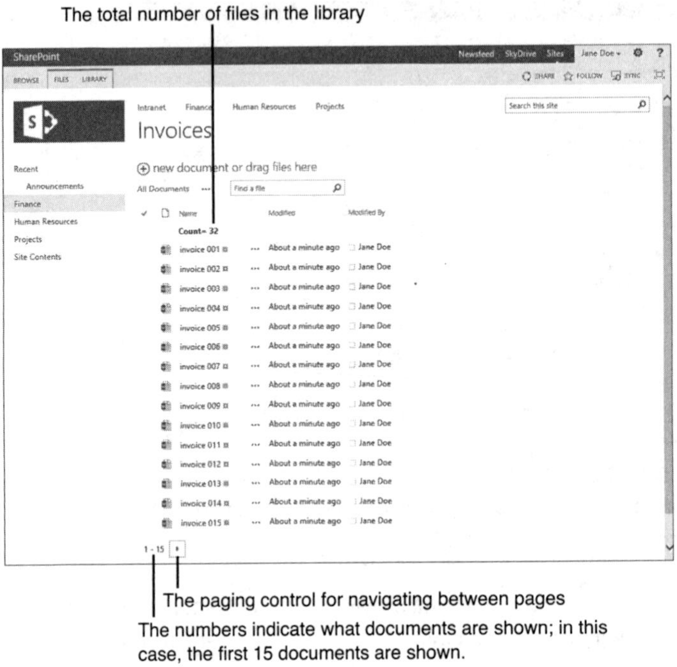

The total number of files in the library

FIGURE 1.18   The first page of a view of a document library with 32 documents, showing the first 15 documents.

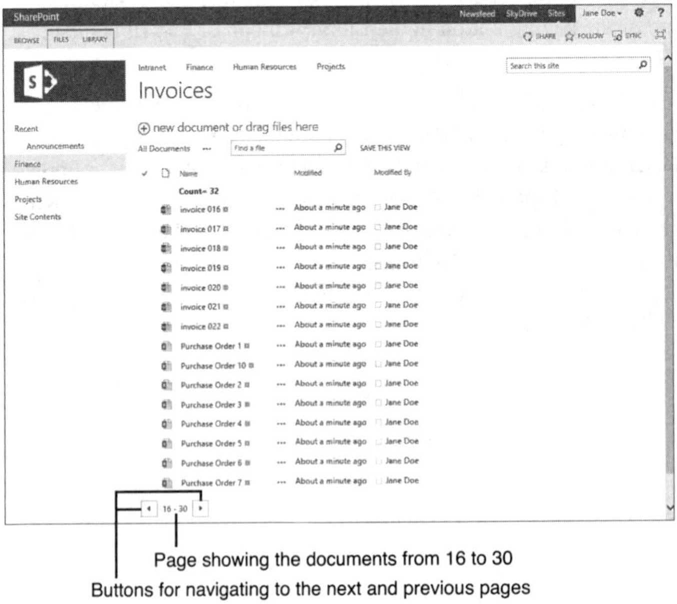

The paging control for navigating between pages

The numbers indicate what documents are shown; in this case, the first 15 documents are shown.

Page showing the documents from 16 to 30

Buttons for navigating to the next and previous pages

FIGURE 1.19   The second page of the view of the document library shows the next 15 documents.

Finally, advanced users can create custom views by using Microsoft SharePoint Designer. Custom views can look totally different from anything that is available for regular views. This book does not cover the use of SharePoint Designer.

What Are Web Parts?

Web parts are the building blocks of pages in SharePoint. They are components that show data, and they can be placed in certain regions of a page—known as web part zones, or as part of text in certain page editing controls. A page can hold many web parts, in different zones or in the same zone, or as part of a piece of text. They may be one under another in some zones and side by side in other zones, and text may flow around them or be separated by them.

For example, to show on the home page of a site the contents of a list of links, you can use a web part that displays the content of a list. Figure 1.20 is a web part that you have already seen in this chapter—it is the web part that shows views of lists and libraries.

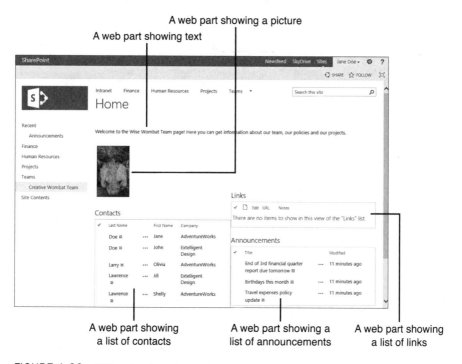

FIGURE 1.20   Different web parts on a page.

SharePoint developers can develop web parts, and the data and functionality that web parts offer to visitors of a SharePoint site is limited only by what develops can create. The following are some other examples of how web parts could be used:

▶ To show search results (see Figure 1.21)

▶ To show a picture

▶ To show the users of a site

▶ To show the content of a site

Although web parts are a part of SharePoint, they can show information that is from outside SharePoint. For example, a special web part may be developed to show information from a corporate application for timesheets or project management. The web part may even offer interaction with the data, allowing users to modify data in the corporate application. In this case, the data itself is not in SharePoint. However, such web parts usually have to be developed, and most of the web parts that come with SharePoint out of the box are used to display data that is stored in SharePoint.

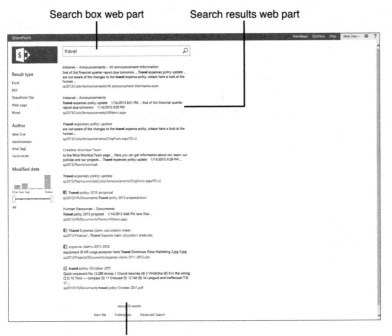

FIGURE 1.21   Search-related web parts.

Although web parts might be important building blocks for a SharePoint page, other components also make the pages what they are. Not everything you see on a SharePoint page is a web part, but identifying web parts is usually easy—especially if you have the permissions to edit a page, in which case the page editor shows you the web parts that are on the page, with options to remove them, move them around, and add additional ones.

You learn to use web parts in Chapter 9.

What Are Alerts?

Using alerts is a great way to be notified by e-mail or SMS of changes in lists and libraries or even specific documents or list items.

SharePoint has a built-in alert mechanism that allows users to register for different kinds of alerts. Basically, a user selects the piece of content she wants to be alerted on and requests that SharePoint send her an e-mail or SMS when that content changes.

For example, you might use alerts with a document library that is supposed to have documents regarding a specific topic. You might want to know immediately when a new document is added to that document library. As another example, you may want to know when a particular policy document is changed (for example, the corporate travel policy might be important to people who travel a lot). Alerts allow you to request to be notified when changes like these occur.

What Is a Site Column?

A site column is a column for a list or a document library that can be used in all document libraries or lists in the site in which it is created, as well as in the subsites for that site.

A site manager can define a specific column of data once and manage it from a central location instead of creating that column many times in many lists and libraries. In addition, content types can only use site columns. (In lists and libraries, on the other hand, columns can be created separately.)

Using site columns is covered in Chapter 7 and Chapter 13, "Customizing a SharePoint Site."

What Is a Content Type?

As mentioned earlier in this chapter, lists and document libraries can store different kinds of content, known as *content types*. A site manager can create and manage the content types in a site. The content types are then available in that site and in all the sites under it. The different types of content can have different site columns and/or different settings, such as policies and workflows, associated with them.

Content types can use site columns only for column definitions. This means that to create a content type, you have to choose what site columns should be included in that content type.

A simple example of a content type is a list of contacts that stores two types of contacts—an internal contact and an external contact. The Internal Contact content type is used for a contact inside the company—and as such does not need the company property because all internal contacts are from the same company. However, the External Contact content type does require the company property because every contact might be from a different company. Hence, a single list has two different column requirements.

As another example of the use of content types, consider a document library where you store many different types of documents. Some documents are presentations and some are financial reports, whereas others are user guides and product whitepapers. The differences between those content types are possibly more than just different columns: The content types might also specify different templates that users should use when creating documents of these types. For example, when creating a presentation, a Microsoft PowerPoint template will be used. When creating a financial report, a user will get a specific Microsoft Excel workbook as a template to start from. User guides might be from a certain Microsoft Word template, whereas product whitepapers might be PDF documents. Some of these examples are shown in Figure 1.22, which shows the content type options for creating a new document in a document library.

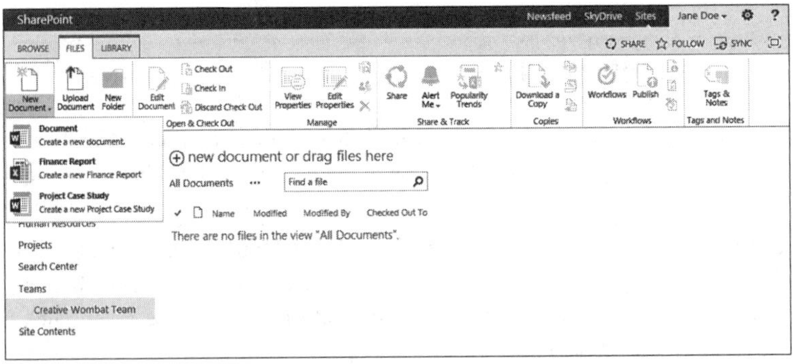

FIGURE 1.22   Choosing a content type when creating a new document in a document library.

Content types can be created in each site, and every subsite under that site can then use the content type. The subsites can either use the content type as it is defined in the parent site or create their own content types.

Content types are hierarchical, which means they can inherit from other content types. For example, the External Contact and Internal Contact content types can both inherit from the Contact content type. This way, if changes are made to the Contact content type (for example, if a property birthday date is added), both child content types may get the update (depending on whether the person who applied the update to the Contact content type chose to apply the update to content types that are inheriting from that content type).

Because the content type of an item or file says a lot about what the item actually is, it is an important piece of data associated with an item. This makes it important that authors (that is, people adding information to SharePoint) choose the right content type when creating data in SharePoint. However, sometimes content types are not used. A list might use the basic Item content type or a library might use the Document content type and add columns to the list itself—not impacting the content type itself. This means that all the columns are defined in the list or library and are added to all the items or files in it.

Content types use site columns to define the properties that the files or list items of that content type will have. Site columns are explained later in this chapter, in the section "What Is a Site Column?"

Chapter 7 shows how to add and remove a content type to a list or document library.

What Is Tagging?

Tagging is a social web mechanism available in Microsoft SharePoint 2013 Server (not in SPF) that allows you as the user to tag a document or a list item or even a page—in the SharePoint site or outside it. This mechanism needs to be turned on by the server administrator, so you might or might not be able to use it.

You can tag something to help remember it and find it more easily later on.

For example, you can tag a page of a document library with the tags describing the common denominator for the images in that library as shown in Figure 1.23 for example. You can use whatever tag keywords you want, and you can later remove or rename tags.

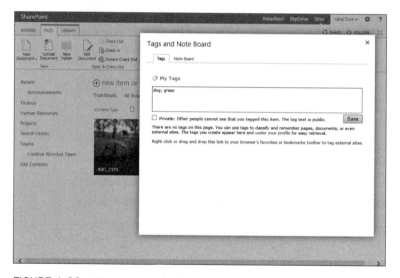

FIGURE 1.23   The document library is tagged with two terms—*dog* and *grass*—to help users find it later on based on the terms.

You can also add notes to an object, including saying what you like or dislike about it, or any other kind of notes. These notes are displayed to other people who look into the notes that you write, and you can view them as well. You can therefore keep working notes on documents or pages you are working on without those notes being part of the actual document or page.

Chapter 3 explains in detail how to add tags to content. Chapter 5 explains how to use tags and notes from your personal site to find content you tagged or commented on.

What Is Managed Metadata?

Available only through Microsoft SharePoint 2013 Server (not SPF), and in some plans of SharePoint in Office 365, managed metadata is a mechanism that allows administrators to create hierarchical term sets that can then be used in document libraries and lists as columns.

A term set is similar to a list that contains items, except that these items can contain more items under them in a hierarchy. For example, if you have a term set called *Products*, you could have a term for each product that you have in the organization.

By using managed metadata, you can create the list as a hierarchical list, grouping the products into categories (creating terms for the categories and then terms for the products under them) or into product groups, as shown in Figure 1.24.

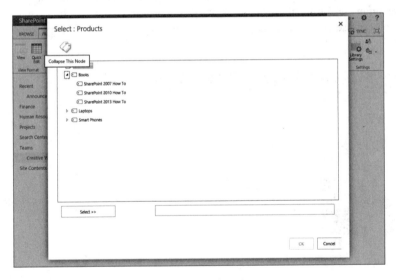

FIGURE 1.24   A managed metadata list of products.

You can then choose whether the terms that are categories (and not products) are available to the users as options. You can therefore allow the users to tag a document as belonging to a category of products (for example, Books), or you can let them tag a document as belonging to a specific product (for example, SharePoint 2013 How To).

Managed metadata in SharePoint 2013 can also be used to manage the navigation of a publishing site, where the navigation bar shows links from a certain term set. This can prove useful if you want different sites to share the same navigation, while managing it from a central location.

As you can see, managed metadata can be quite useful for tagging and then finding documents and list items. Chapter 7 describes how to create managed metadata columns and how to define term sets for those columns. Chapter 13 explains how a site manager can use managed metadata to drive the navigation in a publishing site.

What Are Versions?

Document libraries and lists in SharePoint have an option to track versions. This option stores old versions of files or items each time a change is made. For example, if a user uploads a document, and then another user edits the document and saves it, SharePoint saves the original document as a version of the file. Later, users can look at the version history of the file and choose to open a specific version or restore it (that is, make that version the current one).

SharePoint supports two types of versioning. In the first type, each change is regarded as a major change, and the version numbers go from 1 (the first time a document was uploaded) to 2 (after the first change) and then 3 and 4 and so on as shown in Figure 1.25. In the second type, each change is regarded as a minor change, unless the user specifies that it is a major one. The version numbers go from 0.1 (the first time a document was uploaded) to 0.2 (the first change) and so on, until a user selects the option to perform a major change, and the version number changes to 1.0, and subsequent changes raise it to 1.1, 1.2, and so on.

Version History				×
Delete All Versions				
No. ↓ Modified	Modified By	Size	Comments	
3.0 1/14/2013 10:21 PM	☐ Administrator	116.4 KB		
2.0 1/14/2013 10:20 PM	☐ Administrator	116.4 KB		
1.0 1/14/2013 10:20 PM	☐ Jane Doe	225.9 KB		
Title	Employee Profile - Ishai Sagi, SharePoint Architect			
Products	SharePoint 2013 How To			

FIGURE 1.25   Viewing the lists of versions for a document.

For information about how to work with versions, see Chapters 3 and 7.

What Does Check-in/Check-out Mean?

Check-in and *check-out* are common terms in many document management systems, including SharePoint. Their purpose is to prevent conflicts in an environment where multiple people might want to edit the same piece of content (in SharePoint, list items or files) at the same time. The term *check-in* describes the process of adding a new or modified item or file to a document library or a list to replace the previous version.

The term *check-out* describes the process of locking a version of a document or list item in a list or library. By checking out an item or a file, a user can prevent others from editing that content. By checking in the item, the user can allow others to edit the content, without needing to worry about overriding changes that others have made.

Usually when an item or a file is checked out to a user, that user can work on that item or file, and other users cannot. Other users have to wait for the user to check the item or file back in (that is, perform a check-in) before they can edit the item or file. While the item or file is checked out, other users usually can see only the last version that was checked in; they can't see the changes that the current user has made on the file while it's been checked out.

Pages in SharePoint can be in document libraries—and often are. This means that pages can be checked out and in, allowing page editors to change a page (for example, add or remove a web part), but the users cannot see the changes until that editor is happy with the changes and checks the page in.

> **NOTE** SharePoint does not require a check-in and check-out on all lists and libraries. This is a setting that the list or library manager can set.

When versioning is activated on a document library or list, a check-in creates a new version. See "What Are Versions?" earlier in this chapter.

What Is a Workflow?

In SharePoint, a workflow is a series of steps—some automatic, some manual—that need to be performed as part of a business process for a document or a list item.

For example, the most common workflows for documents are review and approval. Some important documents (for example, contracts) need to go through several steps of approval from different people before they can be officially considered final and published. Figure 1.26 shows an example of starting an approval workflow.

Another example is pages in a site itself. In some SharePoint environments, each change to a page needs to be approved by the site's manager to make sure the contents of the page comply with the company's policies.

SharePoint allows developers to develop workflows and attach them to documents or list items. End users might be expected to interact with a workflow, either approving documents or items or triggering a workflow to start or stop.

Chapter 11, "Workflows," covers the common tasks involved with workflows.

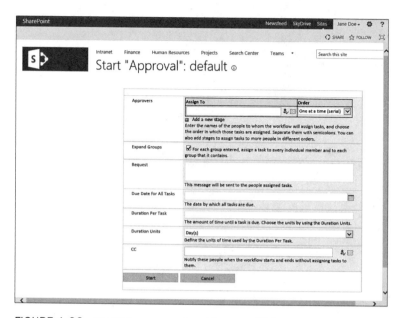

FIGURE 1.26   Starting an approval workflow to publish a page.

What Are Catalogs?

In SharePoint 2013 you can make any list or a library into a catalog. This makes the content of the list or library available across the entire system to be displayed. This way, you may have a list of products in one site (a product catalog), and display the products' information in other sites across the environment using special web parts—without duplicating the content.

CHAPTER 2

Finding Your Way Around a SharePoint Site

IN THIS CHAPTER

This chapter shows you how to get around a SharePoint site, with some common tasks that you might want to do in every SharePoint site you use. It explains how to log on to a SharePoint site and the different navigation options in SharePoint sites.

Get to a SharePoint Site

Scenario/Problem: The most basic thing when working with SharePoint is getting to the SharePoint site and opening it.

Solution: How you get to a SharePoint site depends on the location of that site. Most often, your system administrator will give you the location. Your company might have several sites, and an administrator should supply you with links to the sites you should be aware of. Possible examples of such links are http://*portal* or http://*home* or http://*companyname* or, if the SharePoint site in question is an Office365 SharePoint site, the address might be http://companyname.sharepoint. com. This book uses http://sharepoint as the example link.

NOTE SharePoint sites can have subsites. If there is a subsite under sharepoint called sample, for example, the path to the site would be http://sharepoint/finance or http://sharepoint/sites/finance.

To get to the site itself, you open the link supplied to you in any Internet browser, such as Internet Explorer, Chrome, or Firefox.

Depending on the setup of the site itself, you might or might not be prompted for a password. Because SharePoint is often configured to automatically identify you, the likelihood is that you will not be prompted, and SharePoint will log you on with the user name and password you used when you logged on to your computer. If you are prompted, fill in the user name and password that your administrator advised you to use (see Figure 2.1). If the site in question is an Office 365 site, you might have to use a different user name and password—using the email address that was used to register with that site. This is known as your Microsoft Live Account. If you are not sure what user name and password to use, contact your administrator.

If for some reason you do not have permissions to the SharePoint site you are trying to open, SharePoint displays an Access Denied page, telling you that you don't have permissions, or, if the site allows it, will ask you to let the site managers know why you need access to the site (see Figure 2.2).

After you are logged on, the SharePoint site opens. SharePoint sites look different from one another, depending on the way the site managers set up the sites.

FIGURE 2.1   The prompt for credentials when connecting to SharePoint.

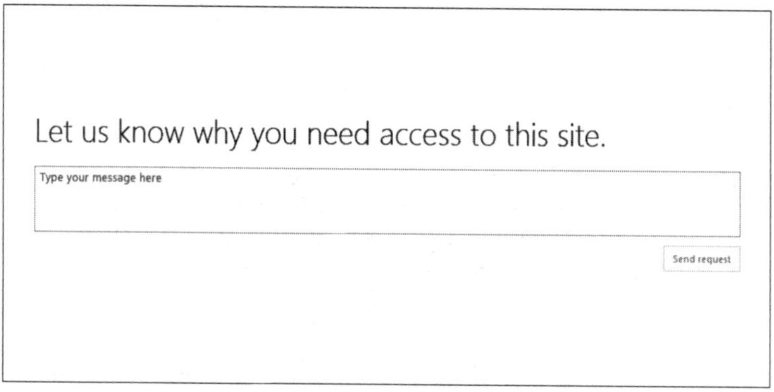

FIGURE 2.2   The Request Access screen.

Sign Out of a Site

Scenario/Problem: Sometimes when you are viewing a SharePoint site, you might want to sign out. For example, say that you logged on as a different user, and you now want to sign out completely.

Solution: After you have logged on to a SharePoint site, you might want to sign out. You do this by clicking the [*your name*] link at the top of the page to open a drop-down menu and then selecting Sign Out from the options (see Figure 2.3). After you click on that option, the window shows a message that you have been signed out, and it closes itself if your browser allows it to.

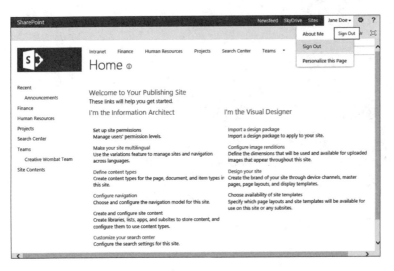

FIGURE 2.3   How to sign out of a site.

Use the Ribbon

Scenario/Problem: Any page in SharePoint might have several ribbons with different command buttons and actions. Often you will want to either show the ribbon to expose editing options on a page, or manually switch to different ribbons to find the actions or the information that those other ribbons offer.

Solution: By default, when you browse through a SharePoint site, the ribbon switching controls are hidden and you are shown the default ribbon that displays the site's name, logo, and navigation. As you navigate through the site, SharePoint attempts to detect what ribbon you need to see based on what you select in a page.

To show the ribbon controls if they are not visible, you must click on the Settings icon that looks like a cogwheel at the top-right corner of the page, and then select the Show Ribbon command from the drop-down menu that opens, as shown in Figure 2.4.

If the ribbon is already shown, the command displays Hide Ribbon instead. After ribbons are made visible, you can use the ribbon controls to switch between the different ribbons.

NOTE   Site administrators might choose to disable the Show Ribbon option in some sites. If they did, you will only see the ribbon options if you are in a page that SharePoint requires a ribbon to be displayed in.

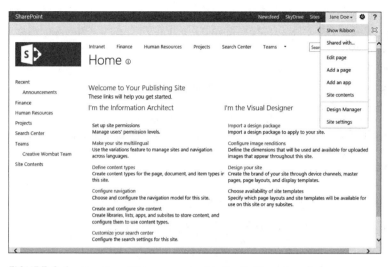

FIGURE 2.4   The Show Ribbon command in the Settings drop-down menu.

The control that allows you to switch between ribbons is usually shown at the top of the page, listing the names of the available ribbons as tabs. For example, in most pages, you see the tab for Browse (see Figure 2.5). (This tab shows the navigation ribbon that contains the site title, breadcrumbs, and top-level navigation. All these concepts are explained later in this chapter, in the section "Navigate Through a SharePoint Site"). This is the default ribbon in most scenarios.

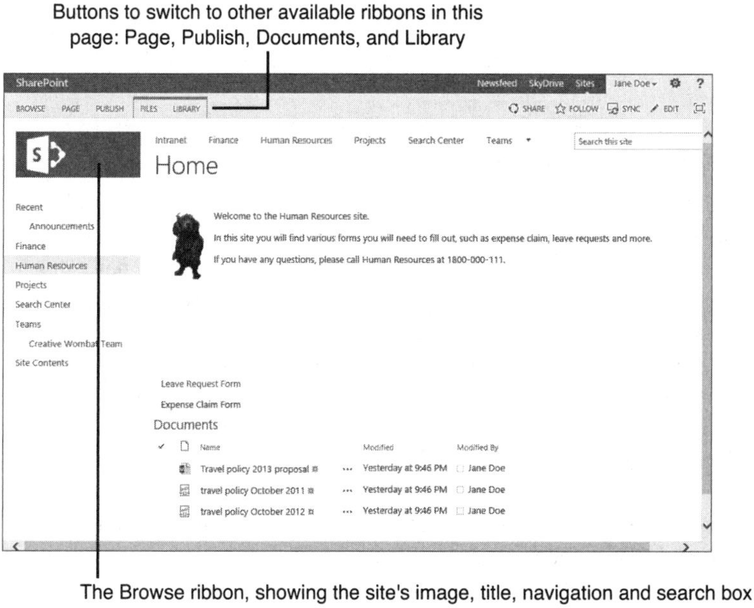

Buttons to switch to other available ribbons in this
page: Page, Publish, Documents, and Library

The Browse ribbon, showing the site's image, title, navigation and search box

FIGURE 2.5   The ribbon interface, showing the Browse ribbon and buttons to switch to other available ribbons.

To switch between ribbons, you click on the name of the ribbon you want to switch to. For example, when viewing a site's home page, you can usually switch to the Page ribbon to see buttons that allow you to e-mail a link to the page or make the page your browser's home page.

Depending on where you are in a site, or what you click in a page, different ribbons will appear and disappear. Figure 2.6, for example, shows the ribbons that will be shown when you view a Calendar list—with special buttons to change how you view the calendar. The Calendar ribbon has buttons under the Scope sections that allow you to switch from the monthly view to the weekly and daily views. This is specific to calendar lists.

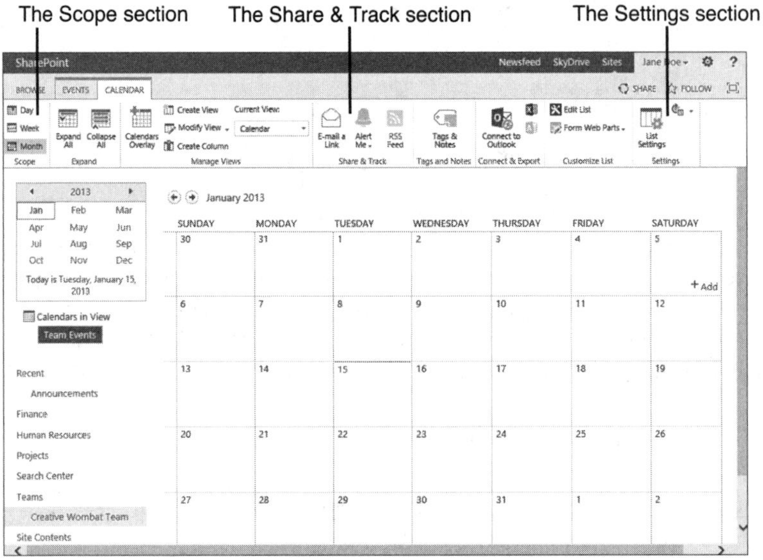

FIGURE 2.6   The Events and Calendar ribbons are available when viewing a calendar.

The ribbons provide links and buttons to different functionality. However, sometimes your screen is not big enough to display all the buttons that appear on a ribbon. This is why the ribbon is split into sections, as shown in Figure 2.6. The sections group various buttons and controls together. If the screen is not big enough to display all buttons in all sections, SharePoint automatically shrinks as many sections as needed so that the sections are still visible, and the buttons are accessible through a section button. Figure 2.7 shows an example of this, with the same page as shown in Figure 2.6 displayed in a much smaller screen. As you can see, the Scope section is compressed to display the buttons without their text next to them, and the Expand section is shown collapsed, as a button. Clicking on the Expand button reveals the two buttons that exist in that section, as shown in Figure 2.8.

FIGURE 2.7   The Calendar ribbon, in a smaller screen, showing the Scope and Expand sections compressed to save screen space.

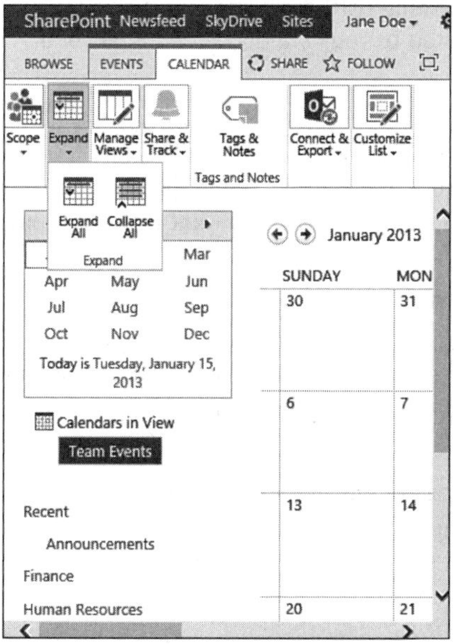

FIGURE 2.8   The Expand section as a drop-down button, showing the buttons under it when clicked.

> **NOTE** The images in this book were taken on a small screen to make them easier to read. If you have a bigger screen, the ribbons shown on your screen will probably show more buttons, and they will be bigger.

When you want to return to the default ribbon to see the navigation toolbars, you click on the Browse tab, and the Navigation ribbon appears again.

Change Language and Regional Settings

> **Scenario/Problem:** When you are working in an environment that has sites from all over the world, you might want to define in a specific site that you want the date formatting to appear in the way you are used to—for example, with the month before or after the day in a date. You might also want to show time data in your time zone, and not in the time zone that the site manager set. For example, when viewing a list of events, you might see an event scheduled to start at nine in the morning. But if the site was created by someone in Japan, and you are in the United States, you need to know whether that time is based on the time zone in Japan or in your time zone.

Solution: Depending on the configuration of the SharePoint environment, you might be able to define your own regional settings for that environment (which will affect all sites in that environment) or for the specific site (which affects just that site). Doing this changes the way the site is presented to you, without affecting anyone else's view of the site.

When you change the regional settings, you can define how you want dates and numbers to be shown to you, the default sort order that will be used in the site when you view lists, what calendar format you want to see, and how you want to define your work week days.

For example, in a calendar list of events, when the regional settings are set to Australian regional settings, the events are shown with the day before the month. But if you change the settings to the American regional settings, the date will show the month before the day, and the times for the events will change, to show when the events occur in the selected time zone.

To change the settings, you click on the [*your name*] link at the top of the page to open a drop-down menu. Depending on the environment's setup, you will see either a My Settings link or an About Me link (see Figure 2.9).

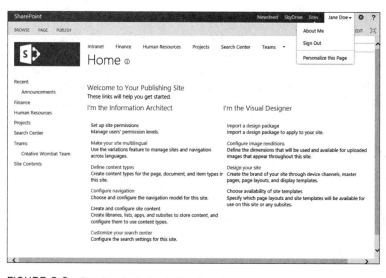

FIGURE 2.9   The About Me link in the drop-down menu.

Change Settings Only for Current Site

If you click the My Settings link, SharePoint opens a page showing your details as they are saved in the system (see Figure 2.10). When you click on My Language and Region, SharePoint opens the Language and Region configuration screen, where you can choose the settings you want. The default option is to always follow the settings defined for the website. Unless you clear this option (called "Always follow web settings"), you will not be able to set any personal setting for yourself.

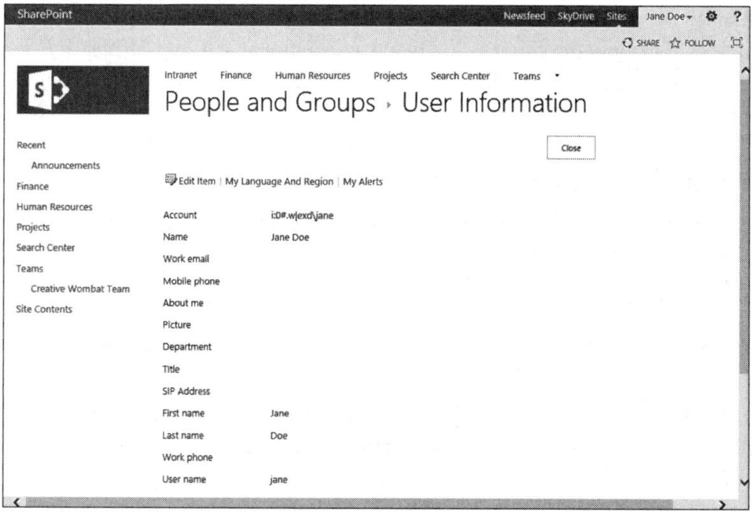

FIGURE 2.10   The Language and Region page.

Change Settings for Entire Environment

If you click the About Me link, SharePoint opens your personal site, showing a page with your details, and a link to edit your profile. Click the Edit link to see a few tabs of profile information to edit (more information about editing your profile is available in Chapter 5, "Social Networking, Personal Sites, and Personal Details in SharePoint Server"). Click on the link showing three dots—this opens a drop-down menu with the option Language and Region, as shown in Figure 2.11.

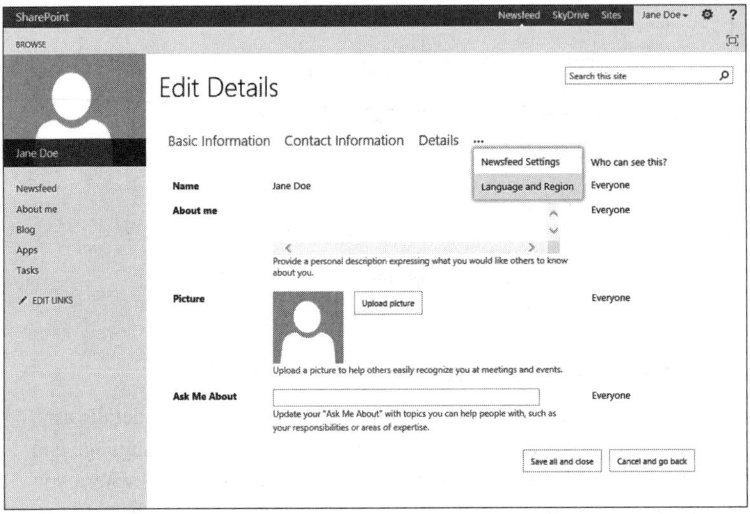

FIGURE 2.11   The Edit Details page, with the drop-down menu open to show the regional settings link.

Click this option to show the configuration options for your regional settings for the entire environment. The default option is to always use regional settings defined by site administrators, and you can override it by selecting "Always use my personal settings" as shown in Figure 2.12.

Regional Settings You Can Change

The following are the settings you can configure on either of those pages after you override the site's regional settings:

▶ **Locale**—Sets the formats of dates, numbers, and sorting order.

▶ **Time Zone**—Sets your time zone so that times (for example, time for a meeting) will be displayed to you in your time zone.

▶ **Set Your Calendar**—Allows you to select a different calendar format (for example, the Jewish calendar or Arabic calendar) to be displayed instead of the default one.

▶ **Enable an Alternate Calendar**—Allows you to select an alternative secondary calendar that will be displayed in addition to the default one.

▶ **Define Your Work Week**—Allows you to select your work week and working hours (which changes how calendars are colored when displayed to you).

▶ **Time Format**—Allows you to select whether the time format should be 12-hour format (for example, 01:00 PM) or 24-hour format (for example, 13:00).

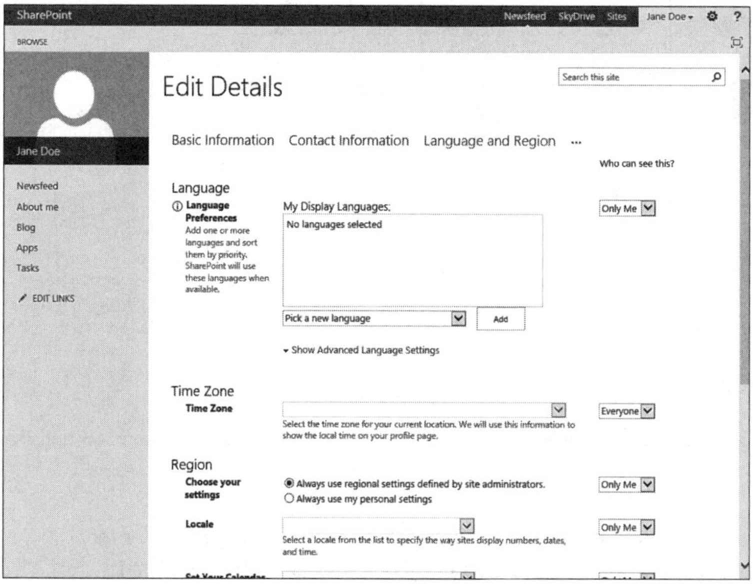

FIGURE 2.12   The Edit Details—Language and Region page.

Navigate Through a SharePoint Site

Scenario/Problem: Information is the focus of a SharePoint site. Each site might contain different information in different places. You need to know how to navigate a site to find the information you need.

Solution: This section explains the different mechanisms that help you to navigate through a site. Most sites use the navigation ribbon (also known as the Browse ribbon) to show navigation controls on the top of the page—including a top navigation bar and the breadcrumbs. Often there is also a side navigation bar that shows more navigation options on the left of the page.

A site manager can change the navigation bars to show different links to different parts of the site. The navigation bars should be your primary source of information about what you can view in the site.

Figure 2.13 shows an example of a site that shows both navigation bars, along with the breadcrumbs. In this figure, the top navigation bar shows links to subsites that exist under the current site.

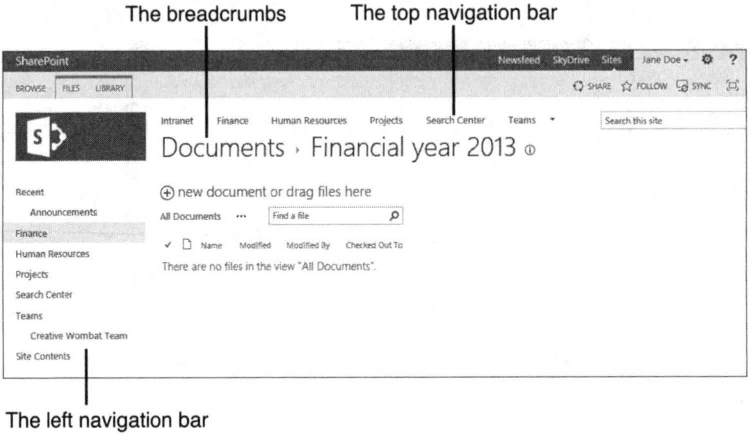

FIGURE 2.13   The three navigational aids: the breadcrumbs, the top navigation bar, and the left navigation bar.

Sometimes the navigation in a site is configured to display the pages and/or the subsites of the subsites, resulting in a hierarchy of sites that is displayed as fly-out menus. These menus show the subsites for a site when you hover the mouse over the link for that site, as shown in Figure 2.14.

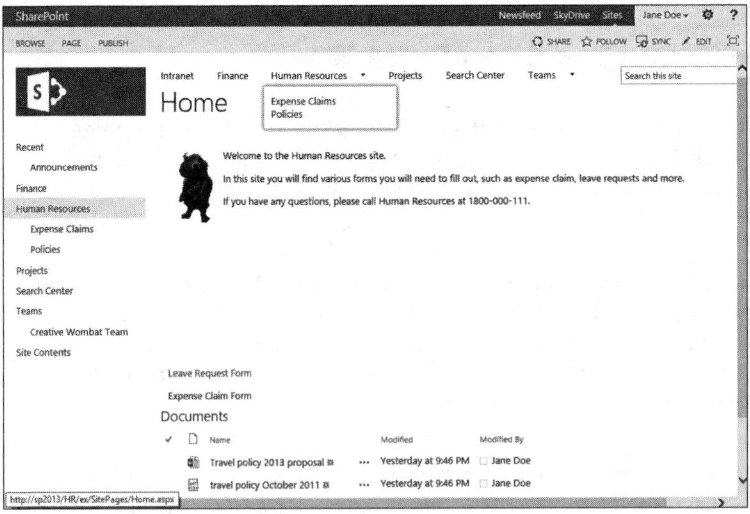

FIGURE 2.14   The top navigation bar, showing fly-out menus for the subsites under the Human Resources site.

To navigate to a subsite, you can click on the links to that subsite in either navigation bar. Depending on how your administrator set up the navigation, the subsites might show the same top navigation bar but a different left navigation bar—one that is specific to the current site. However, the administrator can choose that a subsite will display the same left navigation as the top site, making it look as if you are still in the same site, except for the fact that the current site that you are on is highlighted in the top navigation bar.

Use the Left Navigation Bar

The left navigation bar is also known as Current Navigation. It is usually used to show content that exists in the current site and sometimes content from subsites. The content is usually (but not always) lists and libraries, and it is usually grouped so that document libraries are shown under a Documents header, lists under a Lists header, discussions under a Discussions header, and so on.

The left navigation bar highlights where you are in the navigation—but only when you are on a page that is shown in the navigation (see Figure 2.15).

The parent site of the current site is
highlighted in the top navigation bar.

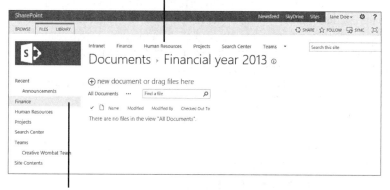

The current document
library is highlighted in
the left navigation bar.

FIGURE 2.15   The left navigation bar, with the current document library highlighted.

The left navigation bar is meant to be used as a quick launch bar—a useful list of links in the current site, and sometimes the sites under it. It might even contain links to content that isn't in SharePoint (for example, an Internet site).

> **NOTE**   Some sites and some pages do not show a left navigation bar. In that case, you have to rely on the information on the page to find your way around the site.

Use the Top Navigation Bar

The top navigation bar is also known as Global Navigation, and it is usually used to show links to sites that are at the top level of the site hierarchy. This allows you to quickly see what important sites the site administrator wants you to see that are available globally.

This menu bar supports fly-out menus. These menus become visible when you hover with the mouse over the parent menu item. You can sometimes tell when menus have fly-out menus because they are usually marked with a triangle pointing to the direction in which the fly-out menu opens.

> **TIP**   The top navigation bar can be customized to show many levels of sites, and sometimes other links. If you see the small triangles or arrows, hover over them with your mouse to find out what navigation item is under them.

Use the Breadcrumbs

The breadcrumbs mechanism is commonly used to navigate websites. It shows you where you are in the site, so you can go "up" the hierarchy all the way to the home page of the site. For example, if you are viewing a folder in a document library, the breadcrumbs will show you the list of folders that are above the current folder, and then a link to the document library's root folder (as the name of the document library). To navigate back to the site's home page, you can click on the site's logo or name, which is usually to the left of the breadcrumbs (see Figure 2.16). Depending on the site's configuration, the breadcrumbs might start in different places. By default the breadcrumbs in SharePoint 2013 show you where you are within a folder structure (which is usually in a document library).

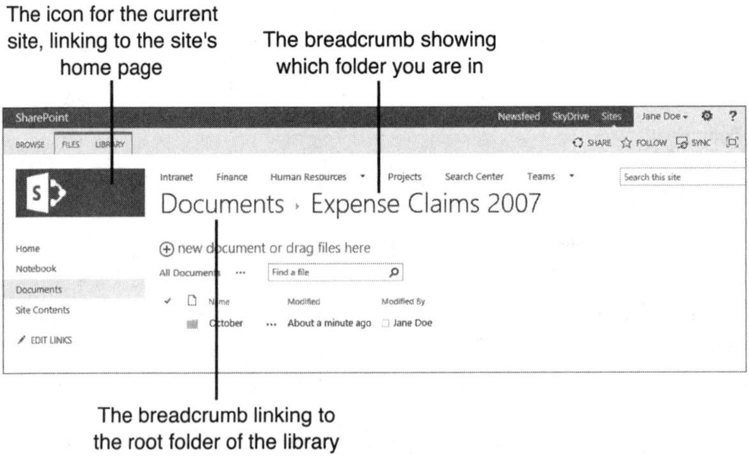

FIGURE 2.16   The breadcrumbs navigation interface for the Expense Claims 2007 folder in the Documents library in the Expense Claims site under Human Resources.

In some cases (usually with pages in pages libraries), the breadcrumbs do not show that the page is under a library, but instead display as if the page is directly under the site itself.

As you go deeper into the folder hierarchy, the breadcrumbs by default show the parent folder of the one you are in, allowing you to navigate up one folder at a time. For example, if you navigate into the October folder shown in Figure 2.16—the breadcrumbs then show the name of the current folder (October) preceded by the name of the parent folder instead of the name of the library, as shown in Figure 2.17. Note that this is merely the default behavior, and it is possible for your site designer to change the breadcrumbs to show more information or behave differently.

FIGURE 2.17   The breadcrumbs in the October folder show the parent folder Expense Claims 2007.

To use the breadcrumbs, you just click on the link you want to navigate to.

> **TIP**   When you're in a document library that has folders, using the breadcrumbs is the best way to go back to the parent folder of the one you are currently in.

Use the Navigate Up Breadcrumbs

In addition to the navigation bars and the breadcrumbs, SharePoint 2013 also has a button dedicated to navigation called the Navigate Up button. Although this button is not available by default, a site designer might enable it for you to use.

> **NOTE**   By default, this button is not shown in the SharePoint navigation—if you don't see it, it is up to the site's designer to add it.

This button solves the problem of long breadcrumbs. As mentioned earlier, if you are in a folder in a document library with a lot of parent folders, the breadcrumbs might get too long to display the entire hierarchy.

You can usually find the Navigate Up button in the top-left site of the top navigation bar (see Figure 2.18). It appears as a rectangular icon with a gray arrow pointing up.

Clicking on that button does not take you up but instead shows you a hierarchical view of breadcrumbs—showing you where you are on the site and allowing you to navigate up, the same as the breadcrumbs mechanism described earlier in this chapter.

The Navigate Up breadcrumbs differ from the normal breadcrumbs navigation mentioned earlier in this chapter in two major ways. First, they show the entire hierarchy all the up to the root site in the site collection, and not just to the current site. For example, if you have a site called Expense Claims inside the Human Resources site, the Navigate Up breadcrumbs show Human Resources above Expense Claims in the hierarchy. Figure 2.18 shows the Navigate Up menu for the October folder shown in Figure 2.17.

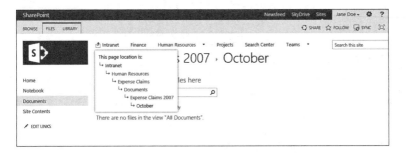

FIGURE 2.18   Using the Navigate Up button allows you to follow the breadcrumb trail all the way to the top site.

Second, compared to the regular breadcrumbs, the Navigate Up breadcrumbs offer more hierarchy detail for pages. Unlike the breadcrumbs mentioned earlier, the Navigate Up breadcrumbs display the entire hierarchy structure for the page you are viewing. For example, if you are viewing a web part page in a pages library, the normal breadcrumbs will show the site name as the parent for the page, while the Navigate Up breadcrumbs show you the library the page is in as the parent of the page. This allows you to go to the library as well as to the site, but it can make the hierarchy in this control very long if the page you are viewing is deep inside the hierarchy.

Follow a SharePoint Site

Scenario/Problem: Keeping track of all the sites you regularly use is difficult.

Solution: SharePoint 2013 introduces a mechanism called "Follow" that allows you to mark sites as sites you are following—similar to the concept of favorites in your browser. When you mark a site as a followed site, it is added to a list of sites that are shown to you in your personal site (for more details about viewing your followed sites, see Chapter 5).

To follow a site, open that site, and click the Follow button on the top of the ribbon, as shown in Figure 2.19.

The Follow button for a site

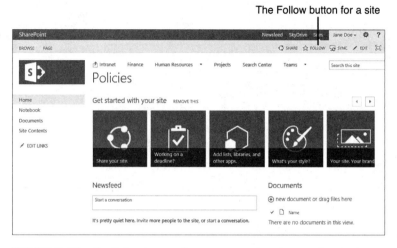

FIGURE 2.19   The Follow button allows you to mark a site as a favorite for your personal site.

CHAPTER 3

Solutions Regarding Files, Documents, List Items, and Forms

SharePoint is most commonly used to store information in the forms of either list items or files (which can be documents, forms, or any other type of file).

This chapter explains how to perform common tasks in SharePoint that you as an end user would need to know, such as creating list items, viewing files and their properties, and setting up alerts that let you know when there are new files or list items or when specific files or list items have been modified.

Most importantly, this chapter also covers how to switch between list views so you can see the content in a list in various ways and therefore find the content you are looking for more easily.

If you are looking for more author-oriented tasks, such as uploading files or creating new list items, see Chapter 6, "Creating and Managing Files, List Items, and Forms in SharePoint."

See What Lists and Document Libraries Are in a Site

Scenario/Problem: When you're in a SharePoint site, you often want to see what is beyond the home page of the site. What document libraries are there to store information, and what lists and surveys exist?

Solution: You can see what lists and document libraries are available in a site in several ways. The following sections demonstrate how you can use various methods to view the content of a site.

Use Direct Links in the Left Navigation Bar

Site managers can use the left navigation bar to show various links in different categories. Document libraries are usually shown under the Documents header, and lists are usually under the Lists header, as shown in Figure 3.1.

View All Lists and Libraries

Not all the document libraries and lists are shown in the navigation bar. Which ones are shown depends on how the site administrator set up the navigation bar.

To see all the libraries and lists apps available, you use the Site Contents link in the left navigation bar (refer to Figure 3.1). SharePoint takes you to the Site Contents page, which lists all the content in the site, as shown in Figure 3.2. Different app types show with different icons next to them, so you can tell which is a document library app and which is a list app, and sometimes more specific icons will be displayed.

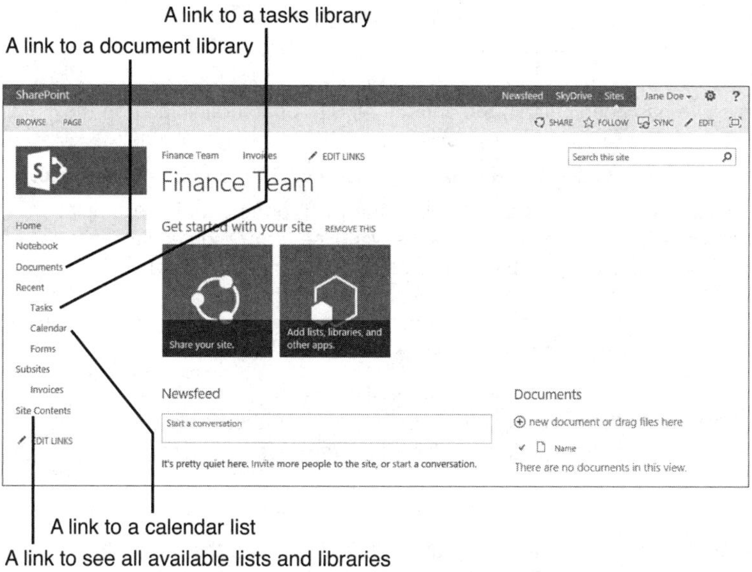

A link to a tasks library

A link to a document library

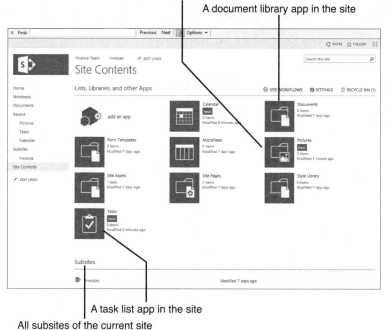

A link to a calendar list

A link to see all available lists and libraries

FIGURE 3.1   The left navigation bar's links to document libraries and lists.

An image library app in the site

A document library app in the site

A task list app in the site

All subsites of the current site

FIGURE 3.2   The Site Contents page.

You click on the link to the document library to view the documents in them, or click the link to a list to see the list items in it.

> **NOTE** If the site has been customized and the All Site Content link isn't on the page, you can try to get to this page by using one of the following methods:
>
> ▶ Open the Site Actions menu and click on the View All Site Content option there.
>
> ▶ Type **_layouts/viewlsts.aspx** at the end of the path to the site. For example, if your site is at http://sharepoint/finance, you type http://sharepoint/finance/_layouts/viewlsts.aspx in your browser to get to the All Site Content page.

Open a Document for Reading

> **Scenario/Problem:** When viewing a document library, either in the home page or in a library view, you need to open a document in order to see its contents.

Solution: When you're in a document library, you just click on the link to the document you are interested in (see Figure 3.3). If the file is a Microsoft Office file, and if the SharePoint environment supports it, the file may open in the browser, in what is called a Microsoft Office Web App. If it is a different file type or if the environment doesn't support Microsoft Office Web Apps, then depending on your machine's configuration, the document opens either in a new window or in the associated application (Word documents open in Word, Excel workbooks will open in Excel, and so on).

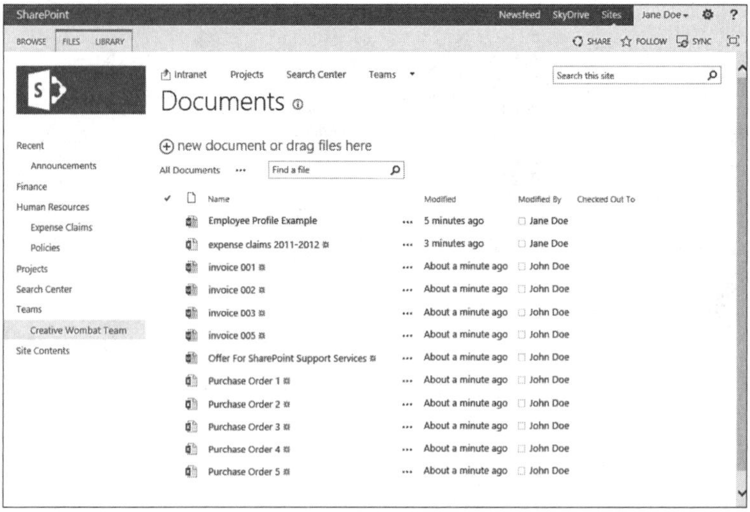

FIGURE 3.3   Open a document for reading by clicking the document's filename in the document library.

Also, depending on the installed applications on your machine and on the level of permissions you have, you might be prompted to make a choice about how to open the file. You should also get a warning that files from websites may contain viruses (as shown in Figure 3.4), and you will be asked to confirm that you indeed want to open the file.

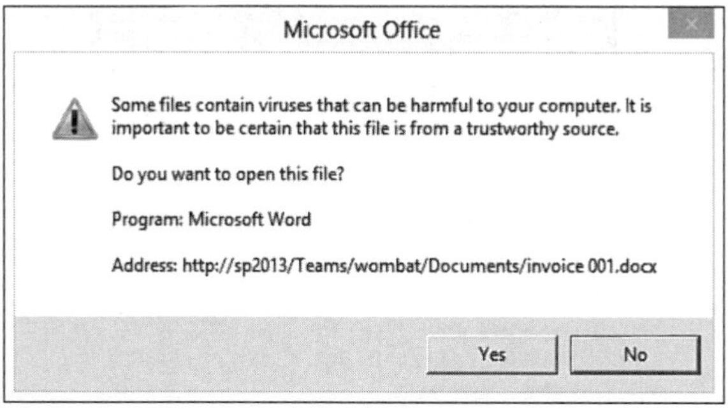

FIGURE 3.4   Microsoft Office's warning when opening a document from a SharePoint site.

View Properties of a Document

Scenario/Problem: When viewing a document library in either a web part on the home page or in one of the list views of that library, you might want to see more details about a document before choosing what to do with it. These details might include who wrote the document, its subject, and maybe additional pieces of metadata describing the document (for example, the client it was written for, the date it expires).

Solution: You can view the properties of a document in two ways: using the ribbon interface or using a drop-down menu.

Using the Files Ribbon

To view the metadata of a file by using the ribbon, you click on the row for that file—but not on the link to the file itself. To help you select a line, when you hover the mouse over a row, the row is highlighted, and you see a tick sign on the left that means clicking it will select the file row.

After you select a file, switch to the "Files" ribbon by clicking the Files header to switch to it. On the Files ribbon, click the View Properties button to view the file's properties as shown in Figure 3.5.

The three dots next to a file's
name open the file's preview dialog.

The tick mark showing
which row you selected

FIGURE 3.5   Select a single file by clicking a row, and click the View Properties button in the Files ribbon.

Using a Context Popup Menu

To view the metadata of a particular file, you click on the three dots next to the file's name (refer to Figure 3.5) to open the file preview dialog. In this dialog you might see an actual preview of the file (shown in Figure 3.6), if, as was explained before, the environment you are viewing has Microsoft Office Web Apps. If not, you will see an empty box above some of the file's properties such as who was the last person to change it, and who has permissions to see the file. The choices in the dialog depend on the permissions you have on the file, on the applications installed on your computer, and on the applications installed in SharePoint. You might see more or fewer options than Figure 3.7 shows—and each file might present you with a different menu.

At the bottom of the dialog is a row of links that enable you to perform several types of actions on the file. One of these links is again just three dots. Clicking on these three dots opens the context popup menu for the file, as shown in Figure 3.7.

The file preview dialog

A preview of the file

Click the three dots next to a file's name to open a popup menu.

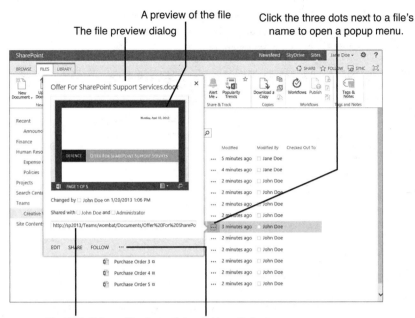

The file's link   The three dots next to a file's name open the Context popup menu.

FIGURE 3.6   The file preview dialog.

The view properties menu option

The file's context popup menu

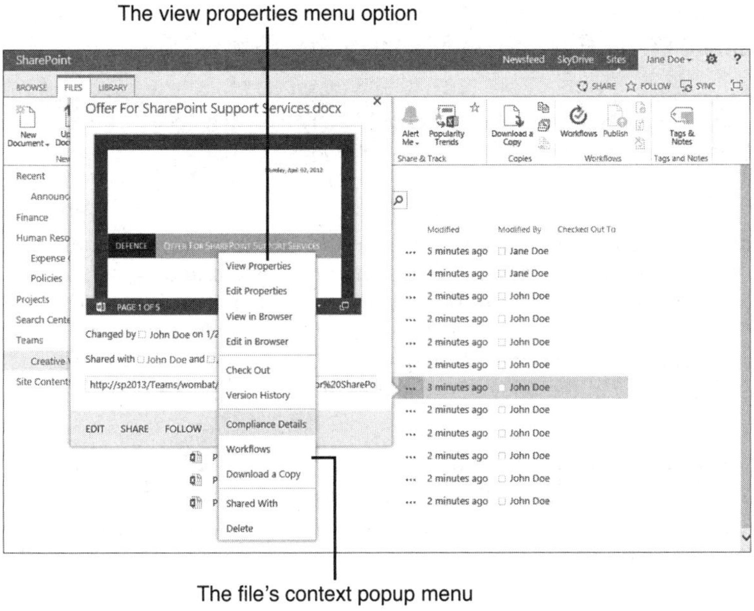

FIGURE 3.7   Click the three dots in the dialog menu to open a drop-down menu with more options.

In that menu, select View Properties to open the properties page (shown in Figure 3.8), which shows all the properties the document has. You can click Close in this page to return to the document library view you were on.

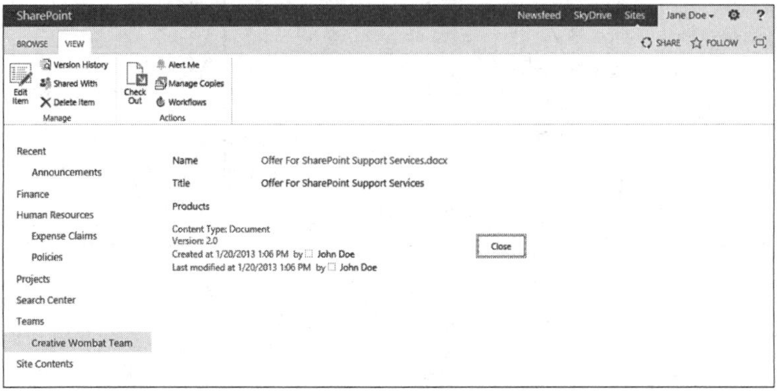

FIGURE 3.8   The file properties page.

> **NOTE** When you set properties on a Microsoft Office file, the properties are copied into the file itself. When you upload a file to a document library that has properties with the same names as the file's properties, they are copied back. This means that if you download a file and then upload it to a different document library that has the same properties, the data of the properties is retained.

Send a Link to a File or a Library by E-mail

> **Scenario/Problem:** When viewing a document library, you might want to select a single file in that library and send a link to someone via e-mail.

Solution: You can e-mail a link to a file by copying the link from the file's context popup menu for the file as was shown in Figure 3.6 and paste it into an email message. If you want to send a link to the document library instead of the file, you can find an E-mail a Link button in the Library ribbon, which appears under an envelope icon (see Figure 3.9). This opens your email client and creates a new message with the link to the library in the body of the message.

When you click on the E-mail a Link button in the "Files" ribbon or in the context popup menu option, your default e-mail application opens a new message with a link pointing directly to the document. You can choose who to send the link to and send the message as you would any other e-mail.

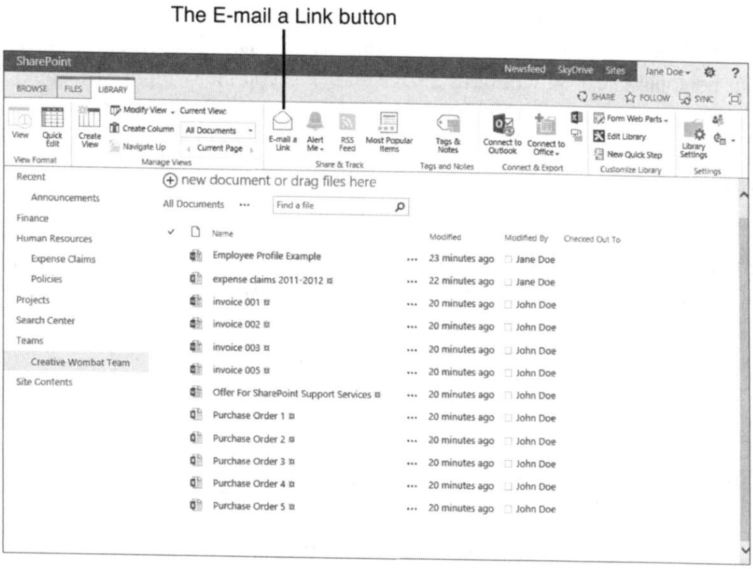

The E-mail a Link button

FIGURE 3.9   The E-mail a Link button in the Library ribbon.

Tag a Document, List Item, or Page

Scenario/Problem: You find that a specific document, list item, or page is useful to you, and you want to be able to mark it so that you can easily find it in the future. You might also want to share this mark with other people.

Solution: As mentioned in Chapter 1, "About Microsoft SharePoint 2013," tagging is a useful mechanism that helps you find content quickly. This mechanism is available only in SharePoint 2013 Server, not in SPF.

TIP   Tagging is not just for highlighting something as useful. It has many different uses! For example, you might want to tag some documents and items as "unhelpful," or "redundant," or maybe "not relevant." Doing so will allow you to compile a list of documents that you think should be removed, and you can then report them to the site manager.

When tagging an item, you can write basically anything that you want that will help you find that item later on. Then, when you go to your personal site, you can see the phrases that you used, and the documents you tagged with those phrases. You will also be able to use the tags when searching for documents, items, and pages. (For more information, see Chapter 4, "Searching in SharePoint.") Tagging can target a document, a list item, a page, or even sites—including external sites.

For example, if you tag two documents in different sites with the phrase "my important presentations," and another document with the phrase "a template for invoices," when you go to your personal site, you will have a page showing you the two phrases, and when you click on one of them, you see links to the documents you tagged with that phrase.

For more information about how to use the tags in personal sites, see Chapter 5, "Social Networking, Personal Sites, and Personal Details in SharePoint Server."

To tag an item or a file with a different phrase, you select the row for that document or item (see "Using the Files Ribbon," under "View Properties of a Document" earlier in this chapter, for a detailed description of how to do that) and switch to the Files ribbon. In the ribbon, you will see the Tags & Notes button, as shown in Figure 3.10.

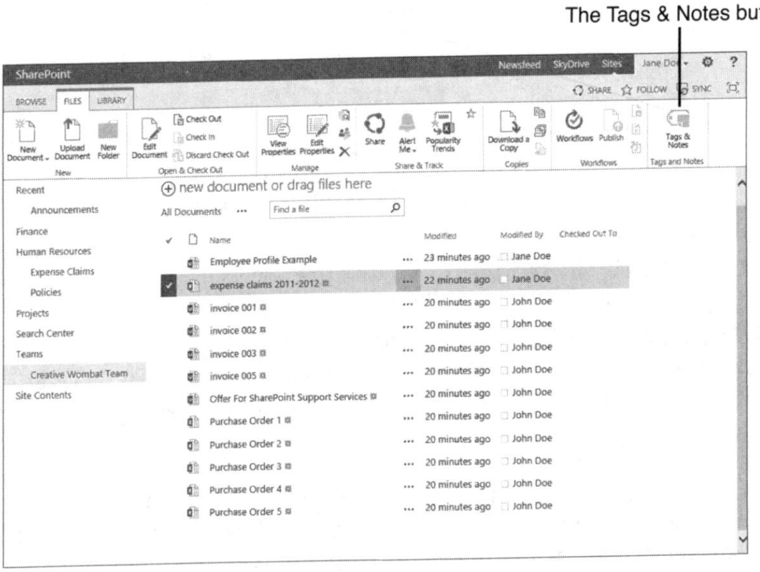

FIGURE 3.10   After selecting a single document, you can click on the Tags & Notes button.

After you click the Tags & Notes button, a window appears, showing the tags that you and other users have attached to the document or item (see Figure 3.11).

To write a tag, you type the tag's text in the text box and click Save. Alternatively, you can click on a tag from the Suggested Tags list at the bottom of the dialog to quickly add tags that you or others have used in the site most frequently. You can add separate tags by using the semicolon character to separate them. For example, writing "Important; Exciting" tags the item with the two separate words *Important* and *Exciting*. The My Tags box at the top shows the tags that are already set on the file or item. You can choose to make a tag private so other people will not see it.

When you click Save, the tags you added become underlined to signify that they have been added. You can close the dialog by clicking the X button in the top-right corner.

When you open the dialog again, you see the same tags, and the Recent Activities list on the bottom of the dialog shows the date you added the tags.

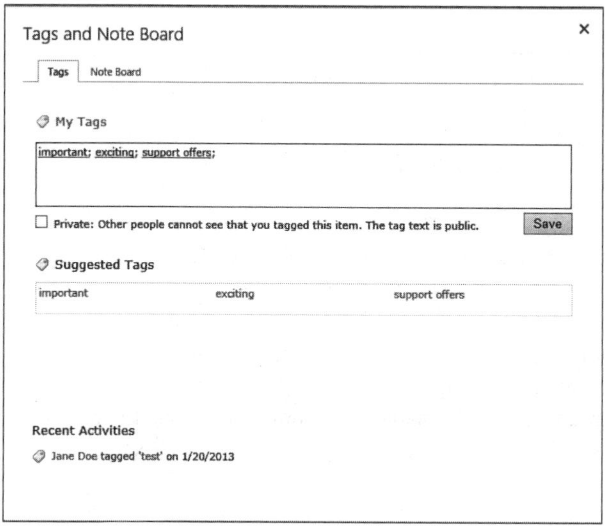

FIGURE 3.11   The tagging dialog, showing the Tags tab.

> **TIP**   Tagging a page in SharePoint is possible, but not all pages show the buttons that allow you to tag it. Pages that do allow this usually have the buttons as part of the navigation ribbon. If you cannot find the link, you can still tag the page by using the instructions in the following section.

Tag an External Site

> **Scenario/Problem:** You find a site that is useful. However, this site is not hosted in SharePoint, and it's not even part of your corporate site. You want to be able to find it again using the tagging mechanism. For example, say that you are tagging documents that are important for your day-to-day work as "Useful for my project," so that you can access them quickly from one location in your personal site. You might also want to add an Internet site to the list of useful items for the project.

Solution: In SharePoint Server 2013, you can tag any link from any site, whether it is hosted in SharePoint or not. To be able to tag external sites, you need to open the tagging dialog by using the Tags & Notes button on the Library or Files ribbons in a document library. SharePoint opens the tagging dialog in page tagging mode, and it provides a link that says "Right click or drag and drop this link to your browser's favorites or bookmarks toolbar to tag external sites," as shown in Figure 3.12. You follow the instructions in the dialog to add the sites to your browser's favorites, and then you are ready to tag external sites.

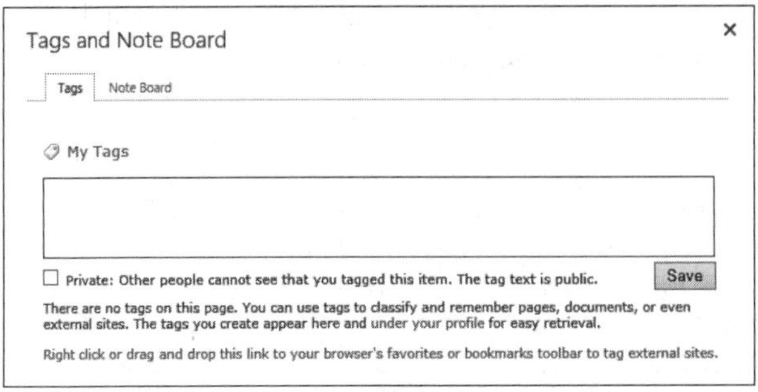

FIGURE 3.12   The tagging dialog, when opened from the Files ribbon for a file with no tags, shows the option to add a special link to your browser's favorites for tagging external sites.

When you want to tag an external site's page with a tag, you browse to that page, open your browser's favorites, and click on the link you added. SharePoint directs you to the same tagging dialog you saw earlier in this chapter that allows you to tag the page or site. You can also view or add notes to it, as described in the following section.

View/Add Notes to a Document or List Item

Scenario/Problem: You want to see whether any notes exist about a document or a list item, and you want to add notes about a document or list item.

Solution: In SharePoint Server 2013, you can add notes to a document. These notes are available for other people to read. You can use this feature, for example, to provide feedback on a document without actually changing the document and without having to check out the document or even have editing permissions to the document.

To add notes to a document, you select the document in the web part or list view that displays the document to switch to the Files ribbon. In the ribbon, you find and click the Tags & Notes button to open the tagging dialog. In the dialog, you select the Note Board tab. This tab allows you to type notes about the document or view notes that other users wrote for that document, as shown in Figure 3.13.

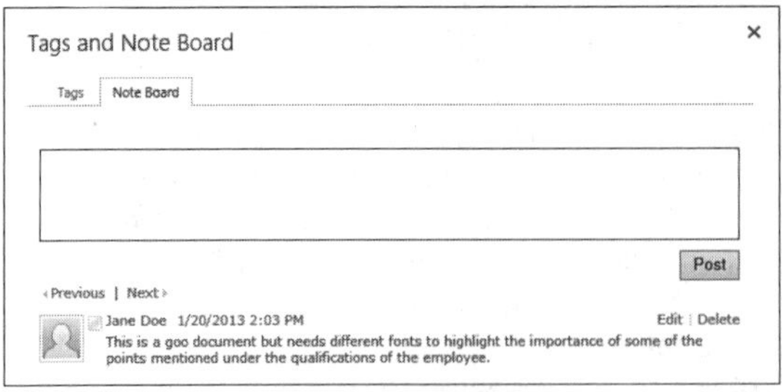

FIGURE 3.13   The Note Board tab of the tagging dialog. Existing notes are shown, with options to edit or delete them.

View Past Versions of Documents

Scenario/Problem: Some document libraries support versioning, which means that every time a file in the library changes, the old version is stored. Sometimes you might want to view an old version of a document without restoring it to be the current version.

Solution: To view the past versions of a specific document, you select the document to switch to the Files ribbon, and then you click on the Version History button. Alternatively, you can open the popup dialog menu for the file and choose Version History from the drop-down menu (see Figure 3.14).

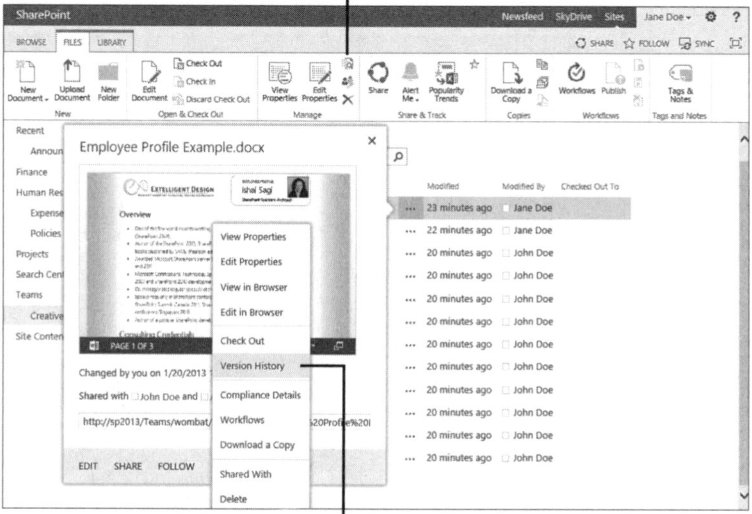

The Version History button in the Files ribbon

The Version History option in the files's context drop-down menu

FIGURE 3.14   The two options to view the versions of a file.

The version history dialog opens, showing past versions of the document (see Figure 3.15).

By default, the Version History dialog displays the list of versions in the order of the version number, with the earlier versions at the bottom of the list. You can change the sort order by clicking on the header links of the version table.

The versions are shown as dates, representing the date the version was created. If you hover the mouse cursor over one of these dates, you can open a menu for the document that allows you to view the version (see Figure 3.16).

The fourth (and last) version of the file

The first version of the file

FIGURE 3.15   The Version History dialog, showing the four versions of a file.

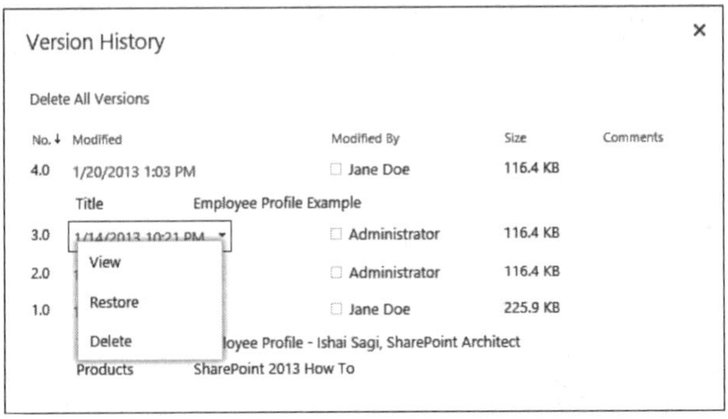

FIGURE 3.16   The drop-down menu for a version appears if you hover over the date for that version and click the arrow. In the menu you can choose to view the selected version.

View Properties of a List Item

Scenario/Problem: The list views or web parts might not show all the columns defined in a list. When you're viewing a list in either a web part on the home page or in one of the list views of that list, you might want to see more details about a list item. For example, a web part or a list view showing a contact list item might show only the contact's first and last names, and you might want to see more details about the contact, such as the address and phone number.

Solution: When viewing in a list view or a web part, you can click on the title of the list item to see its details. Alternatively, you can use the View Item button in the Items ribbon or select View Item from the item's drop-down menu which, similarly to viewing a document's properties, you can open by clicking the three dots next to the item's title as shown in Figure 3.17.

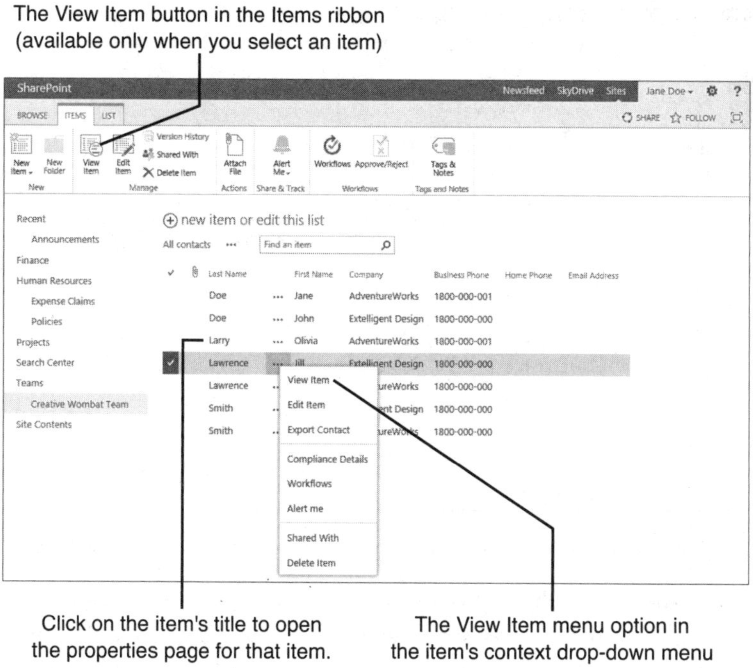

The View Item button in the Items ribbon
(available only when you select an item)

Click on the item's title to open   The View Item menu option in
the properties page for that item.   the item's context drop-down menu

FIGURE 3.17   The drop-down menu for a list item, showing actions that readers can
perform, including View Item and the Items ribbon.

Either method opens a properties page showing the metadata of the list item, with all of
its properties.

View a Microsoft InfoPath Form

Scenario/Problem: As explained in Chapter 1, form libraries are used to host
Microsoft InfoPath forms. In many cases, you will want to open one of the forms
in a form library to view its contents.

Solution: The form libraries behave much the same as document libraries. Viewing
a Microsoft InfoPath form that is in a form library is much like opening a document
for reading: You just click on the link that is the form name (see Figure 3.18).

NOTE   Some forms are configured to allow the data that is in the form to be
displayed as a column in the form library. This allows you to preview the data that is
in the form without opening it. It can also help you more easily find a specific form.
In Figure 3.18, you can see that certain data from the form is displayed, such as the
total of the expense claim, as well as the start and end dates for the expense claims.

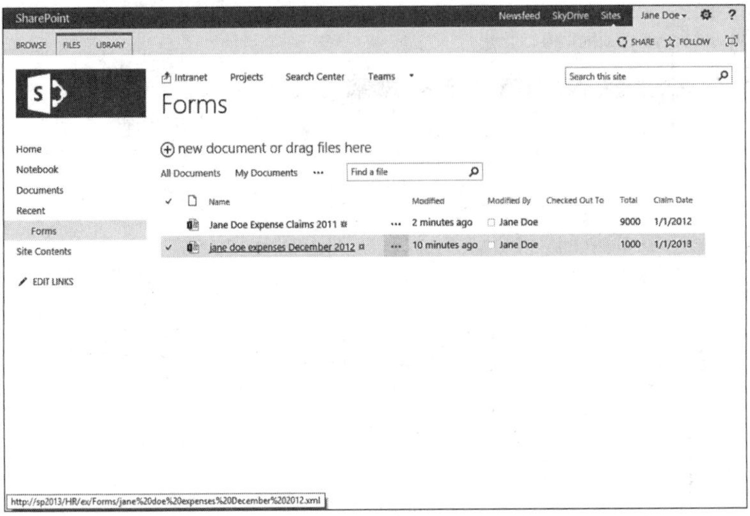

FIGURE 3.18   A form library with two forms. Click on the name of the form to open it.

If the site you are using does not have SharePoint Server installed, or if the form or form library has not been configured to make forms open in the browser, clicking on a form opens it on your computer in Microsoft InfoPath. If you don't have Microsoft InfoPath installed, the form just downloads to your computer.

If the site is using SharePoint Server, and the form and the form library are both configured to show the form in the browser, then clicking on the form opens it using the browser interface.

To close the form and go back to the form library, you either close the Microsoft InfoPath application (if the form was opened with the application) or click on the Close link on the top of the form if it was opened in the browser.

Change Sorting and Filtering of a List or Library

Scenario/Problem: When in a large document library or a list, finding the piece of information you are looking for can be tricky. To help you find what you are after, you might want to sort a specific column differently from its default sorting order or filter a column on a specific value. For example, in a document library, you might want to sort the documents based on the date they were changed so you can easily see the last one that was changed. Or in a contacts list you might want to filter the Last Name column to display only people with the last name Doe.

Solution: When viewing a list or a document library, you can change the view in several ways to find the specific item or document you want. The following sections discuss the possibilities.

> **NOTE** The changes you make are not permanent. Only you see them, and when you close the browser and navigate to the list again, the default sort order and filters that the list manager has defined are applied again.To learn how to save a sort order or filter, see Chapter 8, "Creating List Views."

Sort

To sort a list view on a specific field, you click on the heading for that field. Clicking on the field header causes the list to be sorted based on that field, either in ascending or descending order. A small arrow appears to signify the sort order. Using this mechanism, you can only sort based on one field at a time.

Another way to define the sort order is to open the column's drop-down menu and click on the sort order you want.

Filter

To filter on a column, you move your mouse cursor over the heading for that column, which causes a drop-down menu to appear. You click on the drop-down menu and choose the filter value from the list (see Figure 3.19).

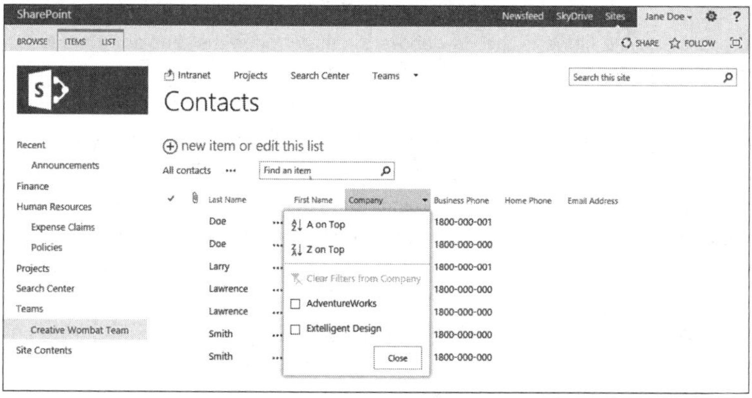

FIGURE 3.19   Choosing the sort order for the Company column in a contacts list.

> **NOTE** When there are many items to display in the filter options drop-down, SharePoint does not automatically display them in the menu. Instead, you see a button that allows you to load the items. This prevents you from waiting for the long list of items to load if you just want to sort the list and not filter it.

Switch List Views in Lists and Libraries

> **Scenario/Problem:** Most lists and libraries have different list views that show different columns and apply different sort orders, filters, and styles. Switching to a different list view can help you more easily find information in the list or library.

Solution: You can switch views in several ways. First, above the web part showing the items or files, the different views will be displayed as navigation—allowing you to switch from one view to another simply by clicking the view's name. If more views are in the list than can be displayed, only the first few will be displayed, and the rest will be in a view selector control, requiring you to click on the three dots and open a drop-down menu with the rest of the views, as shown in Figure 3.20.

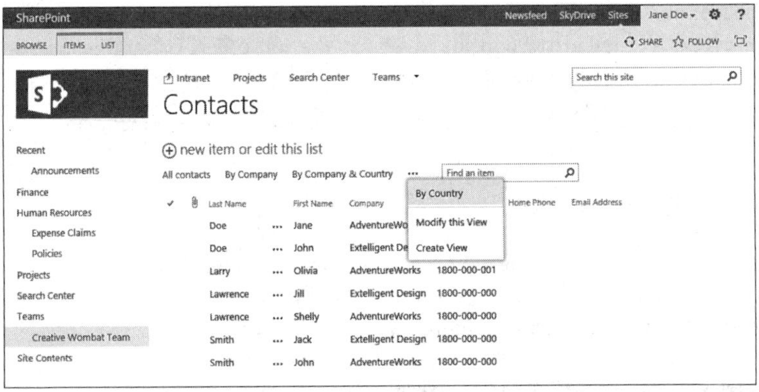

FIGURE 3.20   Click on the name of the view above the list or open the drop-down menu to show other views you can switch to.

In some lists, the views are not shown above the list items. In those cases you can switch to the List or Library ribbons. In the ribbon, you locate the Current View drop-down menu, which is usually to the left of the E-mail a Link button. When you open this drop-down menu, you see the names of all the views that are available for you in the list (see Figure 3.21).

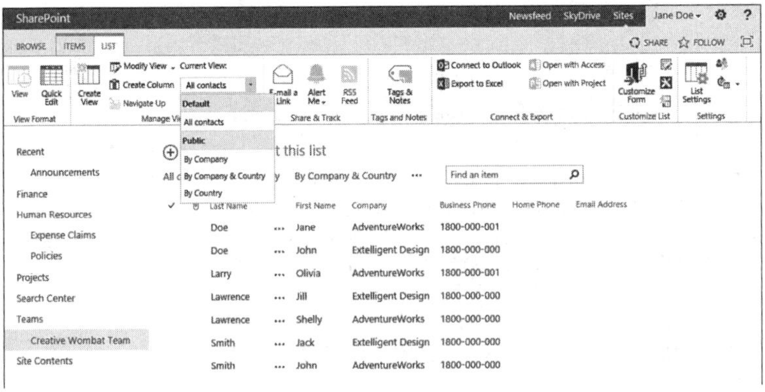

FIGURE 3.21   The view selector drop-down menu in the List ribbon.

> **NOTE** The ribbon name might change depending on the type of list or library. For example, in calendar lists, the name of the ribbon is Calendar, whereas in most other lists, the name of the ribbon is List.

These views are either public views (that everyone sees on that list) or a private view that you have created for yourself. For more information on list views, see Chapter 1 and Chapter 8. To switch to the view you want, you click on the view name that you want, and the view changes.

> **TIP** Investigate the different views. Some views might be more efficient and helpful for you to quickly find data. You can do some things beyond filtering and sorting that you can do only by creating views, so take a look at your options.

Some special instances of views have subviews. Subviews offer other ways to see the same view. For example, in calendar views, you can switch between the daily subview, the weekly subview (see Figure 3.22), and the monthly subview by using buttons on the ribbon. These subviews show the information that is defined in the view itself (filtering the items, ordering the items) but in a different manner.

To switch between the subviews of a calendar view, you use the Day, Week, and Month links in the Calendar ribbon when in a calendar view.

The available subviews of a calendar view

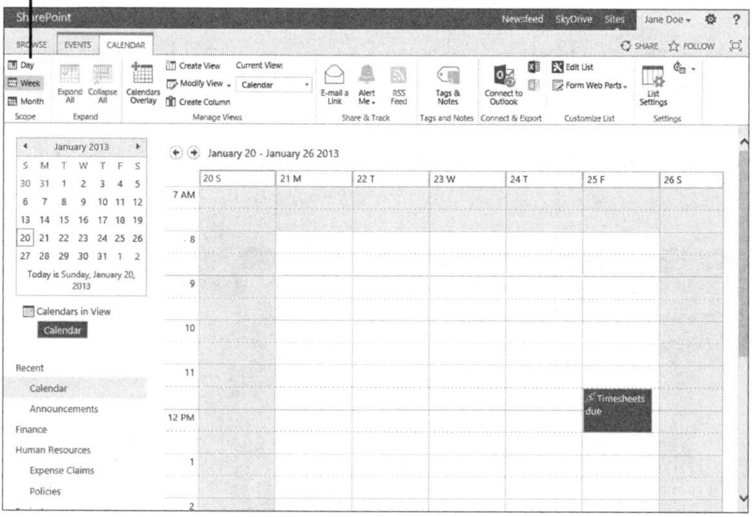

FIGURE 3.22   The weekly subview of a calendar.

> **NOTE** Survey lists are unique in that they do not offer ribbons (at the time of this writing). Instead, this type of list offers a toolbar at the top of the list view with buttons that allow you to do most of what is available in the corresponding ribbons in other lists and libraries.

Switch to the Quick Edit View

As explained in Chapter 1, the quick edit view is a special type of view that looks like a spreadsheet. It allows you to copy information from the list to spreadsheet applications or do some calculations on data in the list. To switch to the quick edit view, you switch to the List or Library ribbon and click on the Quick Edit button (see Figure 3.23).

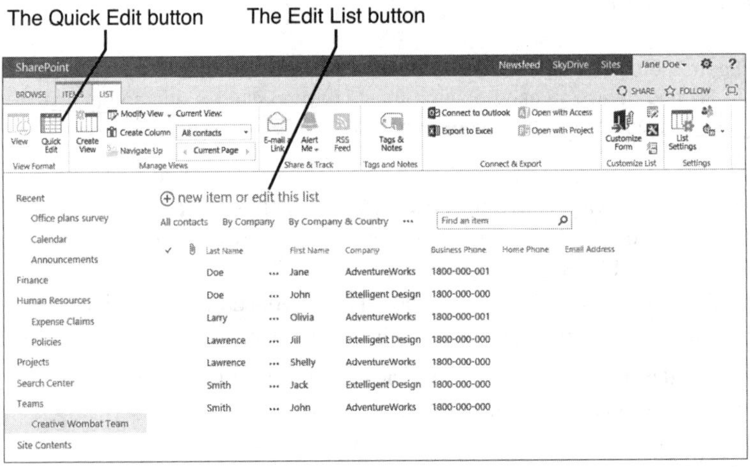

The Quick Edit button   The Edit List button

FIGURE 3.23   The Edit List link and the Quick Edit button in the List ribbon.

> **NOTE**   The Quick Edit view is only available if you have permissions to edit the list's contents. Otherwise, it will be grayed out.

As shown in Figure 3.24, the Quick Edit view displays all the columns from the standard view.

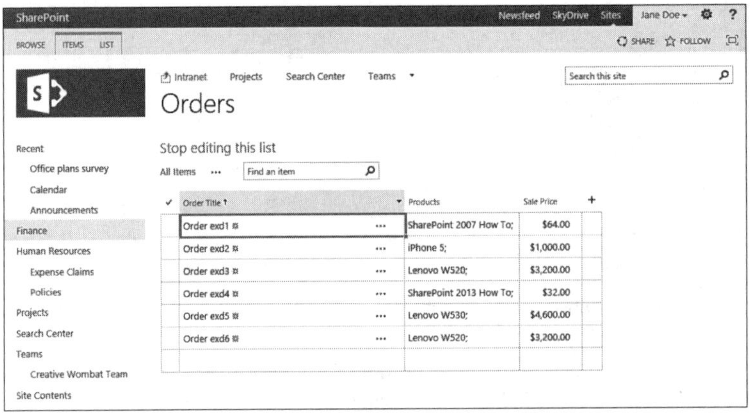

FIGURE 3.24   The Quick Edit view, showing the list in a spreadsheet format.

Use Alerts

Scenario/Problem: Information in sites changes often. Lists and libraries get updated with new items or files, and existing items and files get updated or deleted. Often, you need to know if something important to you is changed or updated. For example, if a document containing a policy that heavily impacts your work is updated, you want to know immediately. Or if a new list item is entered into a contacts list used to track potential customers, you want to know about it so you can call the customer.

Solution: You can set up alerts that notify you when some changes are made in SharePoint document libraries or lists or on single items. When you create an alert, you are asking the system to send you an e-mail or send a text message (SMS) to your mobile phone when a specific change occurs. The following sections explain how you can create alerts on different kinds of data and how to manage your alerts.

NOTE Alerts by text messages (SMS) to mobile phones requires special configuration by the administrator, so that option might not be available to you.

Create an Alert

You can create an alert on a file or a list item and also on a library or list. The following sections provide the details of how to perform each task.

Create an Alert on a File or List Item

When you set up an alert on a document or list item, SharePoint e-mails you when changes are made to that document or item. To set this type of alert, select the document or list item and switch to the Files or Items ribbon. On the ribbon, you click the Alert Me button and select Set Alert on This Document or Set Alert on This Item (see Figure 3.25).

Alternatively, you can open the properties dialog for the list item or file (refer to "View Properties of a Document" and "View Properties of a List Item" previously in this chapter), the Alert Me button is shown in the ribbon (see Figure 3.26).

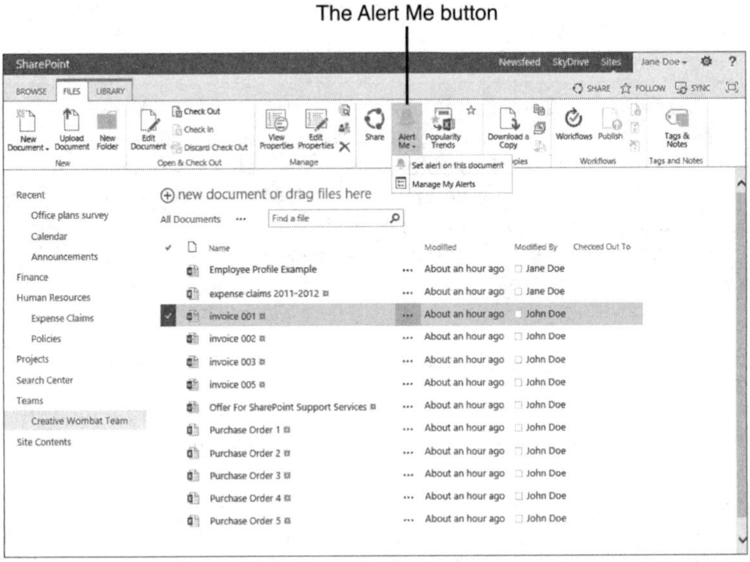

The Alert Me button

FIGURE 3.25   The Alert Me button in the Files ribbon when a document is selected.

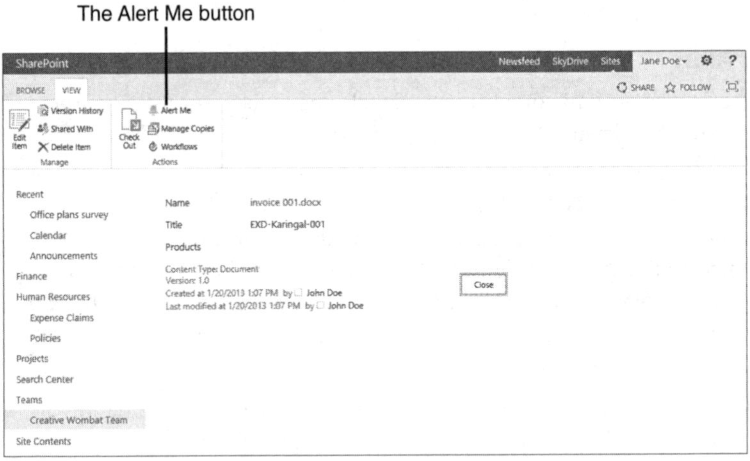

The Alert Me button

FIGURE 3.26   The Alert Me button in the View ribbon for a file.

When you select this option, the New Alert dialog appears, and in it you can define what sort of alert you want to get on the item (see Figure 3.27). If your site supports sending text messages, you can select to have the alert sent using a text message to a phone number in the Delivery Method section of the dialog.

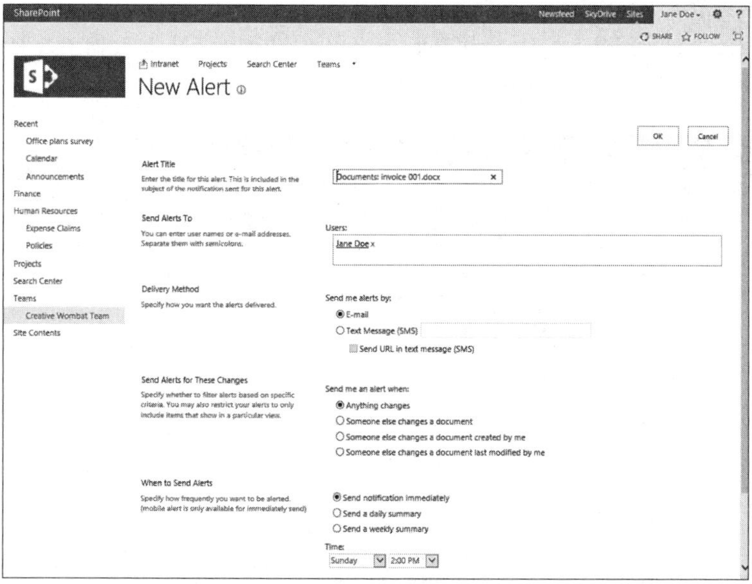

FIGURE 3.27   The New Alert dialog for a file, showing options for a new alert.

Under the Send Alert for These Changes section, you have multiple options to choose from. For example, you can choose to be notified just when someone else changes the item or whenever the item is changed (even when you're the one who changes it). The other options in this section are not relevant for alerts on documents and items.

NOTE   Different list types have different options in the Send Alert for These Changes section. For example, a calendar list has an option to get an alert when the time or location for an event is changed.

In the When to Send Alerts section, you can define when the e-mail for a change will be sent. If you choose Immediately, an e-mail is sent to you whenever someone changes the document—one e-mail per change. Selecting a daily or weekly summary reduces the number of e-mails you get; you receive only a summary e-mail of all the changes.

After selecting the options that you want, a confirmation e-mail is sent to you, to tell you that the alert has been set up. Receiving this message might take a few minutes.

Create an Alert on a Library or List

When you set up an alert on a list or library, SharePoint sends you an e-mail or a text message when changes are made to the list or library (that is, when items are added, removed, or changed).

To set up this type of alert, you switch to the List or Library ribbon, click on the Alert Me button, and choose Set Alert on This List or Set Alert on This Library (see Figure 3.28).

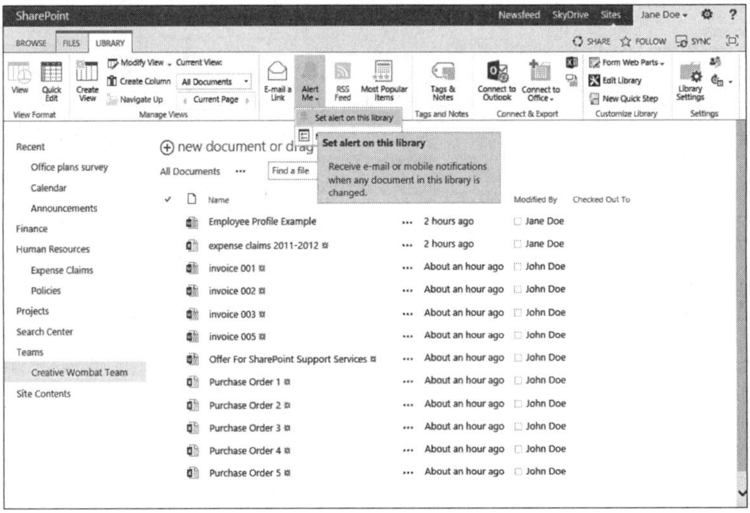

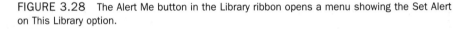

FIGURE 3.28   The Alert Me button in the Library ribbon opens a menu showing the Set Alert on This Library option.

When you select this option, the settings dialog for the alert appears, and in it you can define what sort of alert you want to get. If your site supports sending text messages, you can select to have the alert sent using a text message to a phone number in the Delivery Method section of the dialog.

In the Change Type section, you can choose what kind of change you want to be alerted on. For example, you can select to be alerted only when new items are added, only when items are deleted, or when anything happens (that is, for all changes).

Similarly to setting up an alert on a list item, you can choose when the alert will be sent—either immediately or as a daily or weekly summary.

> **NOTE**   Different list types can have different options in the Send Alert for These Changes section. For example, a task list has an option to send an alert when a high-priority task changes or when someone changes a task in a specific view. This allows you to create more complex alerts for different list types.

After you create an alert, you get a confirmation e-mail. Alert e-mails for lists look exactly the same as alerts on list items.

> **TIP**   Don't forget that alerts can be annoying if you get too many e-mails. Creating an alert on a "busy" document library and setting it to e-mail you immediately on every change can overload your mailbox. Consider the daily or weekly e-mail options unless you really need to know about new documents or changes as they happen.

Modify or Remove an Alert

To modify or remove an alert, click on the Modify My Alert Settings link that the alerts sends to you. Doing so opens the site where that alert was created, in the alert management screen. In this screen you can either click on an alert to change its settings (for example, when it should send the e-mail, what changes it should alert on), or you can select the alert and delete it by using the Delete Selected Alerts button.

Alternatively, you can browse to the list or library on which the alert is set, switch to the List or Library ribbon, click the Alert Me button, and select Manage My Alerts. This opens the same dialog, allowing you to edit or delete any of the alerts you have set in that site.

Manage My Alerts in a Site

To see what alerts you have in a site and manage them without going through a list, as you've done up to this point, you can navigate to the site's My Alerts on this Site page by adding _layouts/mysubs.aspx to the path to the site where the alerts are set. For example, if the site containing your alert is at http://sharepoint/sample, you type http://sharepoint/sample/_layouts/mysubs.aspx to get to the alerts page as shown in Figure 3.29.

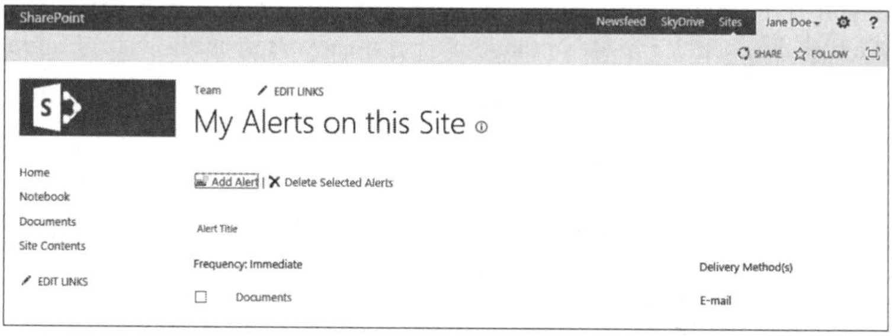

FIGURE 3.29   The alert management page allows you to click on an alert to edit it or select an alert to delete it.

Export the Contents of a List to Microsoft Excel

Scenario/Problem: You want to take a snapshot of a SharePoint list and copy its contents to a Microsoft Excel spreadsheet, either to analyze the data or to print it using Excel.

Solution: You can export the contents of a list or a document library to an Excel spreadsheet by clicking the Export to Excel button under the List or Library ribbons, as shown in Figure 3.30. The export opens a new Excel spreadsheet with the meta-data of the list or library. In the case of document libraries this does not export the files themselves, just the columns of data about the files.

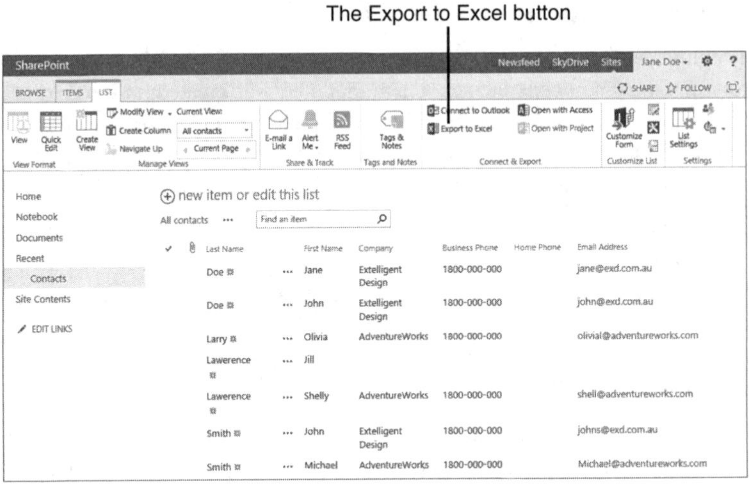

The Export to Excel button

FIGURE 3.30   The Export to Excel button in the List ribbon for a contacts list.

When you click the button, your browser might ask you to download or open a file. Select Open, and wait for Excel to open. Excel might show you a security notice prompt letting you know that the information Excel is trying to open is from a nonsecure location (a website). Click Enable in that dialog if it shows up, as shown in Figure 3.31.

FIGURE 3.31   The Security Notice dialog that appears when you open the exported list.

NOTE   Depending on the security configuration of your computer, Excel might ask you to enter your username and password when opening an exported SharePoint list.

After it's opened, the data from the list is available in Excel, including all the columns that were available in the list view you started from, as shown in Figure 3.32. (See "Switch List Views in Lists and Libraries," earlier in this chapter to learn how to switch to different views, or see Chapter 8, if you want to create a view that displays more or less information to be exported.)

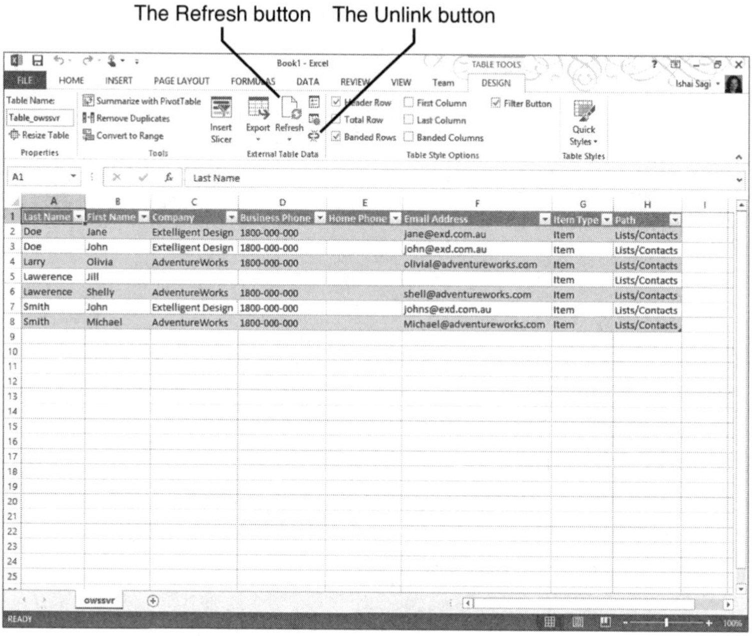

The Refresh button   The Unlink button

FIGURE 3.32   The contacts list open in Microsoft Excel.

The list in Excel is now connected to the list in SharePoint. If someone makes a
change to the list in SharePoint, the change will be reflected in your Excel document
if you reopen the file or click the Refresh button in the External Table Data section of
the ribbon (refer to Figure 3.32). You can use the Unlink button in the same section
to disconnect the spreadsheet from the SharePoint list and continue working on it
separately.

CHAPTER 4

Searching in SharePoint

SharePoint has a built-in search engine that allows you to search for files or pages that are in SharePoint or even in other sites or file storage applications. However, the different SharePoint interfaces—SharePoint Server and SPF—have different ways to search and display the search results. This chapter explains how to search using SharePoint's different interfaces.

Search for Documents and List Items

Scenario/Problem: You want to find a piece of content that exists in your corporate network, but you're not sure where in the network it is. It might be a document stored in SharePoint or in a file share, or a list item in SharePoint or in an application database.

Solution: SharePoint has a built-in search facility that allows you to find content in SharePoint (and, sometimes, also content that is not in SharePoint, depending on the configuration the search administrator set up). The search user interface can be customized, so the search screen in your SharePoint site might look different from what's shown in this chapter. Such customization doesn't change how you search, however.

Note that searching in SPF is different from searching in SharePoint Server. Indeed, one of the main reasons corporations buy and install SharePoint Server is that the search options that come with this product offer much more for the administrator and for you, the end user, to use.

Searching for a File or List Item Within a Specific List or Library

When you're in a document library or a list, a simple search box on the top of the list view (next to the view names) enables you to search for a file or an item in that list or library. This filters the list view to show only the items that contain the term you searched for.

Searching for a File or List Item in the Entire SharePoint Environment

The basic search in both SharePoint Server and SPF is the same: You type the search keywords in the search box and click the search icon. However, SharePoint Server has an additional Advanced option that enables you to search for items using their properties, and a Preferences option that enables you to set the languages you are using to search, the default language, and whether you want to see search suggestions in the search box. SharePoint Server also enables you to search all the SharePoint sites (unlike SPF, which allows you to search only the site you are currently in) as well as content that exists outside SharePoint.

To search for anything, you usually just type in the search box a keyword that represents the item you want to search for and click the search button, which usually looks like a magnifying glass. The location of the search box can vary, and if you are using SharePoint Server, you might have other options about how to search, including the Advanced link (for advanced searching), a Preferences link (for setting preferences, as mentioned earlier), and dedicated search pages. These options are covered later in this chapter.

The simplest form of searching in SharePoint—the method just described—is known as a *keyword search*. The keyword can be a word that appears in the document (part of the document's contents) or in the document or list item's properties (for example, a document name, a contact's company name, or anything else the search administrator decided should be included in the search scope). Figure 4.1 shows an example of a keyword search.

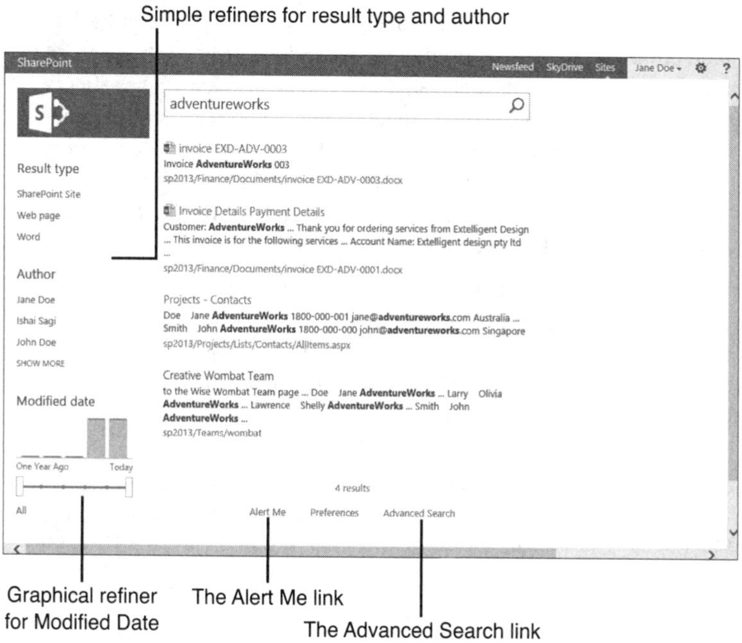

FIGURE 4.1   Searching for the word *adventureworks* produces results that include documents that have the word in its contents, a list view, and a site whose home page has the same word.

TIP   Because search results can sometimes be documents, sometimes list items, and sometimes web pages or list views, what you get when you click on a search result will vary.

When opening search results, you might want to open the result in a new window (or a new tab, in some browsers) so you don't lose the search results page you are viewing. To do so, you right-click the link and choose Open in New Window. You also can Shift+click the link to open it in a new window; Ctrl+click opens it in a new tab in some browsers.

You can search for more than one word. The search results contain everything that includes any of those words.

> **TIP**   Searching for the words *mountain bikes* results in all the documents that have either the word *mountain* or the word *bikes* as well as *mountains* and *bike* and other forms of the two words. If you want to search only for an exact match for a phrase, you surround it with quotation marks (for example, "mountain bikes"). Alternatively, you can use the advanced search (described later in this chapter) to accomplish the same effect.

By default the search results are sorted by relevance; the document you are most likely looking for should be the first in the list. SharePoint calculates the relevance of the documents based on many things, but basically, a document with more instances of the word you searched for should be highest in a list sorted by relevance.

In some instances, SharePoint recognizes that the search you conducted can be filtered on some common property such as the result type (Word documents, web pages, site names, and so on) or the author of the content. These filters, also known as refiners (because they refine your search) appear on the left side of the screen, and you can simply click the value you want to filter the results to. For example, to filter the results to content authored by John, click on John's name under the Author refiner as shown earlier in Figure 4.1. Some refiners have the Show More option, which enables you to manually specify a value instead of selecting one from the list.

Some refiners are more sophisticated than a simple value list. For example, the Modified Date refiner shows a graph of values—the more items were modified on a specific date, the higher the graph bar is. You can then click on the bar to filter the results to that date range. Additionally, a sliding bar at the bottom of the graph lets you drag two lines to specify a start and end range for the date.

> **TIP**   Depending on the configuration of the search page, you might have an option to choose a different sorting order—to sort by modified date. If the page was configured to have this option, you see a drop-down menu with the title Sort By and in it the option Modified Date. You can select this option to reorder the search results.

In addition, the search results page in a SharePoint Server configuration offers a way to be notified when a new search result for your search is added in the future by clicking the Alert Me link. For example, if you search for *AdventureWorks* and you want to know when new documents or list items are created in the future, you can use this option.

The Alert Me option is similar to the alert functionality for other objects in SharePoint (such as documents or lists; see Chapter 3, "Solutions Regarding Files, Documents, List Items, and Forms," for more information) but has fewer options, as shown in Figure 4.2.

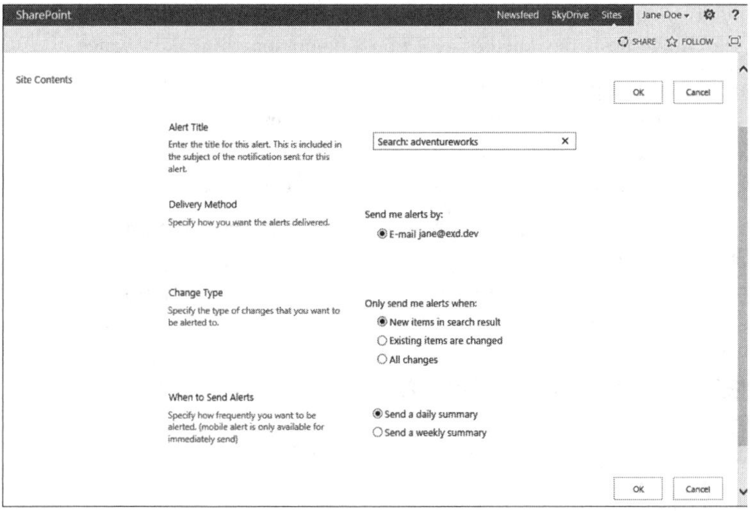

FIGURE 4.2   The search alert settings page.

In the Change Type section, select whether you want to be alerted only on new items, on changed items, or on both. In the When to Send Alerts section, you select whether you want daily alerts or immediate alerts when there is something to be alerted on.

> **NOTE**   Alerts from searches are never immediate. An e-mail is sent to you only when the change has been picked up by the search engine. Depending on the search configuration that the administrator set up, that can take a while.

Search Using the Search Center

> **Scenario/Problem:** When you are using a SharePoint site that is hosted on a server that has SharePoint Server installed, the search options are different and more versatile than if you have just SPF installed. (See "How to Tell Whether a Site Is Based on SPF, SharePoint Server, or SharePoint on Office 365" in Chapter 1, "About Microsoft SharePoint 2013," for more information.)

Solution: A variety of options exist in SharePoint Server sites for executing different types of search queries. You can search in SharePoint Server in many ways. The simplest is exactly like in SPF: You use a search box at the top of the page that allows you to type and search.

> **NOTE**   Depending on the scope you choose and on how the search administrator set it up, you may be directed to a different search results page.

A search option available in SharePoint Server is to use the Search Center. This site is dedicated to searching and is designed to give you a better searching experience.

If your organization is using the Search Center, you can usually get to it by either finding it on the navigation bar, usually under the name Search. You can also get to the Search Center by performing a simple search from any site; if the site administrator configured it, you will be directed to the Search Center when you do that.

Some Search Centers have an option to display several search results of different types in different tabs, or search pages (see Figure 4.3). Each of these tabs can be configured to display search results from different sources of content. The site administrator can create other tabs, and these tabs can be configured to show different search results.

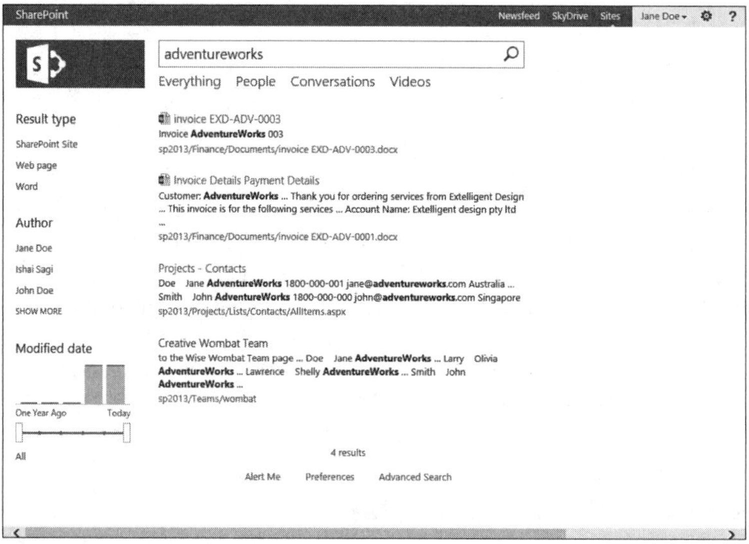

FIGURE 4.3   The default Search Center has a search page for people, conversations, videos, and a search page for other content.

To switch between tabs, you just click on the tab name. The term you were searching for is automatically transferred to the new tab, and a search is performed on it.

> **TIP**   By default, the Search Center template is configured not to display any navigational aids. This makes going back to the site you started from difficult. To do that, you can either click the Back button in your browser or manually change the address of your browser to the site you want to navigate to.

Use the Advanced Search (in SharePoint Server)

Scenario/Problem: Sometimes when you want to search for a document or a list item, you don't want to use free text to search on the content of the document or the list item. Instead, you might want to restrict the search to the metadata—the information stored about the document or list item in the columns of the list or library. For example, if you want to search for documents written by John Doe, performing a simple search for the words "John Doe" returns documents that were not written by that person. Instead, it returns any document that has the words "John Doe" in the body of the document, as well as in other columns, such as the column showing who modified the document last.

Solution: Advanced searching allows you to search for documents or list items in a more organized manner than just typing keywords. It lets you focus your search on a particular property of the documents or list items. For example, you can search for documents that person X wrote or documents that were created after the date 1/1/2008 or list items that have the word *AdventureWorks* in the company property but not in other properties.

To get to the advanced search page, you navigate to the Search Center and click on the Advanced button (see Figure 4.4). Depending on the configuration of the site, you might also have other links to the advanced search page.

The Advanced Search link in the Search Center
The Preferences link in the Search Center

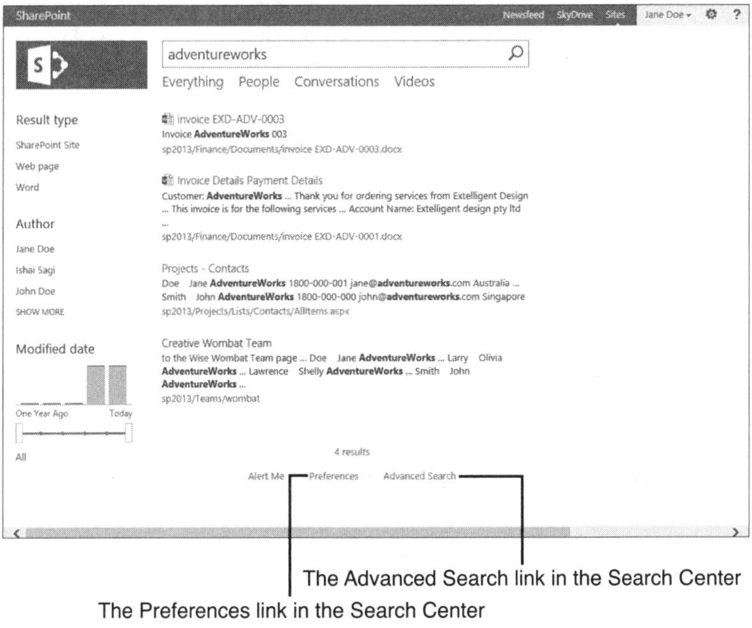

FIGURE 4.4   The Advanced link in the Search Center.

The advanced search page allows you to search more specifically and in a more exact manner on parts of the document or list item (see Figure 4.5).

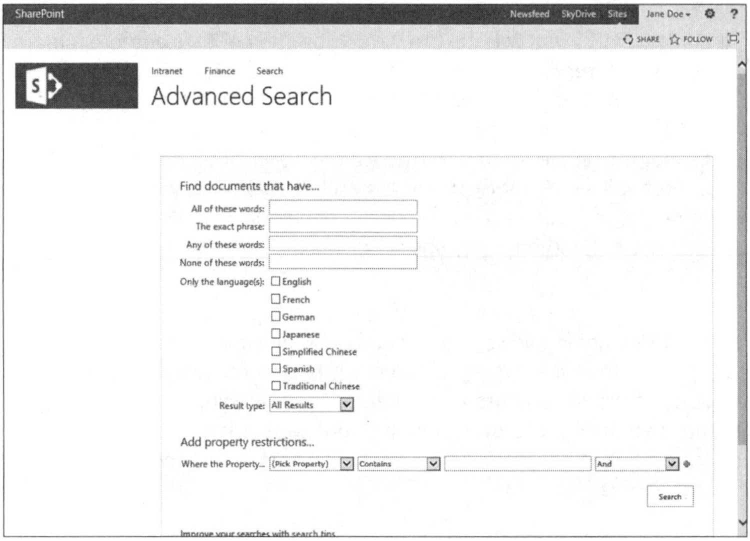

FIGURE 4.5 The Advanced Search page.

In this page, you can specify to look for words exactly as you do with the simple search option. When you type words in the Any of These Words box, the search results contain only documents or list items that have all the words that you type, but not necessarily in the same order. You can use the other options to refine your search. For example, if you select The Exact Phase, you can type a few words, and items will be returned in the results only if they contain the exact phrase. You can also specify words that you don't want in the documents and select the None of These Words box.

Another way to narrow a search is to specify a language. This option is usually used for web pages and not for documents, unless the documents have a property called Language.

You can specify the result type to search for example, for Microsoft Word documents, Microsoft Excel documents, or Microsoft PowerPoint documents. Or you can just select Documents to make sure your search returns only documents—and not list items (see Figure 4.6). The site administrator can customize this box to include more types.

Finally, you can specify a search on specific properties that the site administrator configured for you to search on. You can add up to five conditions, such as Property X Equals/Does Not Equal Y, as shown in Figure 4.7.

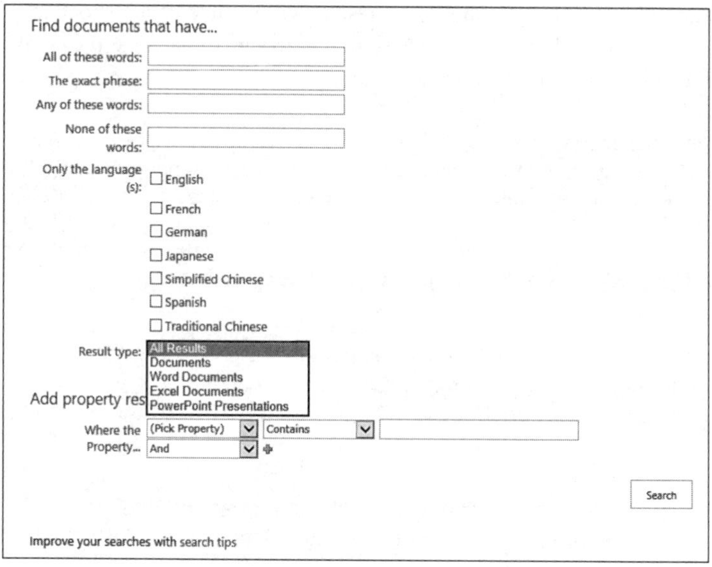

FIGURE 4.6   Selecting the result type.

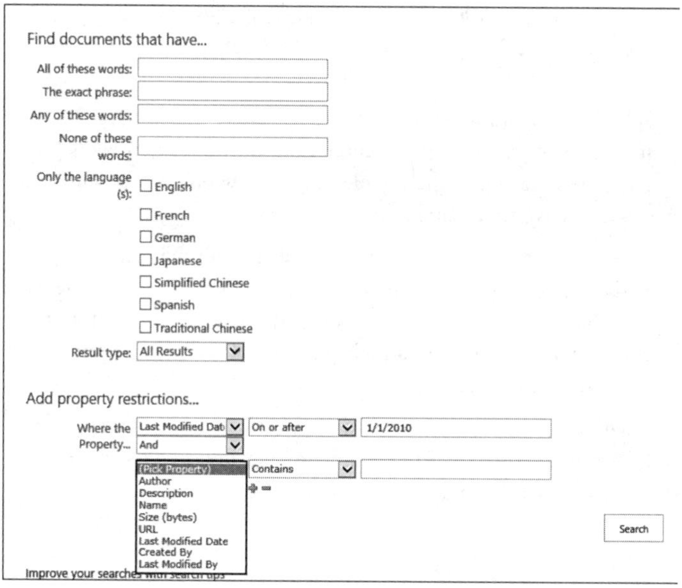

FIGURE 4.7   Searching on properties.

As shown in Figure 4.7, you can chain a few conditions together and choose whether they should be chained by using an Or operator or an And operator. For example, if you specify Author Equals John and Title Equals Example, the only results will be the ones whose author is John and whose title is exactly Example. But if you search for

Author Equals John *or* Title Equals Example, the results will include documents that have been authored by John and documents whose title is Example—not just the documents where both conditions are true.

> **NOTE** Site administrators often customize this interface. The possibility exists that your search experience here will be very different from what is shown here. You might, for example, be able to choose different operators, such as Contains.

Search for People (in SharePoint Server)

> **Scenario/Problem:** You might want to find the contact details of people who work with you in the organization. You might need to know someone's phone number, department, manager, and so on.

Solution: SharePoint Server has a user profile database that stores information about users. For more information about this feature, see Chapter 5, "Social Networking, Personal Sites, and Personal Details in SharePoint Server." If this feature has been set up, you have the ability to search for people and view their details. Also, if someone has created a personal site, you will be able to view the public view of that personal site. (For more information about personal sites and how to create them, see Chapter 5.)

You can perform a people search from most SharePoint Server sites by typing the name of the person you want to search for in the search box. If your search takes you to a Search Center, you can then switch to the People tab to show only users with that name, and not documents that have that name in them.

As with documents and list items, you can search by keyword using the same box, and refiners might appear to further filter your results. For example, you might be able to filter based on the office location property or the person's job title, as shown in Figure 4.8. Depending on whether the person uploaded their picture to their profile, you might see the image as part of the search results.

In the search results shown in Figure 4.8, hover the mouse over a person's name to see a dialog with information about the person, links to documents authored by the person, and links to the person's profile and to follow the person.

FIGURE 4.8　The People search results with refiners in the Search Center.

CHAPTER 5

Social Networking, Personal Sites, and Personal Details in SharePoint Server

IN THIS CHAPTER

Microsoft SharePoint Server 2013 offers social networking features that allow employees of a company to stay connected and update each other on what they are doing. Using these features, you can track newsfeeds about subjects that interest you (for example, items you tagged, colleagues whose status changed, new blog posts) and comments about items that you want to track.

On top of that, in some Microsoft SharePoint Server 2013 implementations, the option to create personal sites is enabled. In this case, you can create a SharePoint site that is totally under your control. You can upload documents to be stored in the site instead of on your desktop and manage your private lists, such as lists of favorite links or lists of friends. You can also microblog—publish short public messages (similar to Twitter) and follow what your colleagues are saying.

In addition, with SharePoint Server you get a user profile that stores information about you, such as your phone number, e-mail, and other details that would be useful for people in your organization. This chapter explains how to use the social features, how you can view personal details of yourself or of others, and how you can edit your own details, as well as how to create and navigate around a personal site.

Get Started with Social Features

Scenario/Problem: You want to use SharePoint Server's social features to manage your colleagues, set your status, microblog, and see the organization hierarchy.

Solution: You can get to your social networking pages from a SharePoint site a few different ways. The first is the top bar above the ribbon, which shows some handy links to certain locations in your personal site: Newsfeed links to your social newsfeed, SkyDrive links to personal document library, and Sites links to a page showing you the sites you chose to follow.

Additionally, you can click the [*your name*] button at the top-right corner of a SharePoint site's page and from the menu that opens and choose the option, as shown in Figure 5.1.

If the various links do not appear, it could be due to one of two reasons: Either you are working on a site that has SPF only (and not SharePoint Server) or the site manager disabled the option to have a personal site.

Clicking the About Me link opens your profile page. By default, clicking the About Me option *does not* create a personal site for you but instead opens the social networking home page, shown in Figure 5.2. This page allows you to navigate through various social apps and to edit your profile.

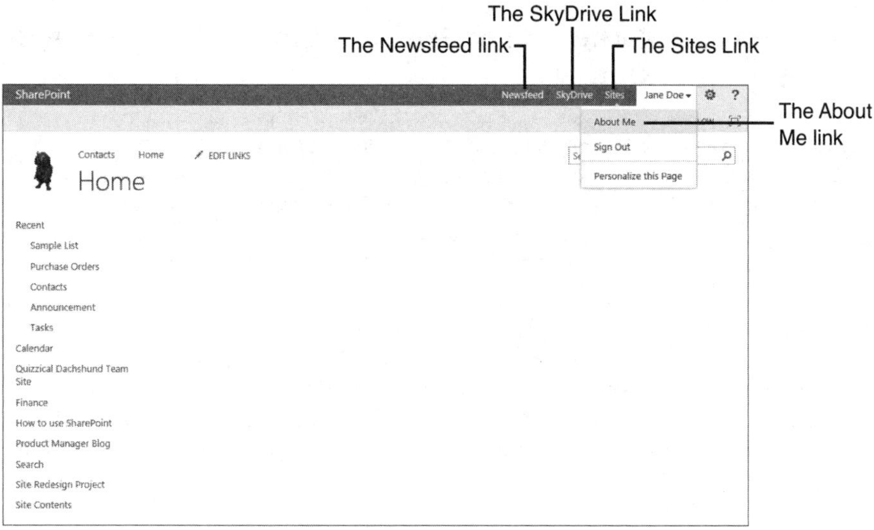
The SkyDrive Link
The Newsfeed link
The Sites Link
The About Me link
SharePoint
Newsfeed
SkyDrive
Sites
Jane Doe
About Me
Sign Out
Personalize this Page
Contacts
Home
EDIT LINKS
Home
Recent
Sample List
Purchase Orders
Contacts
Announcement
Tasks
Calendar
Quizzical Dachshund Team Site
Finance
How to use SharePoint
Product Manager Blog
Search
Site Redesign Project
Site Contents

FIGURE 5.1 Selecting My Profile or My Site from the menu.

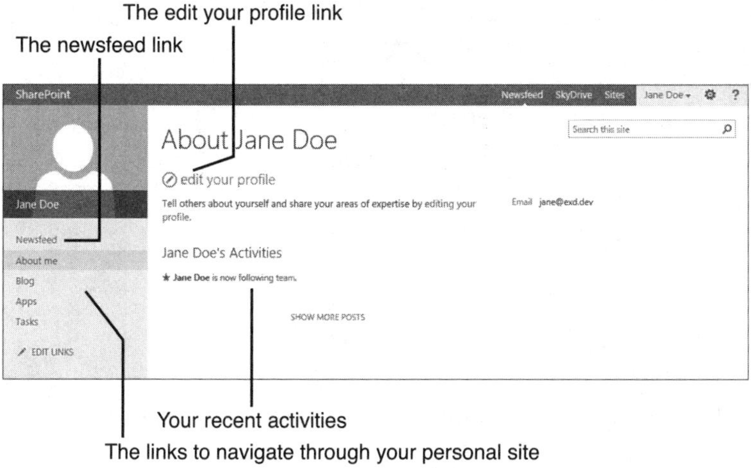
The edit your profile link
The newsfeed link
SharePoint
Newsfeed
SkyDrive
Sites
Jane Doe
About Jane Doe
Search this site
edit your profile
Tell others about yourself and share your areas of expertise by editing your profile.
Email jane@exd.dev
Jane Doe
Newsfeed
About me
Blog
Apps
Tasks
EDIT LINKS
Jane Doe's Activities
Jane Doe is now following team.
SHOW MORE POSTS
Your recent activities
The links to navigate through your personal site

FIGURE 5.2 The social networking home page.

The following sections describe how to perform some of the most common social networking tasks.

Use Microblogging to Let Others Know What You Are Doing or Thinking

Scenario/Problem: You want to use SharePoint Server's social features to share a thought with everyone in the organization, or just with people who visit a particular site. This can be used to start a conversation, either work related or not.

Solution: To microblog, either click the Newsfeed link at the top of any SharePoint page or from your About Me page (refer to Figures 5.1 and 5.2). A page opens showing you posts that other people whom you follow have posted, and your old posts. You can then type your message in the "start a conversation box," as shown in Figure 5.3, and click the Post button. You can also attach images to your post by using the camera icon.

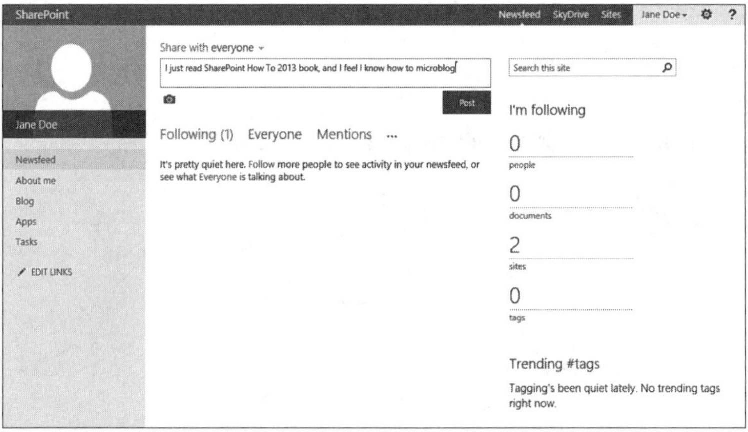

FIGURE 5.3   The Newsfeed page allows you to post a message to anyone who is following you.

This is similar to status updates in social networking Internet sites such as Facebook and Twitter. You can write a small description of what is on your mind or what you are doing, and people in your social network who are tracking your status can see on their newsfeed that you have a new status. Like Twitter, you can tag a term in the text by using the hashtag (#) prior to a word, allowing you and other people to follow specific tags and see it in your newsfeed if anyone else uses the same hashtag in their posts. To manage those hashtags, see "Manage Followed Hashtags" later in this chapter, under "Manage Newsfeed Settings."

TIP   Remember that everyone can see your status unless you specify otherwise!

> **TIP**   If you want to make sure a particular person sees your post, you can mention them in your post, prefixed with the @ sign (for example, "@john" is a mention of john).

Follow Colleagues to See What They Are Posting

Scenario/Problem: You want to use SharePoint Server's social features to follow another colleague and see what they post in their microblogging.

Solution: Navigate to the Newsfeed page (refer to Figure 5.3) and on the right side of the page, under the I'm Following heading, click on the number of people whom you are following (this number will be 0 if you are not following anyone). This opens the People I'm Following page shown in Figure 5.4. In this page you can click on the "follow" button (highlighted and with a star icon next to it), which opens a dialog in which you specify the names or email addresses of people whom you want to follow, as shown in Figure 5.5. You can specify one or more people to follow.

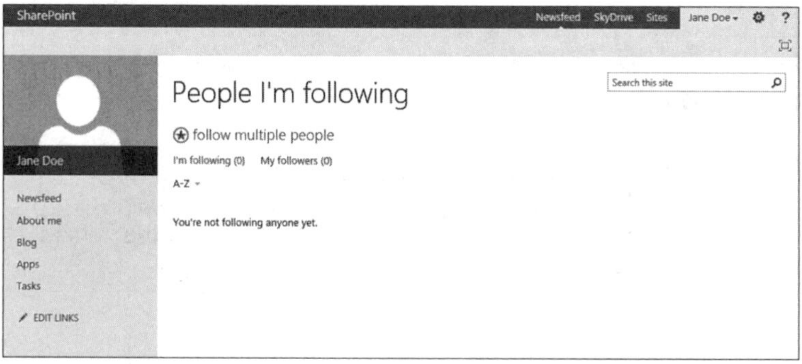

FIGURE 5.4   The People I'm Following page.

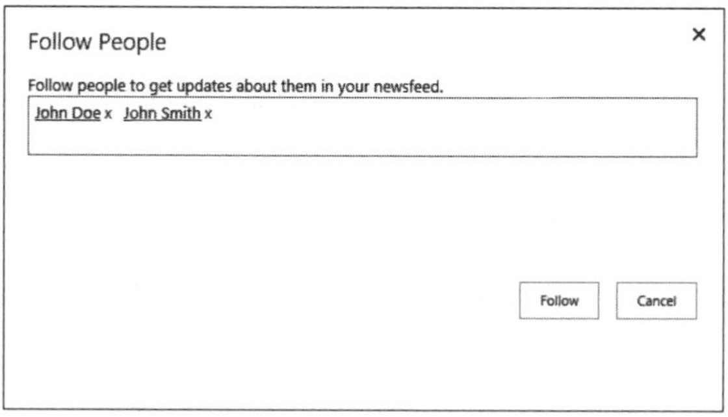

FIGURE 5.5   Use the Follow People dialog to specify whom you want to follow.

After you click Follow, the people you chose will be added to the list of people you are following, and their microblogging updates will appear in your newsfeed, giving you the ability to reply to it or like it, as shown in Figure 5.6.

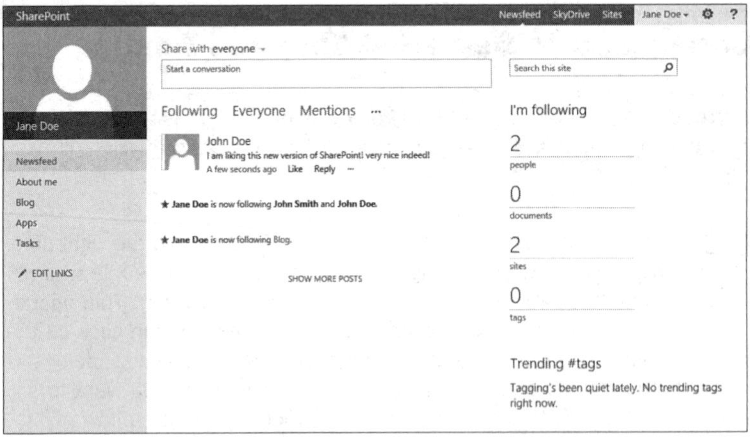

FIGURE 5.6   A post from John Doe appears in Jane's newsfeed.

Manage Tags and Notes

Scenario/Problem: You have added tags on items, documents, and pages. Now you want to find the items you tagged, change whether they are private or public, and maybe remove them. Similarly, you have added notes to the items, and you want to review and manage those notes.

Solution: SharePoint offers a page that allows you to review your tagged items and your notes. However, the link to that page is not always shown in SharePoint pages. To open this page, type **/_layouts/15/thoughts.aspx** after your site's address. For example, if your site's address is http://intranet, you should type http://intranet/_layouts/15/thoughts.aspx in the browser's address bar.

This opens the Tags and Notes page, which lets you find items tagged with specific terms—either by yourself or other people, as shown in Figure 5.7.

At the bottom of the page is a list of activities (by month). This list shows the items you or other people tagged with the term you click on under the Refine by Tag section. For example, clicking on the tag "dog" shows the files or list items or pages that were tagged with that word, as shown in Figure 5.8.

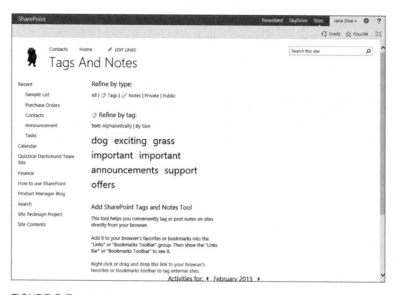

FIGURE 5.7   The Tags and Notes page.

Selecting the "dog" tag

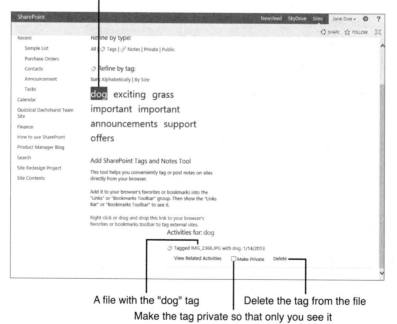

A file with the "dog" tag   Delete the tag from the file
Make the tag private so that only you see it

FIGURE 5.8   Selecting a specific tag.

When you find an item that is tagged or noted, you can click on the link to the item to open the item, or you can remove the note or the tag (by clicking the Delete link). You can also click on View Related Activities to open the tagging dialog for that item to add tags and notes to the file, item, or page.

Add, Edit, and Remove Notes on the Notes Board

Notes are similar to your status, but unlike the status, which is supposed to be a short description of what you are doing, notes can be long. You can use notes to comment on documents, items, and pages—even on external sites. (For more information on how to add notes, see Chapter 3, "Solutions Regarding Files, Documents, List Items, and Forms.")

The notes board is the place in your personal site where you can see all the notes you have written and from which you can easily create more notes that are not related to a specific item, file, or page.

To view the notes board for an item you tagged, either go to that item (or file) and click the tags and notes button. Otherwise, locate the item using the same process you used to find an item by tag (refer to Figure 5.8) but click on the "notes" filter at the top of the page. After you find an item, click View Related Activities to open that item's notes board where you can create a new general note by just typing in the box and clicking the Post button. The page also includes a list of all the notes you have created under the new note text box.

To delete a note, click the Delete link next to it. To edit a note, click the Edit link next to it.

> **TIP**   Remember that everyone can see your notes.

View Sites You Are Following

> **Scenario/Problem:** You want to see what sites you are following.

Solution: In most SharePoint environments the Sites link is at the top of the page. This link redirects you to a page in your personal site that shows you the list of sites you are following and suggestions of sites you might want to follow, as shown in Figure 5.9.

This page serves as a sort of favorites list where you can either click the title of a site to go to that site, or delete the link to the site by clicking the Stop Following link under the site's address.

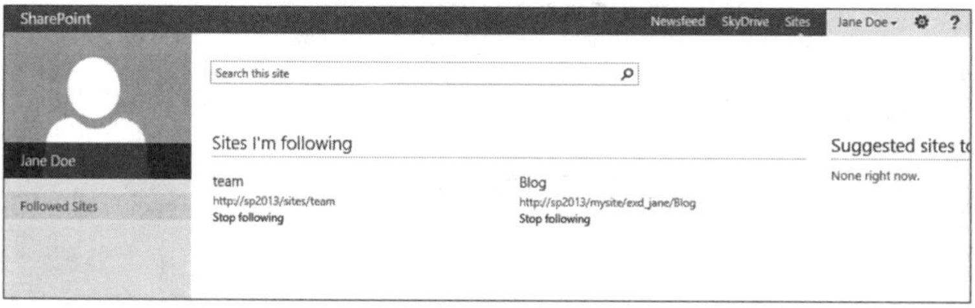

FIGURE 5.9   The Sites I'm Following page.

Edit Your Details

> **Scenario/Problem:** The details that other users see about you are no longer up to date, and you want to update them to reflect recent changes. For example, you might have been promoted, and your job title has changed, or maybe you have a new manager. Editing your details is important because it allows other people in your company to find you quickly using the people search.

Solution: This section explains how you can change the details that appear to other users or are searched in the people search. The details that you can edit are different in every company, so the details you can fill in when you open your details page might differ from what's shown in this chapter.

To edit your details, you open the My Profile page as explained earlier in this chapter in the section "Get Started with Social Features." There you see the Edit Your Profile link at the top of the page, under your name (refer to Figure 5.2). Clicking this link redirects you to a page where you can edit your details. As mentioned previously, these details vary depending on your company's configuration. Figure 5.10 shows how to enter text in an About Me section. You can upload a picture by clicking the Upload Picture button (see Figure 5.11 for the dialog that comes up). You can set your mobile phone number, fax number, and home phone. You can see more profile details by clicking the tabs at the top of the page. For example, the Contact Information tab enables you to update your mobile phone number, whereas the Details tab might ask you for your birthday.

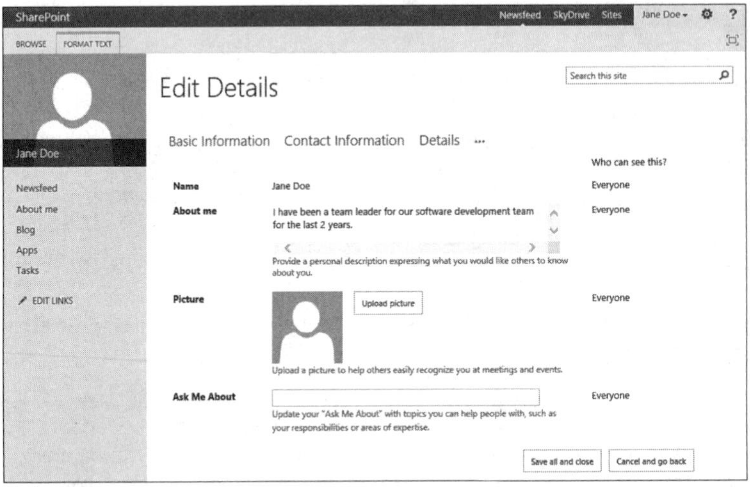

FIGURE 5.10   The Edit Details page enables you to edit some details about yourself.

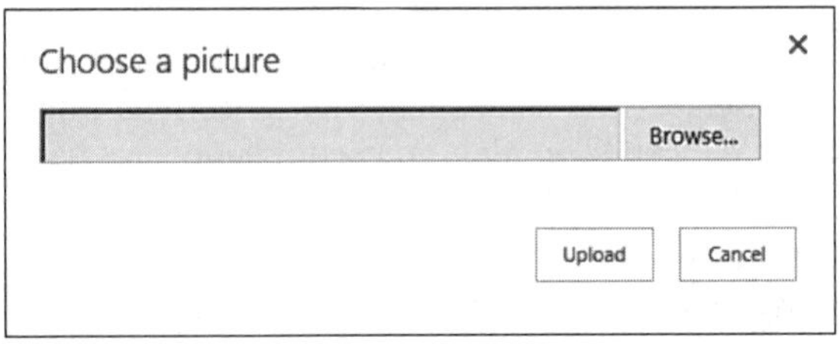

FIGURE 5.11   The upload picture dialog enables you to choose a picture of yourself for your profile.

Manage Newsfeed Settings

Scenario/Problem: You want to change the settings of your newsfeed, so that on certain events—for example, someone mentioning you in a microblogging update—you get notified by email. Also, you want to configure what is shared with other people who follow you. You might also want to configure the newsfeed so that when someone uses a specific hashtag in their microblogging posts, you want that post to be shown to you in your newsfeed.

Solution: To configure your newsfeed settings, navigate to the Edit Details page (refer to Figure 5.10) and click on the three dots in the tab list (to the right of Details). A drop-down menu opens with additional tabs—one of them is the Newsfeed Settings tab, as shown in Figure 5.12.

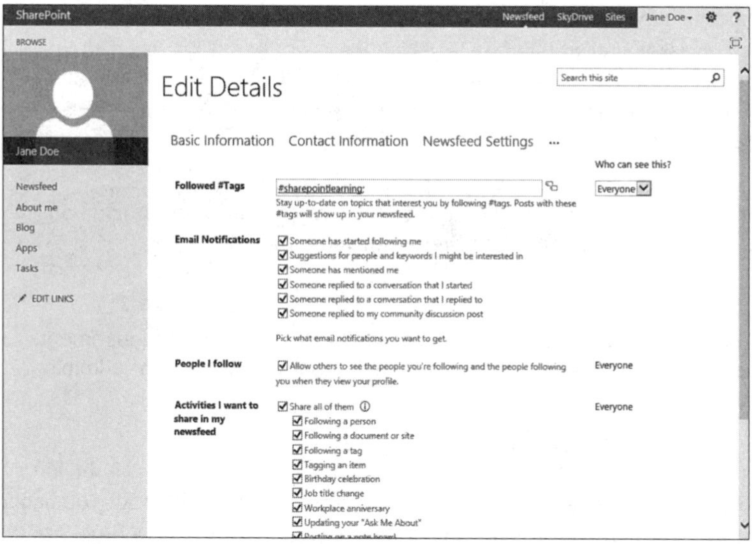

FIGURE 5.12   Selecting the Newsfeed Settings tab in the Edit Details page.

The following sections explain what you can configure on this page.

Manage Followed Hashtags

Under the Followed #Tags section of the Newsfeed Settings tab, you can see the list of hashtags in which you have already specified an interest (either by adding them through this page, or by clicking on them in a microblogging post). In the text box you can either type additional hashtags in which you are interested, or delete the existing ones.

You can also specify who can see what hashtags you are following by using the Who Can See This drop-down menu.

Manage Email Notifications

In the Email Notifications section you can configure the system to automatically send you an email when someone starts following you, when someone mentions you, or when someone replies to you, for example. To disable one or more of these alerts, simply uncheck the box next to that option, and click Save at the bottom of the page.

Manage What Information You Share

Under the People I Follow section you can specify whether you want to allow other people to see who you are following. This can be useful if you don't want people to ask you why you are following someone else and not them, for example.

The next option is to choose what activities you do that will automatically be posted as a microblogging update by you to people who follow you. For example, if you start following someone, anyone who is following you will automatically see that fact in their newsfeed unless you clear that box.

Create a Blog

Scenario/Problem: You want to create a site where you can write articles on topics related to your work and share them with your coworkers.

Solution: A blog is the most appropriate type of site for this kind of requirement. You can usually create a blog under your personal site if the SharePoint administrator has allowed it.

To create a blog, navigate to your personal site and click on the Blog link on the left panel (refer to Figure 5.2). Clicking that link automatically creates a blog for you under your personal site. For more information about the blog site, see "Create a Blog Site" in Chapter 12, "Creating Subsites."

Use SkyDrive Pro to Share a Document

Scenario/Problem: You want to share a document with one or more colleagues, but not in an existing site or library.

Solution: As explained in Chapter 1, "About Microsoft SharePoint 2013," SkyDrive Pro is a private document library in your personal site that allows you to quickly share a document with people in your organization.

To get to SkyDrive Pro, click the SkyDrive link at the top of any SharePoint page (if that link is not available, your administrator has disabled this feature). This opens a document library called Documents in your personal site to which you can upload documents. By default, this library has a folder called Shared with Everyone, which allows anyone in the organization to read any document you upload. At this point you can either choose to upload your document to that folder and send a link to your colleagues, or upload it to another folder (for example the root folder) and use the Share button to grant your colleagues permissions and send them a link to the document (see "Grant Permissions to a File or a List Item" in Chapter 10, "Managing Security").

CHAPTER 6

Creating and Managing Files, List Items, and Forms in SharePoint

IN THIS CHAPTER

SharePoint is most commonly used to store files, list items, and forms. This chapter covers tasks for the authors of files or list items, such as how to upload a file, create a new list item, edit the properties of list items, and publish the results to share them with other users.

Upload a File

Scenario/Problem: You want to upload a file to a document library in a SharePoint site.

Solution: Uploading a file to SharePoint is an easy process. There are three ways to do so. If you are writing a document in a Microsoft Office application, an easy way is to upload the document straight from the application by saving it directly into SharePoint.

If the file you want to upload is not an Office file, or if you prefer to upload the file without opening it in an Office application, you can upload the file using the web interface with your Internet browser.

The third option, which is a bit more advanced, enables you to upload the file to a library as if that library were a folder on your computer. This method is known as using *web folders*, and it requires that some components be installed on your machine. When these components are installed, web folders are easy and efficient to use.

Upload a File from the Web Interface

To upload a file from the web interface using your web browser, you browse to the library to which you want to upload the file, and then go to the folder where you want to put the file. If you have the required permissions to add files to the folder, you will see above the list of documents a New Document link and next to it text that says "or drag files here" as shown in Figure 6.1.

You can either drag and drop one or more files from your desktop into anywhere in the list view, or you can click the New Document link in the list view or Upload Document button in the ribbon. The different interaction options for each choice are described in the following section.

Dragging and dropping is simple: locate the files you want to upload in your file browser, select them, and drag them onto the list view. The list view will change to say Drop Here, and then you can release and drop the files. The list view then changes to Uploading; when the upload completes, the list view changes to say Upload Completed.

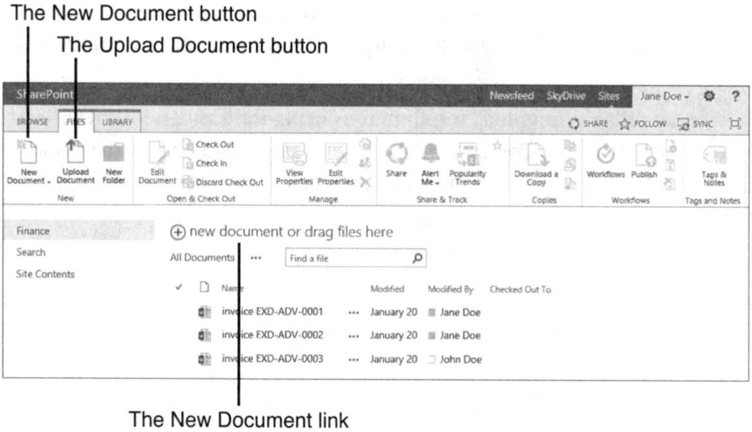

The New Document button
The Upload Document button

The New Document link

FIGURE 6.1   The Files ribbon with the New Document and the Upload Document buttons.

If you click the New Document link in the list view, a dialog appears, allowing you to create new files or upload an existing document as shown in Figure 6.2. Click on the Upload Existing File link at the bottom of the dialog to open another dialog that allows you to browse to an existing file as shown in Figure 6.3. This dialog is the same one you will see if you click the Upload Document button in the Files ribbon shown in Figure 6.2. Using this dialog is described next as part of using the Upload Document button.

Create new files options

The Upload Existing File option

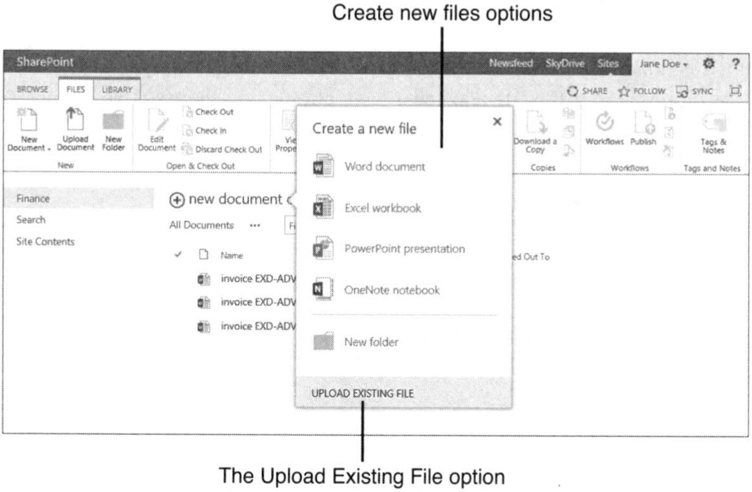

FIGURE 6.2   The Create a New File dialog opens when you click on the New Document link in the list view.

Clicking the Upload Document button in the Files ribbon opens the Add a Document dialog, where you can choose a single file by using the Browse button (see Figure 6.3).

If you are using a compatible browser and have the required components, the option in the Add a Document dialog to upload multiple files using the Upload Files Using Windows Explorer Instead link becomes available. This copy-paste button opens the document library in a Windows explorer window, allowing you to copy paste into the document library.

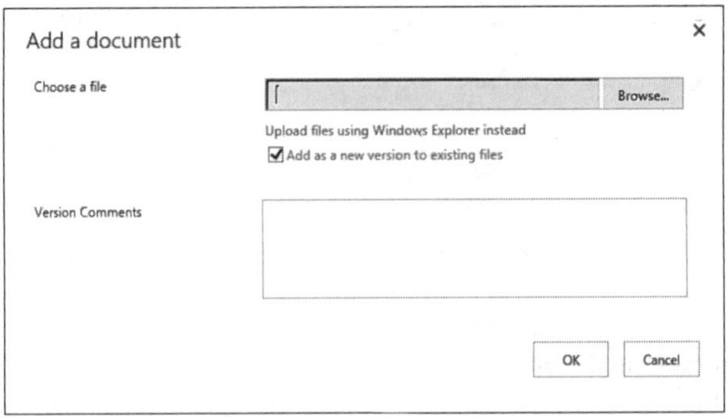

FIGURE 6.3   The Add a Document dialog, with the Upload Files Using Windows Explorer Instead link, enables you to use regular copy-paste to the document library.

If you selected a single file, click OK to commit the upload. This process can take a while, depending on the speed of the network, the size of the file, and the load on the server.

When the upload is done, depending on the setup of the document library, you might be prompted for properties for the file and see a Save button (see Figure 6.4).

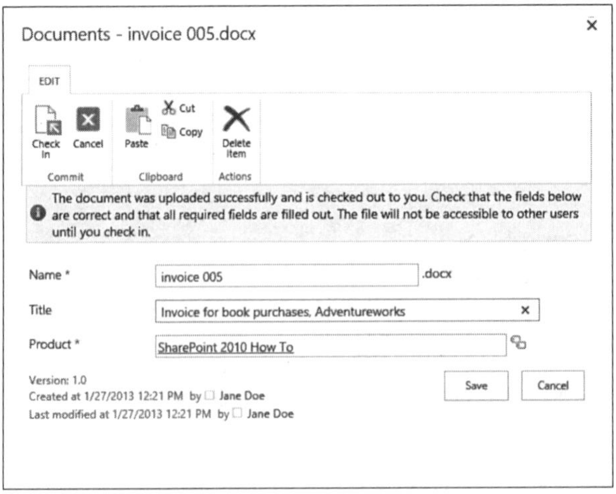

FIGURE 6.4   After the file is uploaded, you might be prompted for more information about the file. In this example, you are asked for information for the Title and Product columns.

> **TIP**   If you change your mind about uploading the document at this stage, you have two choices available in the dialog's ribbon: Cancel and Delete. If you cancel, the document is still in the document library, but it stays checked out to you as a draft document. If you choose Delete, the document is removed from the document library.

If the library supports multiple content types for files, you might have to select what content type this file belongs to, and that might change the properties that you are asked for (see Figure 6.5).

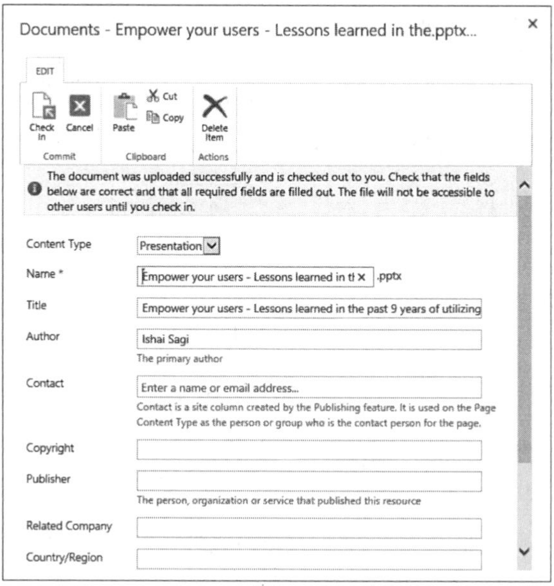

FIGURE 6.5   The properties entry screen when the Presentation content type is selected.

If you uploaded multiple files using either the drag-and-drop method or the Windows explorer copy-paste option, you are not asked for properties for the files, and the files are all uploaded but not checked in to the document library. You still need to check in each file that you uploaded and set the properties for each one separately.

Of course, if check-in is not required on the document library in question, you don't need to check in the files, but setting the properties (for example, the titles for the files) might be a good idea. See "Edit the Properties of a File or List Item" and "Check In and Check Out a File or List Item," later in this chapter, for more details on how to do this after you upload the files.

Upload a File from an Office Application

Office 2003 and later versions have built-in functionality that enables you to save files straight into SharePoint. Different versions might present different user interfaces for doing this, but the principle is the same in all versions.

The latest version, Microsoft Office 2013, has features in it to make finding SharePoint sites and libraries that you commonly use easier for you, and you can add links to libraries to those menus as explained later in this chapter under "Add a Document Library to Microsoft Office."

To save a document from an Office application such as Word, PowerPoint, or Excel, you use the Save or Save As functionality of the application. In Office 2013 you have a choice of where to save the document: one of those choices might be the site that you want to save it in. If it is, select it and continue to save the document. In earlier versions of Office, or if the library or site is not there, proceed to browse to the website as explained in the following section. In Office 2013, you can do that by selecting the Computer option, and then the Browse button. When the Save As (browse) dialog appears, in the File Name box you type the path to the SharePoint site into which you want to save the file and then you click Save or press Enter (see Figure 6.6). (This step does not save the document yet because you have not given it a name.)

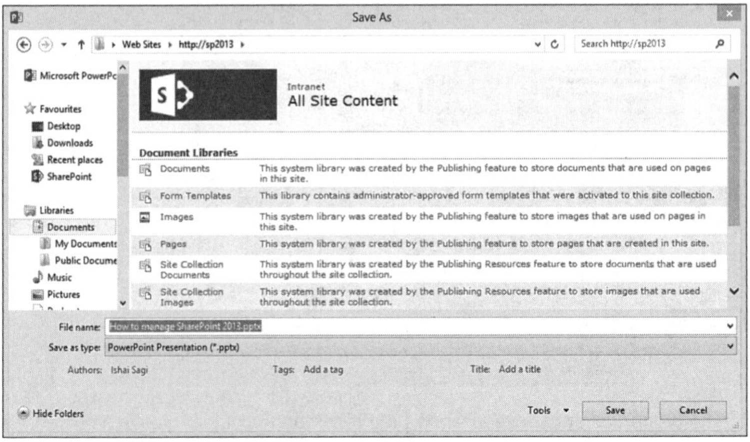

FIGURE 6.6   Clicking Save after typing the path to a SharePoint site displays the document libraries in the site inside the Save As dialog.

This action opens the site's structure in the dialog box and shows you the document libraries in that site, as well as the subsites under that site (see Figure 6.7).

You can now navigate to the document library that you want by double-clicking its name (see Figure 6.8), or you can browse the subsites by double-clicking them and selecting a document library from there.

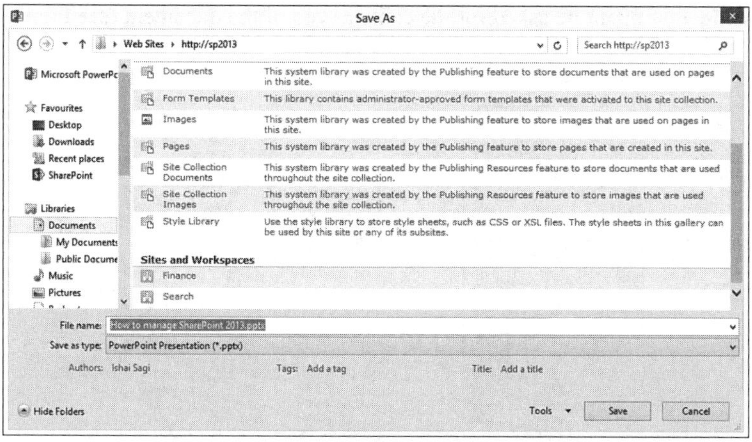

FIGURE 6.7   To see the subsites, scroll down the window.

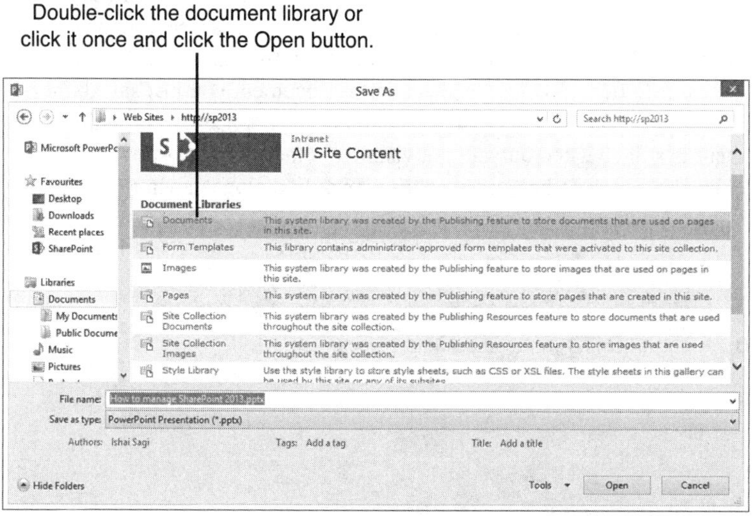

Double-click the document library or
click it once and click the Open button.

FIGURE 6.8   To open a document library and browse its folders, either double-click it or single-click it to select it and click Open.

Alternatively, if you know the path to the document library or folder you want to save to, type that in the File Name box and click Save to open the folder directly. When you have browsed to the folder to which you want to save, give the file a name in the File Name box and click Save to save it to the folder.

Depending on the configuration of the document library, you might be presented with several different dialogs, which look different in Microsoft Office 2003, 2007, 2010, or Microsoft Office 2013. The following figures, for example, show the dialogs presented to Microsoft Office 2013 users.

In the first dialog, you might be asked for the content type of the document (see Figure 6.9).

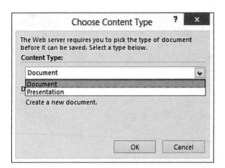

FIGURE 6.9   A dialog that asks for the content type of the document.

Finally, when you are done with all the dialogs, your document is in SharePoint but still checked out. You can check it in from the web interface (see "Check In and Check Out a File or List Item," later in this chapter) or from the Office application. In some versions of Microsoft Office, to help you check in the document you just saved, the Microsoft Office application displays a bar at the top of the application to remind you that the document is still checked out and not visible to other users, as shown in Figure 6.10. You can use the Check In button to see the Check In dialog, shown in Figure 6.11.

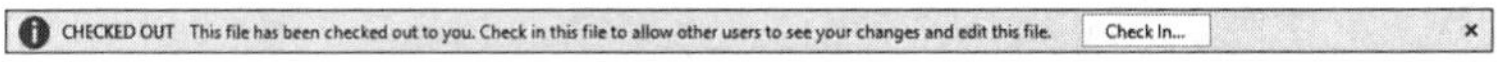

CHECKED OUT This file has been checked out to you. Check in this file to allow other users to see your changes and edit this file.   Check In...   ✕

FIGURE 6.10   A bar to remind you to check in the document.

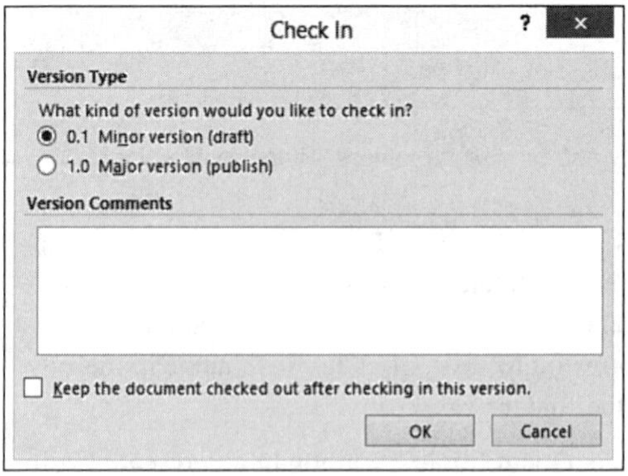

FIGURE 6.11   The Check In dialog.

To check in the document without using the bar, you use the Check In option. This option appears in different places, depending on the version of Microsoft Office you are using. In Microsoft Office 2003, it appears just under the File menu as the Check In menu option. In Microsoft Office 2007, it appears under the Microsoft Office button and then under the Server menu option. In Microsoft Office 2010 and 2013, it appears under the File menu and then under the Info option (see Figure 6.12).

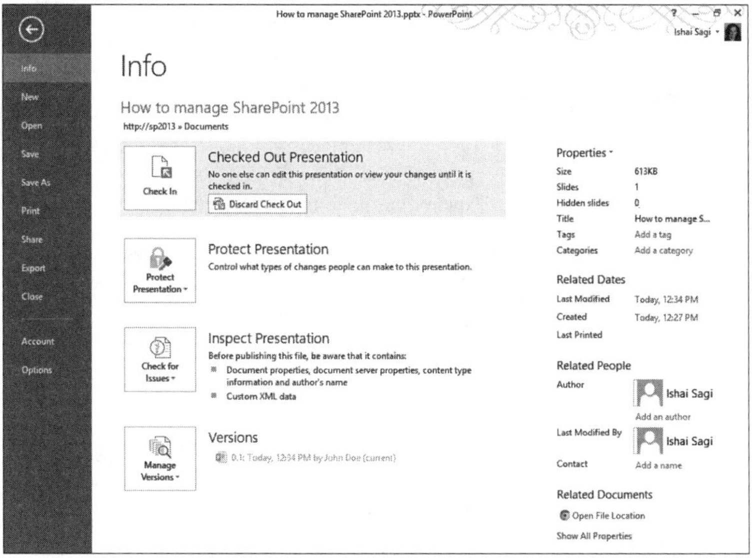

FIGURE 6.12   The Check In option under the Info menu in Microsoft Office 2013.

Selecting Check In prompts you to make sure you want to check in and prompts for check-in comments.

Upload a File Using Web Folders

Web folders are an interface in SharePoint that is usually installed as part of Microsoft Office but might be distributed by other applications. This interface enables you to browse a SharePoint site as if it were a folder on the network. This capability can be useful for copying and pasting a large number of files to or from SharePoint and even for deleting files.

The easiest way to open a document library as a web folder is to switch to the Library ribbon and then click the Open with Explorer button option in the Connect & Export group, as shown in Figure 6.13.

Selecting this option opens the document library, allowing you to copy and paste files into the library or one of the folders (see Figure 6.14).

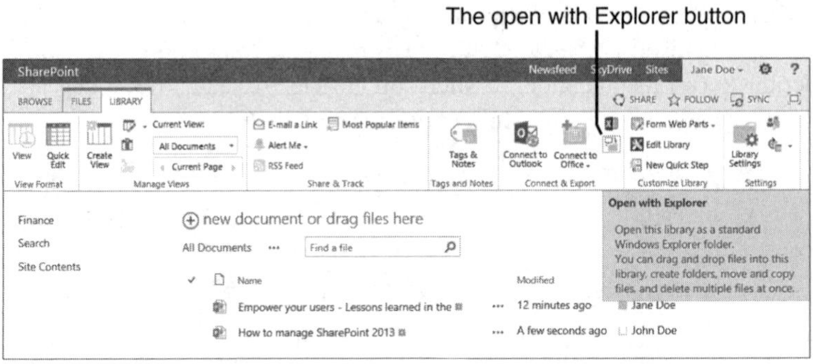

The open with Explorer button

FIGURE 6.13   Selecting the Open with Explorer button in the Library ribbon.

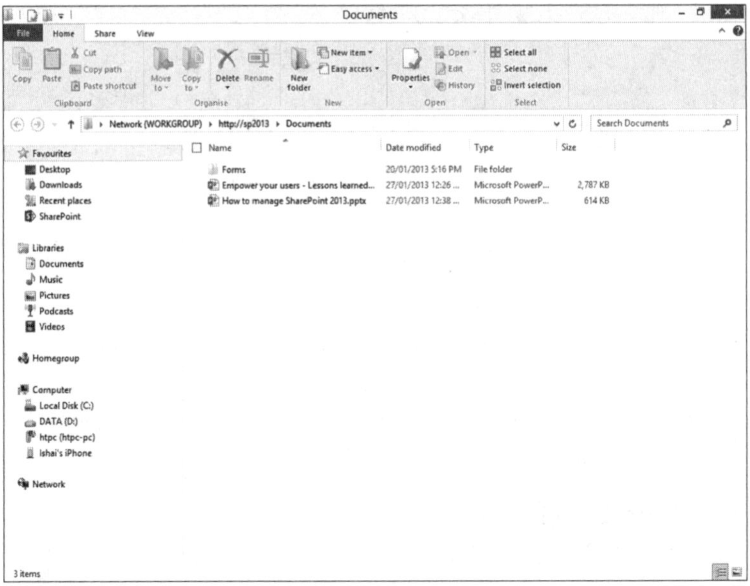

FIGURE 6.14   In this view of the document library, you can copy or paste the files you want to use.

NOTE   Note that uploading files through web folders does not provide you with an interface for specifying the files' properties, and you still need to edit the properties of the files through the web interface. (See "Edit the Properties of a File or List Item," later in this chapter, for information.)

Upload a Picture to a Picture Library

Scenario/Problem: You want to upload a picture to a picture library.

Solution: Picture libraries are almost identical to document libraries, and the process of uploading a picture to a picture library is the same as adding a file to a document library. The main differences are that in a picture library the New Document button is called New Picture, and clicking it doesn't offer the option to create new types of documents; instead, it just opens the Add a Document dialog (refer to Figure 6.3).

Create a New Document

Scenario/Problem: You want to create a new Microsoft Office document (for example, a Microsoft Word document or a Microsoft Excel workbook).

Solution: To create documents in document libraries, you can either use the New Document button in the Files ribbon or the New Document link above the list view.

Clicking the New Document button in the ribbon opens the Office application and the template that was specified by the manager of that document library. For example, if the manager specified that the default template for a document library is a Microsoft Excel template, Excel opens and creates a new file using that template.

Clicking the New Document link above the list view opens a dialog showing you several options for creating documents (refer to Figure 6.2). You can pick one of them to open the application related to the type of document you chose.

When you are done authoring the document, you click Save in the application, and the document is automatically saved in the folder where you started. For more information about saving files into SharePoint, see "Upload a File from an Office Application," earlier in this chapter.

The New Document button offers more choices of templates if the manager configured additional content types for the document library. If that is the case, clicking the New Document button creates a new document based on the template of the default content type. Using the drop-down menu for the New Document button enables you to select other content types that might use different templates and different applications (see Figure 6.15).

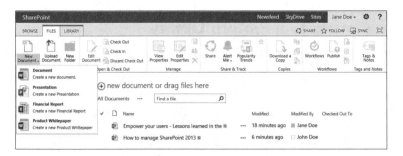

FIGURE 6.15   Use the New Document drop-down menu to select a content type for a new file.

For example, the Presentation content type uses a Microsoft PowerPoint template, Financial Report the content type uses a Microsoft Excel template, and the Product Whitepaper content type uses a Microsoft Word template.

Create a New List Item

Scenario/Problem: You want to create a new list item (for example, add a contact to a contacts list or a new event to a calendar list).

Solution: When you're working in a list, you create a new list item by using the New Item button in the Items ribbon or using the Add New Item link that might be shown under the view displaying the existing list items.

However, unlike with documents, using the New Item button (above the list view or in the Items ribbon) does not open another application but rather redirects you to a form that allows you to fill in the properties or columns for the new list item (see Figure 6.16).

Because each list can have different properties (or columns) in different orders, the screen can look totally different in each list. For example, the announcements list has properties such as Title and Body (see Figure 6.17), whereas the contacts list has properties such as First Name, Last Name, and Business Phone (see Figure 6.18).

Similarly to document libraries, lists can also support multiple content types. This means that the New Item button in the Items ribbon might also offer a drop-down menu of options for you to choose the sort of list item you want to create (see Figure 6.19). Depending on the content type you select, the properties fields might change.

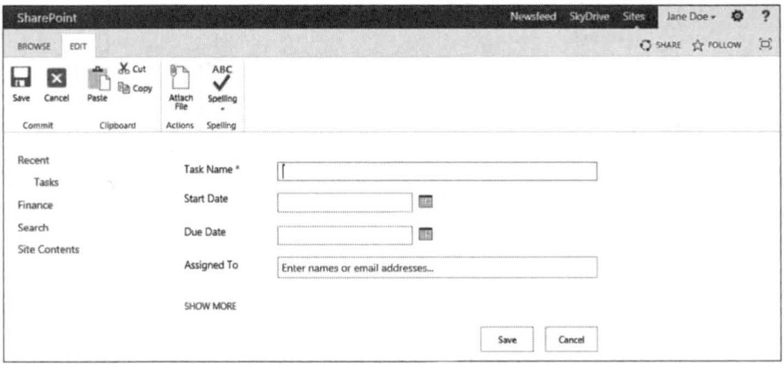

FIGURE 6.16   A sample properties page for creating a new task.

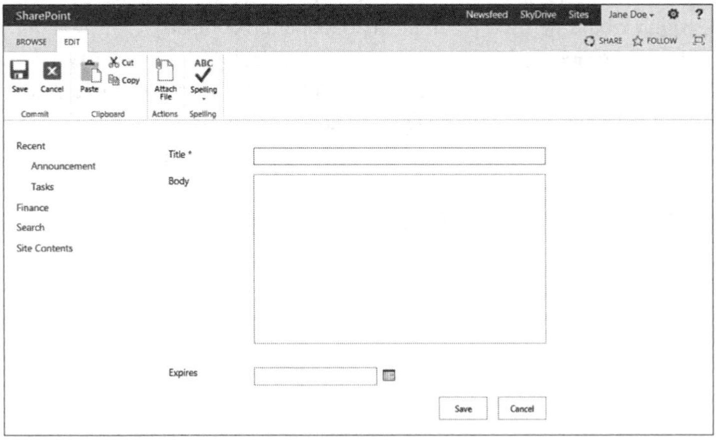

FIGURE 6.17   A sample properties page for creating a new announcement.

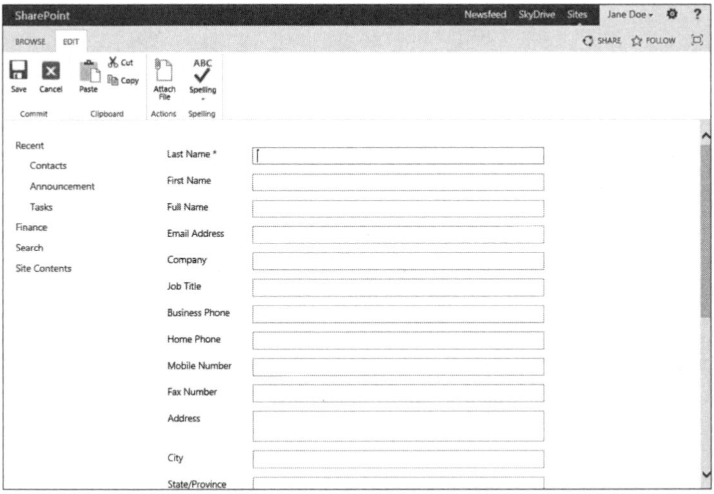

FIGURE 6.18   A sample properties page for creating a new contact.

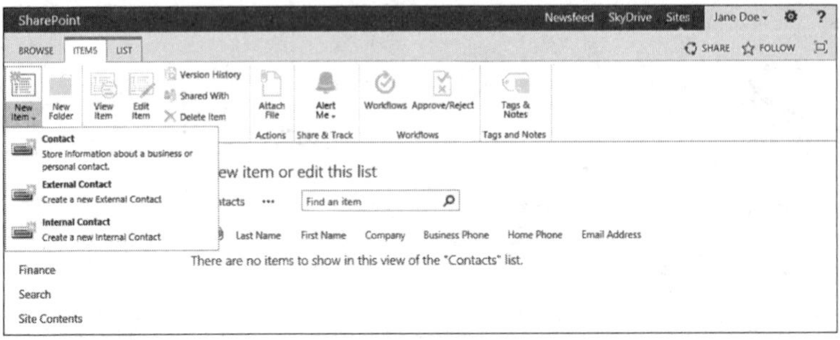

FIGURE 6.19   Choosing content types for creating different types of contacts.

For example, a contacts list might give you the option of creating an item of type External Contact, which would be used for contacts outside the company. This content type asks you to fill in the property for Company (see Figure 6.20). An item of type Internal Contact, on the other hand, does not ask for that property because it assumes that the contact belongs to your company. Instead, it has the property Department (see Figure 6.21).

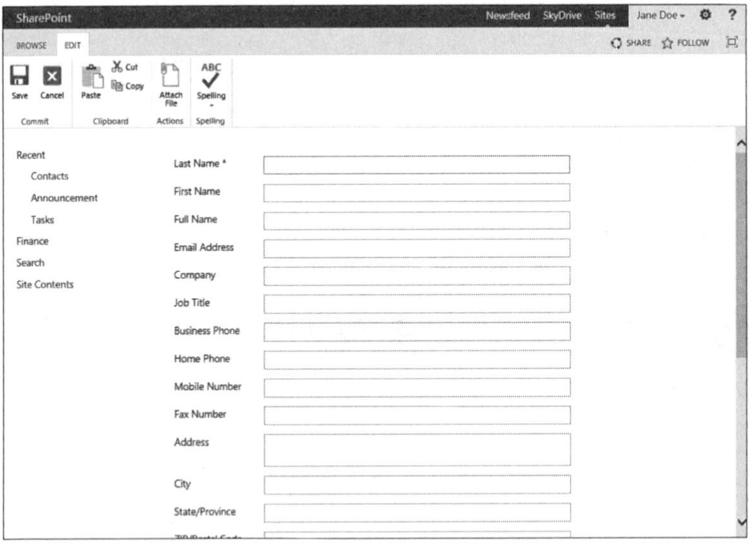

FIGURE 6.20   A sample properties page for creating a new external contact has the Company column.

Another way to create new list items is to use the quick edit view. This is described later in this chapter, in the section "Use the Quick Edit View to Add, Edit, or Delete Items and Files."

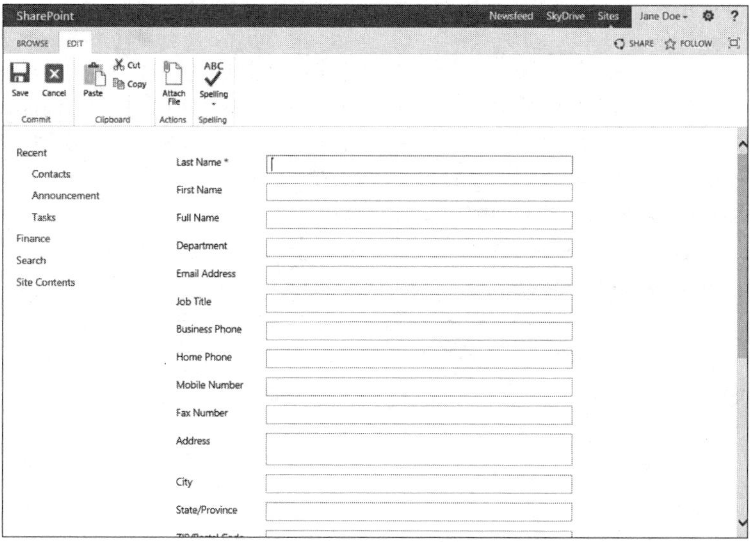

FIGURE 6.21   A sample properties page for creating a new internal contact has the Department column.

Fill a Form

Scenario/Problem: You want to fill a form in a SharePoint form library.

Solution: In a form library, you can fill a form by clicking the New Document button in the Files ribbon. Clicking this button opens the form either in the browser or in Microsoft InfoPath, depending on the configuration of the form and on whether you have Microsoft InfoPath installed (see Figures 6.22 and 6.23).

If the library is configured to have more than one form, you can open the drop-down menu for the new form, the same way you do when creating items or documents from different content types.

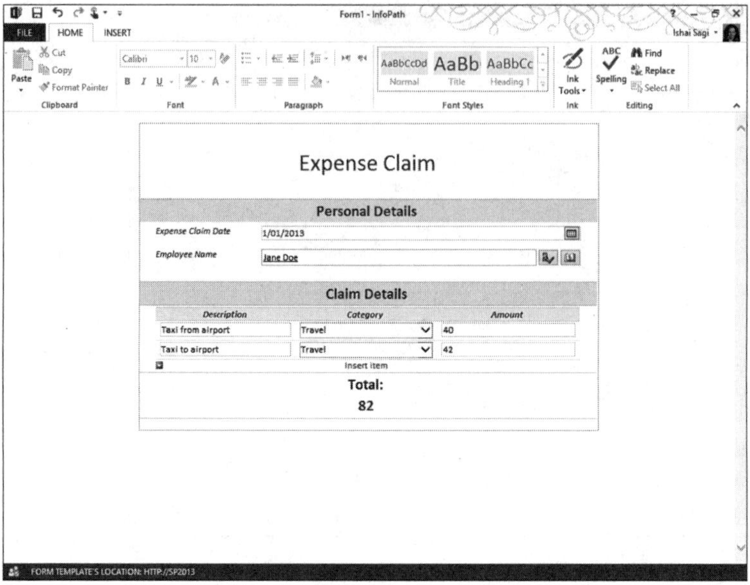

FIGURE 6.22   A form open for editing in Microsoft InfoPath Filler.

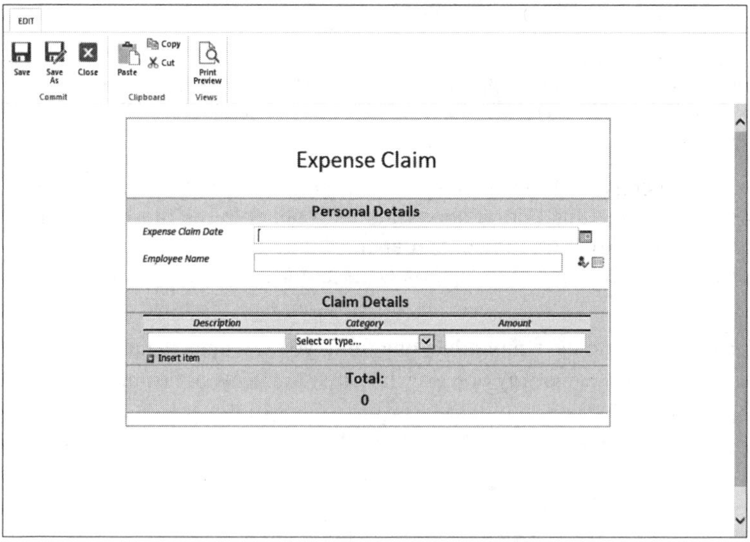

FIGURE 6.23   A form open for editing in the browser.

Add a Document Library to Microsoft Office

Scenario/Problem: You want to add a link to a document library to Microsoft Office 2013 to be able to save documents to that library quickly.

Solution: Microsoft Office 2013 applications can show a list of sites that you commonly save documents to. This list shows up when you click the Save or Save As options under the File menu.

If your SharePoint environment is configured to allow it, your Microsoft Office applications can register to download the list of sites and libraries from your personal site. To do that, open a document library you want to add to the list in Microsoft Office, and from the Library ribbon, under the Connect & Export category, click on the Connect to Office button to open a drop-down menu as shown in Figure 6.24.

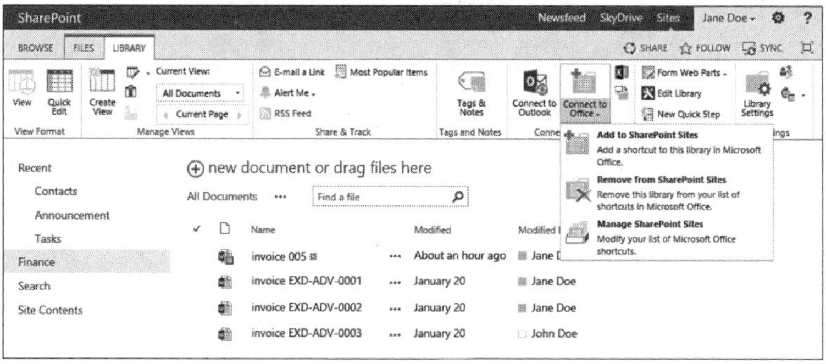

FIGURE 6.24   The Connect to Office drop-down menu.

From this menu, select the Add to SharePoint Sites option. If your computer is not already configured to use that specific SharePoint environment, you will get prompted to allow Microsoft Office applications to trust your personal site. Click Yes in that dialog, and your Microsoft Office applications should start showing the list of sites and libraries in the Save dialogs.

You can add Office 365 SharePoint sites to the sites list, using the Microsoft Office 2013 application itself by clicking Add a Place, and selecting Office 365 SharePoint from the options that appear. This method requires you to log in using your Microsoft Live account that has permissions to the Office 365 site.

Delete a File or List Item

Scenario/Problem: You want to delete an existing file from a document library or delete a list item from a list.

Solution: To delete a single file or list item, you highlight that file or list item by clicking on the row for that item or file, and then switch to the Files ribbon or the Items ribbon. In the ribbon, you click the Delete Document button, shown in Figure 6.25. You are prompted to confirm the deletion.

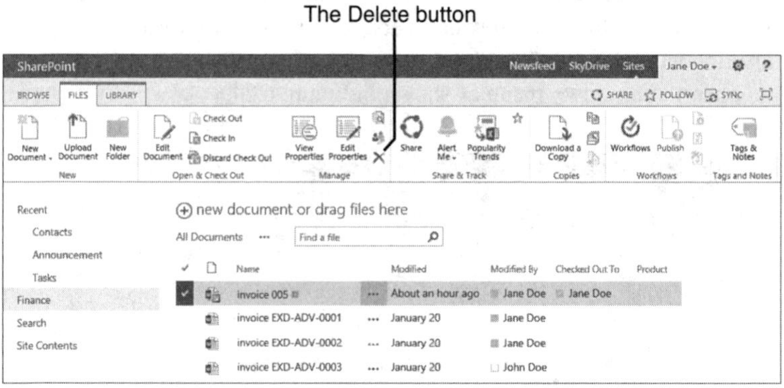

The Delete button

FIGURE 6.25   Selecting Delete Document from the Files ribbon when one or more documents are highlighted.

> **NOTE**   Deleting files requires a different set of permissions than editing, so you might not see the Delete option in the menu. In that case, you should ask the manager of that list to delete the item.

An alternative way to delete a single item or file is to click on the three dots next to the item or file's name. With list items, this opens a drop-down menu (see Figure 6.26). From this menu, you choose Delete Item or Delete. With files, this opens a dialog with information about the file, and another link with three dots on it. Clicking that link opens a similar drop-down menu as shown in Figure 6.26.

You can also delete several files or items at once by selecting those files or items using the check boxes that are shown on the left of the view displaying those items or files (see Figure 6.27). The check boxes become visible if you hover your mouse's cursor over the row for an item or file. After you select several files or items, you use the Delete Document button on the Files ribbon or the Delete Item button on the Items ribbons to delete them all at the same time.

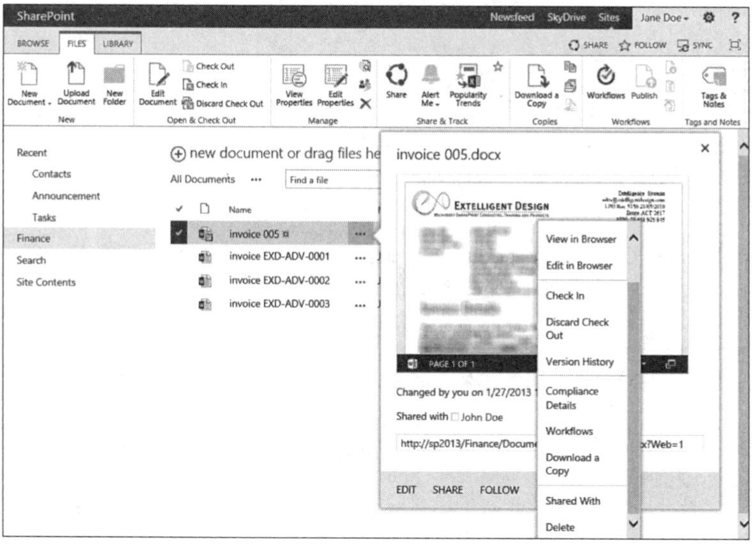

FIGURE 6.26   Deleting a single list item by opening the drop-down menu for that file. In this image, the three dots are hidden behind the opened menu.

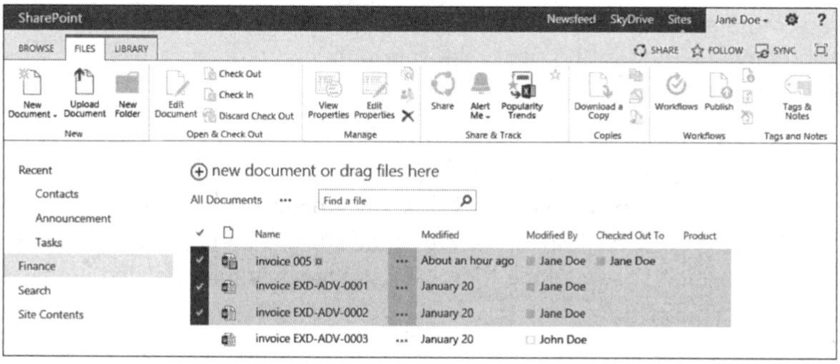

FIGURE 6.27   Selecting multiple files by using the check boxes.

Another method for deleting multiple files or list items is to use the Quick Edit view. For more information, see "Use the Quick Edit View to Add, Edit, or Delete Items and Files," later in this chapter.

Finally, in document libraries, you can also use the Open with Explorer option in the Library ribbon. This opens the document library in Windows Explorer, just as it would any folder on your computer, and it allows you to select the files you want to delete and either press the Delete key on the keyboard or right-click the files and choose Delete from the context menu (see Figure 6.28).

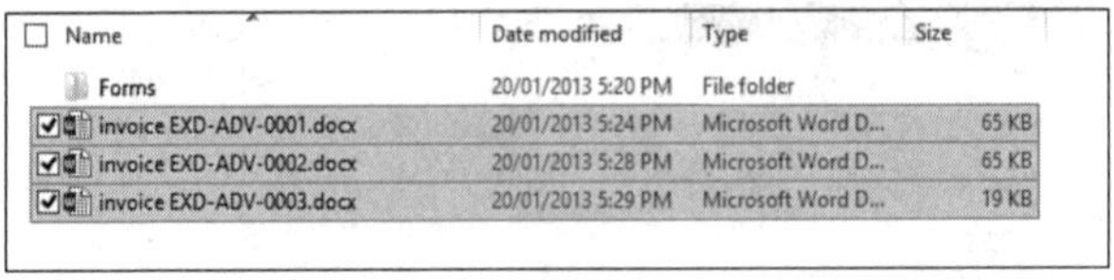

Name	Date modified	Type	Size
Forms	20/01/2013 5:20 PM	File folder	
☑ invoice EXD-ADV-0001.docx	20/01/2013 5:24 PM	Microsoft Word D...	65 KB
☑ invoice EXD-ADV-0002.docx	20/01/2013 5:28 PM	Microsoft Word D...	65 KB
☑ invoice EXD-ADV-0003.docx	20/01/2013 5:29 PM	Microsoft Word D...	19 KB

FIGURE 6.28   Selecting multiple files using Windows Explorer.

When items or files are deleted, by default they are stored in the site's Recycle Bin for 30 days, and you can restore them during that time. See the following section.

Recover a Deleted File or List Item

Scenario/Problem: You have accidentally deleted a file or a list item that you need.

Solution: SharePoint has built-in Recycle Bin functionality that allows you to retract deletions. By default, files and items that were deleted are kept in this Recycle Bin for 30 days, but the site you are using might have different settings. After this time, they are moved to the site administrator's Recycle Bin. So if you don't see a file or list item that you have deleted in the past, ask your administrator to recover it for you.

To restore a file, navigate to the Site Contents Page (refer to "View All Lists and Libraries" in Chapter 3, "Solutions Regarding Files, Documents, List Items, and Forms"), and click the Recycle Bin link at the top of the page. Clicking this link opens the Recycle Bin page, which shows all the files and list items you have deleted in that specific site (see Figure 6.29).

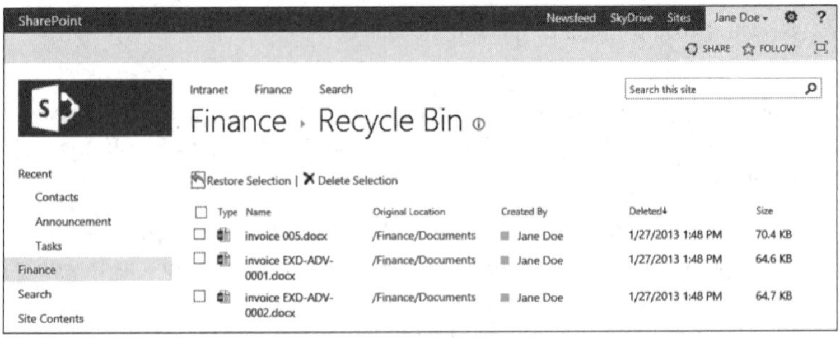

FIGURE 6.29   The Recycle Bin page.

In the deleted items list, you can see the name of the deleted item or file, the original location (site and document library or list and folder), and other data about the file or item, such as who created it in the first place, when it was deleted, and, for files, what size it was.

To restore one or more files and items, select the check box next to each item you want to restore and click Restore Selection. The item or file is restored with all its versions and properties.

You can also permanently delete an item or file from the Recycle Bin by selecting Delete Selection.

Edit the Properties of a File or List Item

Scenario/Problem: You want to change some of the values that have been entered into the columns for a specific file or list item. For example, you might want to change the details for an event in a calendar list or the name or title of a document in a document library.

Solution: Lists and document libraries in SharePoint might be configured to ask you for properties for files and list items. This data appears when you view the properties of a file or list item (see Chapter 3) or as columns when you view the document libraries or lists. This data might also be shown when you search for documents using the advanced search (see Chapter 4, "Searching in SharePoint").

Properties information is useful when you are looking for a file or a list item. You might be able to search for it based on the value that is set in its properties.

To edit the properties of a file, you locate the file in the folder where it was saved and highlight that file by selecting the check box that appears to the left of the file or item when you hover the cursor on the row for that file or list item. Then, switch the ribbon to the Files ribbon. If you have permissions to edit that file's properties, the Edit Properties button is available in the ribbon (see Figure 6.30).

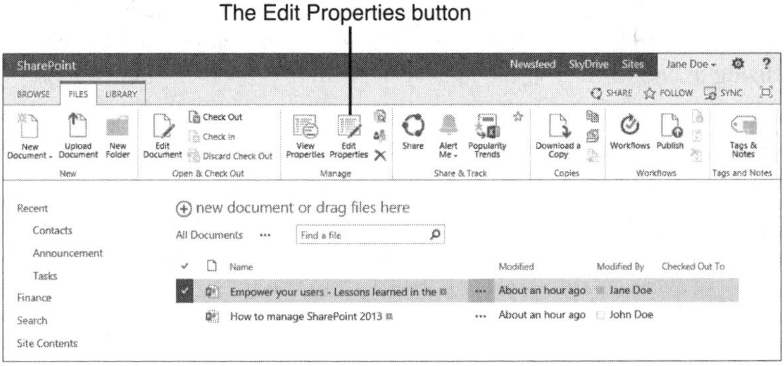

The Edit Properties button

FIGURE 6.30   The Edit Properties button in the Files ribbon.

NOTE Confusing the Edit Document button with the Edit Properties button is easy to do. The Edit Document button opens a document for editing, whereas the Edit Properties button opens the document's properties page.

Alternatively, you can click the three dots next to a file's name to open the file information dialog, and then click on the three dots in that dialog to open a drop-down menu. If you have permissions to edit that file's properties, you see the Edit Properties option in this menu (see Figure 6.31).

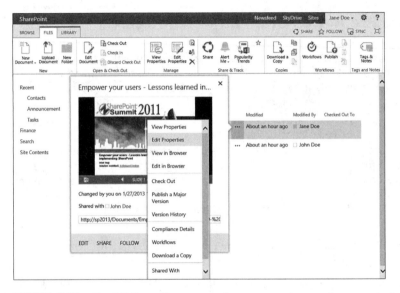

FIGURE 6.31   The Edit Properties menu option appears when you have permissions to edit a document or a list item's properties.

With list items, the procedure is slightly easier than with files. Although you can go through the same process as for files (described in the preceding paragraph), you can also simply click the title of the list item to open the dialog that shows the item's properties and then choose Edit Item from the available ribbon. Clicking this button switches the dialog to one where you can modify the current properties of the file or list item.

When you're editing the properties of a file or a list item, properties that are mandatory are marked with an asterisk (*), and you must fill in those properties before you can save your changes (see Figure 6.32). If you don't fill in those properties, SharePoint does not let you click OK and tells you what properties are not filled in.

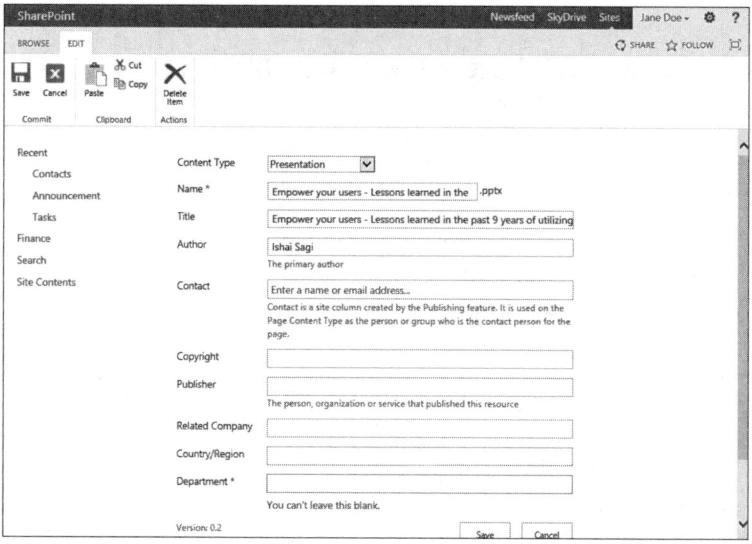

FIGURE 6.32 When you do not fill in a required property, SharePoint prompts you to do so when you try to save.

File and list item properties can be of different types, and each type has a different way of capturing data (see Figure 6.33). For example, a text property displays a text box for you to enter data. A date property can appear as a text box (for the date) with a button next to it that looks like a calendar that allows you to choose a date, and it might even have two drop-down menus for selecting a time. A yes/no field appears as a check box.

SharePoint also validates the properties based on the types. This means, for example, that you cannot write text in a date field or in a numeric property. If you do so, SharePoint shows you a red error message under that field and prevents you from saving the properties until you fix the problem.

In addition, the document library or list manager might choose to impose additional conditions on some of the properties. For example, it might state that the title of a file should be fewer than 43 characters long. SharePoint also alerts you if you try to save the properties when one of those conditions is not met, and it tells you what field is not set correctly and what limitations are configured for that field.

An important action when creating a new file in some document libraries is choosing the content type for the file. Different content types require different properties, so it is recommended that before you enter the other properties, you select the content type first. This should not be a problem because the Content Type property is always the first one to appear in the list of properties if the document library was configured to use more than one content type, as you can see in Figure 6.34.

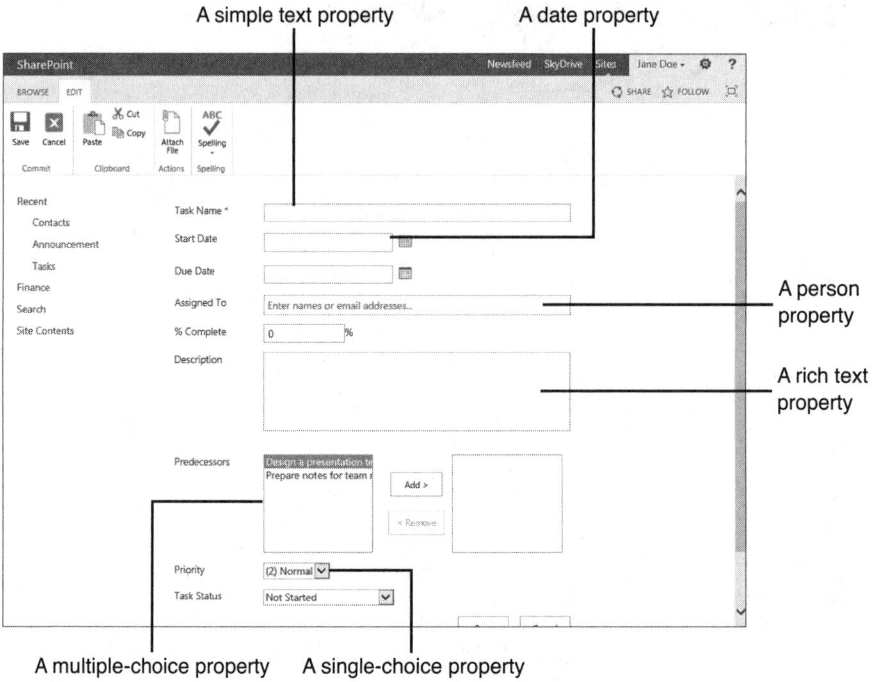

A simple text property   A date property

A person property

A rich text property

A multiple-choice property   A single-choice property

FIGURE 6.33   For different property types, you enter or select data in different ways. In this task form, you can see seven different types.

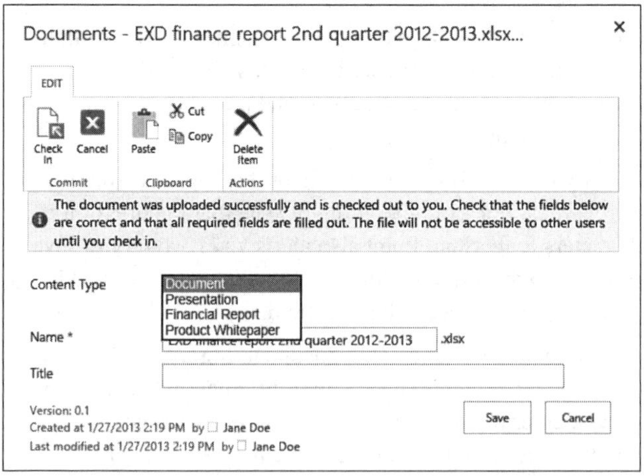

FIGURE 6.34   The content type is the first thing you need to choose when uploading a file.

Changing the content type causes the properties page to refresh and load the properties that are required for the selected content type. However, if the new content type has some of the same properties as the old one, the values in those properties are not lost. You can therefore switch between content types without worrying about losing the information.

After you have filled in all the properties you want, you click Save at the bottom or the top of the page to save the changes.

If the document library is set up to require you to check in and check out files, you must check in the file after changing its properties. See "Check In and Check Out a File or List Item," later in this chapter, for more information on how to do so.

To edit the properties of multiple list items or files, you can also use the Quick Edit view. For more information on this, see the next section.

Use the Quick Edit View to Add, Edit, or Delete Items and Files

Scenario/Problem: You want to add, edit, or delete multiple items in a list or library in an easy way. The details that you want to modify are similar, and you don't want to have to click each one to edit or delete it separately. You also don't want to click the New button many times.

Solution: The Quick Edit view, as explained earlier, is similar to a Microsoft Excel datasheet and allows copying and pasting of data into the list or library (see Figure 6.35).

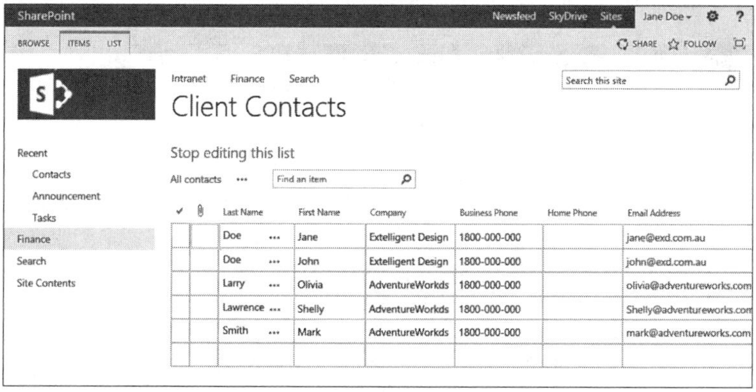

FIGURE 6.35   A Quick Edit view showing a contacts list.

This interface makes adding, editing, and deleting multiple list items or files a lot easier. You can create list items by copying data from Microsoft Excel or another spreadsheet application. You can edit the properties of many list items or files by copying cells, and you can delete many files in one action.

Switch to Quick Edit View

Some views are built to be Quick Edit views by default. In this case, just switching to the view displays the datasheet interface. For more information about how to switch between views, see "Switch List Views in Lists and Libraries" in Chapter 3.

However, you can also switch to a Quick Edit view version of any standard view even if the view creator did not create it as a Quick Edit view. To switch to the Quick Edit view from a standard view, you switch to the List ribbon or Library ribbon and click the Quick Edit view button in the View Format section of the ribbon (see Figure 6.36). To switch back to the standard view, you click the View button in the same ribbon (see Figure 6.37).

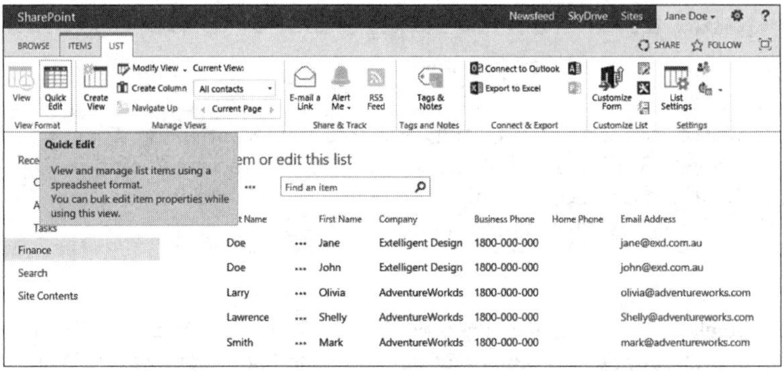

FIGURE 6.36   The Quick Edit button at the left side of the List ribbon is available when you are in a standard view.

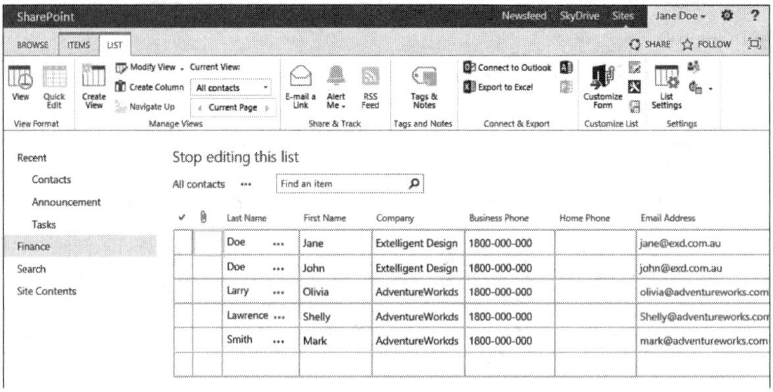

FIGURE 6.37   The View button at the left side of the List ribbon is enabled when you are in a Quick Edit view.

Add a List Item Using Quick Edit View

You can use Quick Edit view to add list items. This approach doesn't work with document libraries because they require you to upload a file for each row, and the Quick Edit view doesn't have an interface to upload a file. Because list items are made strictly of data in columns, you can create new ones from Quick Edit view.

> **NOTE** When some columns are mandatory and the view doesn't show these columns, Quick Edit view doesn't let you create new items. To be able to create new list items in Quick Edit view, you must use a view that displays all the mandatory columns.

To create a new list item in Quick Edit view, you just type values in the last row (the one marked with an asterisk) in the datasheet. The list item is created with the values you typed in. To finish adding the list item, you press Enter or click another row in Quick Edit view. The datasheet creates the list item (see Figure 6.38).

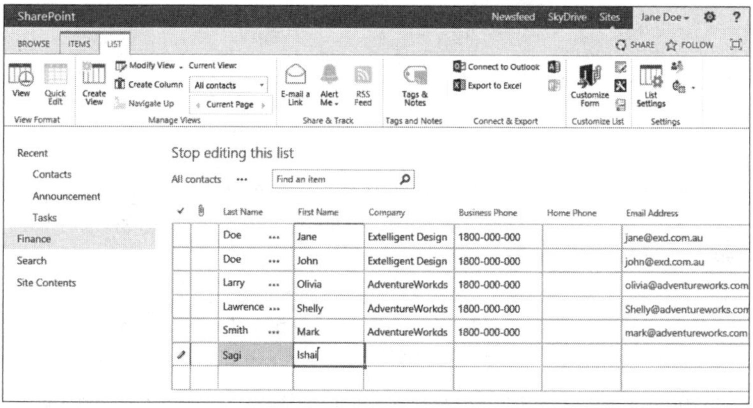

FIGURE 6.38   Creating a new list item using Quick Edit view.

Add Multiple List Items from Microsoft Excel by Using Quick Edit View

A useful way to use Quick Edit view is to populate a list with the data from an existing spreadsheet. If you have a spreadsheet with many items, instead of typing them one by one using the method described in "Create a New List Item," earlier in this chapter, you can use Quick Edit view to paste in the values.

For example, if you have a Microsoft Excel spreadsheet that contains information about products, and you want to copy that information to a SharePoint list, you can use Quick Edit view to copy the information to the list, even if the columns are not the same. To do this, you open the spreadsheet and select the information you want to copy (see Figure 6.39), and then select Copy from the Edit menu.

Next, you switch the SharePoint list to Quick Edit view, which shows the columns you want to paste into. Remember that the view must be showing all mandatory columns for that list.

If the columns in Quick Edit view are not in the same order as in the Microsoft Excel spreadsheet, you must reorder them in Quick Edit view. To do this, you will need to edit the view settings (refer to "Specify the Order of the Columns in a View" in Chapter 8, "Creating List Views"). The column order must be the same so that when you paste the information, the information goes in the correct columns.

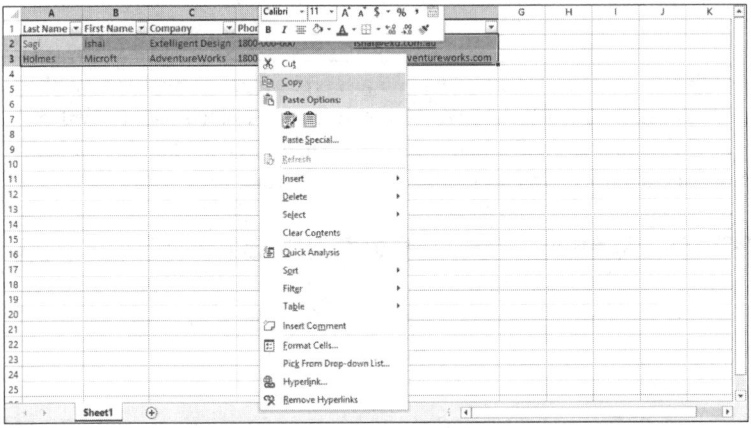

FIGURE 6.39   Select the Microsoft Excel information that you want to copy to the SharePoint list and then copy it.

When the Quick Edit view is ready for the data, click on the first cell, and press the key combination Ctrl+V to paste.

The information from the Microsoft Excel spreadsheet is pasted into the list. Because this can be a lot of information, SharePoint might take a while to create the list items. You must wait until SharePoint finishes creating all the items before you close the window or navigate to a different page.

Check In and Check Out a File or List Item

Scenario/Problem: Some document libraries and lists require you to check out a file or list item before changing it. (*Changing* includes changing the properties of a file or list item and editing a file's contents as well.) You want to make changes to the file or list item and then share the changes with other people working on that site.

Solution: Checking in documents from the Office interface is mentioned earlier in this chapter, in the section "Upload a File from an Office Application." You can use the method described there, and you can also use the same process to check out a document: Just open the document using the Microsoft Office application and select the Check Out option from the menu. If you choose Edit from the document's or list item's drop-down menu, usually the document or list item automatically checks itself out for you. However, check-out and check-in are also offered on the web interface because not all files are Microsoft Office documents, and sometimes you do not want to open a Microsoft Office application just to check out a document (for example, just to make sure no one else is modifying it). When you are done making changes and want other people to see your changes, you should check the document back in.

To check out a document, select the file or list item by clicking on the row of that file or item and switch to the Files or Items ribbon. If the check-out mechanism is enabled, the Files ribbon or Items ribbon shows the Check Out and Check In buttons under the Open & Check Out section of the ribbon (see Figure 6.40).

The Check Out button might be grayed out if the document or item is already checked out to another user, and the Check In button is clickable only if the document or list item is currently checked out to you.

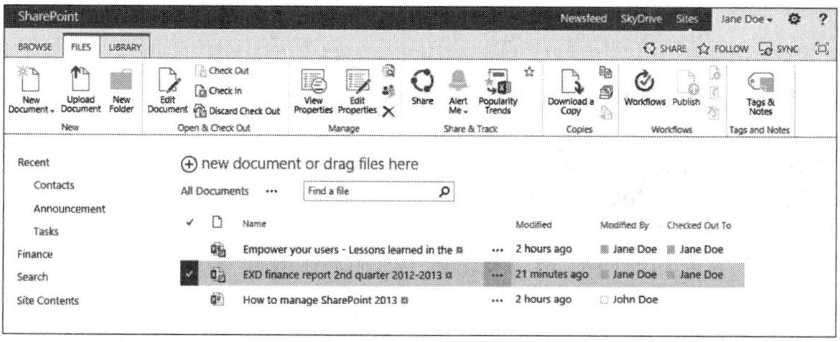

FIGURE 6.40   The Check Out and Check In buttons in the Files ribbon.

> **TIP**   The Check Out and Check In options are also available from the drop-down menu for files and list items. This is similar to the Edit Properties and Delete actions. Figures 6.27 and 6.28, earlier in this chapter, show those options in the menu and how to get to the drop-down menus of a file or a list item.

Checking in a file increases the version number of the file. The amount of increase depends on the settings for the list or document library. With the simplest setting, every time you check in a file or list item, its version is increased by 1. However, some document library settings can change this and you will be asked to choose more options when checking in, as shown in Figure 6.41. The next section provides more information on how different settings can affect the check-in process.

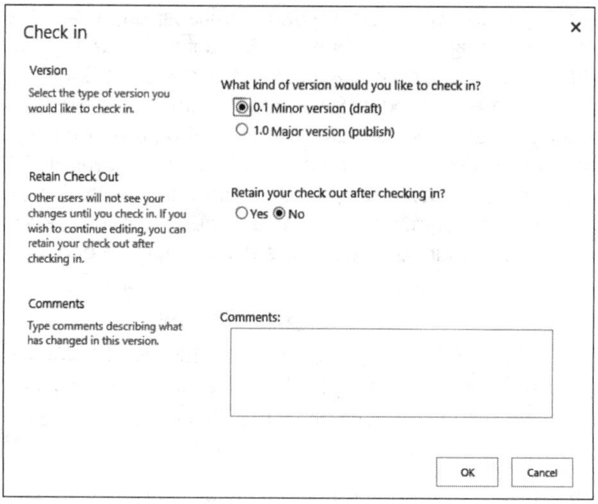

FIGURE 6.41   The Check In dialog offers various options when checking in a file in some libraries.

Publish a File or List Item

Scenario/Problem: A document library or list requires you to publish a file or list item that you have created or modified before it shows the new file or item to other users.

Solution: Some document libraries and lists require you to publish files and list items before other people can see them. This is similar to checking in a file or list item, as described in "Check In and Check Out a File or List Item," earlier in this chapter. The big difference is that the list or library manager can choose to set it up so that checking in a file or list item does not make it visible to everyone. It will be visible just to other people who have editing permissions on the library, and readers will be able to see only the last published version. However, the list or library manager might choose to allow everyone to see unpublished versions, in which case the publishing of an item or file is just a way to track version numbers. For example, a regular check-in increments the version number of a file or list item by 0.1, and publishing increments it by 1.

If the document library or list you are working on has the publishing requirement, the Files ribbon or Items ribbon has a Publish button available in the Workflows section. If the selected file or item is checked in but not published or if it is checked out to you, you can click the Publish button (see Figure 6.42). Clicking this button checks in the file again, changes the version number of the item or file, and enables readers to view this version.

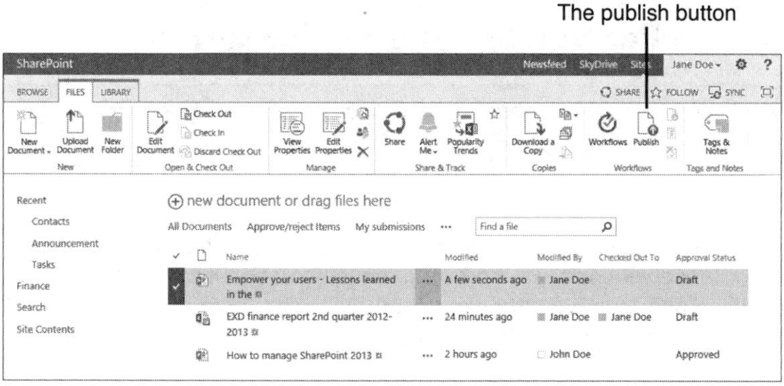

The publish button

FIGURE 6.42   When publishing is required, you must click the Publish button to publish a major version.

If the list or library you are working on is set up to require approval, the file is not published until someone who has the appropriate permissions approves it (see Figure 6.43). This means that despite your publishing the file, readers might still see only the previously published version until someone approves your version. Of course, this also depends on the configuration.

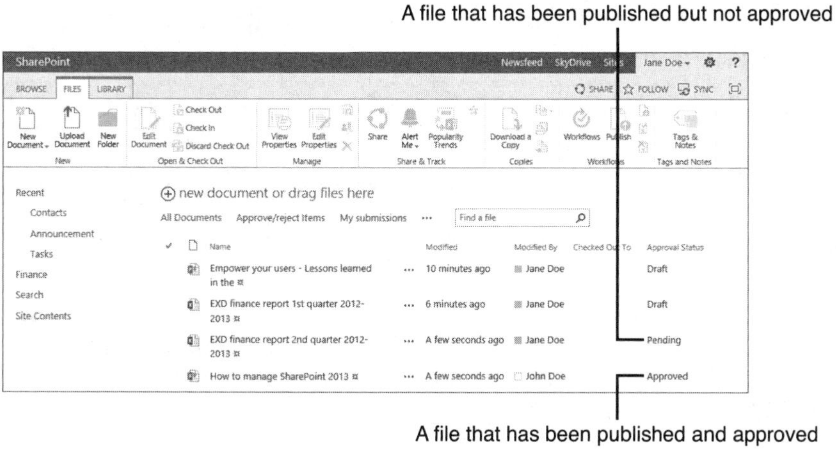

A file that has been published but not approved

A file that has been published and approved

FIGURE 6.43   When publishing and approval are required, checked-in files are still considered to be drafts, and published documents that haven't been approved are considered to be pending approval.

To see how to approve a file that was published, see "Approve or Reject a File or List Item," later in this chapter.

Restore an Earlier Version of a File or List Item

Scenario/Problem: You want to restore a file or list item to an earlier version and make it the current version.

Solution: Chapter 3 explains how to view the earlier versions of files and list items. To restore one of those versions, you hover the mouse cursor over the date and time for that version and then open the drop-down menu that appears. From the drop-down menu, you select Restore (see Figure 6.44).

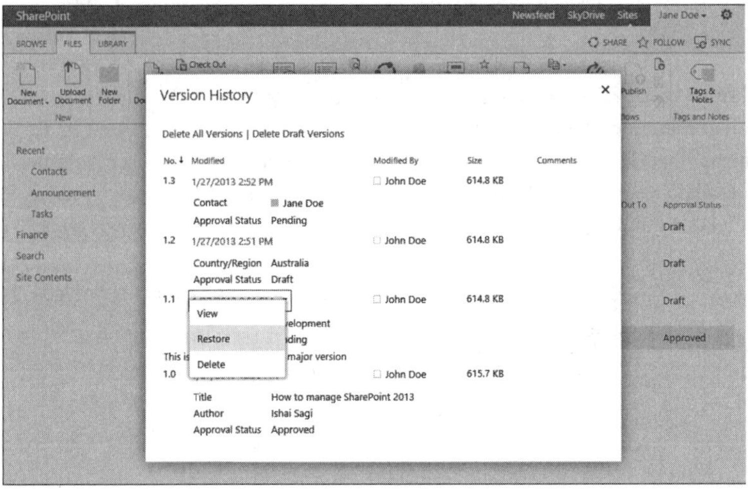

FIGURE 6.44   Selecting Restore brings back an earlier version of a file or list item.

Selecting the Restore option creates a new version for the file or list item and increases its version number. If the list or library requires check-in or publishing, the new version still must be checked in after the restoration. See "Check In and Check Out a File or List Item," earlier in this chapter.

NOTE   A version can be restored only if the file is not checked out by someone else.

Approve or Reject a File or List Item

Scenario/Problem: You are the approver on a list or library, and you need to approve or reject a file or list item that another user has submitted for approval.

Solution: Some file libraries and lists require approval of files or lists. When this content approval setting is enabled, an item or file that has been checked in or published is not published automatically but instead remains in a pending state until it is approved or rejected. This means that the file or item is still considered a draft and is given the Draft status.

To be able to approve or reject files or items, you need specific permissions on the library or list. When a file or an item is approved, it is assigned Approved status in the list or library, and it is displayed to anyone who has permission to view the list or library.

When a file or an item is rejected, it remains in a pending state and is visible only to the people who have permission to view drafts (refer to Figure 6.43).

To approve or reject a file or an item, you select the row for that item and click the Approve or Reject button in the Workflows section of the Files ribbon or Items ribbon (see Figure 6.45). In addition, you can use the Approve/Reject option from the file or list item's drop-down context menu by clicking the three dots next to a list item's title, or the three dots next to a filename to open the file's information dialog and then opening the file's drop-down menu by clicking the three dots in the dialog.

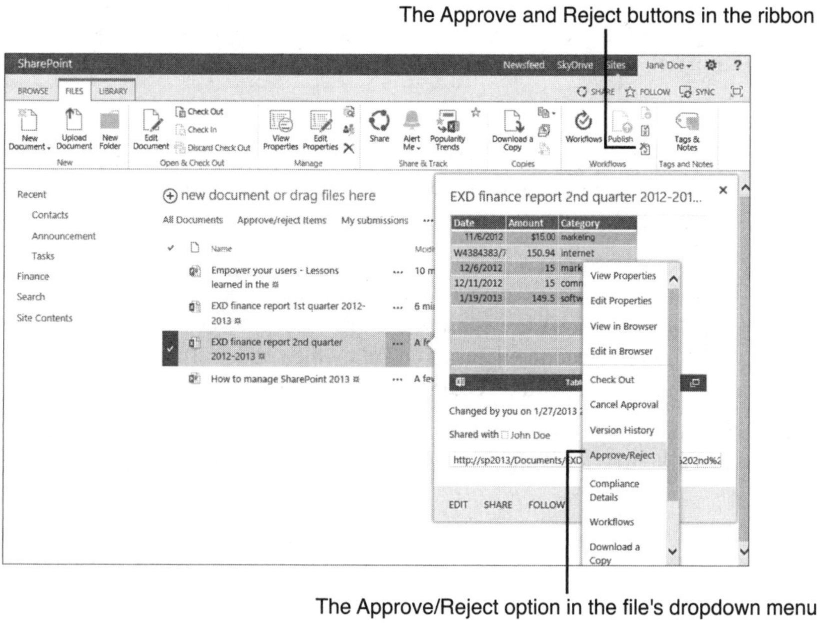

The Approve and Reject buttons in the ribbon

The Approve/Reject option in the file's dropdown menu

FIGURE 6.45   Selecting Approve/Reject from the context menu or from the ribbon.

Clicking the Approve/Reject option or either of buttons from the ribbon opens a dialog where you can choose to approve, reject, or keep the file or item in a pending state (see Figure 6.46). You can also add comments about your decision.

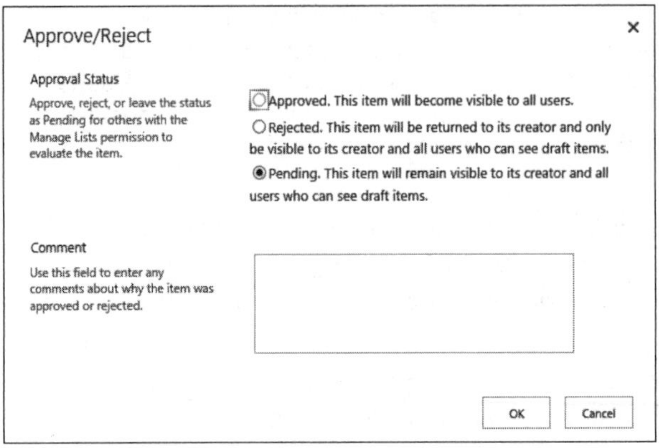

FIGURE 6.46   The screen enables you to change the status of a file or an item.

See What Files or List Items Are Waiting for Your Approval

Scenario/Problem: You are the approver on a list or library, and you need to see what files or list items other users have submitted for your approval.

Solution: When a list or library is set to require content approval, views are added to the regular list views to help you manage the approval of files or list items. You see those views only if you have approval permissions on the list or library.

To see what files are waiting for your approval, switch to the Approve/Reject Items view (refer to "Switch List Views in Lists and Libraries" in Chapter 3). The Approve/Reject Items view shows you all the items, grouped by their status. To see the ones that are awaiting approval, look under the Pending group (see Figure 6.47).

For more information on how to approve or reject a file or list item, see "Approve or Reject a File or List Item," earlier in this chapter.

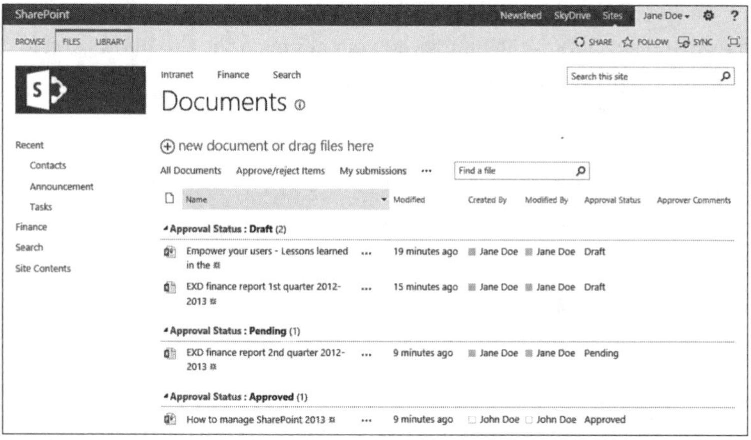

FIGURE 6.47   The Pending group shows files or items awaiting approval.

Synchronize a Library or Folder Using SkyDrive Pro

Scenario/Problem: You want to work on a copy of a SharePoint library or folder offline, and then add, edit, or remove files from that folder or library by working on your local machine.

Solution: With SkyDrive Pro, a Microsoft Office 2013 app, you can synchronize a folder in your desktop to SharePoint. If SkyDrive Pro is installed on your desktop, you can open the document library you want, and click on the Sync button in the top of the ribbon, as shown in Figure 6.48.

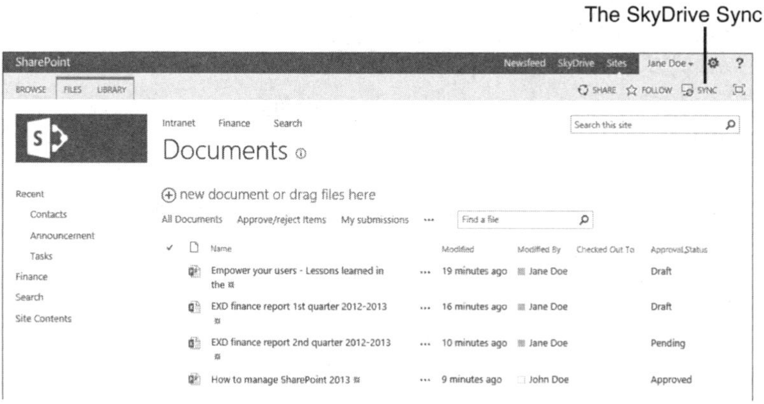

The SkyDrive Sync button

FIGURE 6.48   The Sync button at the top of the ribbon when viewing a document library.

After you click the Sync button, a Microsoft SkyDrive Pro dialog appears asking you to confirm you want to synchronize the library to your computer; it also allows you to set where on your desktop you want the synchronized files to be, as shown in Figure 6.49.

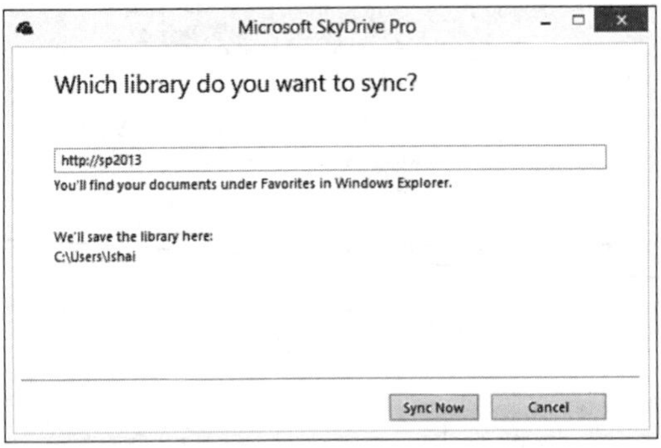

FIGURE 6.49   The SkyDrive Pro synchronization confirmation dialog allows you to change where the files from the library will be copied to on your desktop.

To finish, click the Sync Now button. SkyDrive Pro then copies the files to your desktop. You can click on the Show My Files button in the dialog that opens to open the folder where you chose the files to be downloaded to.

Managing Synchronized Files

When you open a folder that is managed by SkyDrive Pro on your desktop, you will notice that the files' icons have marks on them, signaling their status when compared to the server version, as shown in Figure 6.50.

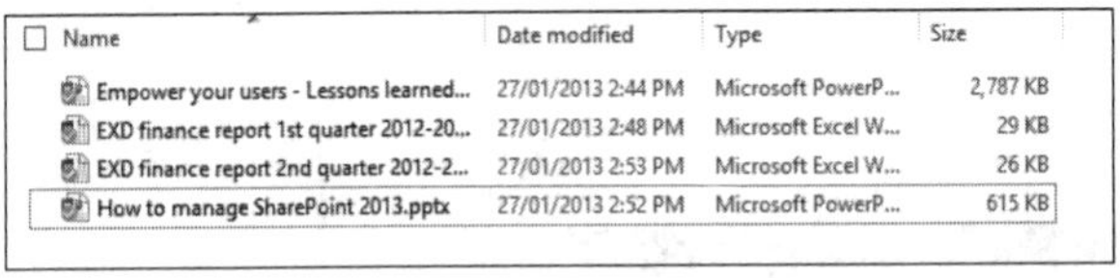

FIGURE 6.50   Synchronized files on your desktop will have different icons signifying their synchronization status.

If you edit a file on your desktop and save it, SkyDrive Pro will automatically attempt to upload the new version to the document library. If you copy a file to the folder, SkyDrive Pro will automatically attempt to upload that file to the document library. While the files have not been uploaded successfully, the files' icons will have a blue mark in the shape of two round arrows pointing at each other on them showing that they are still being synchronized, as shown in Figure 6.51.

☐ Name	Date modified	Type	Size
📊 Empower your users - Lessons learned...	27/01/2013 2:44 PM	Microsoft PowerP...	2,787 KB
📊 EXD finance report 1st quarter 2012-20...	27/01/2013 2:48 PM	Microsoft Excel W...	29 KB
📊 EXD finance report 2nd quarter 2012-2...	27/01/2013 2:53 PM	Microsoft Excel W...	26 KB
📊 How to manage SharePoint 2013.pptx	27/01/2013 2:52 PM	Microsoft PowerP...	615 KB
☑📊 Introduction to SharePoint Developm...	1/02/2011 4:05 AM	Microsoft PowerP...	1,856 KB
☑📊 Lessons learned in the past 10 years of...	6/08/2011 12:17 PM	Microsoft PowerP...	441 KB
☑📊 Migrating Sites to 365.pptx	19/05/2012 12:48 ...	Microsoft PowerP...	545 KB

FIGURE 6.51   The files that have been copied to the folder are being uploaded to SharePoint automatically.

NOTE   If you delete a file from the synchronized folder, it will be deleted from the document library. If you need to recover it, you can either use your desktop's Recycle Bin, or the site's Recycle Bin (as explained in "Recover a Deleted File or List Item" earlier in this chapter).

Managing Synchronized Folders

If problems occurred while a folder was synchronizing, or if you want to view the list of all synchronized folders on your desktop, open the SkyDrive Pro app on your desktop. You can usually find the SkyDrive Pro icon in your taskbar. Right-clicking that icon will give you such options (shown in Figure 6.52) as opening your SkyDrive Pro folder (shown in Figure 6.53, Sync Now, Pause Syncing, and so on).

Open your SkyDrive Pro folder
Sync a new library

Sync now
Pause syncing
View sync problems
Stop syncing a folder...

Help
Exit

FIGURE 6.52   Right-clicking the SkyDrive Pro icon in the desktop's taskbar.

☐ Name	Date modified	Type	Size
📁 Accounting - Receipts	30/12/2012 1:54 PM	File folder	
📁 Accounting - Scans	30/12/2012 3:13 PM	File folder	
📁 Intranet - Documents	27/01/2013 3:08 PM	File folder	

FIGURE 6.53   The list of synchronized folders on your desktop that opens.

If a folders did not synchronize properly, it will have a red mark on its icon. You can then right-click the folder, choose SkyDrive Pro from the context menu, and then choose to view the synchronization issues, which will have various tools to troubleshoot the issues and retry the synchronization.

To remove a synchronized folder, right-click the SkyDrive Pro icon in your taskbar and select Stop Syncing a Folder. This opens a dialog with the list of synchronized folders, allowing you to select the folder and stop syncing.

CHAPTER 7

Creating Lists and Document Libraries

IN THIS CHAPTER

You use lists and document libraries throughout SharePoint to store any information that users need. This chapter explains how to perform basic tasks related to creating and customizing lists and document libraries, including creating columns (metadata), setting the document templates for document libraries, and more.

Open Your Apps Page to Create Lists and Libraries

Scenario/Problem: You want to create a list or a library.

Solution: There are different ways to get to the Add an App page where you can choose from a list of available apps to create lists and libraries as well as other kinds of apps.

The first step is to open the site where you want the document library to be created. In most sites, you see a cogwheel button at the top of the page. This is the Settings icon. Clicking this button opens the Settings drop-down menu. From this menu, choose the Add an App option to open the Your Apps page (see Figure 7.1).

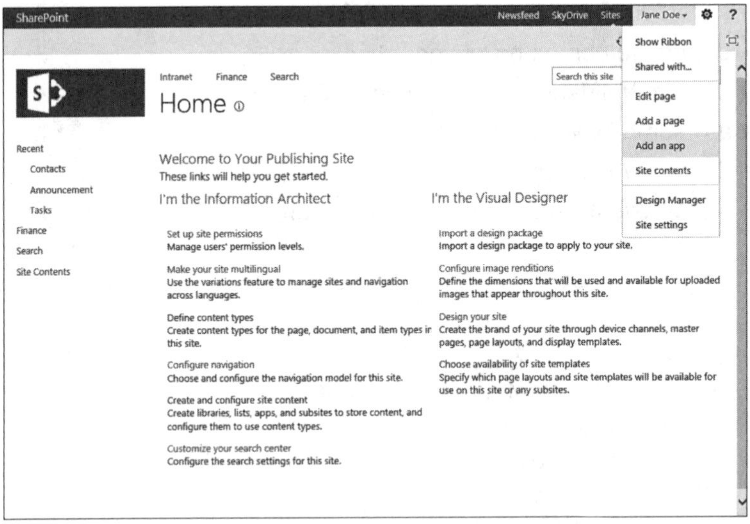

FIGURE 7.1   Open the Settings menu and choose Add an App.

In sites where the Add an App option is missing from the menu, you must use the Site Contents link either on the Settings menu or the link in the left navigation bar (see Figure 7.2). Selecting this option opens the All Site Content page, where you can then click the Add an App link to get to the Your Apps page.

The Your Apps page allows you to create lists and libraries, showing all the different kinds of lists and libraries you can create in that site (see Figure 7.3). Different sites might show different kinds of list and library templates.

View All Site Content in the site actions menu

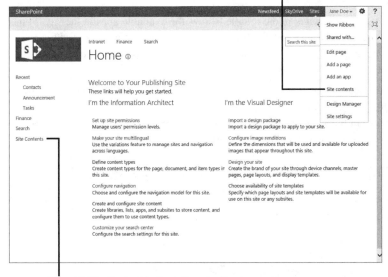

View All Site Content in the left navigation bar

FIGURE 7.2   Use either option to get to the All Site Content page.

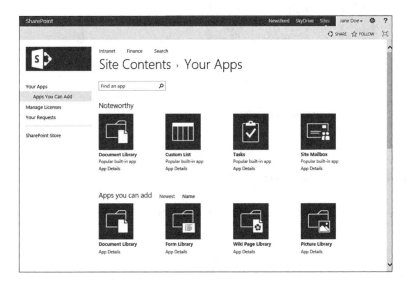

FIGURE 7.3   The Your Apps page.

The Your Apps page shown in Figure 7.3 has three sections. The first section, on the left, allows you to navigate between apps you can add on the current site, and manage App licenses, your app requests, and various app stores, including the SharePoint store. The SharePoint store and other app stores might or might not be available in your environment, depending on the server configuration. The use of these stores is not covered in this book.

The main section of this page, in the middle, shows the available apps in the site. Some of these apps are for creating a list or library in the site. This list of apps might change from site to site. Figure 7.3 shows several library and list templates available by default in SharePoint.

The top of this page provides the option to find the template you are looking for—by searching for a specific template by its name or description. For example, you can type the word *library* in the search box to search the templates. Figure 7.4 shows the search results of seven list templates that have the word *Library* in them.

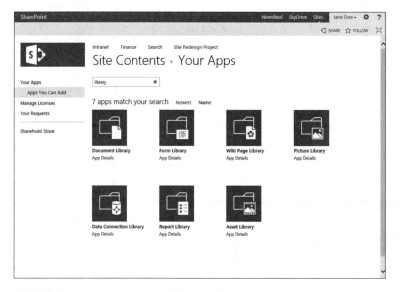

FIGURE 7.4   Searching the list templates.

Create a New Document Library

Scenario/Problem: You want to create a new document library.

Solution: To create a document library, you need to use the Your Apps page as explained in the preceding section.

From the list of apps available, click on the Document Library one and then give the document library a name in the dialog that opens (see Figure 7.5). The name for the document library determines not just the title that the users will see but also the link that will be created to the document library. For example, if you call the document library *Presentations*, the link to the document library is the link to the site and then /Presentations. This is important because although you can change the title of the document library later, you cannot change its link.

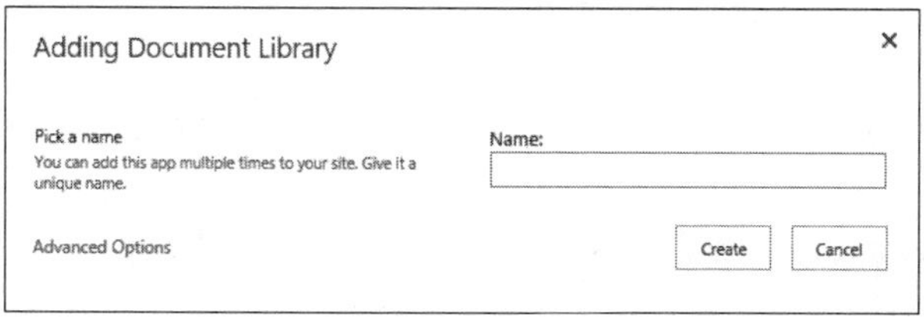

Adding Document Library   ✕

Pick a name   Name:
You can add this app multiple times to your site. Give it a
unique name.

Advanced Options   [Create]   [Cancel]

FIGURE 7.5   The Adding Document Library dialog.

TIP   If you want to avoid creating complicated links, choose a short name for the document library when you are creating it and then later change the title for the document library. For example, if you want to create a document library for human resources policies, you can name it HRP when creating it and then change the title to Human Resources Policies after it has been created. That way, the link is short and easy to type or view (when sending it in e-mail, for example), and the title explains to all users what should be in that document library.

Using this approach can also help you avoid unreadable links. For example, if your document library's name has spaces in it, the link to the document library will have the special character combination %20 instead of the spaces, which will make the link look long and complex. You can create the document library with a short name without spaces and then rename the title to have the spaces. The simpler link will remain.

Although you can have two document libraries with the same title, you cannot have two document libraries with the same link. This means that the link to the document library must be unique, and in this initial screen, you choose the unique name. If that name is already in use, SharePoint prevents you from creating the document library and asks for another name. Remember that you can always change the title later.

After selecting a name for the document library, you can either click Create to create the new document library with the name you chose and the default settings for that kind of library, or you can click Advanced Options to switch to a page with more settings for the new document library, as shown in Figure 7.6.

This dialog might show different options for the document library, depending on the server configuration. For example, some SharePoint servers can allow a document library to have an associated e-mail address and receive e-mails sent to that library directly into the document library itself. If that option is enabled in the server, the settings page asks you for additional information, such as the e-mail address that should be associated with the document library. If the option is not enabled, the setting isn't either (see Figure 7.6).

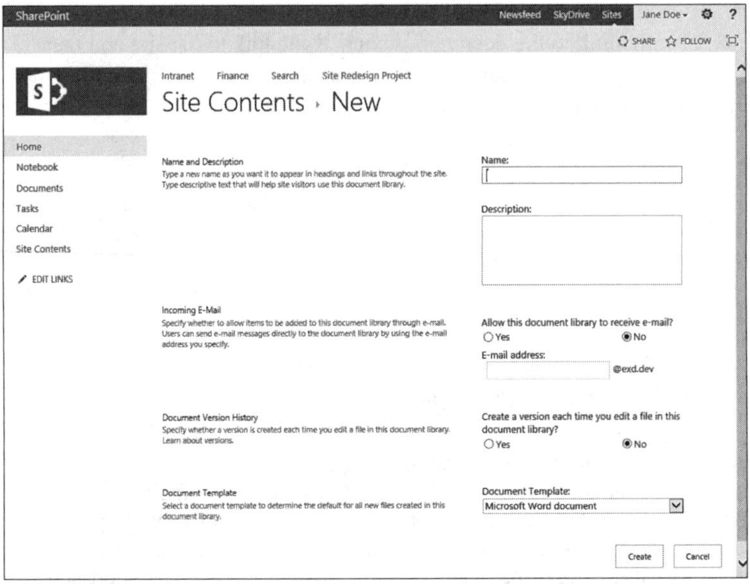

FIGURE 7.6   The Advanced Options page for creating a document library.

First on this page, you can set the description for the library. This description is usually displayed to users in the All Site Contents page next to the library's name. In most cases, it also appears in all the views for the library, just above the view. You can change the description later, in the library's settings.

For more information about how to change the title or description for a list or a document library, see "Rename a List or Document Library or Change Its Description," later in this chapter.

The next choice to make is whether SharePoint should manage versions for documents in the document library. If you choose Yes, all changes in documents will create new versions of the documents. Although you can change this option later, if you choose No, all changes made in documents until you change the setting will not be stored in separate versions. However, if your site has a size quota and you are worried about consuming a lot of space, leaving this setting turned off can save quite a bit of space.

For more information about changing the versioning information for a list or document library, as well as setting some more advanced versioning options, see "Change the Versioning Settings for a List or Document Library," later in this chapter.

The last option, Document Template, enables you to choose the application or type of file that will be used when the user clicks the New Document button in the document library. For example, you can choose Microsoft Word to have SharePoint open an empty Microsoft Word document when the user clicks the New Document button, or you can choose any of the other Microsoft Office applications. For web pages, you can choose Basic Page to create an empty page that you can type text on. Or you can choose Web Part Page to create a page that allows the user to add web parts.

By default, the new document library has only the Document content type associated with it, so the New Document button in the ribbon does not show any options for different kinds of file types, whereas the New Document button in the list view itself will still open a dialog with multiple types. However, here you can set the specific file type that the users can use with the New Document button. You can change this later also, as explained in the section "Change the Document Template for the New Button in a Document Library," later in this chapter.

When you are finished selecting the options, click Create to create the document library. A new, empty library is created with the settings you chose.

Create a New Folder in a Document Library

Scenario/Problem: You want to create a new folder in a document library.

Solution: To create a new folder, navigate to the document library where you want to create the folder and then to the folder in the document library where you want the new folder to be (if you don't want it under the root of the document library). Then switch to the Files ribbon and click on the New Folder button in the New section. A Create a New Folder dialog appears as shown in Figure 7.7, asking for the name for the new folder. Enter the name and click Save to create the folder.

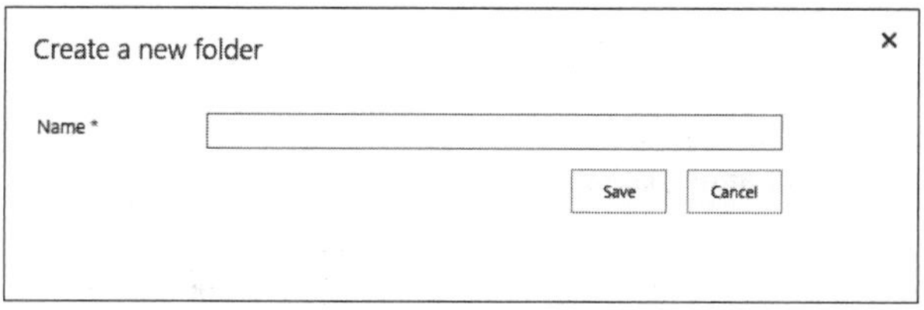

FIGURE 7.7   The Create a New Folder dialog.

NOTE The New Folder button is unavailable if any of the following conditions are true:

- ▶ The document library is configured not to allow creating folders.
- ▶ You do not have permissions to create items in the document library.
- ▶ The current view is configured to display as a flat view (see the section "Specify How Folders Will Be Used in a View" in Chapter 8, "Creating List Views," for more information).

NOTE Folders are handled as list items in the document library. This means that if a library requires approval, the folder is not visible to other users until it is published and approved. For more information about publishing and approving files and list items, see Chapter 6, "Creating and Managing Files, List Items, and Forms in SharePoint."

Create a New List

Scenario/Problem: You want to create a new list.

Solution: As with the process of creating document libraries, to create a list in a site, you open the Your Apps page as explained earlier in this chapter, browse the list of apps to find the type of list you want to create and click it.

For example, you can create a list of events by choosing the Calendar type or a discussion board list by choosing Discussion Board. If you want a list that does not have any specific columns like those lists, you can choose the Custom List type to create a list that has only one column (Title). You can later add additional columns, as explained in "Add a Column to a List or Document Library," later in this chapter.

After you select the template, type a name for the new list in the name box on the right side of the dialog and either click Create to create the list with that name or click the Advanced Options button to switch to the Advanced Options page, which allows you to set more advanced options for the list before you create it. These options might vary depending on the type of list you chose.

Unlike with document libraries, the link to the list (or any other lists) is the site link, then /Lists/, and then the name you choose for the list.

TIP As with document libraries, it is recommended that you choose a short name for a list when you are creating it and after that change the title.

As with document libraries, the name you choose here must be unique in the site. If you choose a name that is already in use in the site, SharePoint does not let you create the list and asks you for a different name. Remember that you can change the title to anything you want after the list has been created.

In the Advanced Options page you can set the description for the list. This description will show up in the Site Content page of the site next to the list's name and in the views of the list. You can modify this later, in the list settings. For more information about how to modify the title or description of a list, see "Rename a List or Document Library or Change Its Description," later in this chapter.

Some lists, such as the survey list, have additional special settings, which are covered later in this chapter, but most lists have exactly the same initial settings.

When you are done selecting options, click Create to create the list. A new, empty instance of the list type that you selected is created, with the settings you chose.

Create a New Survey

Scenario/Problem: You want to create a new survey.

Solution: You create a survey the same way you create a new list, using the process explained in the section "Create a New List," earlier in this chapter.

However, the new list's advanced options page that is shown if you clicked the Advanced Options button has two additional settings for the new survey you are creating. These options appear in the Survey Options section of the page as shown in Figure 7.8.

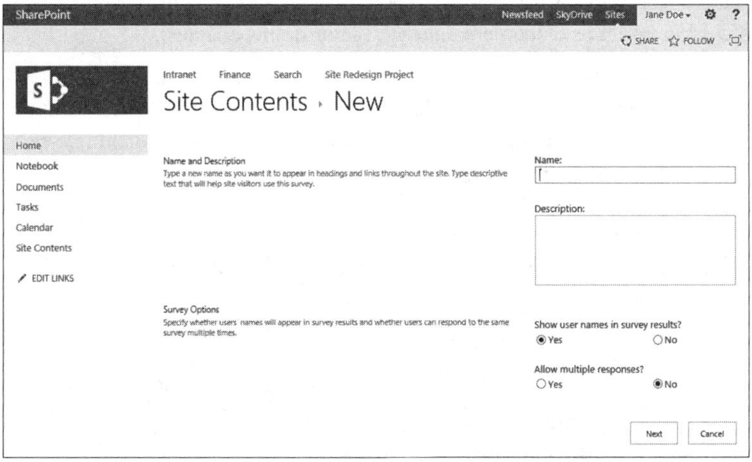

FIGURE 7.8   The Advanced Options page for creating a new survey.

The first option to configure—Show User Names in Survey Results?—enables you to decide whether the survey will be anonymous. If you choose No, the person viewing the results of the survey can't tell who answered what in the survey in any way. This setting is useful if you want to get honest feedback from people who might be concerned about revealing their true opinions (for example, using an employee satisfaction survey).

Choosing Yes tells SharePoint to show the name of the person who answered next to his or her answer in the reports. This setting is useful when you want to track who answered what (for example, in a survey that collects data from employees about what hotel they like to stay in when they are traveling).

The next option is whether to allow multiple responses. By default, a survey allows each person to answer the survey only once—like a voting system. However, you might want to create surveys that allow people to respond multiple times (for example, a survey that asks employees for suggestions for improving the company, where every employee might want to answer several times, every time they think of a new suggestion).

After you finish with the settings for the survey, click the Next button. Unlike with other list types, when you create a survey, you are immediately redirected to create questions for the survey.

The questions are almost identical to list columns, and creating them is almost the same as the process described in the following section. However, surveys also have additional options for column types that are not available in regular lists: the Rating Scale question type and a Page Separator. The section "Choose a Column Type," later in this chapter, describes these options in more detail.

When you are finished configuring the first question of the survey, you can either click the Next Question button to remove a question or click the Finish button to finalize the survey. You can add, modify, or remove questions in the future (see "Change or Remove a Column in a List or Document Library," later in this chapter).

When you create questions for surveys, the questions support another unique option called *branching logic*. This enables you to display different questions to users based on the answers they answered previously. For more information about branching, see "Branching in Surveys," later in this chapter.

Add a Column to a List or Document Library

Scenario/Problem: You want to create a new column and add it to an existing list or document library. For example, you might want to add a date column called Birthday for a contacts list or a choice or lookup column called Client to a document library so that users can choose which client the document is about. (For more information about choice and lookup columns, see "Choose a Column Type," later in this chapter.)

Solution: To add a column to a list or document library, switch to the List ribbon or the Library ribbon and click the Create Column button in the Manage Views section of the ribbon, as shown in Figure 7.9.

NOTE The Create Column option creates a new column in the list or library but does not let you select from the site columns that are already set up in the site. To learn how to add an existing site column to the list or library, see "Add a Site Column to a List or Document Library," later in this chapter.

Choosing the Create Column option opens a dialog where you can define the type of column you want to add, as well as set the settings on that column (see Figure 7.10).

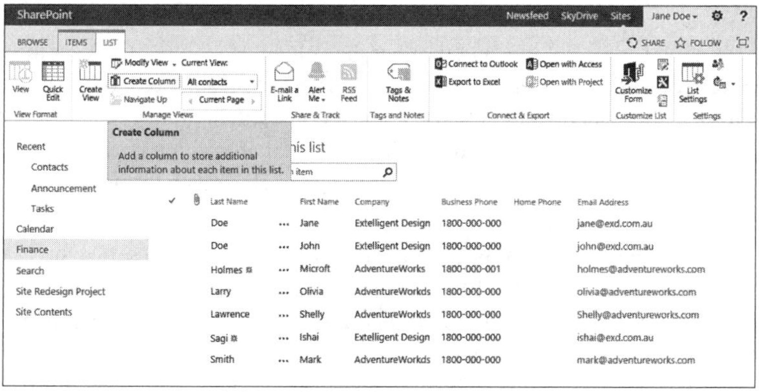

FIGURE 7.9   The Create Column button in the List ribbon.

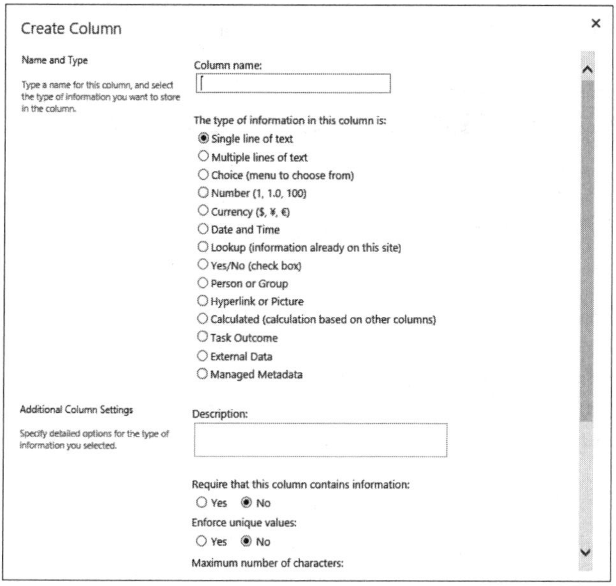

FIGURE 7.10   Creating a new column.

The first choice to make is the name of the column. Column names must be unique in the list; that is, you can't have two columns with the exact same name.

After choosing the name for the column, you must choose the type of the column, as shown in Figure 7.10. Numerous types of columns are available, and developers can add to those types, so you might see more than the built-in types shown in the figures in this book. Also, as mentioned earlier in "Create a New Survey," creating a new column in that type of list (also known as creating a new *question*) shows more options than are available for standard list types.

All column types require you to choose a name for the column. They also allow you to specify the description for the column and whether the column is required (making the column mandatory in the list, forcing the user to fill it in when creating or editing an item). Except for the column type, all options can be modified in the future. Changing the column type for a column is possible but is limited to certain column types. For more information about modifying a column see "Change or Remove a Column in a List or Document Library," later in this chapter.

Additionally, each column type can offer different configuration options for that column. For example, a Single Line of Text column type has a Maximum Number of Characters setting, whereas a Multiple Lines of Text column type has a Configuration option for how many lines it should allow.

Some column types also have an option for more complex validation settings, under the heading Column Validation, as shown a little later, in Figure 7.12. Other columns do not support this type of complex validation.

For more information about choosing a column type and the different configuration options that each type may have, see "Choose a Column Type," later in this chapter.

Add a Site Column to a List or Document Library

Scenario/Problem: You want to add to an existing list or document library an existing site column that has been defined in the site.

Solution: As explained in Chapter 1, "About Microsoft SharePoint 2013," a site column is a column that is defined at the site level rather than at the list or library level. Reusing those columns in lists and libraries makes a lot of sense. If a change to the column setting is required in many lists and libraries, changing the column at the site level once to update all the lists and libraries using that column is possible.

If you want to use an existing site column instead of create a new column, you can open the list's or library's settings page by switching to the List ribbon or Library ribbon and clicking the List Settings or Library Settings button.

In the list's or library's settings page that opens, you scroll down to the Columns section of the page. Here, you see the list of all the columns that have been added to the list or library. In this section, you click the Add from Existing Site Columns link. This selection opens a page that enables you to choose one or more site columns to be added to the document library or list (see Figure 7.11).

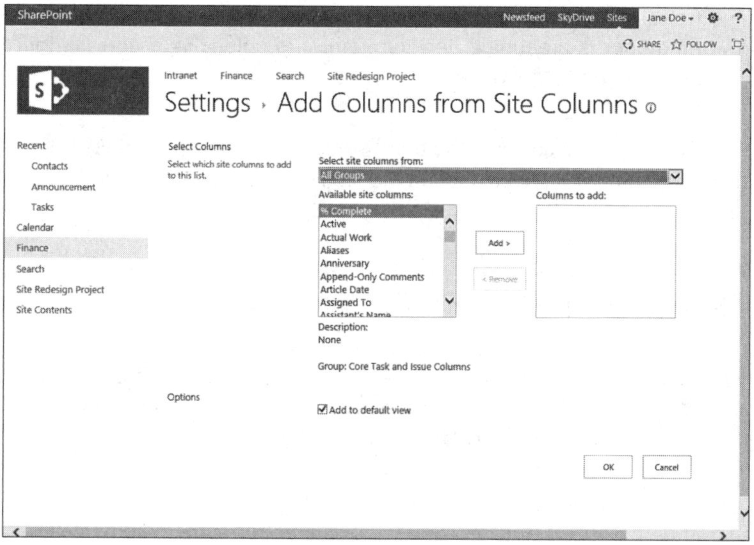

FIGURE 7.11   Choosing site columns for a list or library.

To choose a column, you locate it in the Available Site Columns box, select it, and click the Add button to add it to the Columns to Add box. If you regret your choice and want to undo it, you select the column in the Columns to Add box and click the Remove button.

To more easily find a column, you can filter the columns that are in the Available Site Columns box by choosing the group for the column. Site columns are grouped in logical groups. For example, the Core Document Columns group holds columns that are commonly used by most documents: Author, Comments, Date Created, and so on. By default, you see the site columns from all groups available to you. To choose a different group, you open the Select Site Columns From drop-down box and select a different group.

> **TIP**   When adding a site column, you cannot specify any settings on it because any column settings are defined at the site level. However, after adding the column, you can modify it as you would any other column. (See the instructions in the section "Change or Remove a Column in a List or Document Library," later in this chapter.)

Choose a Default Value for a Column

> **Scenario/Problem:** You want to define a default value for an existing or new column in a library or list. For example, in some instances, you want date columns to default to the current day's date or text columns to default to the current user's name; or for choice columns, where the user can choose from multiple choices, you might want to select one of the choices as the default.

Solution: Some types of columns can have default values. Default values appear in the column when a user is creating a new list item or is uploading a new file, but the user can choose to change the value.

Some column types allow more advanced settings for default values than others. The specifics for those column types are covered in the section "Choose a Column Type," later in this chapter.

Enforce Unique Values on a Column

Scenario/Problem: You want to make sure no two list items in a list or library have the same value in a column. For example, you want to make sure no two files have the same title or no two tasks have the same title.

Solution: The option to enforce unique values is available for some column types (refer to Figure 7.10), including the single line of text, number, choice, and lookup. Selecting Yes in this option tells SharePoint to make sure that users do not enter the same value in two different list items.

Enforce Custom Validation on a Column

Scenario/Problem: You want to set more complex validation rules on a column. For example, in a single text column, you might want to prevent users from entering certain words, such as the word *test*. Or you might want to make sure the user filling in the form types *I agree* before submitting the form to make the user think twice before submitting it.

Solution: Most column types support a rudimentary type of validation, allowing you to select whether the column must have a value (in most cases). Some columns are even more specific, requiring you to, for example, specify a minimum and a maximum for a Number column. (For more details, see "Number (1, 1.0, 100)," later in this chapter.) However, sometimes you need more validation options than are available.

Some SharePoint columns support a formula-based validation mechanism similar to Microsoft Excel formulas. This mechanism is available for columns under the Column Validation heading, and this heading is collapsed by default. Expanding this section reveals two additional settings that you can set for the column.

The first option is the formula. Here you can type a formula that is evaluated when the user tries to save the value for that column. For example, you can add a formula to prevent the word *test* from being used as a value:

```
=[column_name]<>"test"
```

In this example, you replace `column_name` with the name of the actual column you are validating, as shown in Figure 7.12.

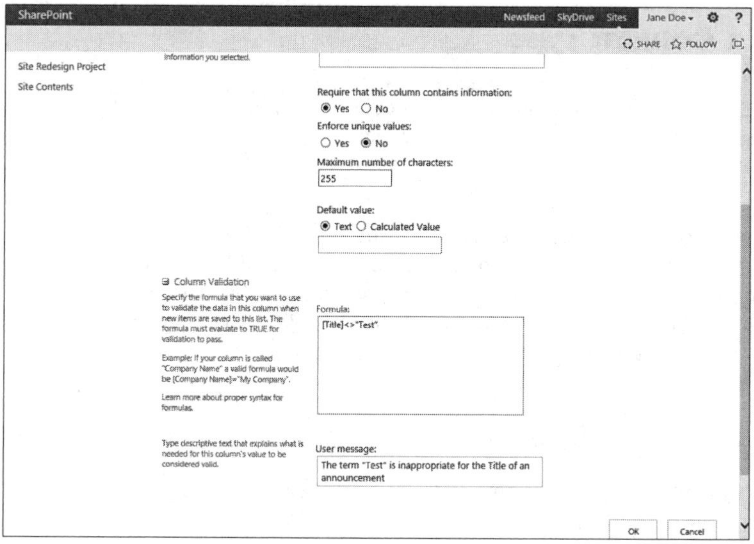

FIGURE 7.12   Setting custom column validation on a text field.

The second option you can set in this section is the message that is displayed to the user when validation fails. For example, you can write **The term "Test" is inappropriate for the Title of an announcement**. This message is displayed to the user below the column in red text, as shown in Figure 7.13.

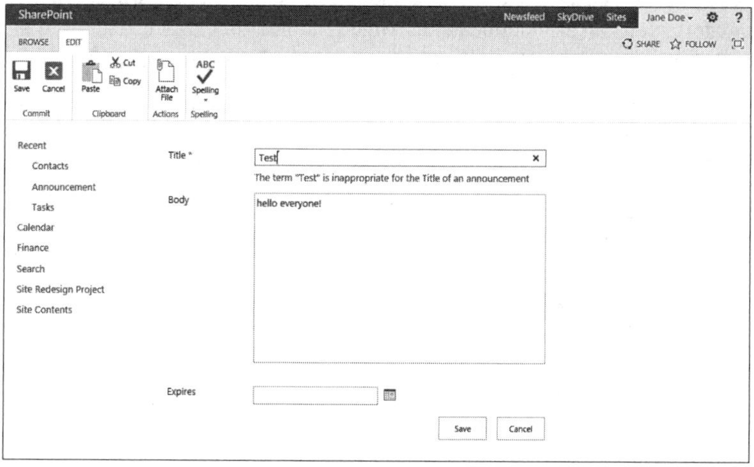

FIGURE 7.13   The column validation prevents a user from submitting an announcement with the title `Test`.

You can also enforce validation based on comparison between two columns. This is covered later in this chapter, in the section "Enforce Custom Validation on a List or Library."

Choose a Column Type

Scenario/Problem: You are creating a new column in a library, list, or site, and you have to select a column type for the new column.

Solution: When you're creating a new column, the first thing you need to decide in addition to the name for the column is its type. The type of the column defines what kind of data can go into it, and SharePoint has a lot of different built-in column types for you to choose from. The following sections explain each built-in column type and the different settings you can define for each one.

Single Line of Text

You use the Single Line of Text column type when you want the user to enter simple text, in a single line (that is, no line breaks), as shown in Figure 7.14.

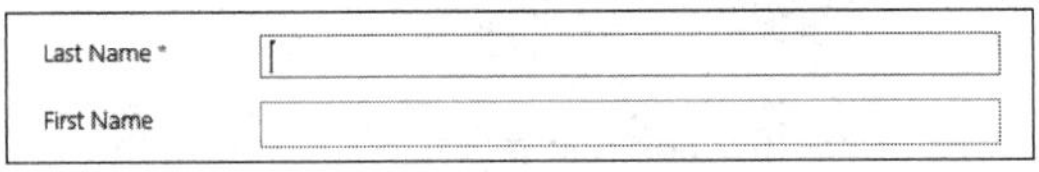

| Last Name * | |
| First Name | |

FIGURE 7.14   The First Name and Last Name columns in a contacts list are examples of a Single Line of Text column.

Aside from the regular settings, such as the description for the column and whether the column is mandatory, you can also define the maximum number of characters allowed in the field (up to 255 characters) and the default value for the column (see Figure 7.15).

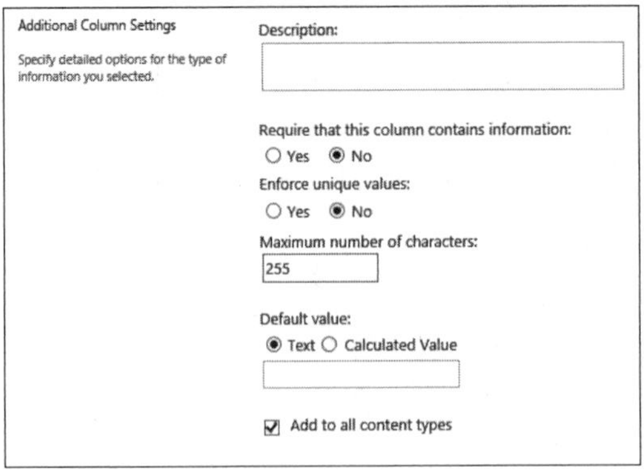

FIGURE 7.15   Defining the settings for a Single Line of Text column type.

The default value for a Single Line of Text column can be either a static piece of text that you type if you select the Text option or a calculated value showing the current user's account name by using the token [Me]. For example, you might want to create a calculated default that will have text (that the user can change) saying who purchased an item. The default is the name of the current user filling the form, but if the user is filling in the form for someone else, the text might need to be changed. Figure 7.16 shows how to configure this, and Figure 7.17 shows how it looks to users.

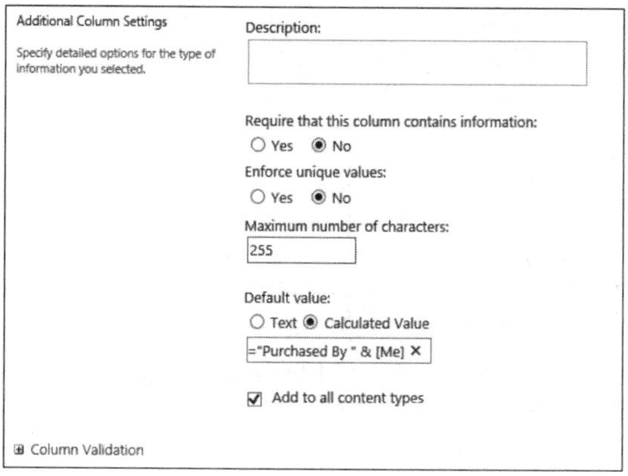

FIGURE 7.16   Defining a calculated default value.

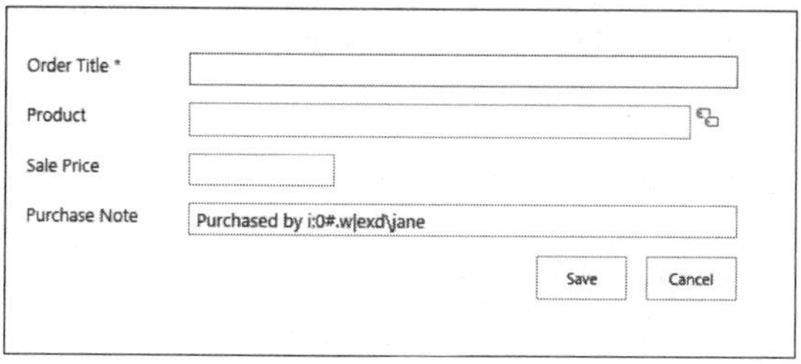

FIGURE 7.17   The calculated default value when a user creates a new item.

Multiple Lines of Text

The Multiple Lines of Text column type allows users to enter text with more than one line (that is, line breaks are allowed). It can be configured to allow different editing options for the user, as shown in Figure 7.18.

As shown in Figure 7.18, the column type can be configured to allow rich formatting of the text: You can make parts of the text bold, underlined, or a different font or color, and you can even include pictures, tables, and links.

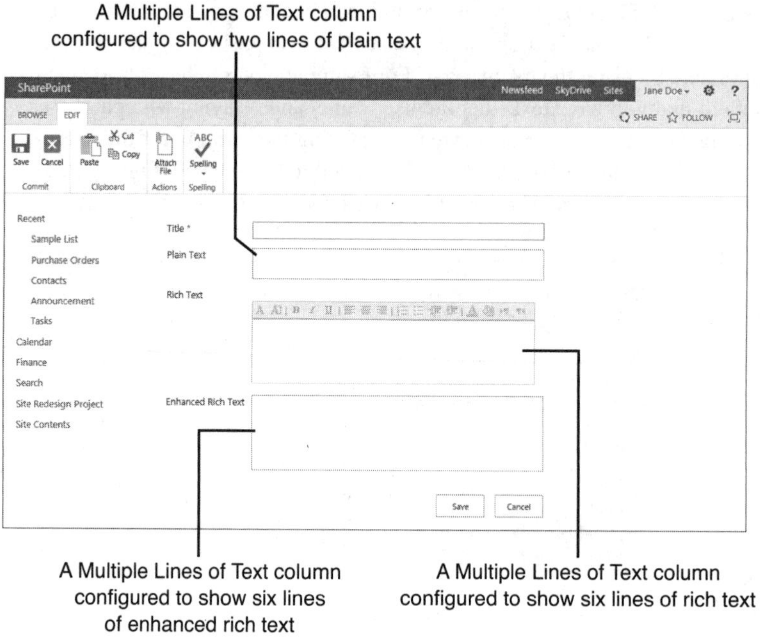

A Multiple Lines of Text column
configured to show two lines of plain text

A Multiple Lines of Text column
configured to show six lines
of enhanced rich text

A Multiple Lines of Text column
configured to show six lines of rich text

FIGURE 7.18   Different configurations of the Multiple Lines of Text column.

The enhanced rich text option shows as an empty text box, but when the user switches to that text box, the Editing Tools ribbon appears, enabling the user to edit the text using the enhanced text-editing options available through that ribbon, as shown in Figure 7.19.

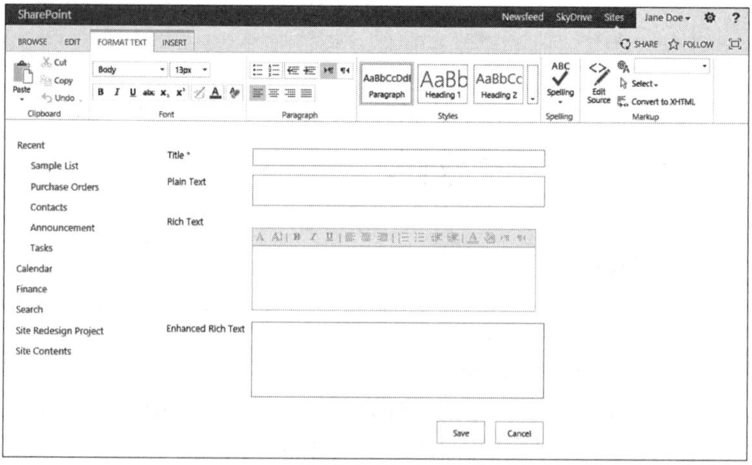

FIGURE 7.19   The Editing Tools ribbon displays to the user when the cursor is in an enhanced rich textbox control.

Figure 7.20 shows the settings for this column type. This column type does not support a default value, so no setting exists to configure one. However, you can configure the column with three settings that are special for this column type, as explained in the following sections.

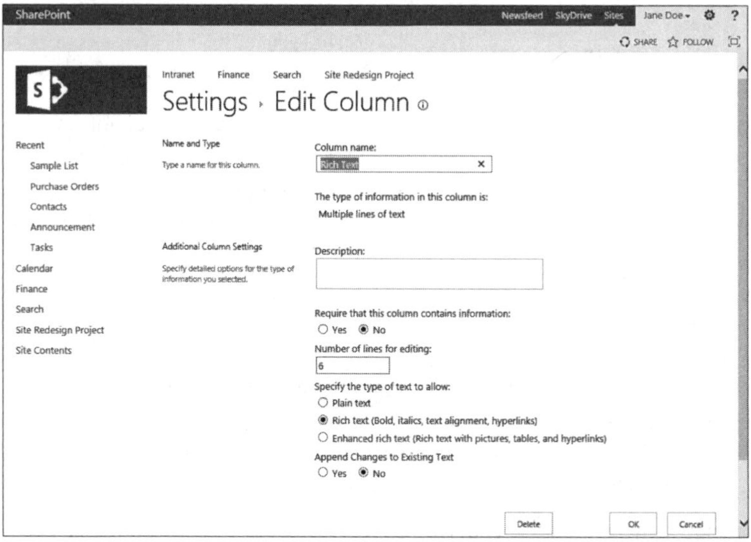

FIGURE 7.20   Defining the settings for a Multiple Lines of Text column type.

Number of Lines for Editing

The Number of Lines for Editing setting determines how many lines are displayed in the editing box for the text. This can be any number from 1 (where only one line will be displayed, but users can scroll down or up in the box) to 1,000. This setting does not affect the length of the text that can go into the column, just the appearance of the editing box (refer to Figure 7.18).

> **TIP**   Keeping the number small in the Number of Lines for Editing setting is recommended so that the column editing box doesn't take a huge amount of space in the editing form.

Specify the Type of Text to Allow

In the Specify the Type of Text to Allow setting, you can specify the type of text that can be entered in the editing box. The simplest option is Plain Text, which allows just simple, unformatted text (refer to Figure 7.18). The users do not have options to make any part of the text bold or a different font.

The next option, Rich Text, enables the users to set formatting on parts of the text and set the font, font size, alignment, color, and other kinds of formatting that are common when writing rich text.

The last option, Enhanced Rich Text, allows even more special formatting, such as making parts of the text into hyperlinks, adding images to the text, and creating tables.

Append Changes to Existing Text

The last option, Append Changes to Existing Text, lets you configure what happens when someone edits the value of the column in a list item or a file. The default setting is No, which means that when someone edits the value, the value just changes to the new value. Users who then view the properties of the list item or file see the new value, not the old one. If they want to see the old one, they must open the list item's or file's version history, if versioning is configured in the document library.

Choosing Yes here changes how the column is displayed when users view the properties of the list item or file. Instead of seeing just the current value, user also see the entire history of what the value was before, including who made changes and when. This option can be turned on only when versioning is enabled on the list or library because SharePoint must track the old versions of the value to show this information. For information about how to configure versioning on the list or library, see "Change the Versioning Settings for a List or Document Library," later in this chapter.

When the Append Changes option is enabled, the old entries and the current one appear under the editing box for the column. If no old entries exist, that is shown also (see Figure 7.21).

FIGURE 7.21   The Address column shows that there haven't been any old values.

When old entries exist, such as corrections to a value, they are shown to a user viewing the item as a list of values, complete with who wrote the value and when (see Figure 7.22).

Address	■ Jane Doe (1/27/2013 5:23 PM):
	15 Mann Street LA
	☐ John Doe (1/27/2013 5:23 PM):
	23/11 Nice Street, Seattle
	■ Jane Doe (1/27/2013 5:22 PM):
	1 wonderful way, New York

FIGURE 7.22   The Address column shows the history of changes when users view the properties of a list item.

When you are editing a list item of a file, the list of values appears below the editing box for the column, and the edit box is empty (see Figure 7.23).

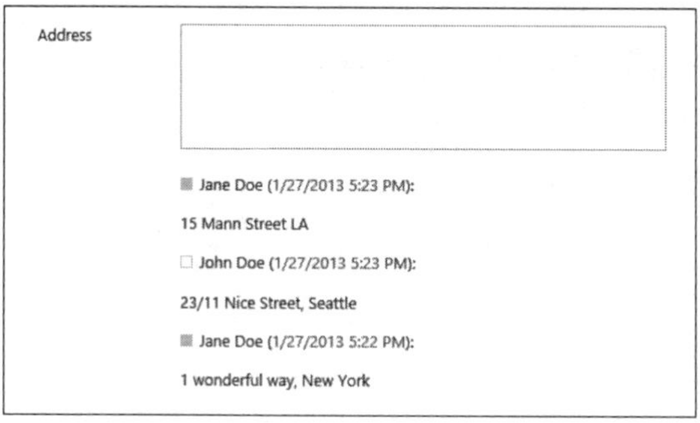

Address

Jane Doe (1/27/2013 5:23 PM):

15 Mann Street LA

John Doe (1/27/2013 5:23 PM):

23/11 Nice Street, Seattle

Jane Doe (1/27/2013 5:22 PM):

1 wonderful way, New York

FIGURE 7.23   The Address column shows the history of changes when editing the properties of a list item.

Choice Column

You can use a choice column when you want users to choose from a list of options for the value of the column in different configurations (for example, a list of regions or countries, as shown in Figures 7.24 through 7.26), with different controls appearing to the user.

Country/Region   ☑ Australia
                  ☐ United Kingdom
                  ☐ United State of America

FIGURE 7.24   A choice column that allows users to select one or more choices from a list.

Country/Region   Australia
                  United Kingdom
Web Page   United State of America   : here to test)
                  http://

FIGURE 7.25   A choice column that allows users to select only one choice, using the drop-down menu configuration.

Country/Region   ◉ Australia
                  ○ United Kingdom
                  ○ United State of America

FIGURE 7.26   A choice column that allows users to select only one choice, using the radio buttons configuration.

Choice columns enable you to specify the values you want the users to choose from, and you can configure them to allow the users to either make a single selection or select multiple values from the list (see Figure 7.27).

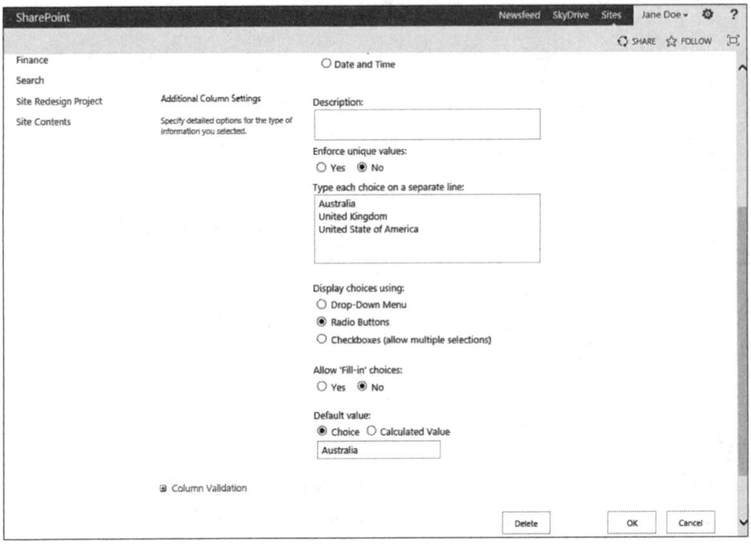

FIGURE 7.27   The configuration options for a Choice column type.

Specify the Choices

To specify the choices that users can choose from, you simply type the choices in the box titled Type Each Choice on a Separate Line (refer to Figure 7.27). You use a line break to separate choices. For example, for a list of countries, you type the countries in the box with a line break between each country name.

Choose How the Choices Will Be Displayed

The next configuration setting you can set is how the choices are displayed to the user. The first two options, Drop-down Menu and Radio Buttons, enable users to select only one option from the list of choices, whereas the last option, Checkboxes, allows multiple selections of values.

The Drop-down Menu option is useful when you have a lot of choices and don't want to overwhelm users. The values appear in a drop-down menu, which opens to reveal the list of choices (refer to Figure 7.25).

The Radio Buttons option is useful when the list of choices is small and will not take a lot of space on the page. The advantage of this option is that the user sees all the options on the page without having to open a drop-down menu (refer to Figure 7.26).

The Checkboxes option is useful when you want the users to be able to choose more than one option (refer to Figure 7.24).

Allow Fill-in Choices

When you choose to allow fill-in choices, the column enables users to type a value if the value they are looking for does not exist in the list of choices you chose (see Figure 7.28). The values that users type are not added to the list.

FIGURE 7.28   When the Allow Fill-in Choices option is enabled, users can type a value manually.

Default Value

As with most other column types, you can type a default value that will be selected when the user creates a new item. If you want nothing to be selected by default, you clear the Default Value box; otherwise, you need to make sure you type in the Default Value box the exact text of one of the choices.

Number (1, 1.0, 100)

The Number column type is useful when you want to capture a numeric value. With this column type, the user is asked to type a number in a text box. For example, you might ask for a 1-to-10 rating for a document or the number of products in stock. Figure 7.29 shows the settings for this column type.

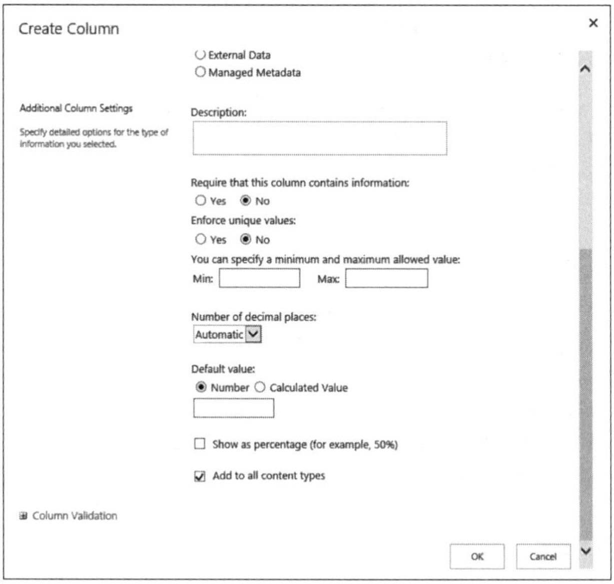

FIGURE 7.29   The configuration options for the Number column type.

Minimum and Maximum

With this option, you can configure for a Number column the minimum and maximum numbers that the user can choose in the value.

Number of Decimal Places

In the Number of Decimal Places option, you configure how many decimal places the value can have. If you choose the value 0, fractions of numbers are not allowed; only integers are allowed. Choosing the value 1 enables users to specify numbers with one decimal place, such as 15.4. Choosing the value 2 allows a precision of two decimal places, and so on up to five decimal places. The default option for this setting is Automatic, which displays how many decimal points are in the entered number.

Show as Percentage

Choosing the Show as Percentage option causes the value entered in this column to be displayed as a percentage.

Default Value

Like other columns, this column supports a default value that you can enter as a static default value or as a calculated value. This column supports many mathematical formulas using standard arithmetic operators (such as +, -, *, and /) to perform calculations. For example, you can have a calculated default value of =128+10, which results in a default value of 138. Another option is to use special functions in the calculation. Number columns support such functions as Pi(), which returns the number for pi; AVERAGE(), which returns the average of the numbers you give it; and MAX, which returns the biggest number in the list of numbers you give it.

> **TIP**   As you can see, having calculated defaults for the Number column is not extremely useful; essentially, you are typing in a static number. However, these formulas do work in this column type, and you might find a use for them. To take full advantage of these formulas, see the "Calculated (Calculation Based on Other Columns)" section, later in this chapter. For more information about the types of formulas and how to use them, see **http://tinyurl.com/SPcalculated2013**.

Currency ($, ¥, €)

The Currency column type is almost exactly the same as the Number column type. The only option that is different in the Currency column type from the Number column type is Currency Format. This option determines what symbol will be used next to the value when displaying the value in the item's or file's properties. For example, choosing United States displays values with the dollar sign ($) next to the value, whereas choosing one of the European countries displays the euro sign (€) next to the value.

Date and Time

The Date and Time column type lets users specify a date or a date and time as the value for the column. For example, in a calendar list, users can specify the start date and time of a meeting. However, for a list of contacts, if you want a column with the birth date of a contact, for example, you need to configure the column to ask only for the date, not for the time. Figure 7.30 shows the two modes for this column.

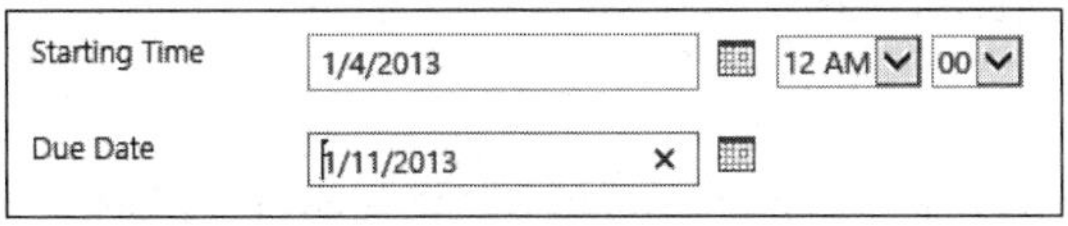

FIGURE 7.30   Two date and time columns: one shows only dates and the other shows date and time.

Figure 7.31 shows the configuration options for this column type.

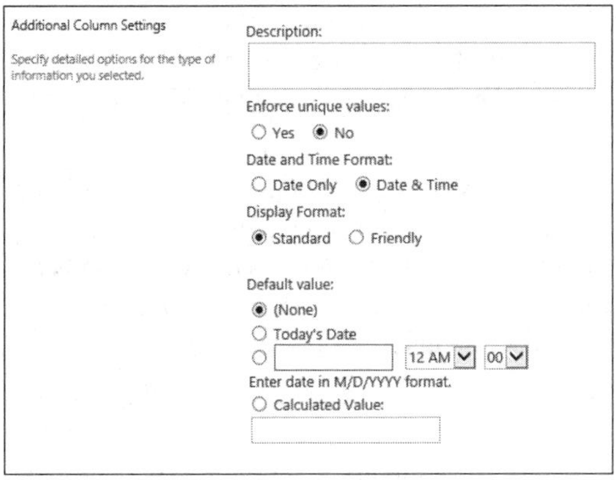

FIGURE 7.31   The configuration options for a Date and Time column type.

Date and Time Format

With the Date and Time Format configuration option, you can choose whether the users can choose just a date or a date and time. This choice changes what the date-choosing control looks like.

Display Format

You can choose between two ways to display the value of the column in list views—this option doesn't change how the date looks when viewing the item itself, or when editing the item. However, if you choose the Friendly format then instead of seeing "1/11/2013" you would see "January 11."

Default Value

You have the option to choose a specific date or make the current date the default. Also, you can use the Calculate Value option and set a default that calculates based on the current date using the [Today] token. For example, to set the default to be two weeks from the current date, you type **[Today] +14** in the Calculated Value box. This capability is useful when you want to use a column as an expiration date, for example, while allowing the users to change the expiration date. You can set the default value to be two weeks in the future from creating the list item or file, but the user can still change the date manually.

> **TIP**   If a user just selects a time and not a date, SharePoint doesn't save anything in the column. To avoid this, you should set a default date value for the column.

Lookup (Information Already on This Site)

Lookup is one of the most useful column types. It is similar to the Choice column type in that the users get to choose from a list of values (refer to Figures 7.24 through 7.26 for examples of how this might appear to users). However, unlike the Choice column type, the Lookup column type does not store the choices in the settings of the column. Instead, the choices are in another list or library.

For example, if you create a SharePoint list in a site and enter a list of countries in that list, you can use the Lookup column type to show values from that list. This feature is helpful when you want other users to be able to manage the list of choices. The other users do not need permissions to change settings on the current list; they just need permissions to change items or files in the list of values (the remote list).

Unlike the Choice column type, though, in the Lookup column, the values that users choose show up as links to the list item or file selected. This can help create a complicated system of lists connected to one another (for example, a list of orders connected to a list of products). When users create a new order, they can choose a product or products, and when they view an order, the product name appears as a link to the product list item.

You can configure a Lookup column to display additional columns from the list to which it is looking up. For example, in an orders list, instead of just seeing the name of the product for an order, you can also see the product ID or when the product expires, as if these were separate columns in the list to which you added the lookup column.

Finally, the Lookup column can enforce relationship behavior. It can control the relationship between the two lists selected. For example, you might want to restrict deleting products while there are still orders referring to those products. This option allows you to do that, and it is explained in more detail later in this chapter.

Figure 7.32 shows the configuration options for this column type.

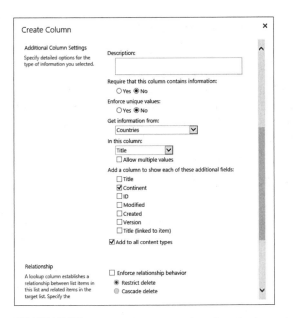

FIGURE 7.32   The configuration options for a Lookup column type.

Get Information From

In the Get Information From field, you specify which list has the information you want to display to the user. The choices here are the available lists in the current site. Referencing a list from another site is not possible.

In This Column

In the In This Column configuration option, you specify which column in the list to which you are connecting will be displayed to the user as the possible values. For example, the most common choice for this setting is the Title column, which displays the titles of the list items or files as the options for the user to choose from.

Allow Multiple Values

As you can do with the Choice column, you can have the Lookup column enable users to choose more than one value. When you select the Allow Multiple Values option, the user interface for selecting values changes, allowing the users to select multiple values, as shown in Figure 7.33.

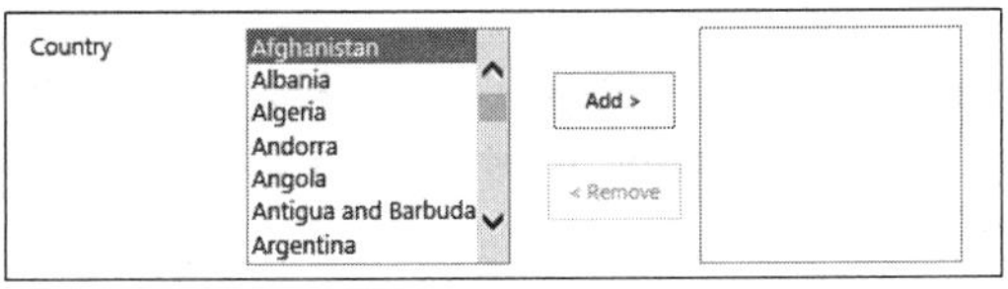

FIGURE 7.33   The user interface for selecting multiple values in a lookup column type.

> **NOTE** Selecting Allow Multiple Values disables the Enforce Unique Values and Enforce Relationship Behavior settings.

Add a Column to Show Each of These Additional Fields

As mentioned earlier, you can configure a Lookup column to display more than just one column (the one selected in the "In This Column" section, mentioned earlier). The additional columns are displayed to users in list views and when viewing the properties of the list items or files, but they are not displayed to users who are editing the properties because they are part of the Lookup column.

The additional columns are displayed with the name of the Lookup column before them, as shown in Figure 7.34.

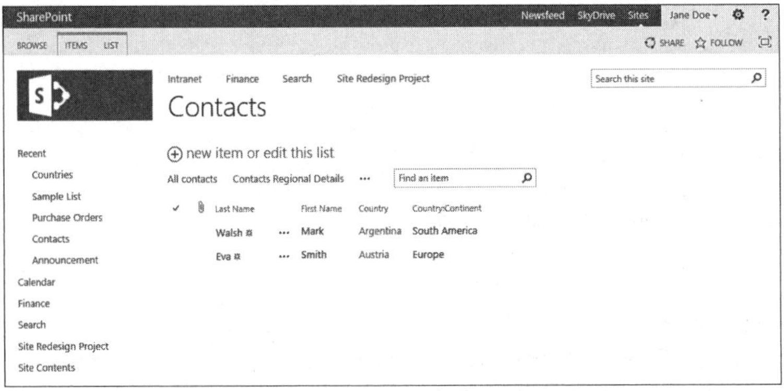

FIGURE 7.34   The user interface displaying additional columns from a Lookup column.

> **NOTE** Not all columns from the looked-up list are available to display under this section. This feature supports only columns from certain column types (for example, date, Number, and Single Line of Text column types).

Enforce Relationship Behavior

The last option on the lookup column settings page is to enforce relationships between the item in the current list and the item or items it is linked to in the looked-up list. This allows you to specify that items that are used as lookup values cannot be deleted when there are items linking to them, or that when you delete them all related items in the current list will also be deleted. For example, if you have a list of companies and a list of contacts, with a column called "Company" in the contacts list, you might want to either restrict deletion of companies while there are contacts that are marked as belonging to the company using the lookup column, or you might want to specify you want to cascade the delete—so that if someone deletes a company SharePoint will automatically delete all the contacts marked as belonging to the company.

Yes/No (Check Box)

The Yes/No column type is one of the simplest column types available. It enables the user to select either Yes or No by selecting or clearing a checkbox. The only configuration option you can set for this column type is the default value for it: Choose either Yes or No.

> **NOTE** A common problem that a lot of people have when creating forms in SharePoint is how to add a checkbox for the user to agree to conditions before saving the form (or a similar requirement). This requirement can be answered with a Yes/No column, combined with list validation (see "Enforce Custom Validation on a List or Library," later in this chapter), or it can be achieved with the Choice column type: You simply specify just one choice (I Agree, for example) and make the column mandatory.

Person or Group

The Person or Group column type enables users to choose a value from a list of users or groups (see Figure 7.35).

FIGURE 7.35   The user interface for entering data in the Person or Group column type.

You can see an example of this column type in the tasks list, where users who want to assign a task to other users choose from the list of users to whom they want to assign the task. The selected values appear as the names of the users chosen when a user views a list item or a file's properties, and the name is a link to the chosen user's properties page. As you can do with Lookup columns, you can configure whether this column type allows multiple selections (see Figure 7.36).

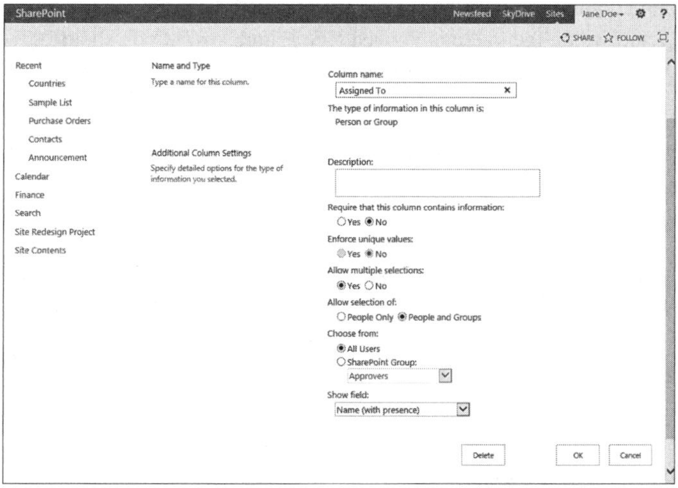

FIGURE 7.36   The configuration options for the Person or Group column type.

Allow Multiple Selections

The Allow Multiple Selections configuration option lets you define whether the column will allow users to choose more than one user in this column.

Allow Selection Of

The Allow Selection Of configuration option defines whether the user will be able to choose only people (other users) or also groups. If you want groups to be selectable, you must change this option.

Choose From

In the Choose From configuration option, you specify what users and groups appear to the user to pick from. By default, this option is set to All Users, which enables the user to choose from the list of all the users that SharePoint recognizes, even users who do not have access to the current site or list. The second option, SharePoint Group, limits the selection to users in a specific security group in the current site or site collection. This option is useful if you want to let users select from a restricted list of users, in which case you should create a security group and set the column to show only users from that group.

Show Field

In the Show Field configuration setting, you define what will be displayed as the selected value when a user views the list item or file properties. The default is the name of the user who was selected, together with that user's presence information (whether that user is online or busy, for example; this requires that special instant messaging software be installed and configured on the user's machine). You can change this option to display other information about the selected user.

Hyperlink or Picture

The Hyperlink or Picture column type enables users to enter data that will be displayed as either a link or a picture when the value is viewed (see Figure 7.37). You should choose this column type when you want users to freely type a link to a web page (in SharePoint or otherwise) or to a picture.

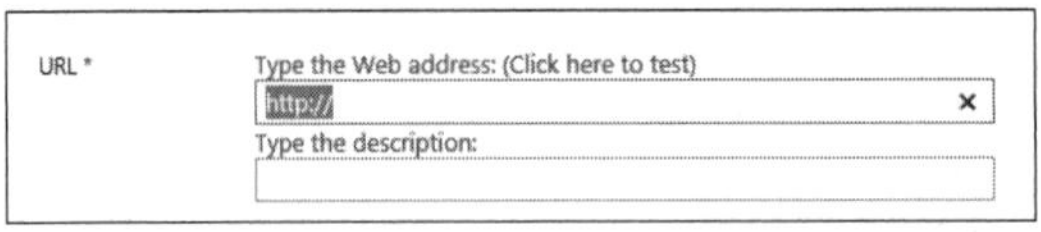

FIGURE 7.37   The user interface for entering data into a Hyperlink or Picture column type.

The only setting to set on a Hyperlink or Picture column type, Format URL As, determines how to format the link that the user types when viewing the list item's or file's properties. The first option is to format it as a hyperlink, which displays the title that the user chose as a link to the page the user chose. The second option is to format as a picture, which shows the picture to which the user typed the link instead of showing the link itself.

Regardless of what settings you choose, the user interface looks the same: The user is asked to enter a URL path and a title (refer to Figure 7.37). However, when you're looking at list views and viewing the properties of a list item or file, the difference is apparent. As Figure 7.38 shows, the same information is shown in two columns of type Hyperlink or Picture, one formatting the information as a link and the other formatting the information as a picture.

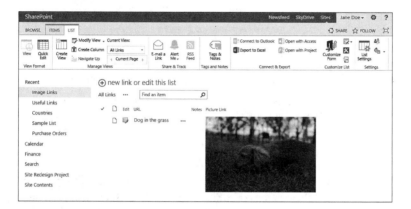

FIGURE 7.38   A view showing one column configured to show the data the user typed as a picture and another column configured to show the data the user typed as a hyperlink.

Calculated (Calculation Based on Other Columns)

A Calculated column type does not allow the user to enter data in it; it is used only to show data based on a calculation of other columns. For example, if you want a Full Name column that displays information automatically based on the First Name and Last Name columns, you can create a Calculated column that concatenates the values in those two columns.

As another example, say that you have a list of orders that has a column for the number of products ordered and another column for the price for a single product. The Calculated column can display the total revenue for the order by multiplying the numbers in the two columns.

The configuration options for this column type include a special formula builder control that enables you to specify the calculation required for the column, as shown in Figure 7.39.

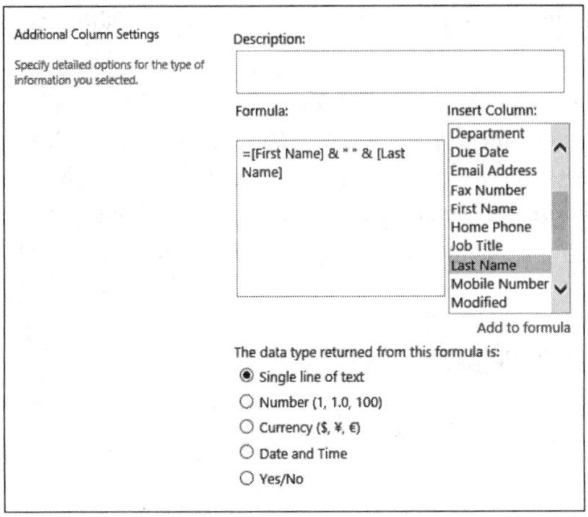

FIGURE 7.39   The configuration options for a Calculated column type. The formula in this figure concatenates two columns and a piece of text.

Formula

In the Formula text box, you can define the calculation that will be performed (refer to Figure 7.39). You can select the columns on which you want to perform a calculation from the list on the right and click Add to Formula to add a reference to that column in the formula.

For example, to concatenate two text columns, you add the two columns from the list and use the ampersand (&) character to connect them. You can also add a piece of text in quotation marks. The value is automatically displayed everywhere, including in list views and views showing the list item's or file's details.

For a complete list of formulas that you can use, see **http://tinyurl.com/SPcalculated2013**.

The Data Type

The second option you need to configure for the Calculated column type is the data type that will be used for the calculation. You select the appropriate data type that matches the data type of the columns for which you are performing an operation. Performing an operation on columns of different types is possible. For example, you can multiply the value in a Number column by the value in a Currency column, but you must decide how the result of the operation will be displayed—either as a number or as currency.

Rating Scale

The Rating Scale column type is available only in surveys. You use it when you want the user to rate several items in a Likert scale control. It's like asking many questions in one column, where the answer for each question is a number. These questions are referred to as the sub-questions of the column.

For example, you might want to gather input on user satisfaction on several aspects of a service, or you might want to know how strongly users agree with certain statements about different aspects of a book (see Figure 7.40).

How helpful did you find the book?						
	Low		Average		High	
	1	2	3	4	5	I don't know yet
The book helped me solve my problem	◎	○	○	○	○	○
The book answered all my questions	○	○	○	○	○	○
The book covers sufficient ground	○	○	○	○	○	○

FIGURE 7.40   The Rating Scale column data entry user interface.

The Rating Scale column type is useful in surveys where you want to assess how users feel about multiple subjects. It gives the user an interface for easily answering many questions quickly. You can configure this column to specify what questions will be included, what ratings the user can choose, and what the values mean. Figure 7.41 shows the configuration page for this column type.

Additional Question Settings

Specify detailed options for the type of answer you selected.

A rating scale question consists of a question and sub-questions that are rated on a scale such as 1 to 5. Type a question into the Question box, and then type sub-questions that support the main question. Select a Number Range to define the number of options that users can choose from. The Range Text appears above the option buttons to describe the meaning of the scale, such as Low, Average, and High or Strongly Disagree, Neutral, and Strongly Agree. Use the N/A option if you want users to select N/A or a similar response, if a question is not applicable.

Require a response to this question:
○ Yes ⦿ No

Type each sub-question on a separate line:

The book helped me solve my problem
The book answered all my questions
The book covers sufficient ground

Number Range:
5 ▾

Range Text:
Low   Average   High

Show N/A option:
☑
N/A option text: t know yet

FIGURE 7.41   The configuration page for the Rating Scale column type.

Type Each Sub-question on a Separate Line
The Type Each Sub-question on a Separate Line setting is where you specify the sub-questions that appear to the user to rate. You type each one in a separate line, as shown in Figure 7.41.

Number Range

In the Number Range setting, you specify the range of numbers the users can choose from when rating your sub-questions. You can choose any number from 3 to 20.

Range Text

In the Range Text setting, you specify the text that will be displayed above the low, medium, and high rating options. This helps the user understand what the numbers mean. For example, in Figure 7.40, number 1 means Disagree, while number 3 means Somewhat Agree and number 5 is Agree.

Show N/A Option and N/A Option Text

Show N/A Option and N/A Option Text enable you to specify whether you want to allow the user to not rate some of the sub-questions. This is useful if the user might not have an answer for one of the sub-questions. If you select that you want the option to be available, you can also change the text shown for the option. For example, in Figure 7.41 the text was modified to I don't know yet. Figure 7.40 shows how the user sees this.

Page Separator

The Page Separator column type is unique to surveys. It enables you to add a page break between questions, so if you have a very long survey, a user is not presented with a single page with all the questions on it, but instead sees a subset of the questions and has a Next button to go to the next page.

A page separator does not have any settings that you need to set. You can't even give it a name.

External Data

The External Data column type is available only when you have SharePoint Server installed. You use it in a similar fashion to the Lookup column type, but instead of allowing the user to select a value from a list in the current site, it shows the user values from a business application that the administrator or developer has set up.

A common example for this is a company that has a database with information about customers. Instead of migrating that information into a SharePoint list, the administrator configures a business data application integration. You can then create columns that allow the users to choose from the list of customers who exist in that database. By default, no external data applications are configured, so this column type is used only after developers and administrators have configured it. Figure 7.42 shows the configuration options for this column type, when an external content type and field are selected.

FIGURE 7.42   The configuration options for an External Data column type, with External Content Type and Field settings selected.

External Content Type

In the External Content Type selection box, you select which external content type the column will connect to. If you click the database icon, a dialog box appears, showing all the content types that you can select from and to which external data source they belong. If no application is configured in your system, the dialog tells you so.

In the dialog you can search for the entity you want to allow the users to select (for example, Product) and select it. After you select an entity, more options you can set on the column become available, the same as in a Lookup type column (refer to Figure 7.42).

Select the Field to Be Shown on This Column

The Select the Field to Be Shown on This Column option enables you to select what field from the database should be used as the title field for the selection that the user made. For example, in the Product entity, choosing the Product Name field makes a lot of sense. However, you might want to choose the Product Serial Number field instead.

Display the Actions Menu

The Display the Actions Menu option enables you to select whether an Actions menu should be displayed when a user moves the mouse cursor over a value in the column. Some entities can have actions that the developer has developed for them, such as Show Product or Delete Product. To see the list of actions available for an entity, you select this option and then see what actions show up.

Link This Column to the Default Action of the External Content Type

The Link This Column to the Default Action of the External Content Type option determines whether the values appear as links. When this option is selected, the user is redirected to a profile page for the entity. For example, when showing the name of a product, the name appears as a link that, when clicked, opens a page with more information about the product and actions to perform on the product.

Add a Column to Show Each of These Additional Fields

You might want to display more information than just the name of the selected entity when users are viewing the list item's or file's properties. The Add a Column to Show Each of These Additional Fields option enables you to select more properties of the entity that will be displayed as if they are separate columns when viewing the properties of the list item or file, even though, when editing the properties, the column is shown as only one. This is displayed in the same way as the Lookup column with the same option selected (refer to Figure 7.34).

This option is visible only after you select a content type and a field.

Managed Metadata

The Managed Metadata column type is available only when you have SharePoint Server installed (not SPF). It is similar to the Lookup column type in the fact that it, too, displays options to the user from a predefined list of options that is not part of the column itself. However, the Managed Metadata column type is more advanced both in the way it is displayed to the end users and in the options administrators have to manage the items available for the users to choose from.

Unlike with a Lookup column, the items the users choose from in a Managed Metadata column type do not come from another list. Instead, the values come either from an enterprise term repository (managed by the administrator) or from a custom term set that you can create in the site collection.

The terms in the term sets can be hierarchical. For example, instead of having a flat list of products for the user to choose from (as in the example in the "Lookup (Information Already on This Site)" section earlier in this chapter), the administrator of the Managed Metadata service can create a term set that has product categories, with products in each category. This can evolve to more levels of hierarchy if required. For instance, you might have a category for Mobile Phones and under it the names of the manufacturers, and under each manufacturer the model numbers of the phones. You can also have a simpler, two-level hierarchy with the first level called Books, and under it a list of book names, as shown in Figure 7.43.

The user interface for this type of column is a textbox with an icon next to it. The user can either write the term in the text box or click the icon to open the dialog that shows the terms that are available, as shown in Figure 7.43.

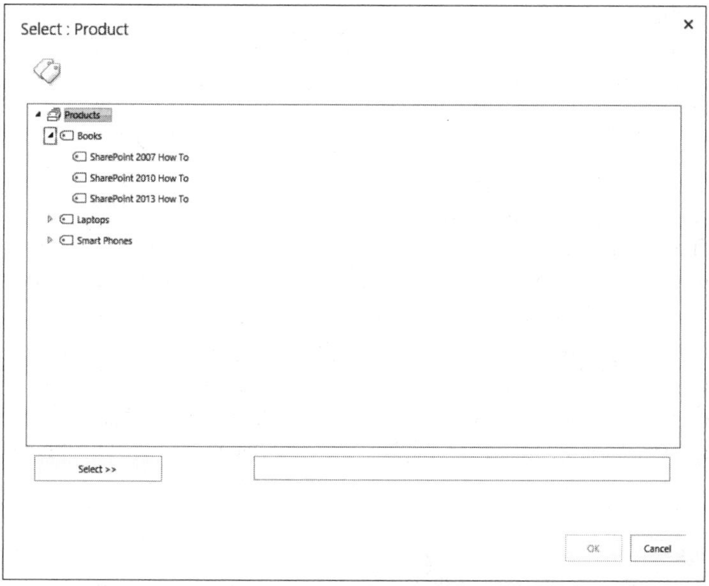

FIGURE 7.43   The user interface for selecting a value from a Managed Metadata column.

Figure 7.44 shows the configuration options for the Managed Metadata Column type.

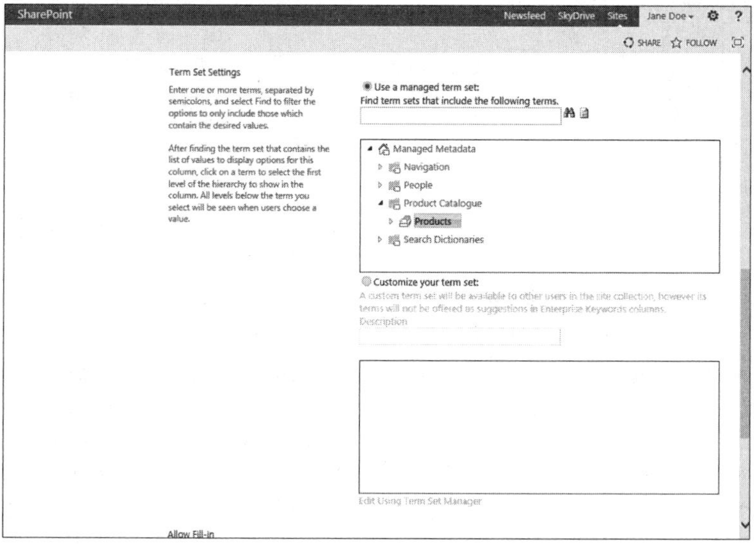

FIGURE 7.44   The configuration options for a Managed Metadata column.

Allow Multiple Values

For the Allow Multiple Values option, you set whether the users can choose multiple terms. You should not select this option if you want the users to be able to select just a single term.

Display Value

The Display Value option sets how the terms will be displayed to a user viewing the properties of the file or list item. Because the terms might be hierarchical, showing just the value of the term (the term label) can lead to confusion if two terms have the same label but are under different hierarchies.

For example, if you have a term set that has mobile phones under the manufacturers, and if two different manufacturers have the same name for a mobile phone, you will not know by looking at the label which mobile phone it is unless you select Display the Entire Path to the Term in the Field, which displays the entire hierarchy as the value of the column.

Term Set Settings

As mentioned earlier, you can connect a column to an existing term set by using the Use a Managed Term Set option. This option allows you to select the existing term set from the box under it, as shown in Figure 7.45.

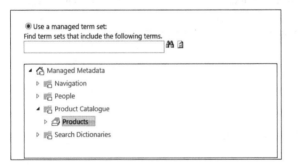

FIGURE 7.45   Selecting an existing term set.

If you want to create your own new term set instead, you select the Customize Your Term Set option. This enables you to create the term set in the box under that option. By default, when you select the Customize Your Term Set option, a new term set is added with the label Untitled. You can rename the term set by clicking on it once and typing the new name. To create terms in the term set, you open the drop-down menu for the term set (hover with the mouse over the name of the term set, and then open the menu that appears) and click Create Term, as shown in Figure 7.46.

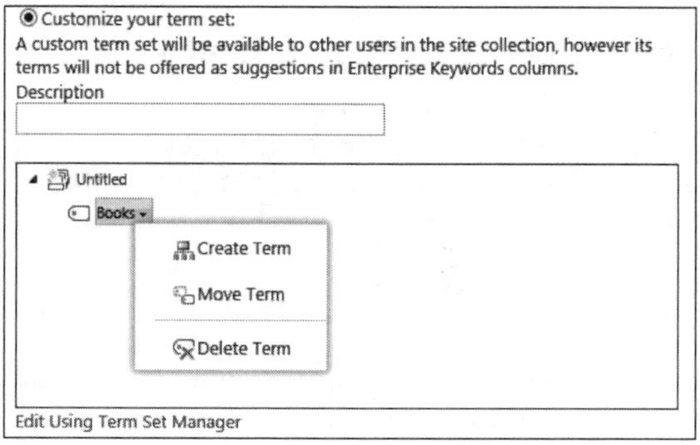

FIGURE 7.46   Creating a new term in a custom term set.

Clicking on the Create Term option creates a new term without a label (name), and you can then give it a name. You can then open the menu for that term and either create terms under it (using the Create Term option), move it, or delete it.

A more advanced way to manage the term set is to click the Edit Using Term Set Manager link at the bottom of the configuration options box. This opens a new page, shown in Figure 7.47, that has more options for managing the term set, including the description for the term set, an ability to lock down the term set, different sorting options, and more.

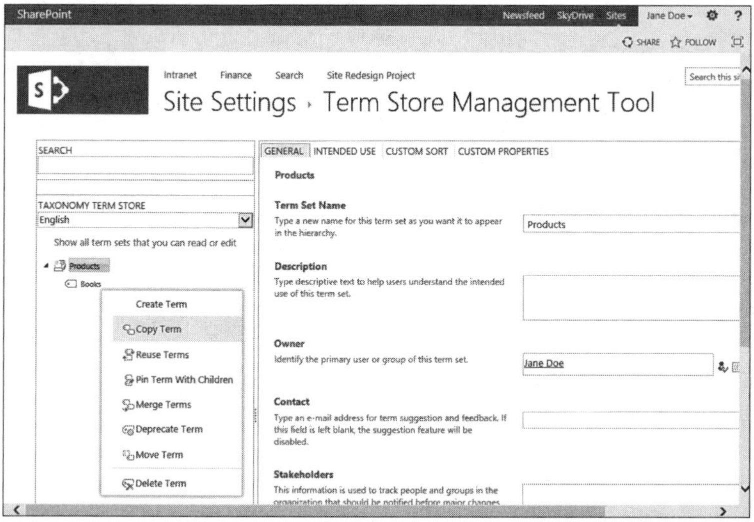

FIGURE 7.47   The term set manager.

Enforce Custom Validation on a List or Library

Scenario/Problem: You want to configure more complex validation for columns to prevent users from entering conflicting information in two different fields. For example, if you have two date columns, Starting Time and Due Date, you want to make sure users enter a bigger value in the Due Date column.

Solution: To configure validation at a list or library level, you open the list or library settings page by switching to the List ribbon or Library ribbon and clicking the List Settings or Library Settings button. In the list or library settings page, you click the Validation Settings link to open the Validation Settings page shown in Figure 7.48.

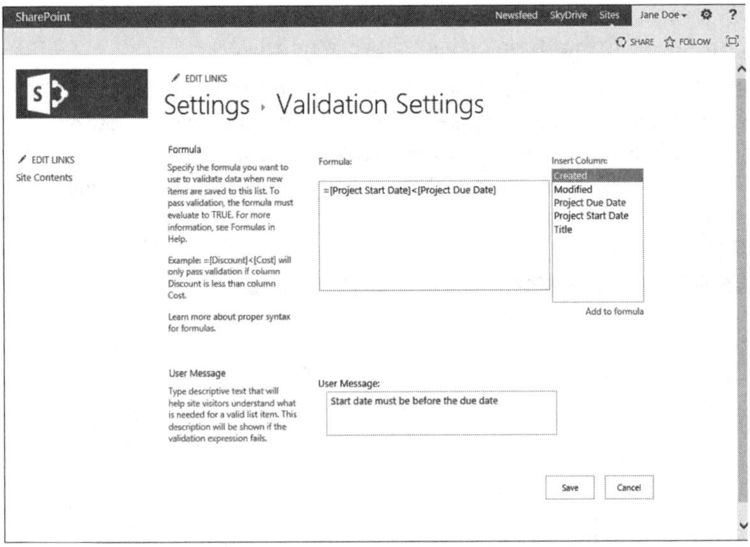

FIGURE 7.48   The list Validation Settings page.

Here you can define a formula that will be evaluated when the user tries to save a new item in the list or library. The formula must evaluate to TRUE for the save to be successful.

For example, if you have two date fields, you select the Due Date column from the Insert Column box on the right and click the Add to Formula link to add it to the box, and you then do the same with the Starting Time column. In this way, you add the column names (surrounded by square brackets) to the formula. You add a > (greater than) sign between them, as shown in Figure 7.48, and click Save.

Another option in this page is to set the message the user sees if the formula fails to evaluate to TRUE. For example, Figure 7.48 is set to display a message to the users that the Due Date must be after the Starting Time.

You can use AND and OR operators to chain validation conditions in the formula. For example, you can have the formula check that either the State/Province column or the Country/Region column has a value and that either Home Phone or Mobile Phone has a value, as shown in Figure 7.49.

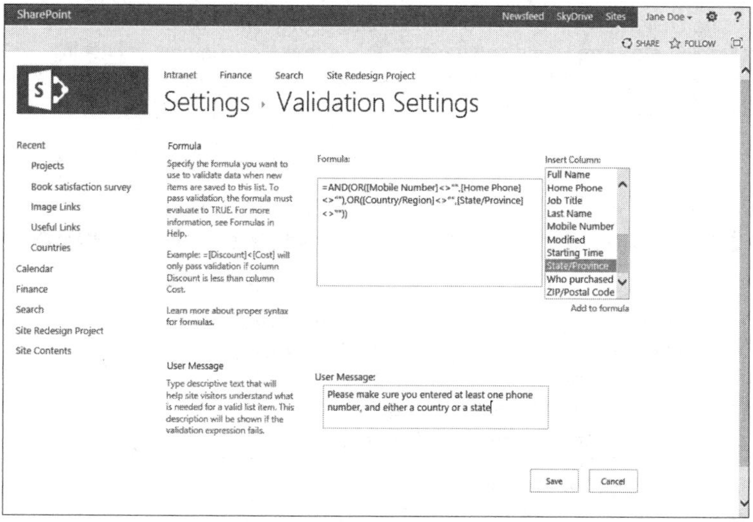

FIGURE 7.49   Chaining conditions by using the AND and OR operators for a complex validation rule.

Change or Remove a Column in a List or Document Library

Scenario/Problem: You want to modify the settings of a column in a list or library. For example, you want to change the default value for the column, change the column's title, or add or remove choices for a choice column.

Solution: To change a column's setting in a list or document library, you go into the list or document library's settings page by switching to the List ribbon or Library ribbon and clicking the List Settings or Library Settings button.

In the list or library settings page, you scroll down to the Columns section of the page. Here, you see the list of all the columns that have been added to the list or library. When you click the title of the column you want to modify or remove from the list or library, the settings page for that column appears. In this page, you can either modify the column (rename it, change its settings, or even change its type) or delete the column by using the Delete button at the bottom of the page.

> **NOTE**   Some columns cannot be deleted, and the Delete button is not displayed for those columns. These built-in columns are an integral part of SharePoint and cannot be removed from lists and libraries.

> **CAUTION**   Changing the type of a column can have significant repercussions. You can lose data if you move from one column type to another. For example, switching from any type of column to a Choice column causes any value that doesn't exist in the choice list to be lost.

Change the Order of Columns in a List or Document Library

> **Scenario/Problem:** You want to change the order in which columns are displayed to users when they're either entering the values for the columns or viewing the details for a list item or file. For example, in a contacts list, you might want the users to enter the first name before entering the last name.

Solution: To change the order of columns in the data entry page for a list or library (but not in the views), you go into the list's or document library's settings screen by switching to the List ribbon or Library ribbon and clicking the List Settings or Library Settings button.

> **NOTE**   For information on changing the order of columns in a view, see "Specify the Order of the Columns in the View" in Chapter 8.

In the list or library settings page, you scroll down to the Columns section. Here, you see the list of all the columns that have been added to the list or library. If the list does not use more than one content type, a Column Ordering link is available under the list of columns. If there is more than one content type, you have to change the column order for each content type separately by clicking on the content type name under the Content Types section above the Columns section. This opens the content type settings page, which also has the columns list and a Column Order link beneath it.

Clicking on the Column Order link opens a page that allows you to reorder the columns (see Figure 7.50).

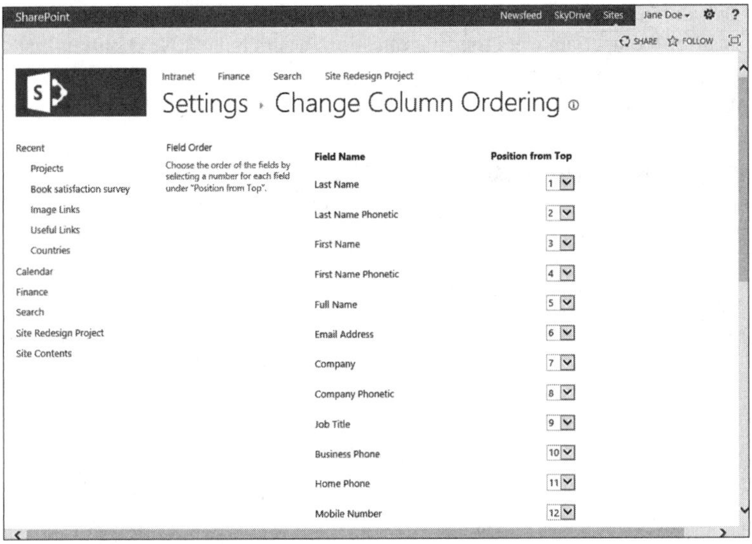

FIGURE 7.50 Reordering the columns in a list or library.

In the Column Order page you can specify the order for each column by using the drop-down boxes to the right of the column names. If you change the order for one column—for example, change mobile phone to be the third column—the column automatically moves to the place you have selected, pushing the other columns down as necessary.

When you are finished ordering the columns to your liking, you click OK at the bottom of the page.

Branching in Surveys

Scenario/Problem: You want to make answering a survey easier for users by displaying the questions in the survey in different pages. Additionally, a survey has a lot of questions, and depending on the answer to some of them you might or might not want answers to other questions.

Solution: As mentioned earlier, in the section "Create a New Survey," surveys have a special capability to redirect users to different questions, based on the answers to previous questions. This is known as *branching*.

For example, if you create a survey with three questions, "Did you read the book?," "Do you plan to read the book?," and "Was the book good?," you can assign a branching on the first question so that a user who answers Yes is redirected to the third question. A user who answers No is redirected to the second question. The second and third questions are not shown when the survey interface is first shown to the users. They are shown only after the user answers the first question. Users have a Next button that allows them to continue to the next question in the branch. Figure 7.51 shows how branching looks to the user.

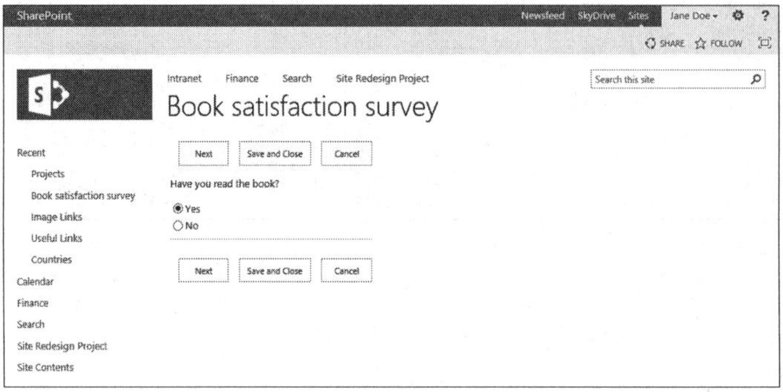

FIGURE 7.51   Branching in a survey. The user sees only the first question, with a Next button to go to the next question, depending on the answer.

NOTE   The branching option is not available for the last question in the survey, because no questions are after it.

To define the branching in a survey, you first create all the questions and then edit the columns you want to be conditional so that they have the branching. You don't need to add page separators unless you want to; the survey automatically splits the questions into pages, depending on the branching. Figure 7.52 shows how to define the branching on the first question to redirect the users based on the answer.

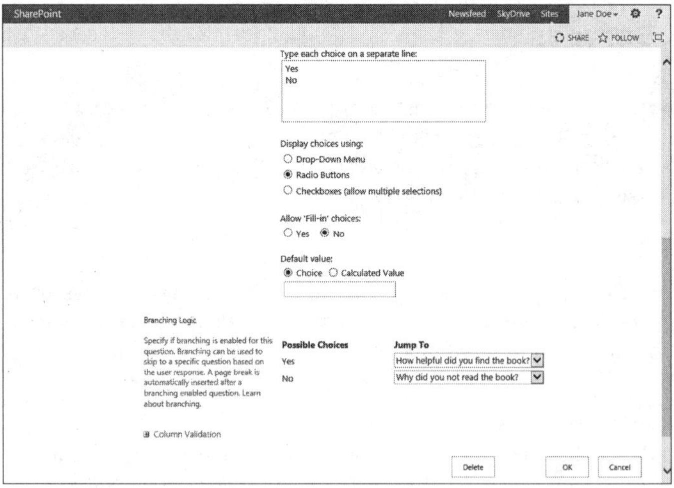

FIGURE 7.52   Defining branching in a survey.

Rename a List or Document Library or Change Its Description

Scenario/Problem: You want to rename a list or document library, or you want to change the description shown for that list or library. For example, say that a library was created with the name Documents, and you want to modify it to a name that tells the user more about the types of documents that should be uploaded to that library—Management Presentations, for example.

Solution: To change an existing list's or library's title or description, you open the list's or library's settings page by switching to the List ribbon or Library ribbon and clicking the List Settings or Library Settings button. At the top of the page that appears, under the General Settings section, you click Title, Description, and Navigation link.

On the page that opens, shown in Figure 7.53, you can set a new title for the list or library, change the description, and choose whether a link to the list or library should appear in the Quick Launch navigation bar.

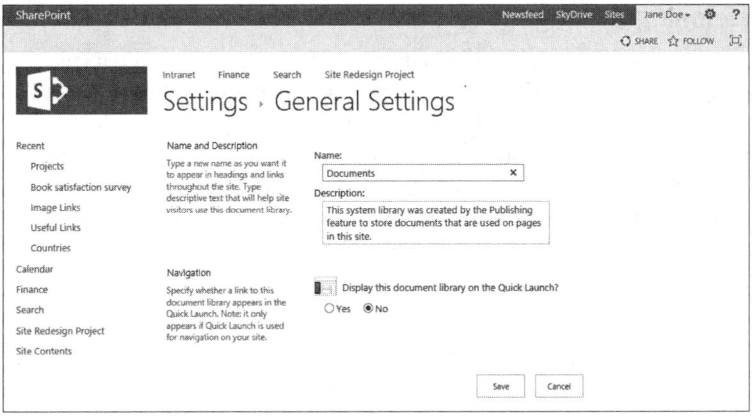

FIGURE 7.53   Changing the list or library name, description, and navigation options.

NOTE   Changing the name of a list or library does not change the link to that list or library. The link stays the same, but the title that is displayed changes.

Change the Versioning Settings for a List or Document Library

Scenario/Problem: You want to change how a list or library deals with storing versions for documents and list items. For example, say that a document library was created with versioning turned off, and you want to turn it on. Or say that a library was created and configured to have versioning but not to support automatic check-out of a document when a user opens a document for editing, and you want to change that.

Solution: To change the versioning settings for a list or library, you open the list's or library's settings page by switching to the List ribbon or Library ribbon and clicking the List Settings or Library Settings button. At the top of the page that appears, under the General Settings section, you click the Versioning Settings link.

In the versioning settings page, you can define how the list or library creates versions for list items or files. This page is different for lists than for libraries because documents and list items behave differently.

Set the Versioning Settings for a List

The first setting for versioning in a list is whether content approval is required (see Figure 7.54). This option is not strictly about managing versions of the list item but rather about the publishing process for a modification to a list item. If you select this option, every time a modification is made to a list item (or when one is created), the list item is not displayed to all users automatically. Instead, the list item gets an approval status of Pending, and no one can see it except its author and people who have permissions to view drafts in the list—until a person with the permissions to approve items in the list approves that item, thereby changing its status from Pending to Approved.

The next section is Item Version History. Here, you can define whether versions should be tracked for the list and how many versions should be kept. This second option is optional, and you can leave it unlimited if you want to. Finally, if you set the Require Approval option, you can also limit the number of approved versions to keep.

The last option on this page, Draft Item Security, is also valid only if you chose to require approval. It lets you define who can see draft items that have not been approved yet. The options are any user who can read items in the list, only users who can edit items in the list (who might need to be able to see the drafts to edit them), or only the people who can approve items in the list (which is the minimum required because they must be able to view the drafts to approve them).

FIGURE 7.54   The Versioning Settings page for a list.

Set the Versioning Settings for a Document Library

The versioning options for a document library are almost identical to those of a list. The only two differences are explained here.

As shown in Figure 7.55, the first option that is different is that, instead of just selecting that the library should store versions, you can select how versions will be stored: either as major versions (which is how lists behave) or so that any change will result in a new version (changing the version number from 1 to 2 to 3, and so on).

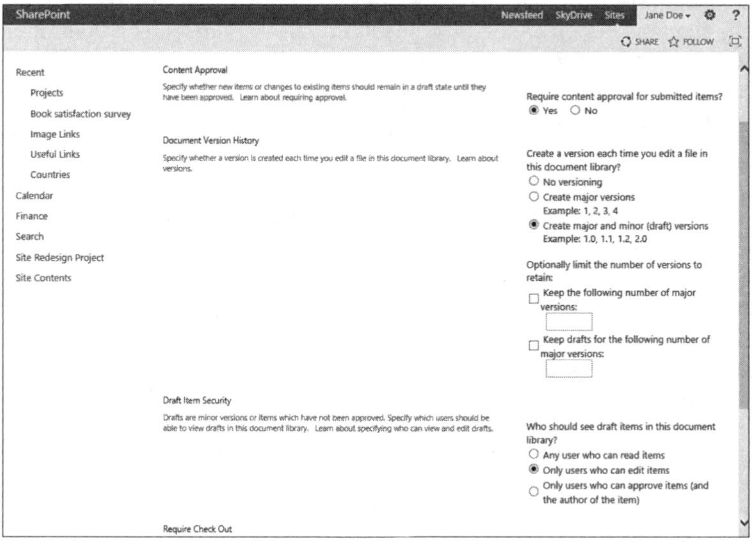

FIGURE 7.55   The Versioning Settings page for a document library.

This setting does not enable you to specify that a certain change is not major enough to warrant an increase of the version number for the document. For example, if you change a document by spell checking it and correcting the spelling or updating the date it was last printed, this change might not be important enough. This is why you might want to choose the option for major and minor versions, which allows users to decide whether the change is major, thereby increasing the version number by 1, or minor, thereby increasing the number after the decimal point for the number.

The second option that you can configure for document libraries only is the Require Check Out option. Selecting this option can help reduce conflicts when several users want to work on the same file. This option forces users to check out a file before editing it by automatically checking out the file for them and preventing others from editing it. This way, users can't forget to check out a file but start to work on it without realizing that another user is also working on the same file.

> **NOTE** It's important to remember that when the Require Checkout option is selected, uploading multiple documents adds those documents as checked out, and they are not visible to other users until you check them in.
>
> There is no automatic check-in of a file because SharePoint cannot know when the editing is done and the user is ready to check in the changes. Users therefore must be aware of this fact and get used to checking in files and not keeping them checked out forever.

Change the Document Template for the New Button in a Document Library

> **Scenario/Problem:** You want to change what kind of document is created when the user clicks the New button in a document library. For example, say that you want to make the New button create a Microsoft PowerPoint presentation out of a specific template in the document library that is specific for presentations. Or say that you want a Microsoft Excel template for expense reports to open in the Expense Reports document library.

Solution: If you want to change the template or application used when a user clicks the New button in a document library, you can specify it in the document library settings. You do so by switching to the Library ribbon and clicking the Library Settings button.

> **NOTE** You might want to show several choices of templates to users as a menu under the New button. That is possible if you use content types. See "Add a Content Type to a List or Document Library," later in this chapter, as well as "Create a Content Type" in Chapter 13, "Customizing a SharePoint Site," for more information.

At the top of the page that appears, under the General Settings section, you click the Advanced Settings link.

On the page that appears, you can either edit the template that is used by clicking the Edit Template link on the right side or link to a Microsoft Office document that you have uploaded to SharePoint (see Figure 7.56). You need to ensure that the link to the document that you entered works by clicking the Edit Template link after adding the link.

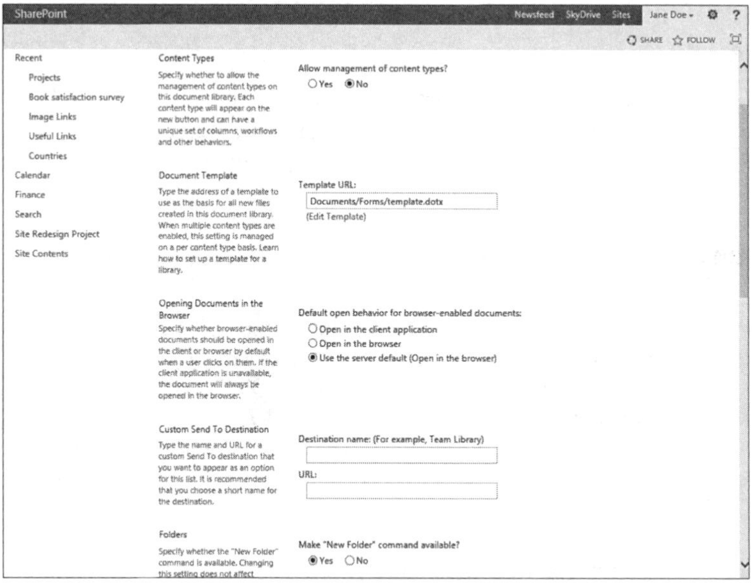

FIGURE 7.56   The Advanced Settings page for a document library, with options to allow content types, set the template URL, and enable or disable the New Folder command.

NOTE The Template URL box is disabled if multiple content types are enabled for the document library. If you want to change the template in that scenario, you have to change it for each content type separately by clicking the content type's link in the library settings page and then clicking the Advanced Settings link in that page (see Figure 7.60, later in this chapter).

You should upload to the Forms folder that exists in any document library. That folder is hidden, and users don't see it in list views, which means they don't see your template as a file to be modified and managed. However, you can decide to put the template in another location, not in the current document library. Just remember that this location must be readable by all users and not just you. Therefore, putting the document in another location can be problematic from a security point of view because you must be sure that all the users who are allowed to create documents in the document library are also allowed to read from the location of the template.

NOTE To get to the Forms folder, you type the link to the document library, followed by /forms/. For example, if the link to your document library is **http://sharepoint-local/Sample/SharedDocuments/**, you type the link **http://sharepointlocal/Sample/SharedDocuments/Forms**. This link opens the Forms folder (which should look empty). You can upload to this folder a document to be used as a template.

The file type you use as a template determines what application is used when the user clicks the New button. For example, if you choose a Microsoft Excel document as the template, the Microsoft Excel application opens when the user clicks the New button.

> **NOTE** Not all file types can be used as templates. You can use only file types from applications that are compatible with SharePoint, such as Microsoft Office applications.

If you want to add several options for templates under the New button, you must do so by adding multiple content types to the document library. See the next section for details.

Add a Content Type to a List or Document Library

> **Scenario/Problem:** You want to add a content type that is defined in the site to a list or library. As explained in Chapter 1, using content types is a useful way to specify groups of properties for files or list items. Content types can also specify a document template for creation of a new document of that content type. For information about creating new content types, see "Create a Content Type" in Chapter 13.

Solution: To add a content type to a list or library, you first enable management of content types in that list or library. To do so, you go to the list or document library settings page by switching to the List ribbon or Library ribbon and clicking the List Settings or Library Settings button.

At the top of the page, in the General Settings section, you click the Advanced Settings link. On the Advanced Settings page, shown in Figure 7.56, you select Yes under Allow Management of Content Types? and click OK at the bottom of the page.

You then return to the list or library settings page, which now has a section for content types (see Figure 7.57).

To add a content type, you click the Add from Existing Site Content Types link in the Content Types section. The content type selection page appears, enabling you to select one or more content types to add to the list (see Figure 7.58).

On this page, the available content types appear in the box on the left. You select the one you want and click the Add button to move it to the box on the right (which shows the types you selected). If you want to remove a content type you added by mistake, you select it from the box on the right and click the Remove button.

When you are finished selecting all the content types you want for the list or document library, you click OK. The resulting list or library settings page shows the list of content types available in the list or library.

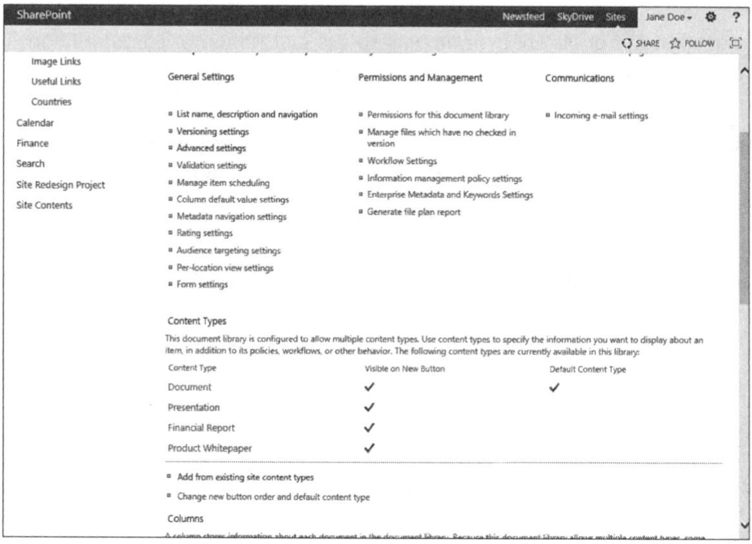

FIGURE 7.57   The Content Types section appears only if content types are enabled for the list or library.

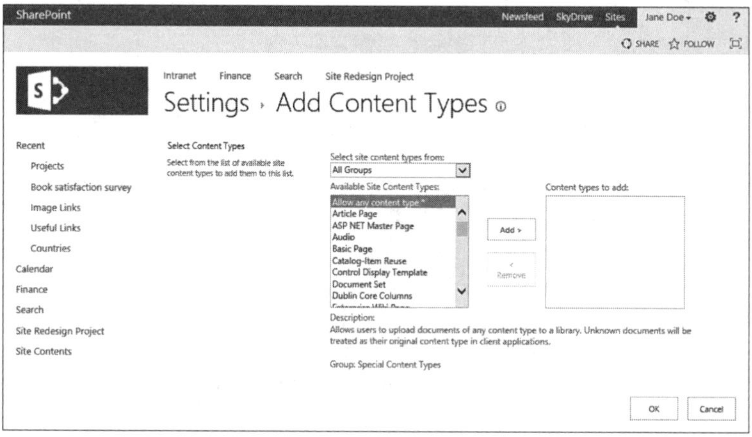

FIGURE 7.58   The Add Content Types page.

Remove a Content Type from a List or Document Library

Scenario/Problem: You want to remove a content type from the list or library so that it is not available for the users in that place.

Solution: To remove a content type from a list or document library, you go to the settings page for that list or library by switching to the List ribbon or Library ribbon and clicking the List Settings or Library Settings button.

The settings page shows the list of content types available in the list or library (if content types are enabled), as you can see in Figure 7.59. To remove one, you click the link to that content type.

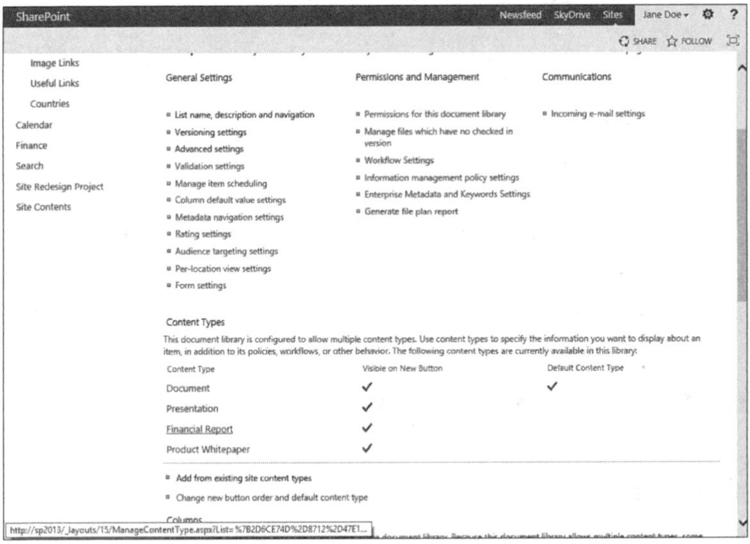

FIGURE 7.59   To remove the Financial Report content type, you click the Financial Report link in the Content Types section.

The configuration page that opens shows the content type for that specific list or library (see Figure 7.60). Changes that you make in this page affect only the list or document library but not other lists and libraries that use the same content type. You can tell this by the fact that the content type has a parent with exactly the same name—and this is possible only when viewing the settings of a content type in a list or library, and not the settings for the content type that is defined in the site. As long as you see this, changing the content type affects only the list or library from which you started.

To remove the content type from the list or library, you click the Delete This Content Type link. Doing so opens a prompt that asks you to confirm the deletion of the content type. You click OK to remove the content type.

> **NOTE**   The Delete This Content Type link does not actually delete the content type; it just removes the content type from the list or library. An easy way to be sure that you are not deleting the content type from the site is to look in the breadcrumbs at the top of the page. If the breadcrumbs show that you are under the settings for the list or library, you are not deleting the content type but instead just removing it. In any case, SharePoint does not let you delete a content type from a site if it is still in use by a list or library, so you can feel safe to click this link.

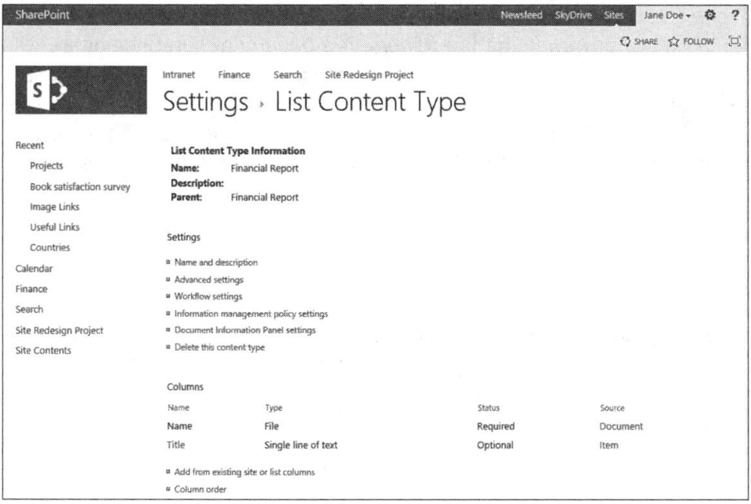

FIGURE 7.60   The Content Type Settings page.

Enable or Disable Folders in a List or Document Library

Scenario/Problem: You want to enable or display folders in a list or library. For example, say that you want to prevent users from creating subfolders in a document library, or you want users to create list items in a folder structure inside a list.

Solution: To enable or disable folders in lists and libraries, you go to the list or library settings page by switching to the List ribbon or Library ribbon and clicking the List Settings or Library Settings button. On the settings page, you click the Advanced Settings link to get to the Advanced Settings page of the list or library (refer to Figure 7.56). On that page, you choose Yes or No for the Make New Folder Command Available option, which is located in the Folders section of the page.

Configure Metadata Navigation in a List or Document Library

Scenario/Problem: You want to make it easy for users to find documents or list items by specific columns, in a better interface than the filtering option available in list views.

Solution: Metadata navigation option is available on some sites (if it is not available in your site, ask the site administrator to activate the "Metadata Navigation and Filtering" site feature). This includes searching for documents that were modi-fied in a range of dates, or navigating the folders in a document library using a tree-like mechanism. Finally, for filtering managed metadata columns this interface is very helpful—showing you the terms from the metadata term set in a tree—allow-ing the user to select a term, thereby filtering the items shown in the list to show only items with that term, or the terms that are under it in the hierarchy as shown in Figure 7.61.

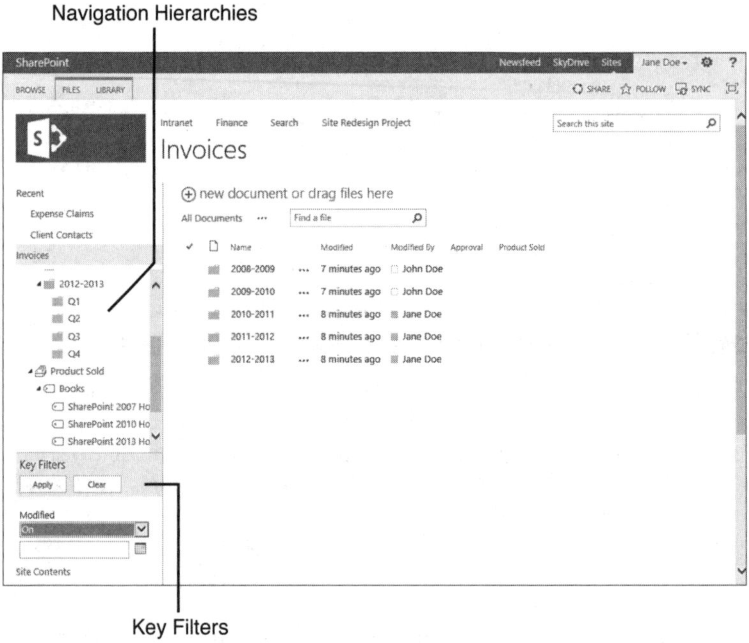

FIGURE 7.61   A library showing managed metadata navigation for folders, products, and modified date.

To configure metadata navigation for a list or a library, open the library or list's settings page by switching to the Library ribbon and clicking the Library Settings button. In the settings page, click on the Metadata Navigation Settings link, as shown in Figure 7.62.

The page that opens allows you to set three different options, as shown in Figure 7.63, and explained in the following sections.

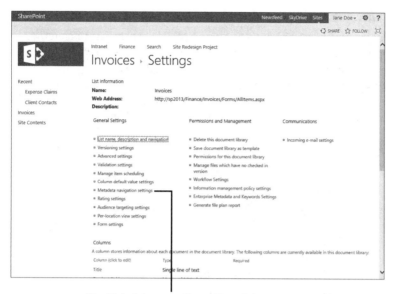

The Metadata navigation settings link

FIGURE 7.62   The Metadata Navigation Settings link in the list settings.

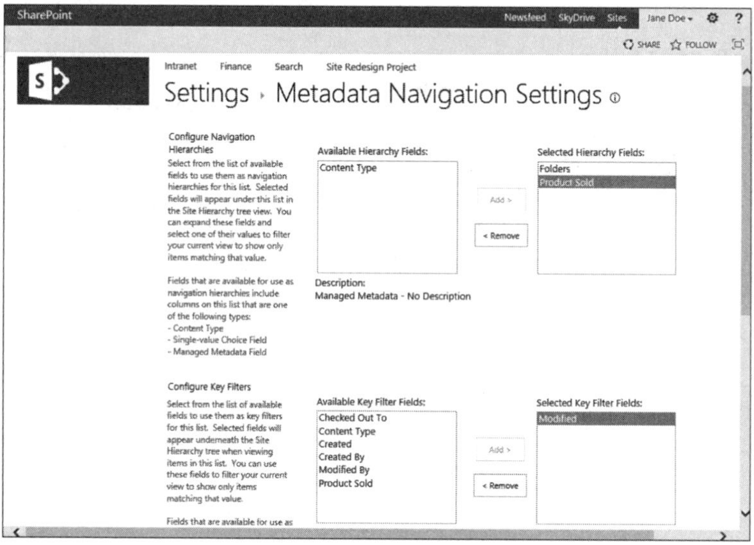

FIGURE 7.63   The Metadata Navigation Settings page.

Configure Navigation Hierarchies

In this section you can choose one or more hierarchy fields. As shown in Figure 7.63, only some types of columns are hierarchical. The columns you choose will be added as a tree structure on the side of the library view, allowing the users to navigate the library or list by clicking on one of the values.

NOTE   If you want to select just the Folders option, you also have to specify a key filter. Selecting just Folders in the navigation hierarchies will not cause the navigation hierarchy to show.

Configure Key Filters

In this section you can choose the columns you want to display in the Key Filters section of the side bar (refer to Figure 7.61). You can select one or more columns and add it to the list of selected key filters.

Configure Automatic Column Indexing for This List

This section allows you to override the default behavior of the managed metadata navigation by disabling it, modifying the column indices automatically. It is recommended you don't change this unless you have a specific need to do so.

CHAPTER 8

Creating List Views

As explained in Chapter 3, "Solutions Regarding Files, Documents, List Items, and Forms," list views are important and help users find the content they are looking for more easily. If you are in charge of a document library or list and want to make it more accessible and more usable to users, you should consider creating list views for the users. Even if managing a particular list is not your responsibility, you will want to learn how to create a personal view that is visible only to you, where you can set the view to display information that is relevant to you specifically and that you often need to find. This view will save you a lot of time.

This chapter covers how to create custom list views, either personal or public ones, and what settings can be set on them.

Create a Personal or Public View for a List or Library

Scenario/Problem: In some lists, you have permissions to create new views: either personal views (that only you are able to see) or public ones (that everyone is able to view). You now want to create a view that will help you or other users find information in the list or library more easily.

Solution: To create new views, either personal or public, go to either the List ribbon or Library ribbon and click the Create View button in the Manage Views section of the ribbon. You also can click on the three dots next to the view names above the list view. This opens a menu in which you choose the Create View options, as shown in Figure 8.1.

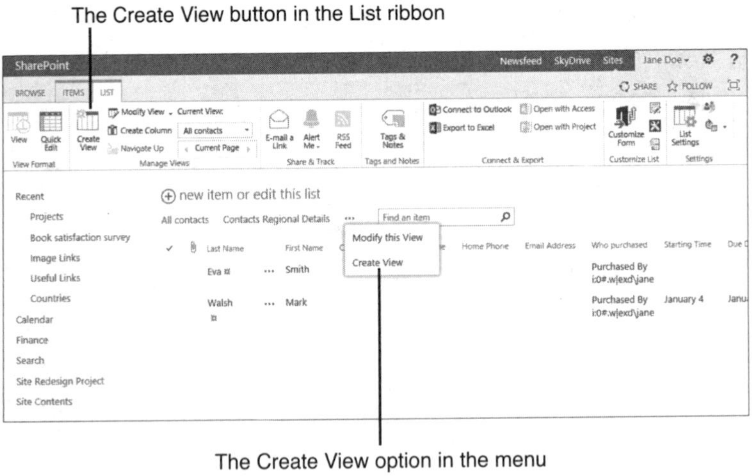

The Create View button in the List ribbon

The Create View option in the menu

FIGURE 8.1   Clicking the Create View option.

On the page that opens, choose from a list of available view types (see Figure 8.2). Different lists can have different types of views. For example, the events list has a special view type for recurring events; this kind of view shows instances of each recurring event as if it were a single event and not relevant to other types of lists.

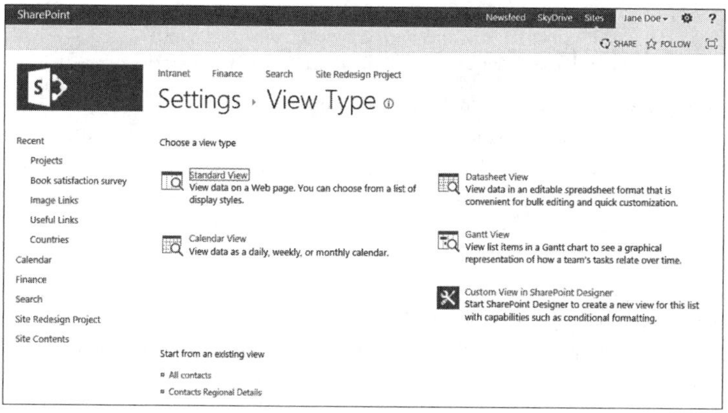

FIGURE 8.2   The View Type selection page.

Create a Standard View

If you want a standard list view, select the Standard View link. The Create View page that appears enables you to name your view if it is going to be the default view for the list (see Figure 8.3). You can also select whether it is going to be a public or personal view and choose the settings for the view.

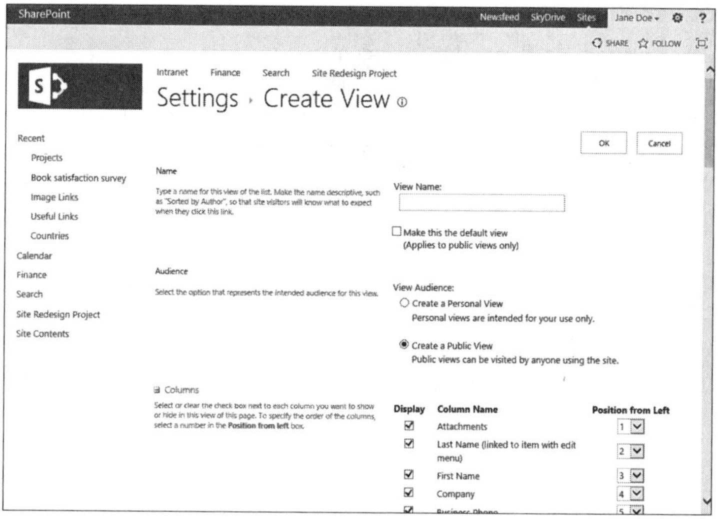

FIGURE 8.3   The Create View page for a standard view.

Select Whether a View Is a Default View

Making a view a default view causes SharePoint to display that view when users navigate to the list or document library. Because that setting affects all users, and not just you, this option is valid only for public views because personal views are visible only to you and not to other users.

Select Whether a View Is a Personal View or Public View

The option to choose between a public view and a personal view is a very important one. If you have the necessary permissions to create public views, consider carefully before creating a view as a public one. After all, creating too many views can confuse the other users of that list or library. If you are creating a view for your own use, keeping the view private is best.

> **TIP**   Naming a view is very important. You will want to know how the view is different when selecting the view from the view picker, and the only thing you see there is the view name. However, you should avoid long names because they are hard to read in the view picker.

If you do not have permissions to create public views, the option to create one is grayed out, and you are able to choose only to create a personal view.

After you fill in the name for the view and select whether it is a personal or public one (and if it is public, whether it should be the default), save the view by clicking OK. The view is created, and you can select it from the view picker. However, you should probably change the view first. The rest of the tasks in this chapter explain what you can change in a view.

Create a Calendar View

Calendar views show information from a list or document library as if this information were events on a calendar. There must be one date column to define as the start date column and one column to define as the end date—the time interval. Having one column to be both the start and end dates is enough. For example, in a document library, you can create a calendar view that shows the documents based on the day they were created (see Figure 8.4).

To create a calendar view, select the Calendar View type. The first two options in the view setting screen are similar to those of the standard view: naming the view and selecting whether it is going to be a default view and whether it is a personal or public view (refer to Figure 8.3). Other options are available for Calendar views to specify what column will be used as the start date, end date, and titles, as shown in Figure 8.5.

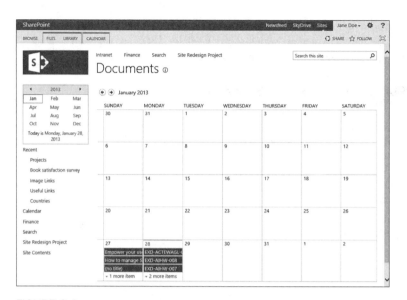

FIGURE 8.4   A document library with a calendar view based on the Created Date.

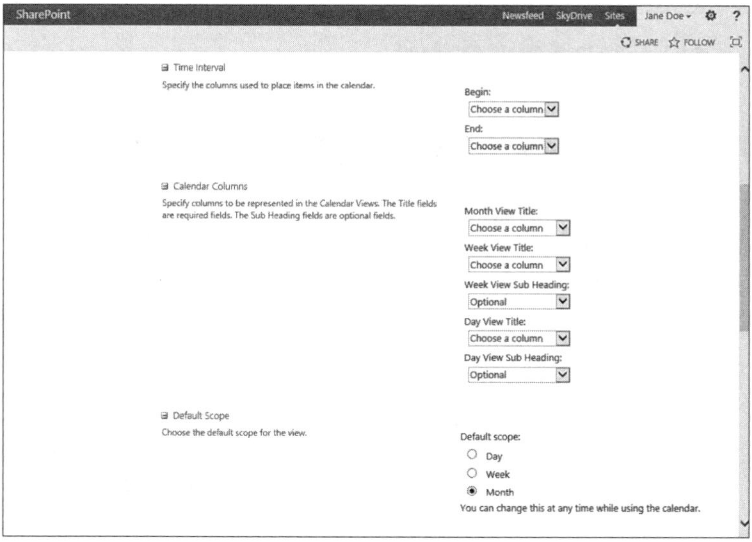

FIGURE 8.5   Configuring a calendar view based on the Created Date for a document library.

As another example, for a tasks list, you can choose the start date of the task as the start column and the due date as the end column to create a view that shows the tasks in a calendar-style view.

Calendar views have three subviews: the daily view, which shows each day separately (see Figure 8.6); the weekly view, which shows week by week (see Figure 8.7); and the monthly view, which shows the entire month (refer to Figure 8.4).

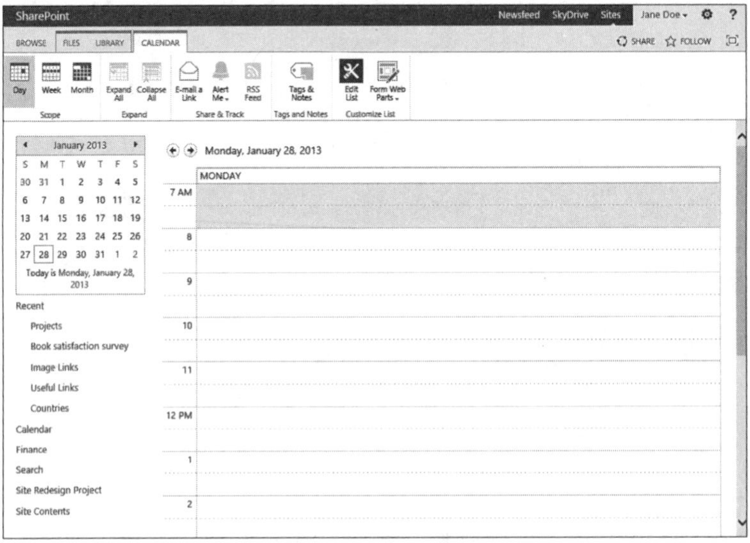

FIGURE 8.6   The daily view for a document library.

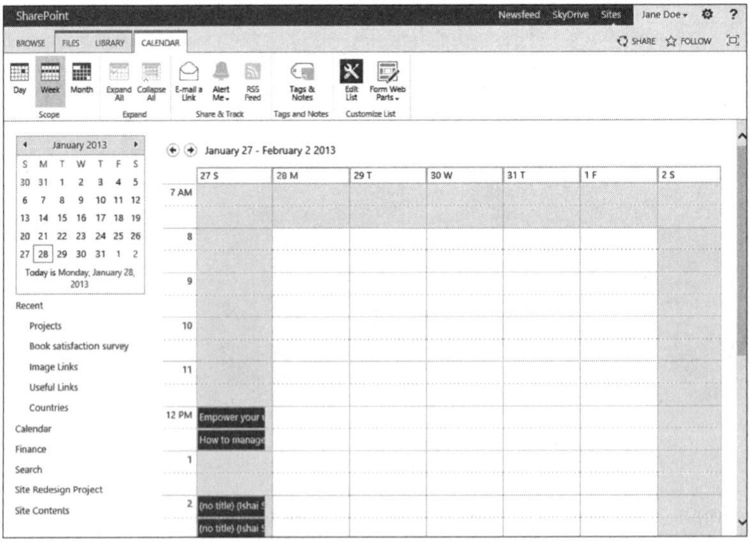

FIGURE 8.7   The weekly view for a document library.

These subviews are part of the view itself and are all configured as part of creating the calendar view. For more information about configuring the subviews separately, see "Specify Columns for a Calendar View," later in this chapter.

Create a Gantt View

A Gantt view displays items based on date columns—much like the calendar view. However, it shows the items in a Gantt chart, where each item is displayed as if it were a task in a project plan. A tabular version of the view appears to the left of the chart, showing more details on the list items (see Figure 8.8).

Creating a Gantt view is similar to creating a standard view. Select the Gantt view type in the view type selection page, and you get the same options as all views to name the view and select whether it should be the default view and whether it should be personal or public.

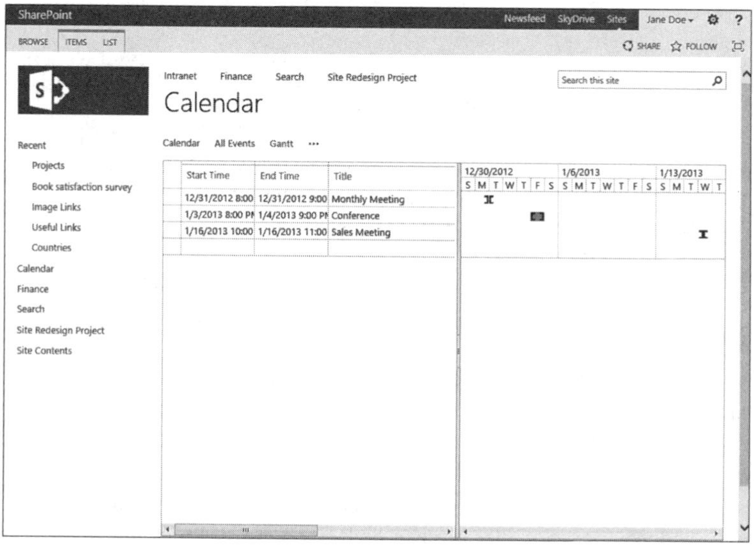

FIGURE 8.8   The Gantt view for an events list.

After configuring those options, scroll down to the Gantt Columns section of the page (see Figure 8.9). In this section, you configure what columns will be used as the title column, starting date column, and due date column. Optionally, you can also specify a percentage column to indicate in the Gantt chart how the item has progressed and the predecessors column. (A predecessors column is a column that specifies for each item which should be completed before it can start. This is most common with tasks that have to be done sequentially.)

The column you select in the Title box is displayed in the Gantt chart as the title of the item. In most cases, this is the title column, but you can also display a different column as the title.

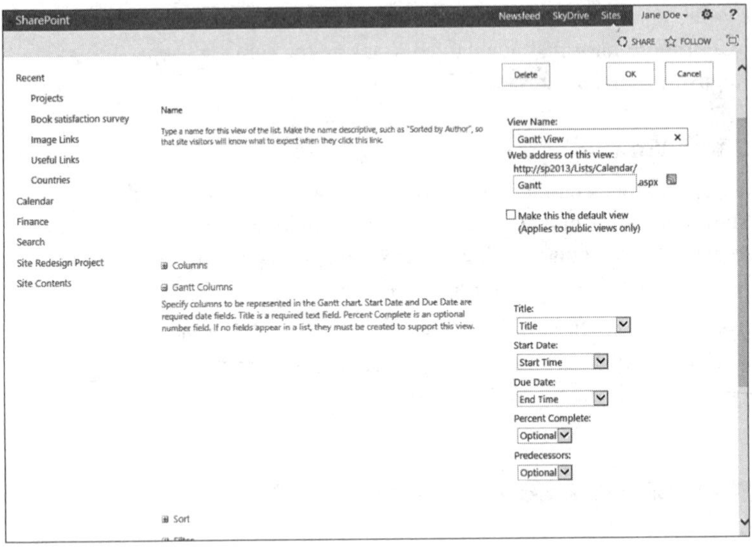

FIGURE 8.9   Creating a Gantt view.

NOTE The Percent Complete option shows only number columns. If you want such a column and the list doesn't have one, you must create one for the list. For more information, see Chapter 7, "Creating Lists and Document Libraries," and Chapter 13, "Customizing a SharePoint Site."

Create a Quick Edit View

Creating a view that opens automatically in Quick Edit mode is called a datasheet view. Creating such a view is exactly like creating a standard view. You select the datasheet view type in the view type selection page, and you get the same options to name the view and select whether it should be the default view and whether it should be personal or public. However, a datasheet view has fewer advanced options to choose from than standard views. For example, you can't specify a grouping for the view (see "Specify How Items in a View Are Grouped," later in this chapter) or the display style for the items (see "Switch to the Quick Edit View," later in this chapter). This is because the datasheet view is displaying the items in a sheet—rows and columns. Refer to "The Quick Edit View" in Chapter 3 for more information about the datasheet view.

Specify Columns for a View to Display

Scenario/Problem: When creating or editing a view in a list or library, you want to specify different columns to be displayed to the users in the view. For example, in a contacts list, you want to display the first and last name columns in the view but not the company.

Solution: The following sections explain how you can select which columns are displayed to the users in different types of views.

Specify Columns for a Standard View or a Datasheet View

After filling in the name for a view and selecting whether it is a personal or public one (and if it is public, whether it should be the default), scroll down to see the list of columns (refer to Figure 8.3). Here, you can choose which columns are displayed in the view and in what order they should appear. To select a column, select the check box next to the column name. To hide a column, remove the check from the check box.

TIP In document libraries, the Title column is separate from the Name column. The Name column holds the actual filename, whereas the title can be blank. When building views for document libraries, remember that the name of the document is more likely what the users are looking for and that, unlike in lists, it is the Name column that can be displayed as the link to the file and not the title column.

Specify Columns for a Calendar View

In calendar views, you can't choose multiple columns to display and order them in the same way that you do for standard views. The reason is that in a calendar, the users see only one column as the heading for the item.

You can set for each subview separately what column will be displayed as the link to the item or file. Normally, you would use the Title column (for lists) or Name column (for document libraries), but you can choose any column you want. That column will be displayed as the heading for the item or document in the view.

Both the daily and weekly subviews support a subheading column, which is displayed beneath the heading. You can either choose a column to be used as a subheading or leave it not configured if you do not want a subheading.

Specify Columns for a Gantt View

In Gantt views, as explained earlier in this chapter, you must choose a column that will be used as the title in the Gantt chart under the Gantt Columns section. However, unlike a calendar view, a Gantt view also shows a tabular view of the items below the chart, which means you can also modify which columns are displayed in that part of the view. To do so, use the Columns section of the page to select which columns will be displayed.

Specify the Order of the Columns in a View

Scenario/Problem: When creating or editing a view in a list or library, you want to specify a different order for the columns that are displayed to the user in the view. For example, in a contacts list, you want the first name to be displayed before the last name or vice versa.

Solution: In standard, datasheet, and Gantt views, you can change the order of the columns you chose to display. For example, you might want to show the title of the item first, followed by the date it was created, and then the date it was modified; or you might want the title to be followed by the modification date and then the creation date.

NOTE In calendar view you don't have the option to reorder columns because only one column appears (two in daily and weekly views).

To rearrange the order of the columns in the view, use the Position from Left drop-down boxes. These drop-down boxes contain numbers that you can choose for the column order. If you want a column to be displayed first, change the number in the drop-down box next to that column to 1. The next column should be 2, and so on. If you change a column that had a higher number to a lower number (say, from 4 to 1), the other columns automatically arrange themselves. For example, changing the Position from Left setting for the Title column that had the value 4 to the value 1 automatically changes the three columns that are before it (Recurrence, Attachments, and Workspace) to be 2, 3, and 4, respectively.

NOTE The Title (or Name, in document libraries) column usually appears three times in this view creation page because three different ways exist to show the title for a list item. The simplest one is just Title, which displays the title of the list item or document as regular text. The second option is Title (Linked to Item), which displays the title as a link to the item. The last option is Title (Linked to Item with Edit Menu), which displays the title as a link but also allows a drop-down menu to open when the mouse cursor hovers over the title. This last one is the default in most views.

Specify How Items in a View Are Sorted

Scenario/Problem: You want to specify how a view should sort the items. For example, in a contacts list, you want it to sort on the Last Name column in ascending order so that Adams is before Brahms. Furthermore, if two people have the same last name, you want them sorted by their first names, so that Anne Adams appears before Brenda Adams.

Solution: SharePoint supports sorting based on up to two columns. To select the sort order, scroll down to the Sort section of the view creation page (see Figure 8.10).

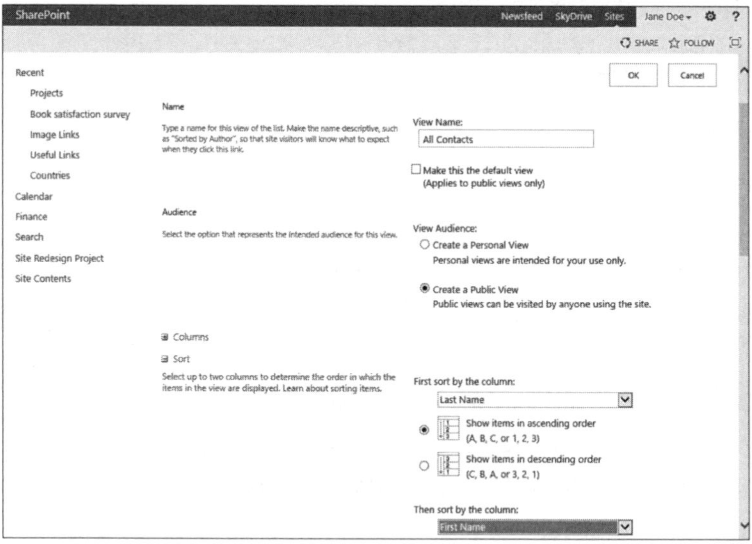

FIGURE 8.10   Changing how items are sorted in a view.

Under First Sort by the Column, choose the column by which the view should sort first and how that sorting should take place (ascending or descending). Then you can optionally select another column to further sort the items, using the second column selection drop-down menu. This determines how items with the same value in the first column you selected will be sorted.

For example, you might want to sort an event list by Start Date column first and Title column second; that way, if two items have the same start date, the one scheduled to start first will appear first.

A different example would be to sort a document library using the Title column (ascending) first and then the Created column (descending) second. That way, if two files have the same title (not name), the one created later would appear before the older one.

> **NOTE**   Some view types do not allow you to pick a sort order. For example, the Calendar view type does not have a sort order because calendars always display the events in them sorted by the start date of the event.

The last option under the Sort section is Sort Only by Specified Criteria. By default, SharePoint views show folders above any files or items, regardless of the name of the folder. If you want the sorting to also affect the position of the folders in the view, select this option, and folders are treated as if they were items when they are sorted. Figure 8.11 shows how a document library with folders is displayed when the view is configured to sort only by specified criteria—sorting on the filename.

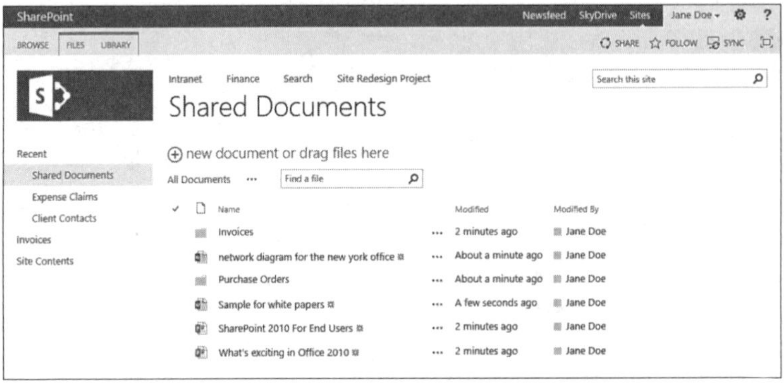

FIGURE 8.11   A view configured to sort only by specified criteria. Folders are sorted as if they were documents and appear in sequence with the documents.

Specify How Items in a View Are Filtered

Scenario/Problem: You want to limit the view so that it shows only items with certain values in certain columns. For example, a common requirement is to display announcements until a certain date, when they then expire.

Solution: Filters determine what items or files are displayed in a view, based on the data that is in the columns. A solution to this problem would be to create a column for the expiration date and add a filter to the view that displays only the announcements whose expiration dates are in the future.

To define filter criteria for a view, scroll in the view creation page to the Filter section (see Figure 8.12). By default, no filter is applied on a new view, so the view displays all items.

To define a filter, use the column picker drop-down menu and select the column based on which you want to filter items. Then choose the operator that you want for the filter and the value you want to use for the comparison. For example, if you want to filter a view to display only items that have a title (excluding the items that do not have a value in the Title column), choose the Title column in the column drop-down menu, select Is Not Equal To, and leave the value box empty (see Figure 8.12). This forms the condition Title Is Not Equal to Nothing.

NOTE   Not all columns can be filtered. The column picker drop-down menu shows only columns that support filtering. For example, columns of type Hyperlink do not support filtering and are not shown in the column picker drop-down.

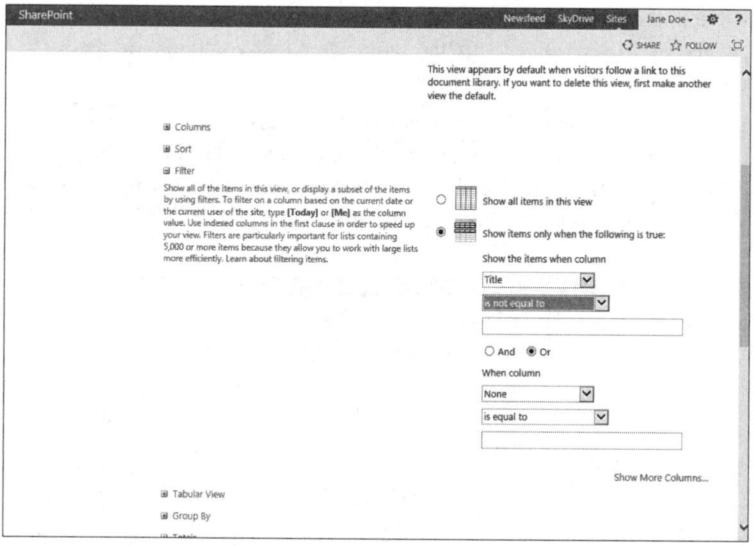

FIGURE 8.12 The Filter section in the view creation page.

Another example for a filter you might want to create on a view would be items that you or another person created. The simplest way to do this is to choose the Created By column in the column drop-down menu, select the Is Equal To operator, and then enter the name of the person you want (either you or anyone else) in the value box (see Figure 8.13).

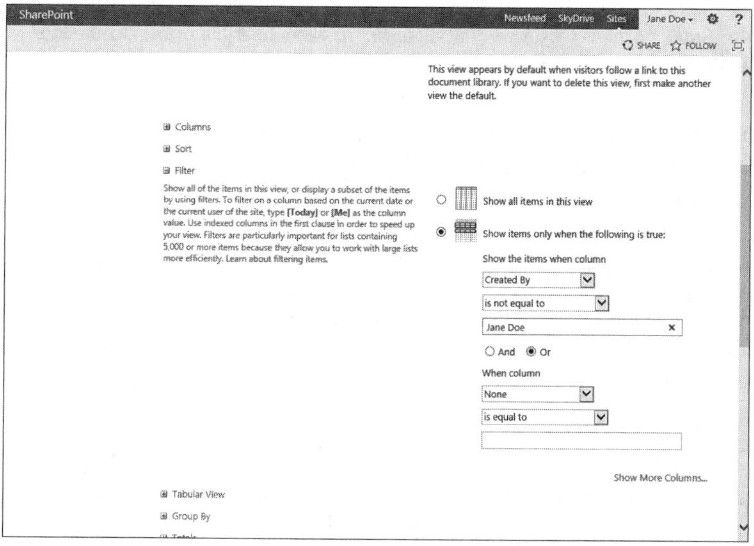

FIGURE 8.13 Setting a filter for the Created By column by typing the name of the person.

When you browse to the new view, the documents (or list items) are displayed only if they were created by a user with exactly the same name that you typed (in this example, Jane Doe).

If you want the filter to be dynamic and change based on the person, you can use a token instead of typing the person's actual name. For example, you can use the [Me] token instead of the value; this is replaced with the name of the user viewing the view and is not limited to a name you chose beforehand (see Figure 8.14).

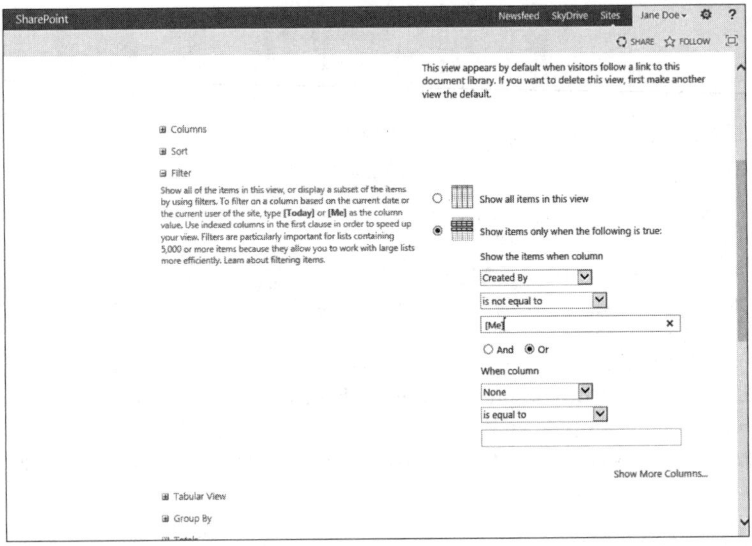

FIGURE 8.14   Setting a filter for a view that displays for every user his or her documents, using the [Me] token.

This capability is useful when you want to set up a public view (for everyone to use) so that anyone visiting the view can see his or her documents or items without requiring you to create a view for each person separately.

> **NOTE**   Another useful token is [Today]. For date fields, it is replaced with the current date. With this token, you could create a view that displays only the documents or items created or modified today, or in a tasks list, you could show all the items that are due today.

You can add, or chain, up to 10 filter conditions in each view. To add an additional filter condition, first decide how the filter will be added—using either the AND or the OR operators. You use the OR operator when you want the items or files to be displayed if they match at least one of the filter conditions.

For example, you can set the first filter column to Created By Is Equal to John Doe and use the OR operator to add the second filter column, Created By Is Equal to Jane Doe (see Figure 8.15). This condition sets the view to display only documents that were created by either John Doe or Jane Doe.

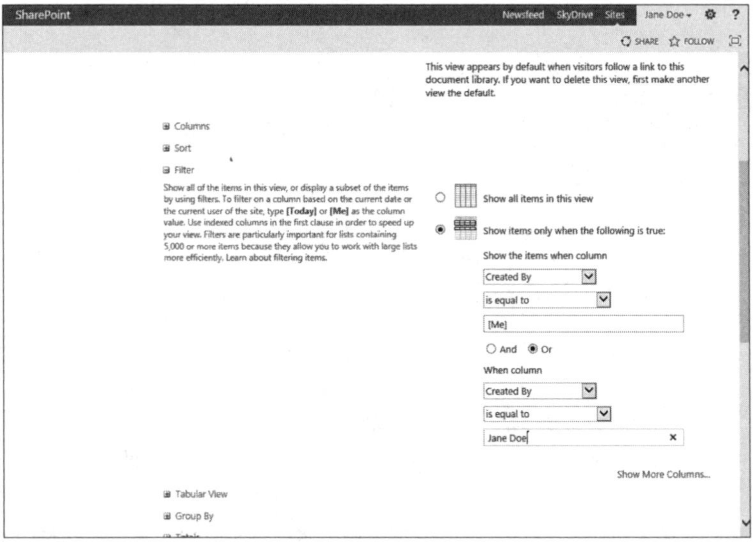

FIGURE 8.15 Setting up two filters, using the OR chaining operator to show documents that were created by either John Doe or Jane Doe.

By using the AND chaining operator, you can create conditions such as Created By Is Equal to John Doe and Created Is Equal to Today. This operator restricts the view to display only documents that match both filters. Another example would be to create the filters Created By Is Not Equal to John Doe and Created By Is Not Equal To Jane Doe (see Figure 8.16). When viewing this view, the users see all files (or items) that have been created by users other than John Doe or Jane Doe.

You can continue and add up to 10 filters, as mentioned earlier. To add additional filters after the first two, use the Show More Columns link below the last filter. Every time you click this link, a new filter criterion section appears.

If you want to remove a condition from the filter, just change the column in the column picker drop-down menu to None. Even though the condition section still shows, the filter does not have that condition when you save the view.

TIP Chaining a lot of conditions can be confusing. The most common mistake people make is choosing AND instead of OR or vice versa. Make sure you select not only the right operator and value but also the right chaining operator.

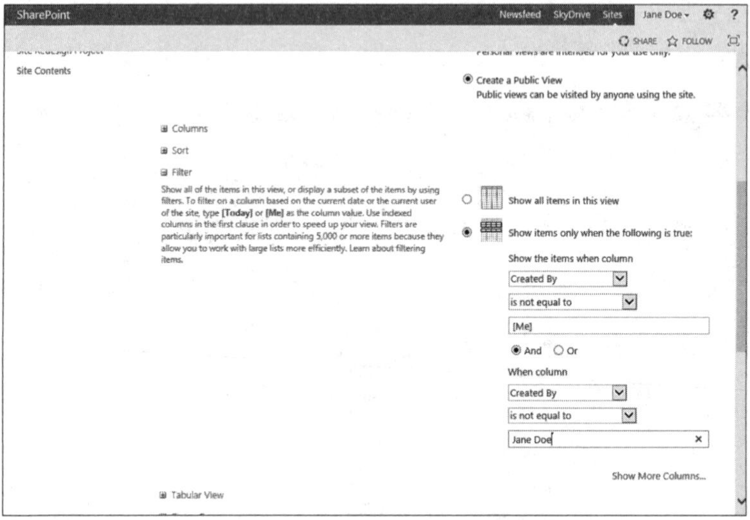

FIGURE 8.16   Adding another filter criterion and joining the criterion with the AND chaining operator.

Specify How Items in a View Are Grouped

Scenario/Problem: You want to group the data shown in a view. Grouping makes getting to the content you want easier.

Solution: SharePoint list views support a feature called grouping that enables you to define a grouping on a column in a list view. For example, grouping contacts by the company to which they belong is a common use of grouping. Grouping documents by the person who created them can be another good idea (see Figure 8.17).

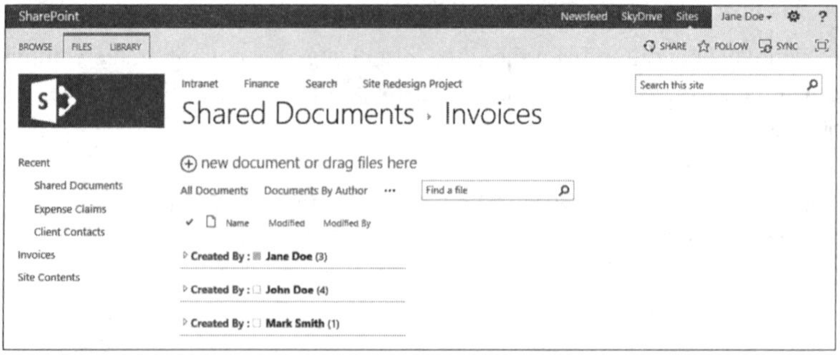

FIGURE 8.17   A view of a document library grouping files by the Created By column.

NOTE Grouping is available only for standard and Gantt view types.

To take advantage of grouping, select the column whose values you want to use as groups. If empty values are in the selected column for some of the items or files in that view, they are placed under a group without a name.

To define the grouping when creating a view, scroll down to the Group By section in the page and expand it by using the plus (+) sign next to the section title (see Figure 8.18). In addition to choosing the column, you can also select the order in which the groups appear: either ascending or descending.

You can specify up to two columns for grouping. The second column's groups appear under each group only if items are in that group. For example, grouping contacts by company and then by country makes finding people easier if you know their company and country (see Figure 8.19).

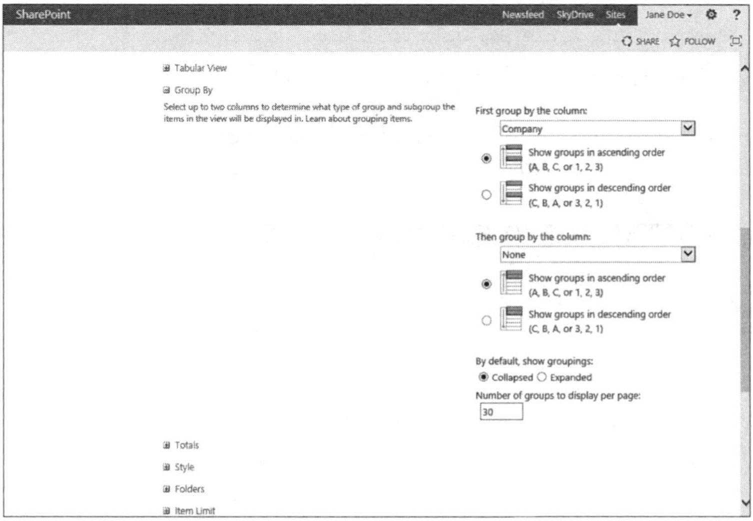

FIGURE 8.18   The Group By section in the view creation page.

TIP When grouping by a column, not displaying that column as part of the view is a good idea because the values appear as a group. For example, if you are grouping by country, you should remove the Country column from the list of columns displayed in the view.

In addition to specifying the columns for grouping and the order of the groups, you can also specify whether the groups show up expanded or collapsed by default. If you choose that columns should be collapsed by default, you can also choose how many groups to display per page. These settings affect both grouping columns.

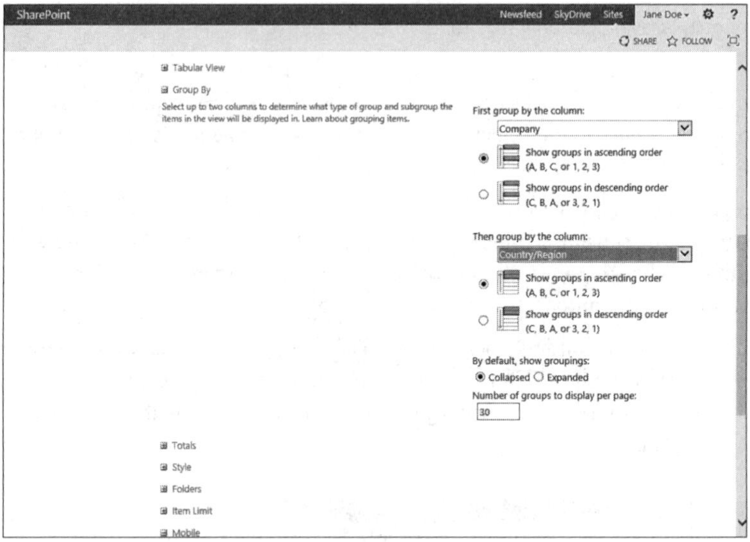

FIGURE 8.19   Grouping by company and then by country/region.

If you choose that the groups should be expanded by default, the view displays the groups with the items shown as soon as users open the view (see Figure 8.20).

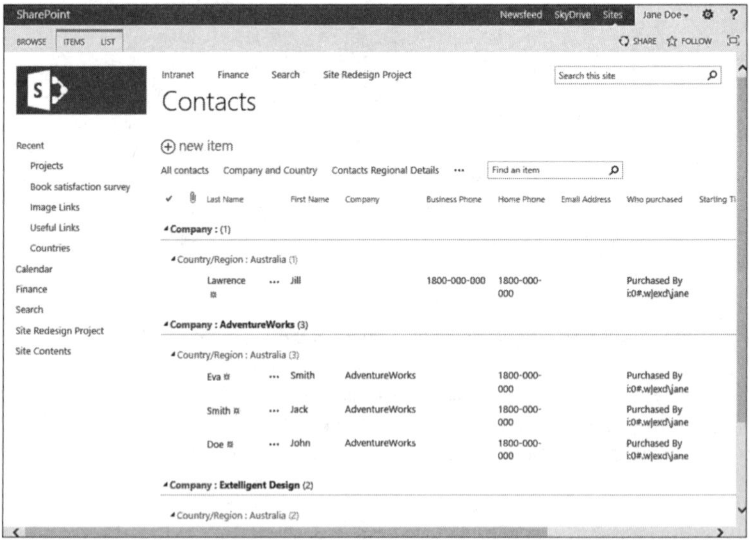

FIGURE 8.20   A view showing contacts grouped by company and then by country, with the groups expanded by default.

If you select that the groups should be collapsed by default, you can also select how many groups will appear per page. If you choose this option, views with a lot of groups still show the users a manageable list (see Figure 8.21).

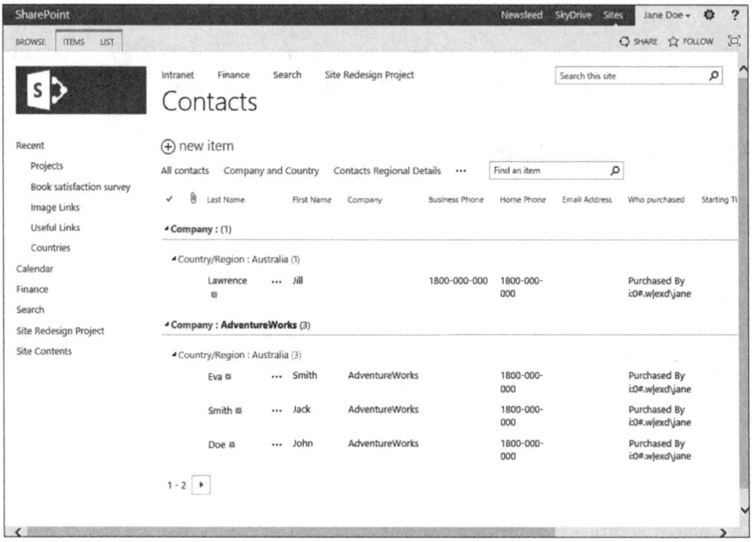

FIGURE 8.21   A view showing the items grouped, with a limit of two groups per page.

The paging mechanism enables users to move back and forth between the pages by using the arrow at the bottom of the view.

Specify Totals for a View

Scenario/Problem: You want to include a mathematical calculation on a column in a view. For example, you want the view to show an average of the numbers in a certain column or the total of another. For example, you have a number column called Number of Leave Days that is used to track how many leave days have been requested by a contact, and you want to create a view that displays the average leave requested by everyone in the list.

Solution: A total is a mathematical calculation that you can add to a view. The result of the calculation shows up at the top of the view, just under the header for the column being calculated. If you want to see some calculations of the values in a column, you can specify this under the Totals section of the view creation page.

Different column types can have different kinds of calculations. For example, a date column can show the count of unique date values in that column, and then average of the date values, and then the largest date or smallest one. A text column can show only the count of unique values because doing mathematical calculations on pieces of text is not possible. A number column can have more functions, such as sum (the sum of all the values in that column), standard deviation, and variance.

For example, if you have a number column called Number of Leave Days that is used to track how many leave days have been requested by a contact, you can create a view that displays the average leave requested by everyone in the list. The average shows up at the top of the view, just under the header for the column (see Figure 8.22).

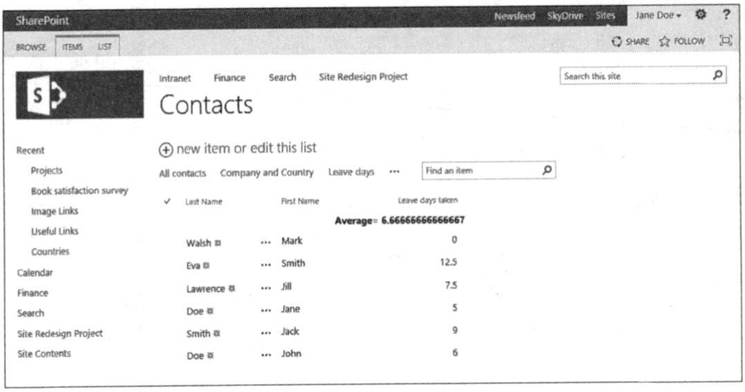

FIGURE 8.22   A view showing the average of a column.

To specify a total for one or more columns, scroll down to the Totals section in the view creation page and expand it by using the plus sign next to the section title. You then see a list of all the columns selected under the Columns section (see Figure 8.23). For each one, you can open the drop-down menu and choose the calculation that will be done for it.

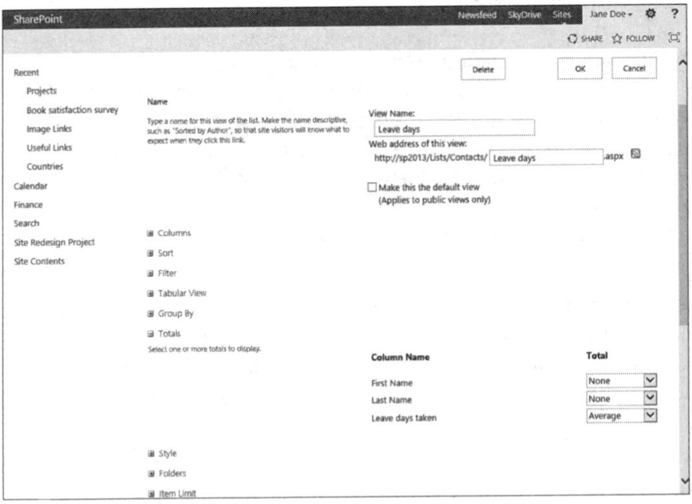

FIGURE 8.23   Creating a view with an average total on a column.

You can specify only one calculation per column. If you want to do different calculations, you must create a separate view for each calculation.

> **TIP**   You can add a total to a column only if it appears in the view. If the column to which you want to add a total does not show up under the Totals section, you need to make sure it is selected under the Columns section.

Specify a Different Item Style for a View

> **Scenario/Problem:** You want to change how a view displays items so that the view does not show them in the regular tabular way in which views normally present items.

Solution: Some view types support displaying items in different styles. This means that instead of showing items in a simple table, you can have the view display the items in a different manner that might make the view easier to read.

A common example is the Shaded style, which shows every other row in the table with a different shade or background color (see Figure 8.24).

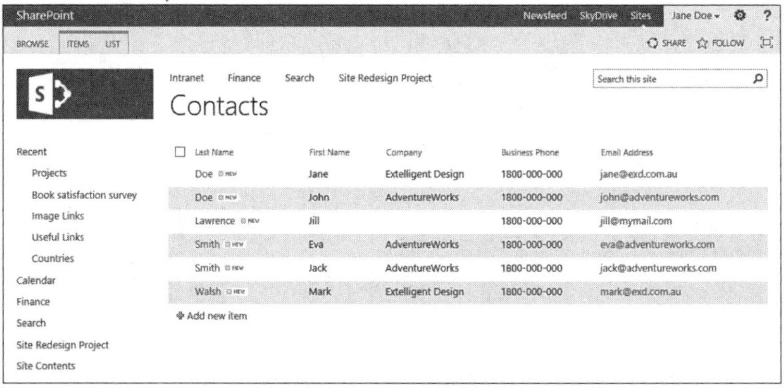

FIGURE 8.24   A view showing contacts with the Shaded style.

Another example is the Boxed style, which displays each item in a box (see Figure 8.25).

To specify the style for the items in a view, scroll to the Style section of the view creation page and expand it by using the plus sign next to the section title. When you see a list of the styles available for that view type (see Figure 8.26), simply select the style that you want.

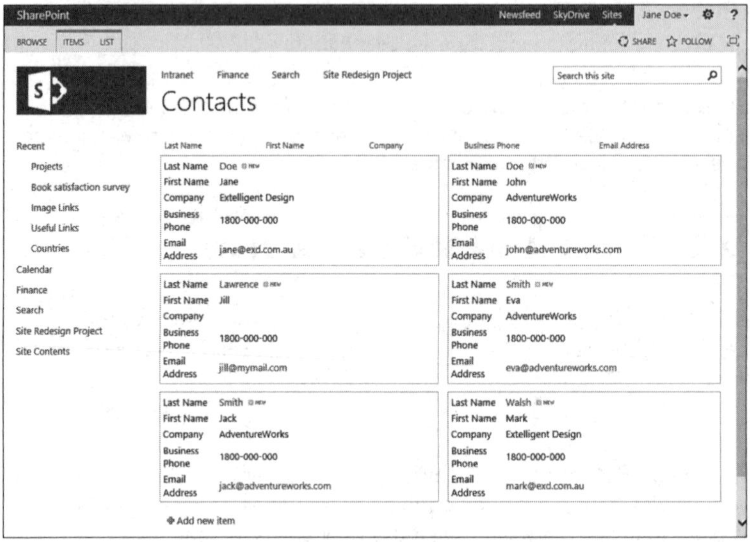

FIGURE 8.25   A view showing contacts with the Boxed style.

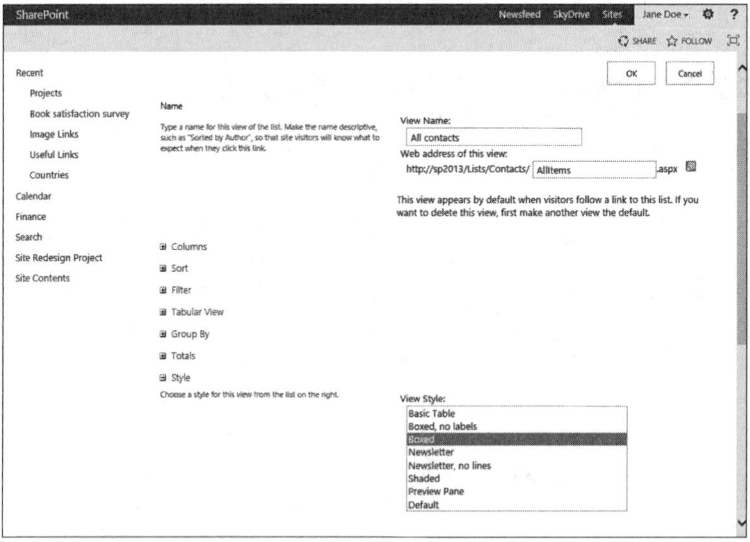

FIGURE 8.26   Specifying the Boxed style for a view.

TIP   Try the different view styles. You might find that one of them is better suited for your purpose than the default one.

Specify How Folders Will Be Used in a View

Scenario/Problem: You want to choose whether a view should display the folders in a list or library or should display all the documents and list items without folders.

Solution: You can choose whether a view shows the contents of the document library or list in folders or shows all the items and files as if there were no folders. A view that is configured to show the items without folders is known as a flat view. By default, views will show folders and files within folders (see Figure 8.27).

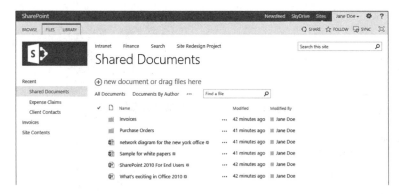

FIGURE 8.27   A view of a document library showing folders.

To specify that a view should not display folders, scroll to the Folders section in the view creation page and expand it by using the plus sign next to the section title. You then have the option of specifying whether the view should display the items in folders (see Figure 8.28).

A flat view displays all the items that are in the list or document library, even if they are not in the root folder of that list or library (see Figure 8.29). Essentially, this view makes it look as if no folders are in that list or library.

TIP   A flat view can be difficult for users who create or upload documents or list items because the flat view does not display the folders, and the user can't specify in which folder a document or list item should be created. It is recommended to create this kind of view only in addition to a view that displays the folders.

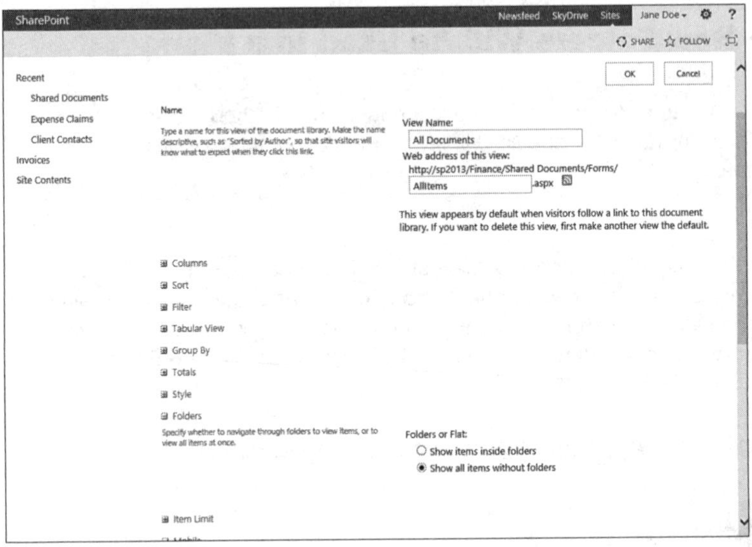

FIGURE 8.28   Configuring a flat view.

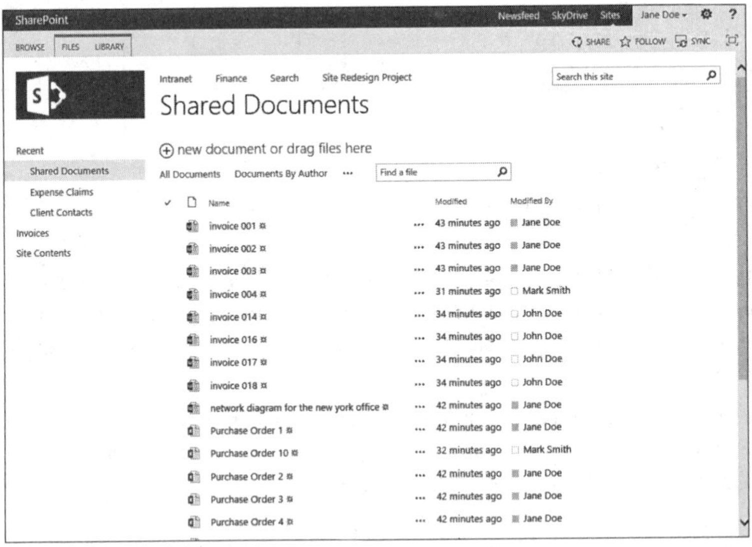

FIGURE 8.29   A flat view of the document library shows all documents from all folders.

Specify the Item Limit for a View

Scenario/Problem: Because many items are in a list or library, you do not want the view to display them all in one page. Displaying them all can cause the page to take a long time to load and makes finding what they are looking for harder for users.

Solution: You can specify an item limit on a view. An item limit on a view enables you to either specify the maximum number of items that are displayed in the view or specify the maximum number of items that are displayed in each page in a view.

For example, suppose you have an announcements list that is used a lot. With at least three announcements made every day, after a year, the list will contain more than 1,000 announcements. Displaying all the announcements in one page makes focusing on the current announcements difficult for users.

A common solution to this problem is to create a view with an item limit that displays, for example, only the last three announcements (see Figure 8.30). To do this, you need to make sure the view sorts the announcements by their creation dates (or modified dates) and then set the item limit to 3.

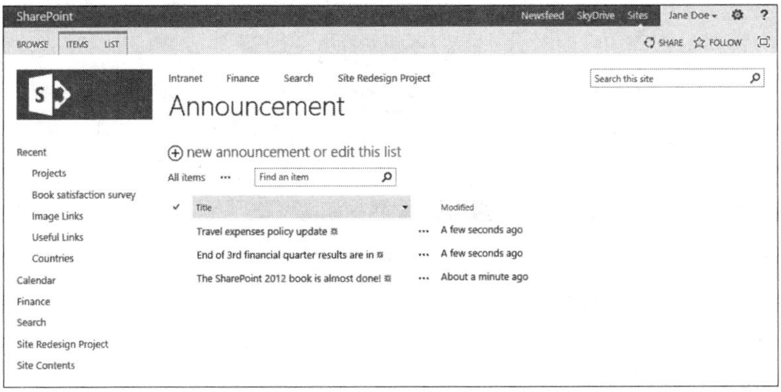

FIGURE 8.30   An announcement list showing only the last three announcements.

To specify an item limit for a view, scroll to the Item Limit section in the view creation page and expand it by using the plus sign next to the section title. You then have the option of specifying how many items should be displayed and whether the view should limit itself to that number or display the items in groups of that number (see Figure 8.31).

If you want to let users see the old announcements, you can choose the Display Items in Batches of the Specified Size option. This makes the view show the items in pages and allows the users to go back and forth between the pages, showing at one time only the number you specified (see Figure 8.32).

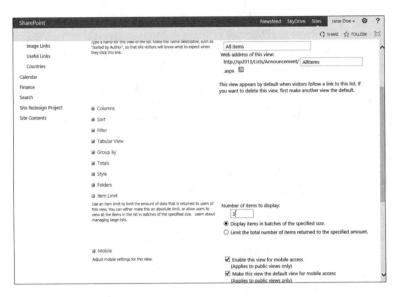

FIGURE 8.31   Specifying the item limit on a view.

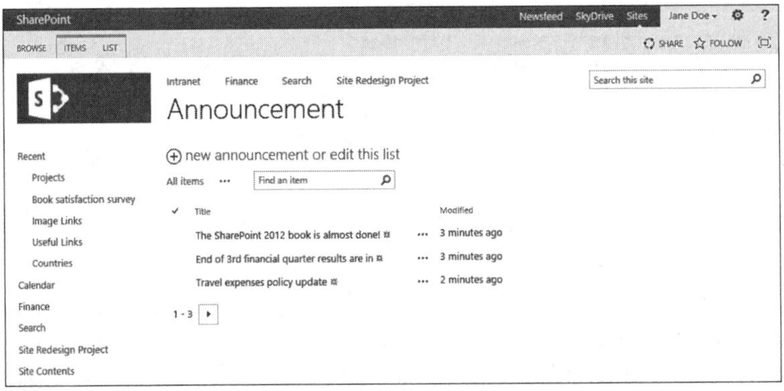

FIGURE 8.32   An announcement list showing the announcements in groups of three.

Enable or Disable Selecting Multiple Items in a View

Scenario/Problem: You don't want users to be able to delete, check out, or check in several files or items at the same time by using the check boxes method described in Chapter 6, "Creating and Managing Files, List Items, and Forms in SharePoint."

Solution: You can disable (remove) the check boxes in a view and prevent users from selecting multiple items. To do so, expand the Tabular View section in the view creation or edit page by using the plus sign next to the section title and either enable or disable the check boxes option by setting Allow Individual Item Checkboxes to the setting you want, as shown in Figure 8.33.

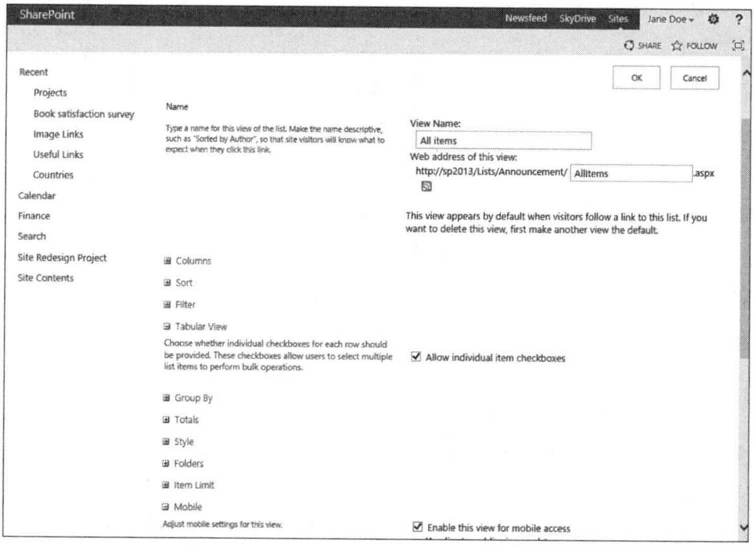

FIGURE 8.33   Enabling the Allow Individual Item Checkboxes options when creating a view.

Create Mobile Views

Scenario/Problem: Today, many people have mobile phones and other small mobile devices capable of displaying websites. However, the size of a device's screen and its resolution limits how much a user can see.

Solution: Creating special views that show information in a more compact way is often a good idea to enable mobile device users to see that information more clearly and to more comfortably navigate in it.

SharePoint attempts to identify whether a device is a mobile device and then switches to a default mobile view that is optimized for that purpose. Nonmobile devices see the view as if it is a regular view. Each mobile view has a special URL that the mobile device is redirected to.

To specify that a view should have a mobile URL, scroll to the Mobile section in the view creation page and expand it by using the plus sign next to the section title. You can create a view and specify it to be the default mobile view for the list (see Figure 8.34), or you can just leave it as another new view in the list.

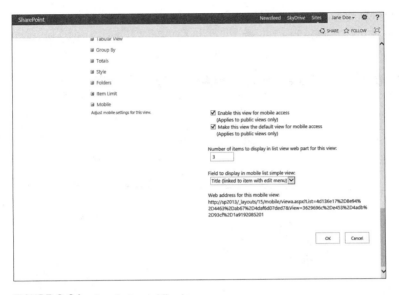

FIGURE 8.34 Creating a mobile view.

Additional options you can set for the mobile view are how many items to show (because you may want to trim a list for a mobile view) and what column to display as the title in the mobile view.

If you don't have a mobile device yourself, and you want to see what the view looks like after it has been created, you must manually type the URL that SharePoint creates for the mobile view. To find out what that URL is, go into the view modification page and scroll down to the Mobile section. The URL for the mobile view appears there as text (refer to Figure 8.34).

To learn how to modify a view, see the following section.

> **TIP** To see what a whole site would look like from a mobile device, you can use the URL that appears when editing a mobile view. That URL is the link to the mobile view of the home page of the site.

Modify a View

Scenario/Problem: You want to change the settings for an existing view.

Solution: The easiest way to change a view is to switch to the view that you want to modify, click the three dots next to the view names, and then choose Modify This View (see Figure 8.35). You can also access this option from the Modify View button in the Library ribbon or List ribbon as shown in Figure 8.35.

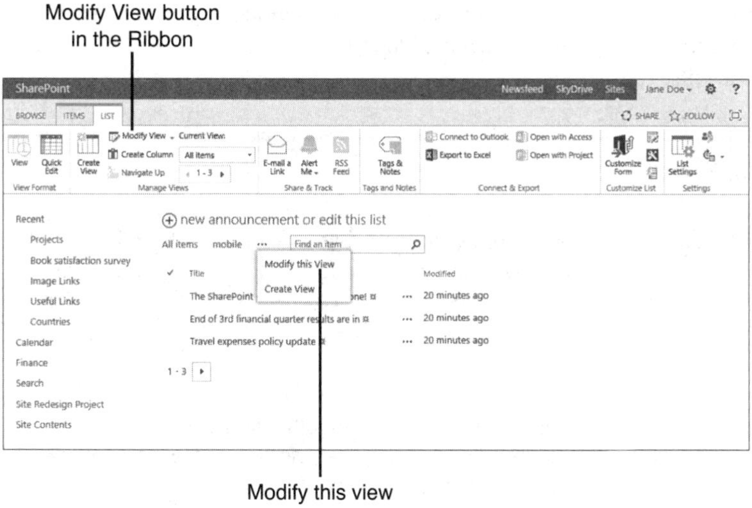

Modify View button
in the Ribbon

Modify this view

FIGURE 8.35   To modify a view, use the Modify View button in the ribbon or the Modify this View link.

Selecting Modify This View or the Modify View button opens the view editing page, which enables you to modify every setting about the view except its type (see Figure 8.36). If you want to switch a view to a different type (for example, change it from a standard view to a calendar view), delete the view and create a new one. For more information about deleting a view, see the next section.

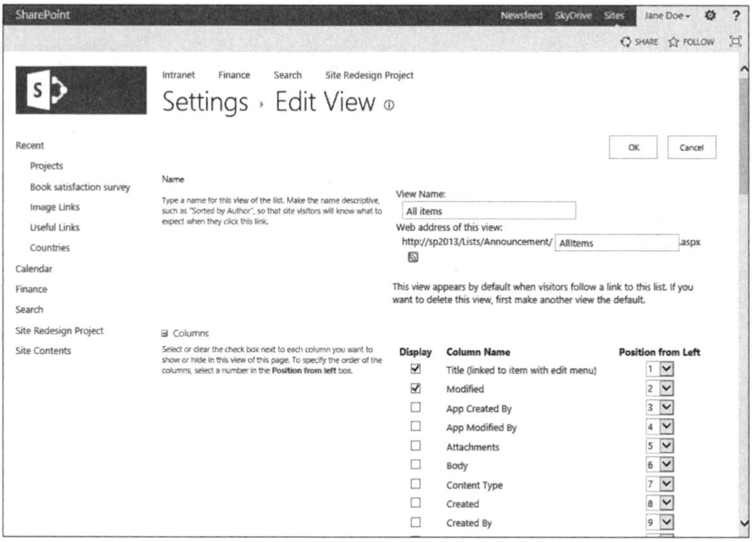

FIGURE 8.36   To change a view's filename, use the Web Address of This View box.

One difference between the view creation page and view editing page is that in the view editing page, you can define the name of the file that the view uses as well as the name of the view itself.

Delete a View

Scenario/Problem: If a view becomes obsolete, you might want to delete it, or you might want to create a view with the same name as an existing view but with a different type, and you need to delete the existing view before you can achieve that.

Solution: To delete a view, navigate to the view's modification page (see the preceding section), and then use the Delete button at the top of the page. You are prompted to confirm that you want to delete the view. If you click Yes, the view is deleted.

NOTE You cannot delete the default view for a list or library. If the view you want to delete is the default view, you need to make another view the default view first by editing the view and selecting the Make This the Default View option, as shown in Figure 8.23. You can then delete the view you wanted to delete.

CHAPTER 9

Authoring Pages

You can modify the contents that SharePoint pages display. SharePoint pages include the home page of a site and other pages that you can add to the site's document libraries and wiki page libraries. By default, a SharePoint site has only one page that you can edit: the home page. However, you can create many more pages and add links to them. Usually, the additional pages are in document libraries or wiki page libraries in the site.

This chapter explains how you can create new pages in a site and how you can edit and author the content in those pages. It covers topics such as editing controls, which are controls that exist on some pages to enable you to specify their content, and some common web parts that you can add to the pages.

Create a New Page

Scenario/Problem: Often, as a site manager or contributor, you want to add more pages to a site. These pages can be used to show information you don't want to display on the home page of the site and can be focused to specific uses, such as articles (where each article is a page) or news items (where each news item is a page).

Solution: You add pages to SharePoint sites by creating new pages in document libraries or new wiki pages in wiki page libraries. In most sites, the option to create a new page is shown under the Site Settings menu as Add a Page (see Figure 9.1). Clicking that option opens a dialog that asks for the page's name and then creates a page of the default type for that site, in the default pages library for that site. For example, in a team site this will usually create a simple wiki page in the Site Pages wiki page library, whereas in a publishing site it creates a publishing page in the Pages document library.

This method of creating pages is the easiest, as it only requires you to specify a filename for the new page, and then the new page is available for you to edit.

Alternatively, if you don't want the page to be created of the default type and in the default location, you can go to the Site Contents page (refer to "See What Lists and Document Libraries Are in a Site" in Chapter 3, "Solutions Regarding Files, Documents, List Items, and Forms"), open the library you want, and use the New Document button in the Files ribbon to create a new page of a particular type, as shown in Figure 9.2.

The Add a page option

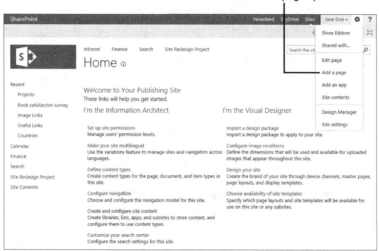

FIGURE 9.1   The Add a Page option in the site actions menu.

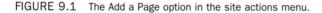

FIGURE 9.2   The New Document button in a Pages library allows you to create pages of different types.

> **TIP**   Short filename (URL names) make the best page names. Try to choose a short filename when you create a page. Some options allow you to specify the filename for the new page (see Figure 9.12, later in this chapter), but even if the interface does not allow you to specify a URL name (for example, see Figure 9.5, later in this chapter), you should choose a short name as the page's name. You can rename the title for the page later on! (See "Edit the Properties of a Page," later in this chapter.)

When creating a page from a publishing pages library, the Create Page dialog opens, allowing you to specify more settings. For more details on these settings, see the "Create a New Publishing Page" later in this chapter.

The Differences Between Different Types of Pages

As explained before, the Add a Page option in the site settings menu creates different types of pages depending on the configuration of the site. Typically, a team site creates a blank wiki page allowing you to freely type text and add web parts to the body of the page as required (see Figure 9.3). However, if you go to the team site's Site Pages library and click on the New Document button in the Files ribbon, you will see two different types of pages you can create: a Wiki Page and a Web Part Page.

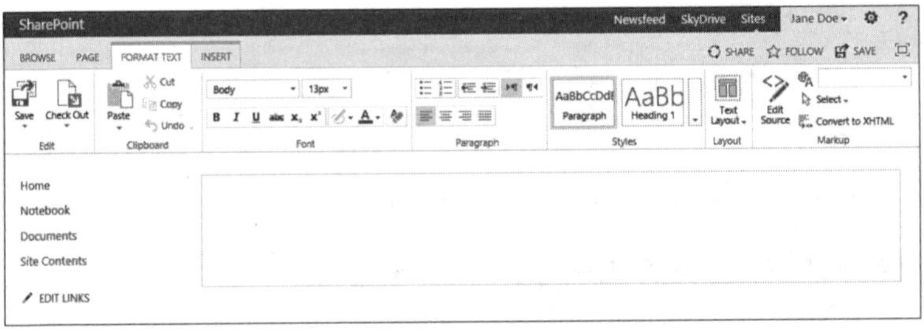

FIGURE 9.3   A new wiki page allows you to freely type text in the page, as well as add other components.

The Web Part Page option creates a web part page. This kind of page does not allow you to type text anywhere in the page but instead requires you to add web parts to the page in zones that are defined by the page's layout (see Figure 9.4). This helps enforce a certain layout for pages in the site.

NOTE   Some web parts allow you to write text in them (such as the Content Editor web part, which is covered later in this chapter, in the section "Use Built-in Web Parts" section). Other web parts show different information or functionality.

The Publishing page option is available only in certain sites with certain features. These pages are designed to enforce certain layouts on the pages in the site and therefore are preferred for sites that need strict structure and consistency between the pages. These pages are usually slightly more complex versions of wiki pages or web part pages or a mix of the two (for example, a wiki page with web part zones in certain places). An example for one of these layouts is the (Article Page) Summary Links layout. A page based on this layout looks similar to a wiki page but with additional controls:

▶ A link list on the right of the page

▶ A control to easily change the page's title

▶ A control to easily change the article date

▶ A control to easily define a byline

▶ A control to set a roll-up image (an image that will be displayed by roll-up web parts that list what pages are there on the site)

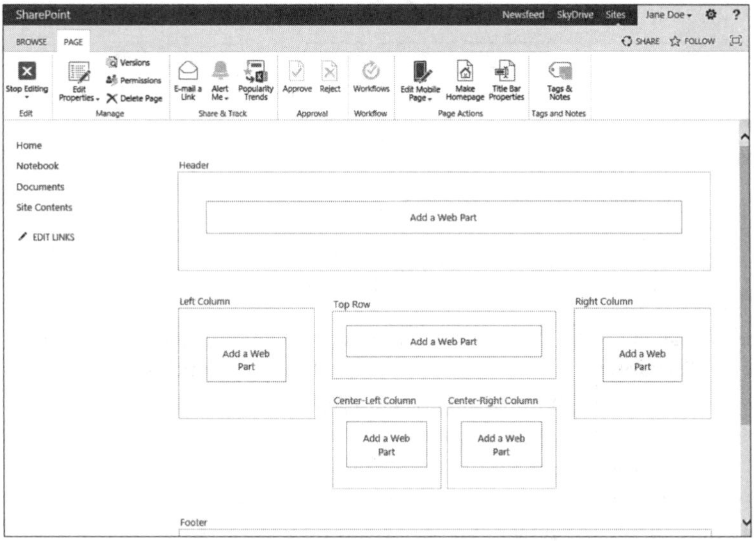

FIGURE 9.4   A new web part page allows you to add web parts in prespecified zones.

Figure 9.5 shows an example of such a page using that layout.

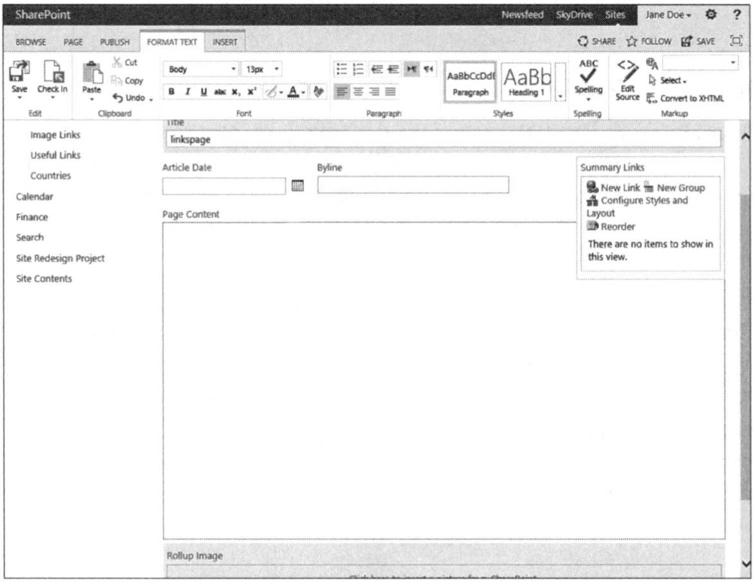

FIGURE 9.5   A publishing page using the (Article Page) Summary Links layout.

Create a New Wiki Page

When you choose to create a new wiki page (using the Add a Page option in the site settings menu, as shown earlier in Figure 9.1), an Add a Page dialog appears, asking for the name for the new page as shown in Figure 9.6.

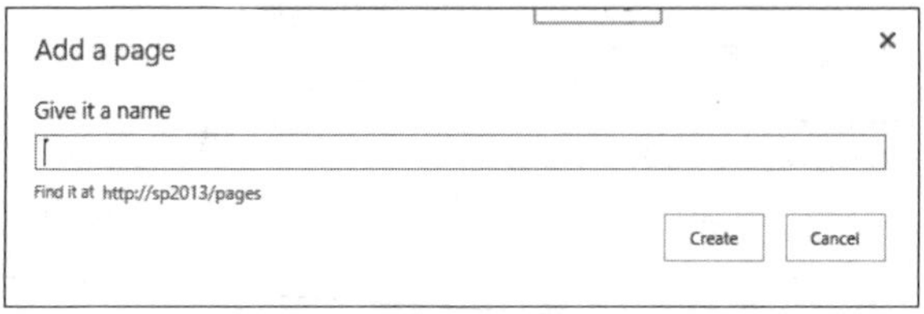

Add a page   ×

Give it a name

[   ]

Find it at http://sp2013/pages

                                                    Create   Cancel

FIGURE 9.6   The Add a Page dialog.

After you type the name for the new page, click the Create button. The name for the page is important because it is used for both the name of the file (which the users type in the address bar of their browsers to open the page) and as the title of the page (which the users see in the navigation bar and in the top of their browsers). You should select a short but meaningful name for the page. You can rename it later, but that can cause links to the page to break. The page is immediately created and opens in editing mode. For more information about editing the contents of pages, see the section "Edit the Contents of a Page," later in this chapter.

NOTE   For more information on how to rename a wiki page, see the section "Edit Properties of a Wiki Page," later in this chapter.

Create a New Web Part Page

When you choose the Web Part Page option via the New Document button in a Site pages library, you are redirected to the New Web Part Page dialog. In this page you must choose a name for the file that will be created for the page. You also choose the layout template for the web part zones on the page and the document library to put the page in, as shown in Figure 9.7.

The different web part zone layout templates are shown in the page under the Choose a Layout Template. Each option in the list box describes the page that will be created in the form of where the web part zones will be located. For example, the layout template called Full Page, Vertical has only one web part zone, spread across the entire page, and any web part that is added to it is vertical, spreading the entire width of the page. Other web parts can be either above it or below it. If you click on the different layout templates, the image on the left changes to show a wireframe of the web part zones layout, as shown in Figure 9.7.

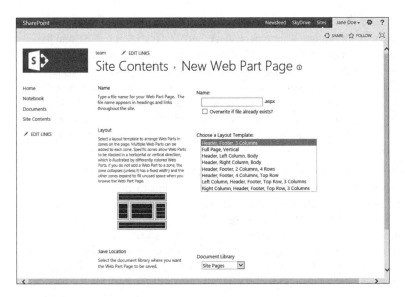

FIGURE 9.7   You use the New Web Part Page dialog for creating a new web part page.

> **TIP**   Choose the layout template carefully because changing the layout of a web part page after it is created is not possible (unlike with a publishing page, as explained later in this chapter). If you create a page with the wrong layout, you have to delete it and create it again with the correct layout.

If any document libraries are in the site, you can choose them from the Document Library option at the bottom of the page. By default, all pages in a site go to either the Site Pages library or the Pages library, if one exists. If you want to create the page in a different library, you can choose it from the box.

After you pick the title, layout template, and document library, click Create. The new page is created in the document library and opens in editing mode. For more information about editing the contents of pages, see the section "Edit the Contents of a Page," later in this chapter.

Create a New Publishing Page

In a site that supports publishing pages, the Add a Page option in the site actions menu (refer to Figure 9.1) will create a publishing page in the site's Pages library. However, if it doesn't, you can still create one by going to the Pages library and using the New Document button in the Files ribbon as shown in Figure 9.2. The process of creating the page is slightly different when you choose the Add a Page option from the menu, however, in that you are not asked what page layout you want for your page, and a default page layout is used. This is useful for site managers who want to make it easier for users to always create the same kind of page, while leaving a more flexible option to create different types of pages by using the New Document menu option.

If you choose to create a publishing page by using the Add a Page option in the site actions menu, you are prompted for a page name only (refer to Figure 9.6), and the page is created with the default layout. You can change the layout of the page later (see the section "Change the Page Layout of a Publishing Page," later in this chapter). The name you choose for the page is used to generate the page's filename (which is displayed to the user in the address bar of the browser). You can change this name later, but changing it breaks users' favorite lists and links to the page, so it is not recommended. The name is also used to set the page's title, which can be changed later with no issues.

You might want to choose the page layout before creating the page, set its description, and set the filename and the title separately. You can do this by going to the site's pages library and using the New Document button in the Files ribbon as explained before (refer to Figure 9.2). After clicking the New Document button itself, or choosing a specific page content type from the menu that opens under that button, you are redirected to the Create Page dialog where you can enter the new page's title, description, and URL name (the name for the file, as just explained), as well as the page layout for the page, as shown in Figure 9.8.

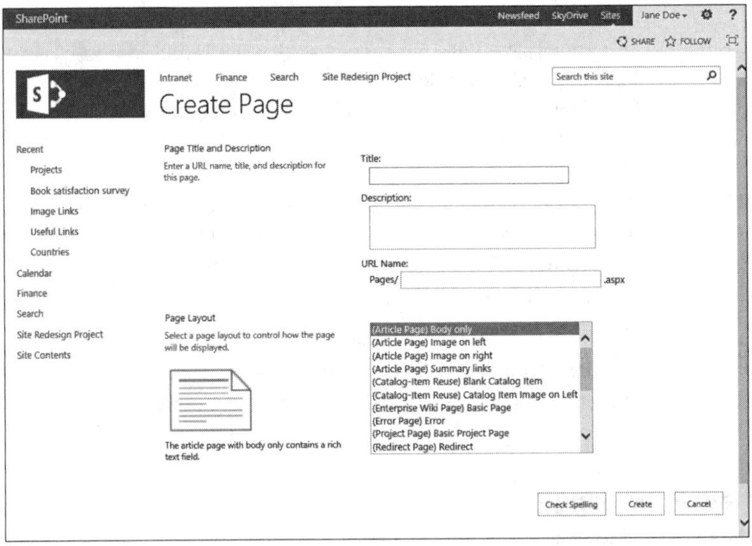

FIGURE 9.8   The Create Page dialog for creating a publishing page.

Because page layouts can be created by developers or removed by administrators, you might see more or fewer options for layouts than you see in this chapter. You should review the options available and choose the one that's closest to what you want to achieve with your page. You can always change the layout of a publishing page at a later stage, a process that is explained later in this chapter. Also remember that a page is just a file in a document library, and you can always delete the page if you choose the wrong layout—just as you would delete any other file in a document library. (See

"Delete a File or List Item" in Chapter 6, "Creating and Managing Files, List Items, and Forms in SharePoint.")

After you select a title, a URL name, and a page layout, click the Create button to create the page and open it in editing mode. For more information about editing the contents of pages, see the section "Edit the Contents of a Page," later in this chapter.

Edit the Properties of a Page

> **Scenario/Problem:** You want to change properties such as the page layout of a publishing page and the title of the page (that is displayed at the top of the user's browser and in the navigational breadcrumbs, and possibly in other locations on the site), the caption for the page, the page's description, and the page's image (which also might appear in different locations on the site).

Solution: How you change the properties of a page depends on what type of page you are editing. The following sections cover the different options.

Edit Properties of a Wiki Page

A wiki page by default does not have any properties except for the filename, which is also shown as the page's title. Selecting a good filename for a wiki page is important because renaming the page breaks links to it.

To rename a wiki page, open it in your browser and switch to the Page ribbon. Click on the Edit button to switch to editing mode, and then switch again to the Page ribbon and click on the Rename Page button, as shown in Figure 9.9.

FIGURE 9.9   The Rename Page button for the wiki page.

If the wiki page library is configured to have properties for the pages, the Edit Properties button in the Page ribbon (refer to Figure 9.9) becomes available. If you click it, you see a page where you can edit the properties of the page.

Edit Properties of a Web Part Page

To edit the properties of a web part page, open the page in your browser and switch to the Page ribbon. In the ribbon, click the Title Bar Properties button in the Page Actions section of the ribbon. A panel opens on the right of the page, allowing you to set the page's title, caption, description, and image (see Figure 9.10). (To set an image, type the link to the image in the Image Link box.)

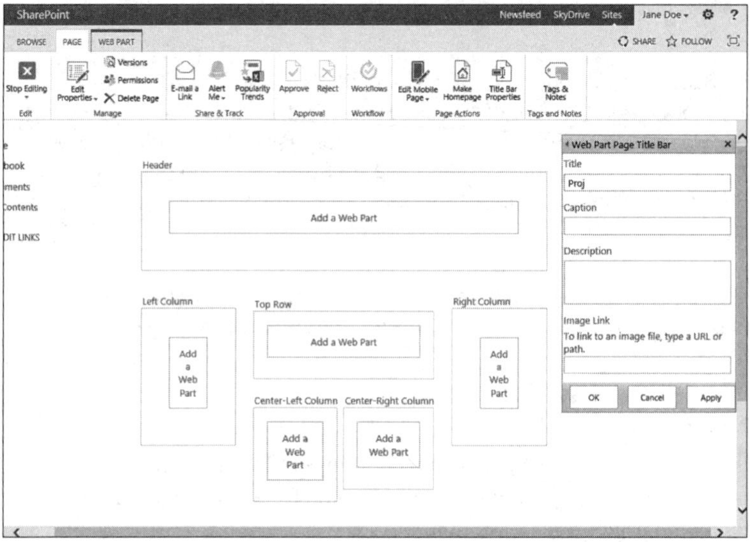

FIGURE 9.10   Editing the properties of a web part page.

Edit Properties of a Publishing Page

To edit the properties of a publishing page, open the page in your browser, switch to the Page ribbon, and click the Edit Properties button, as shown in Figure 9.11.

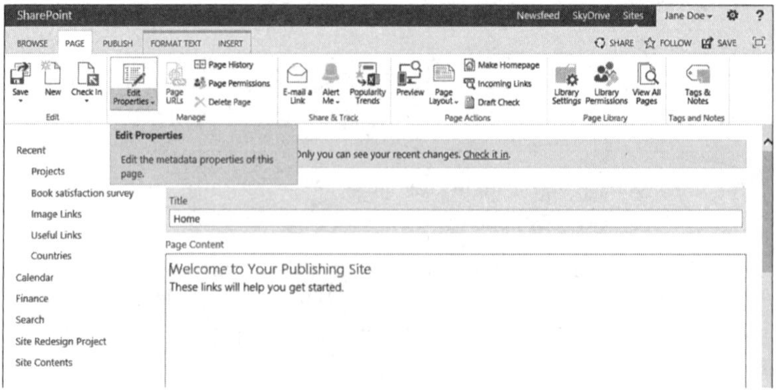

FIGURE 9.11   The Edit Properties button in a publishing page.

The properties page for the page opens (see Figure 9.12). This page allows you to change all the properties set for the page, just as if you were editing a file. You can edit the page's content type, title, and other properties that might be required for that type of page (depending on the selected content type). When you're done, either click the Save button at the bottom of the page or use the Save button in the Edit ribbon at the top of the page.

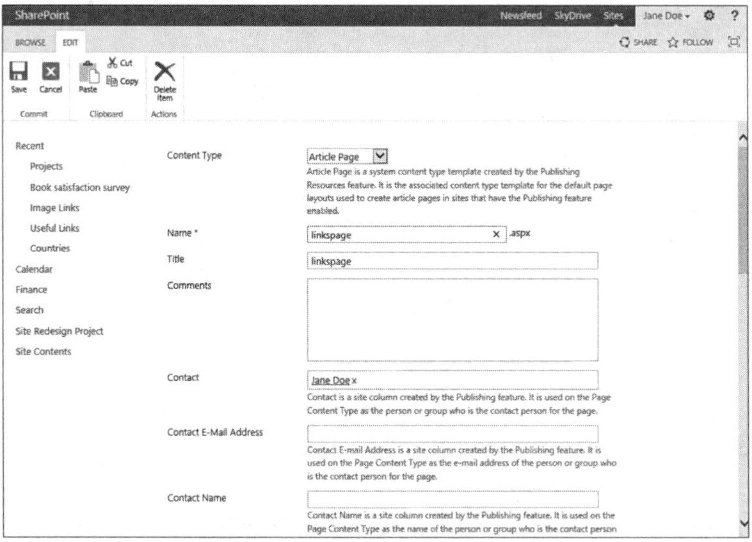

FIGURE 9.12   Editing the properties of a publishing page.

Change the Page Layout of a Publishing Page

Scenario/Problem: You might want to change the page layout that was selected when the page was created. For example, say that a page was created with the "body only" layout, and you want to change it to a layout that includes a web part zone or an image on one side of the text.

Solution: To change the layout of an existing publishing page, open the page in your browser and switch to the Page ribbon. There, click on the Edit button to switch the page into editing mode. This enables you to click on the Page Layout button in the ribbon.

NOTE   In some publishing sites, the ribbon is hidden by default. To get to the ribbon, open the site settings menu and select Show Ribbon (refer to Figure 9.1) from that menu to expose the Page ribbon.

The Page Layout button then shows the various available page layouts for you to choose from (see Figure 9.13).

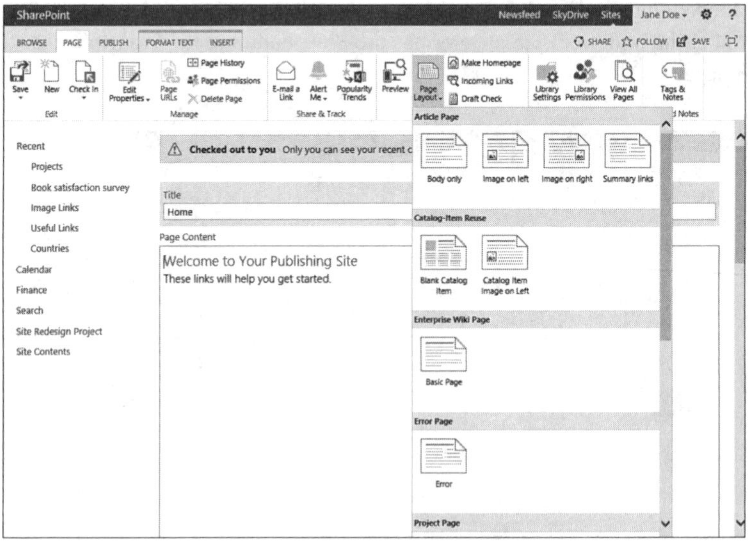

FIGURE 9.13   Choosing a new page layout for a publishing page.

After you click on the layout that you want, you can see it change the page. It is important to note that switching layouts might remove web parts from the page because the web parts are tied to a specific web part zone, and if the new layout does not have the same web part zone, the web parts that belonged in that zone will be removed.

If you are happy with the new layout, click the Save & Close button in the Page ribbon. (The page might still need to be published. See "Publish a Page," later in this chapter.) If you want to revert to the layout that you had before, open the menu under the Check In button and click Discard Check Out. This retracts all the modifications you've made to the page since the last time you checked it out, including the page layout change.

Edit the Contents of a Page

Scenario/Problem: As a site manager, you want to change what is displayed on a specific page in a site.

Solution: To change the display, you must view the page in editing mode—a mode that enables you to edit the page. You can make such changes after you switch to editing mode. (You'll learn how to make specific changes, such as changing text or a picture or a web part, later in this chapter.)

When you have the permissions to edit a page, and if the page is not currently checked out by someone else, you edit the page by navigating to it in the browser, opening the site settings menu, and choosing Edit Page, as shown in Figure 9.14.

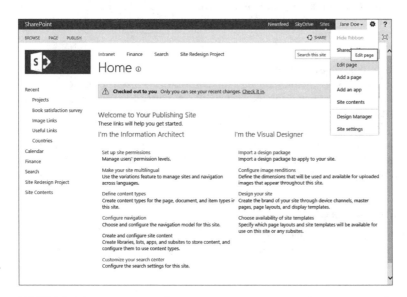

FIGURE 9.14   Opening the site actions menu and choosing Edit Page to get to page editing mode.

> **NOTE**   If the page is checked out to another user, the Edit Page menu option is not available until that page is checked in.

When the page is in editing mode, it looks different than it looks normally, showing either web part zones (where you can add web parts) and/or editing controls, depending on the type of page (refer to Figures 9.4 and 9.5). For example, a wiki page by default has only the page body control—a control in which you can type. Publishing pages might have additional controls, depending on their layouts, whereas web part pages show web part zones to allow you to add web parts, as well as the existing web parts for you to edit.

When you are finished editing the page, save your changes. How you do this depends on the configuration of the library the page is in. In libraries that do not keep track of page versioning and do not require checking in or checking out the page, you can just click the Stop Editing button on the Page ribbon. In libraries that maintain version control over pages, use the Save & Close button in the Page ribbon, along with a Check In button. If publishing is required in the document library, you have a Publish ribbon with buttons for publishing the page after you check it in. For more information, see "Publish a Page," later in this chapter.

Use the Text Editing Control in a Page

Scenario/Problem: When authoring a page, you want to enter or change the text that appears on the page.

Solution: Some pages have text editing controls embedded in them. This is true of all wiki pages and most publishing pages. You can type rich text in these controls, including pictures, videos, links, tables, and even web parts. The following sections explain how you can use this type of control to add or change these elements.

NOTE   Some pages do not have text editing controls. To add text to or edit text in those pages, use the Content Editor web part, as explained in the section "Use the Content Editor Web Part," later in this chapter.

Edit and Format Text

To edit text in a text editing control, simply click anywhere in the control. When you do that, the ribbon switches to the Format Text ribbon, allowing you to format the text as required (see Figure 9.15).

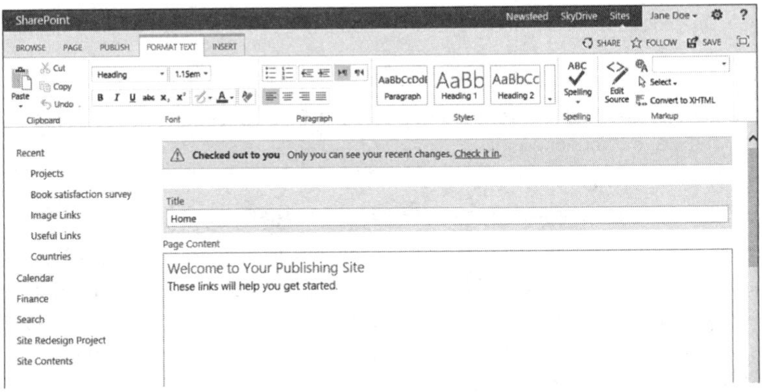

FIGURE 9.15   The Format Text ribbon allows you to set formatting for the text in a text editing control.

You use the ribbon and control as you would use any word processor; for example, to make part of the text bold, highlight it and click the Bold button (labeled B).

Add a Hyperlink

To add a hyperlink to text, highlight the part of the text that you want to make a hyperlink and switch to the Insert ribbon, as shown in Figure 9.16. In this ribbon, you can either click the Link button or open the menu under it to reveal the From SharePoint and the From Address options, as shown in Figure 9.16.

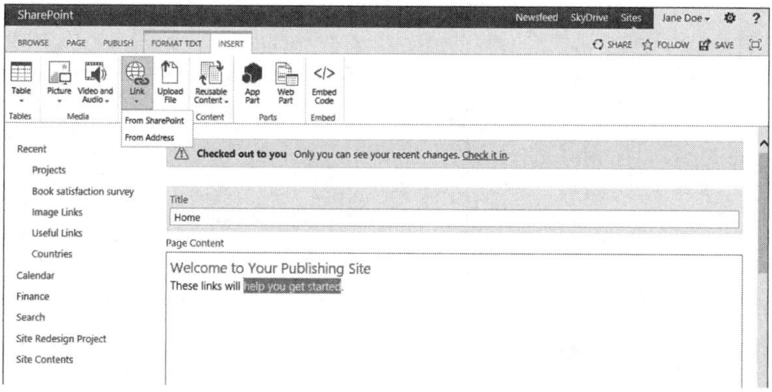

FIGURE 9.16   The Link button's menu.

Selecting the From SharePoint option or just clicking the Link button opens a dialog that enables you to choose where the hyperlink will link to (see Figure 9.17). This dialog presents you with the content in the current site, and you can navigate to content in subsites. You can double-click any site, list, or library to view what is in it, or click a site, list, library, or the items in them to add the link to the selected item to the Location box at the bottom of the dialog. Click OK to close the dialog, and the link is added to the text.

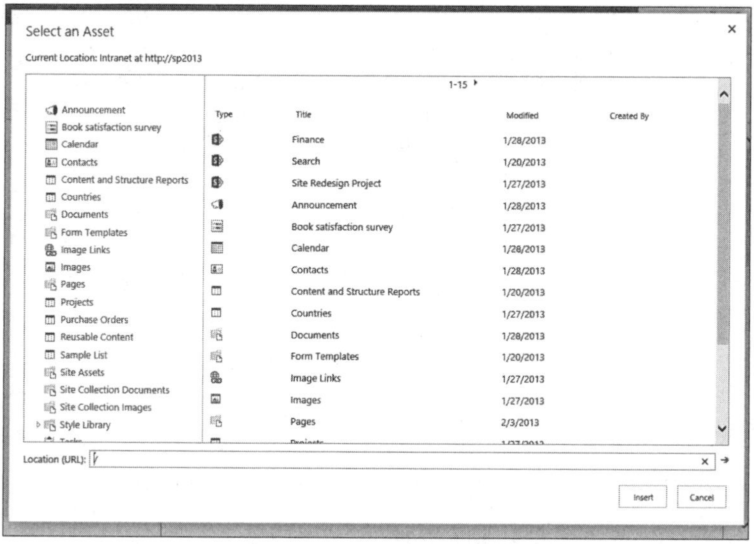

FIGURE 9.17   The dialog for adding a hyperlink from SharePoint.

Selecting the From Address option shows a much simpler dialog that asks you for the text to display for the link and the address that the user will be directed to when clicking on it (see Figure 9.18).

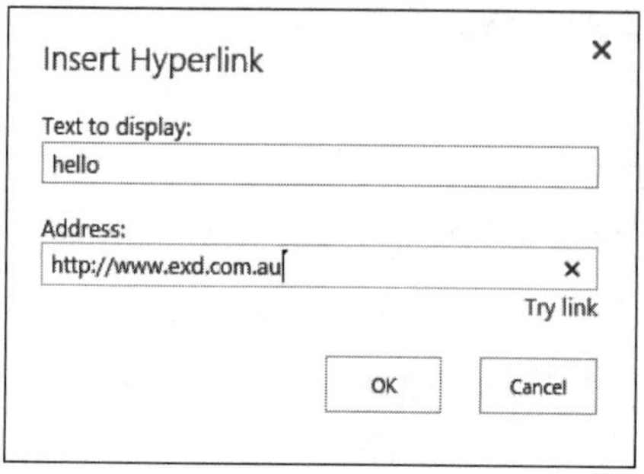

Insert Hyperlink ✕

Text to display:

hello

Address:

http://www.exd.com.au ✕

Try link

OK   Cancel

FIGURE 9.18   The dialog for adding a hyperlink from address.

After you have added the link, clicking on it in the text editing control allows you to switch to the Link tools ribbon (see Figure 9.19). Here you can either remove the link or edit its properties (including the description that is shown when a user hovers over the link). You can also configure how it should behave, such as whether it should open in a new tab (or a new window) and whether it should show an icon next to the text to further signify that this is a link. You can change the icon's image later (see the following section for information about changing existing pictures).

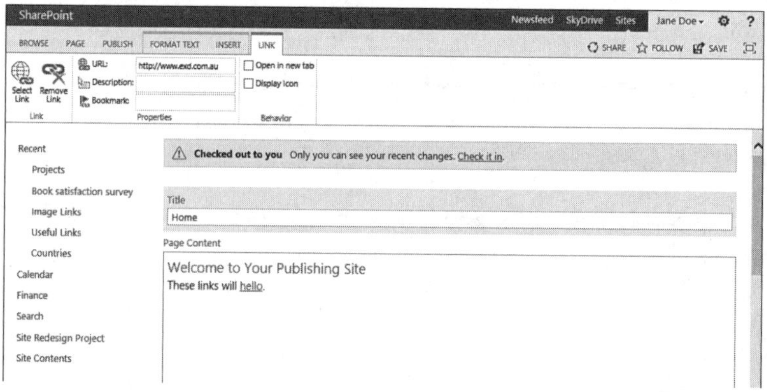

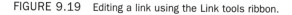

FIGURE 9.19   Editing a link using the Link tools ribbon.

Add and Edit a Picture

To add a picture to a text editing control, place the cursor where you want the picture to be added and switch to the Insert tab in the Editing Tools ribbon. Open the drop-down menu under the button to expose the options to upload an image from your computer (From Computer), select an image somewhere else on the web using its address (From Address), or select a picture that was already uploaded to the site (From SharePoint), as shown in Figure 9.20. This last option is not always available and might be either missing from the menu or disabled, depending on the configuration of the site. The following sections describe these options in detail.

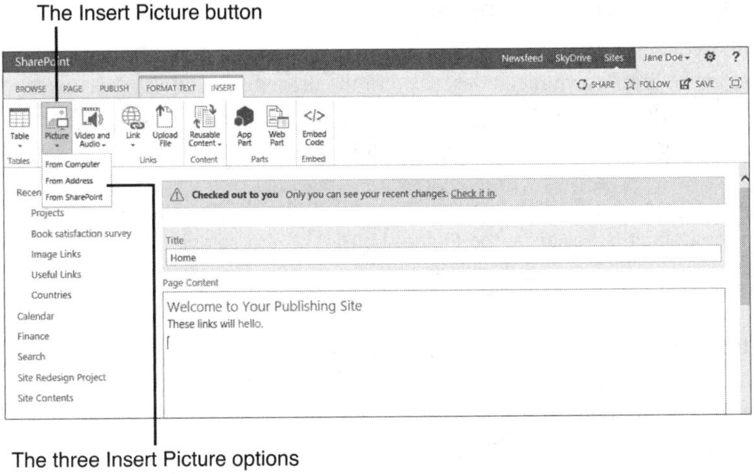

The Insert Picture button

The three Insert Picture options

FIGURE 9.20   The Picture button and the drop-down menu.

After you add a picture to the page, click the picture to expose the Image ribbon (see Figure 9.21). On this ribbon you see the Change Picture button, which works like the Picture button. You also have the option to set the alternative text for the image (for users whose browsers do not support images, or in case the image cannot be loaded) using the Alt Text box. You can also configure the image's size by typing a custom size, and you can resize by dragging and dropping the borders of the image.

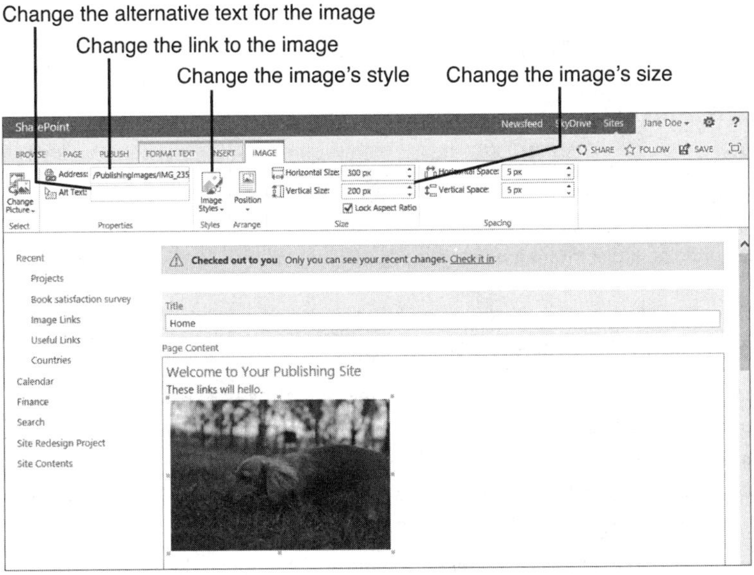

Change the alternative text for the image
Change the link to the image
Change the image's style   Change the image's size

FIGURE 9.21   The Picture Tools ribbon shows when you select a picture.

Use a Picture from Your Computer

To use a picture you have on your computer in a page, choose the From Computer option in the Picture drop-down menu described in the preceding section. This opens the Select Picture dialog, which allows you to specify the picture to upload from your computer and the library in SharePoint to upload it to.

> **NOTE** If the From SharePoint option is not available in the site you are using, From Computer is the default behavior for the Picture button, so you can simply click the button instead of opening the drop-down menu.

You choose the file you want by clicking the Browse button, choosing the library, and clicking OK to upload. Depending on the settings for the library you chose, a dialog might ask for the picture's properties. After you fill in the required properties and click Save, the picture is uploaded to the library and added to the page.

Use a Picture Using an Address

To use a picture that exists on the Web (that is, was already uploaded to the site or on another website), you open the Picture drop-down menu (refer to Figure 9.20) and select the From Address option. The Select Picture dialog opens, which allows you to specify the picture's address and the alternative text that will be displayed if the picture is not available or if the user's browser doesn't support images (see Figure 9.22).

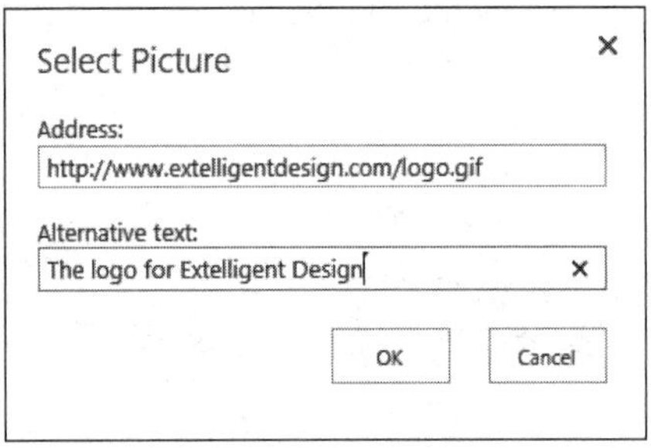

FIGURE 9.22   Adding a picture from a known address.

Use a Picture from SharePoint Server

The last option for inserting a picture is to select one that already exists in SharePoint. (You can use this option only with SharePoint Server, not with SPF.) You can use the From Address option to achieve the same result if you already know the address of the image file, but typing the address is usually a lot harder than browsing to the image file and selecting it, which is what this option allows.

To see the dialog for browsing to an image in the current site, open the Picture drop-down menu (refer to Figure 9.20) and choose the From SharePoint option. This option might be missing from the site if the site does not have all the publishing features enabled. This means that sites that are not running on SharePoint Server—that is, SPF sites—do not have this option at all, and sites that are running on SharePoint Server might still have this option disabled if the publishing features are not enabled on the site.

> **NOTE** If the From SharePoint option is available in the site you are using, it is also the default behavior for the Picture button. It allows you to simply click the button instead of opening the drop-down menu.

Clicking the From SharePoint option opens the Select an Asset dialog, which allows you to browse for a picture that was uploaded to the site. This dialog is the same as the one for adding a hyperlink from SharePoint (refer to Figure 9.17) but is meant to be used to find images.

In the Select an Asset dialog you can select the picture by clicking it once and clicking OK, or you can navigate through the sites to find the picture you want. The links on the left side go to the picture library in the current site and to the library in the root site. If the picture you are looking for is in a different location, click the Up button to see all the contents of the site. You can then navigate through the site and subsites and look in different picture libraries (or document libraries) to select the picture you want. To select a picture, either double-click it or click it once and then click OK.

Add and Edit a Table

To add a table in a text control, place the cursor where you want the table to be added, and then switch to the Insert subribbon in the Editing Tools ribbon and click the Table button. Clicking this button opens a submenu that allows you to quickly add a table by choosing how many rows and how many columns will be in the table by clicking on the squares (see Figure 9.23). Above this quick option is the Insert Table option, which opens a dialog that allows you to specify the number of rows and columns using numbers instead.

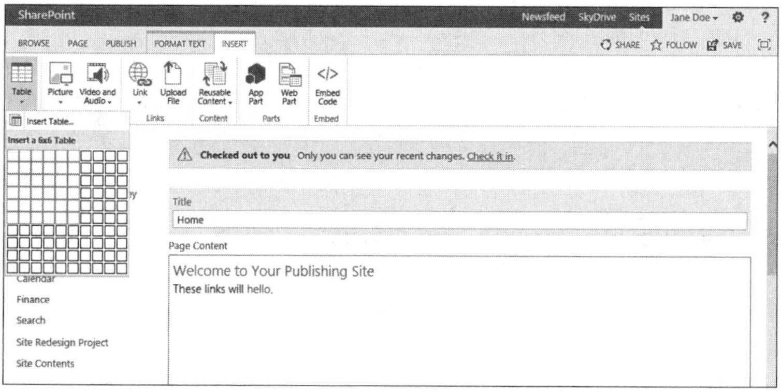

FIGURE 9.23   The Insert Table button menu.

After the table has been added, you edit it by clicking inside it, and then the Table Tools ribbon shows up, with two tabs. The Layout ribbon (see Figure 9.24) allows you to customize the table's layout (inserting/removing rows and columns, specifying width and height for the table and for each row and column, and so on), and the Design tab (see Figure 9.25) allows you to choose styles for the table and specify settings for the current row and column.

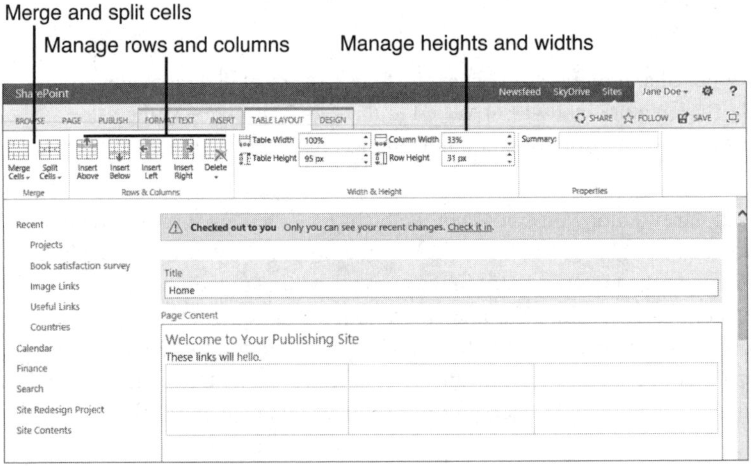

FIGURE 9.24   The Table Layout tab in the Table Tools ribbon.

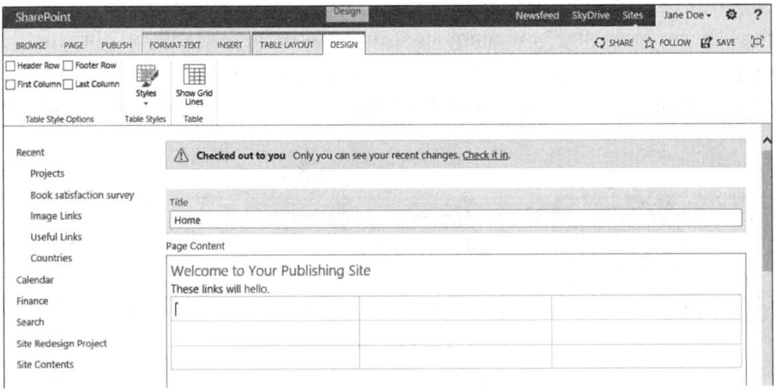

FIGURE 9.25   The Design tab in the Table Tools ribbon.

Use Wiki Syntax to Link to Existing Content and Create Pages

Scenario/Problem: When authoring a page, you realize that a certain piece of text should be linked to a page that is not yet created. You do not want to stop authoring your page, or maybe you are not the right person to author the other page you want to link to.

Solution: Wiki syntax offers quick and easy ways to link to existing content and also to mark a piece of text as one that should have a page created for it. SharePoint then turns terms into special links, that when clicked, allow the user to create pages for the terms. The following sections explain how to use wiki notation to achieve these two simple tasks.

Linking to Existing Content

To link to existing content while typing text in a wiki page, type [[. This opens a pop-up menu that shows a list of existing pages available in the site (see Figure 9.26). To link to one of these pages, simply select it from the menu and add]]. The item is added to the text as [[pagename]], and when you save the document, this is transformed into a link to that page.

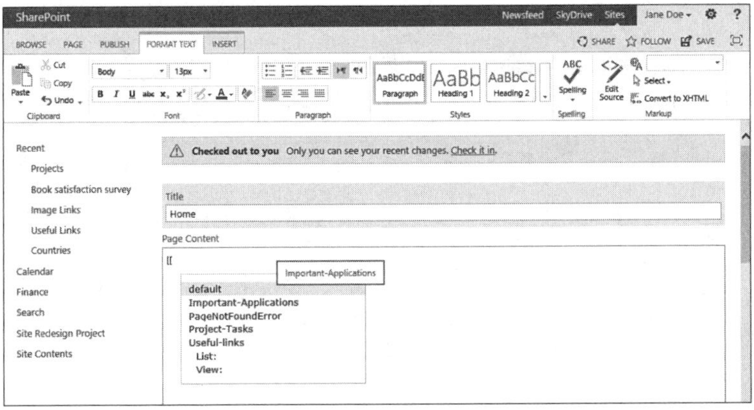

FIGURE 9.26   Typing [[in a wiki page opens a popup menu that enables you to quickly link to another page.

The menu also offers two special options at the bottom: List and View. Selecting one of these is the same as typing [[List: or [[View:. You can then start typing either the name of the list or the view that is in the current site, and SharePoint autocompletes the name of the list as you type it or allows you to choose a list and then an item or view (depending on whether you selected List or View in the first level, as shown in Figure 9.27).

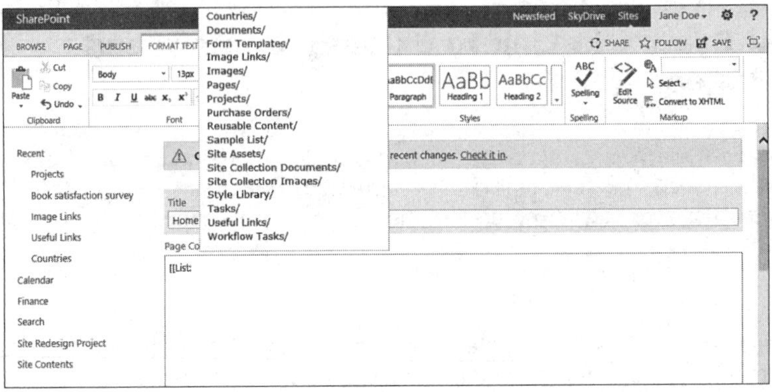

FIGURE 9.27   When you start typing the list name, SharePoint shows you the lists you can choose from.

As before, the text shows as [[List:listname]], and this transforms into a link to the list or view when you save the page. For example, [[List:Documents]] shows up in the page as the name of the list (Documents), and it is linked to the list. Typing [[List:Projects/1|intranet upgrade]] links to the item in the list Sample List with the title Sample Item, as shown in Figures 9.28 and 9.29.

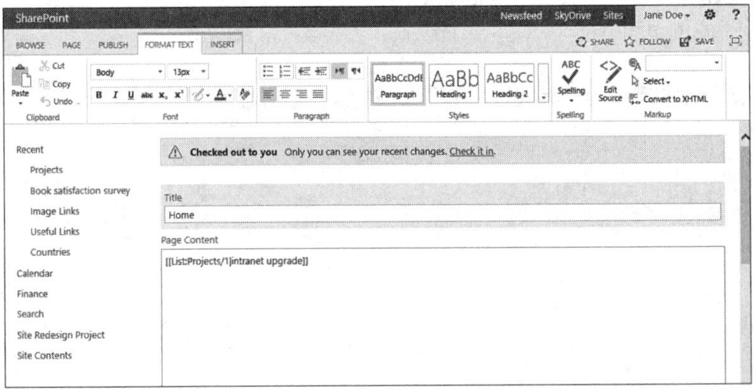

FIGURE 9.28   The syntax to link to a list item in a list.

FIGURE 9.29   The link is shown as the list item's title.

> **TIP**   If the popup menu does not appear, press Ctrl+space to force it to show up.

Creating New Pages

If you are writing something and realize that a certain word or term in your text should link to a page that needs to be created, you don't need to stop and create it right away. Instead, you can use the wiki syntax to mark it as a link and then create it later—or let someone else create it. To do this, simply type the term you want to make into a link inside double square brackets. For example, if you type [[Product X]], the words *Product X* appear on the page as a link, even if no page exists for that product.

When you save the page, the link looks different from other links; it is underlined with a black dotted line, as shown in Figure 9.30. Clicking this link opens the New Page dialog, which allows you (or other users) to quickly create a page for the word (or words) you wrote, as shown in Figure 9.31.

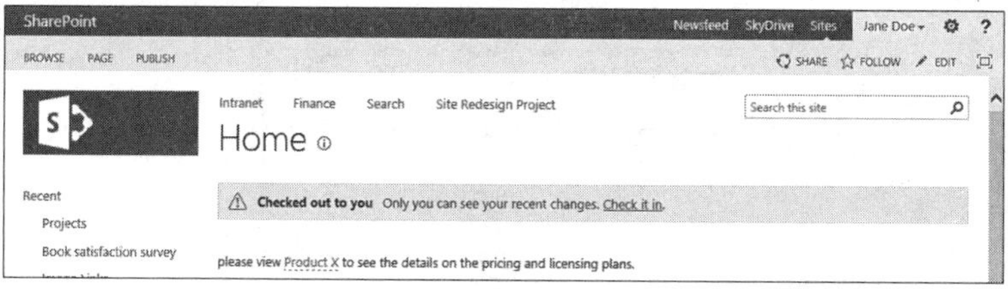

FIGURE 9.30   A link to a page that doesn't exist yet is marked with a black dotted underline.

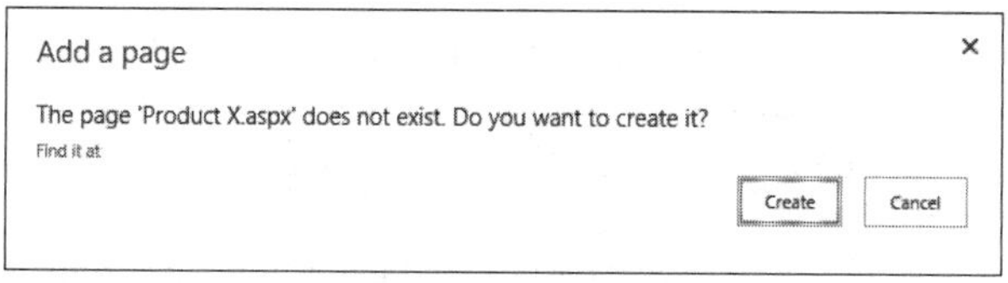

FIGURE 9.31   The New Page dialog for a wiki link.

Use the Picture Editing Control in a Page

> **Scenario/Problem:** When authoring a page, you want to change the picture that appears on the page, but the picture is not in a text editing control.

Solution: A page might have a picture editing control embedded in it. If a picture is not defined for the picture editing control, the control shows a link when the page is in editing mode, allowing you to insert a picture. Clicking this link opens the Edit Image Properties dialog (see Figure 9.32). This dialog allows you to browse for the picture and specify properties for the picture, such as its alternative text, its layout and size, and whether it should be a hyperlink (and if so, whether it should be opened in a new window).

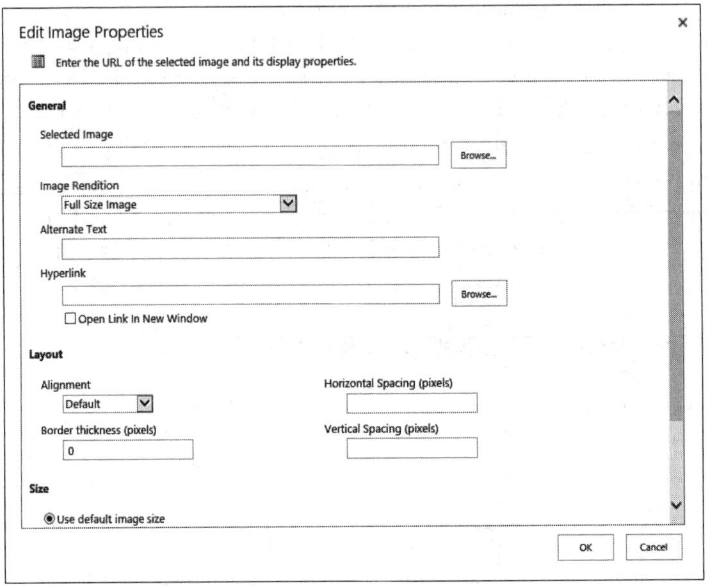

Edit Image Properties

Enter the URL of the selected image and its display properties.

General

Selected Image

Browse...

Image Rendition

Full Size Image

Alternate Text

Hyperlink

Browse...

☐ Open Link In New Window

Layout

Alignment   Horizontal Spacing (pixels)

Default

Border thickness (pixels)   Vertical Spacing (pixels)

0

Size

◉ Use default image size

OK   Cancel

FIGURE 9.32   The Edit Image Properties dialog opens when you use the picture control to insert a picture.

Clicking the Browse button opens the dialog shown earlier in this chapter in Figure 9.17. To edit the properties of a picture after it is added, you use the same method described in the section, "Add and Edit a Picture," earlier in this chapter.

NOTE   Some pages do not have a picture editing control, and the pictures displayed in them are stored in web parts. For information about how to modify web parts, see the sections "Use the Image Viewer Web Part" and "Modify a Web Part," later in this chapter. For information on adding a picture as part of the text in a text control, see "Add and Edit a Picture," earlier in this chapter.

To change or edit an existing picture in a picture control, follow the same instructions as if the picture is in a text control. (See the "Add and Edit a Picture" section, earlier in this chapter.)

If you want to clear a picture control (that is, remove the picture and not replace it), click the picture in the picture control and press the Delete key. The picture is removed, and the next time you enter editing mode for the page, the link to add a picture reappears.

Add a Web Part or an App

> **Scenario/Problem:** When authoring or editing a page, you want to add different kinds of content to different sections of the page.

Solution: Some pages enable you to add web parts to them. To add a web part to a page, you first need to decide where on the page you want it. Depending on the type of page, there might be several web part zones you can add web parts to, or you might have the option to add a web part to a text control in the page. An app part is the same as a web part, and the act of adding an app part is almost exactly the same as adding a web part, but you see slightly different options. The following section concentrates on adding a web part, but the process is similar for adding an app part.

Add a Web Part to a Text Editor Control

To add a web part as part of the text in a text editor control, place your cursor in the location where you want the web part to be and switch to the Insert tab of the Editing Tools ribbon. (See "Edit the Contents of a Page," earlier in this chapter, for instructions on how to do so.) In this ribbon, click the Web Part button to open a new pane under the ribbon that allows you to select the web part you want to add (see Figure 9.33).

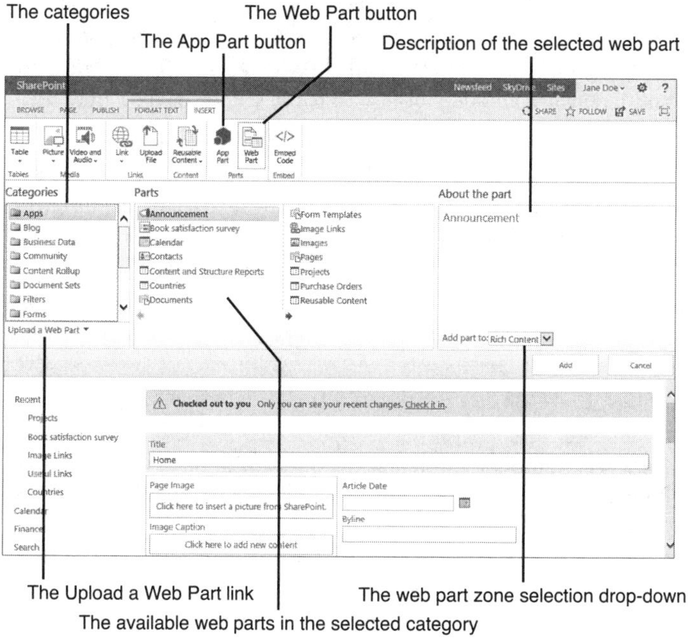

FIGURE 9.33   The Web Part selection pane.

For more information about how to use this pane and how to find the web part you want, see "Choose a Web Part," later in this chapter.

Add a Web Part to a Web Part Zone

Pages that have web part zones show them on the page as a rectangle, with the zone name above the top-left corner of the rectangle. If a web part zone is empty, the zone has another rectangle inside the zone with a link that says Add a Web Part. If the zone already has one or more web parts in it, the Add a Web Part link appears above the existing web parts.

Choose a Web Part

The web part selection pane allows you to find the web part you want, based on the web part's category (shown on the left of the pane) and the list of available web parts in the middle of the pane. When you click one of the web parts, you see the web part's description on the right side of the pane (refer to Figure 9.33). If you click the App Part button (refer to Figure 9.33), you get a similar interface, but without the Categories section, and only the list view app parts in the Parts section.

The pane shows all the web parts available in the current site. Some sites offer different web parts than others. You can browse the categories by clicking on them, and the choices in the middle of the pane change to reflect the category you clicked.

The first category, Lists and Libraries, shows all the lists and libraries that exist in the current site. If you want to add a view of one of those lists or libraries, you can select the list or library from the list of web parts. This kind of web part is known as the Use the List View Web Part or App part, and you can find more information about it later in this chapter, in the section "Use the App Part (List View) Web Part." For more information on some of the other commonly used web parts, see the next section.

To add the web part you selected to the page, click the Add button in the pane. SharePoint adds the web part to the location you chose when you started the process. If you want to add it to a different location, open the drop-down box with the different zones under the About the Web Part section of the pane. For information about changing the location of a web part or its settings, see "Modify a Web Part," later in this chapter.

Use Built-in Web Parts

Scenario/Problem: When authoring or editing a page, you want to add different content to different sections of the page.

Solution: The following sections explain some of the choices you have when adding a web part to a page. Although you can choose from many more web parts, the ones described here are the most common ones.

Use the App Part (List View) Web Part

You can add a list view web part to a page in two ways. The first is to click the App Part button instead of the Web Part button in the Insert ribbon. The second is to select the Lists and Libraries category in the web part selection pane. Both options show you the list of all the lists and libraries available in the current site as web parts. The only difference is that clicking the Existing List button hides the categories, showing you only the web parts that belong to the Lists and Libraries category.

By selecting one of the lists or libraries and adding it to the page, you actually add a List View web part to the page. After you add the web part to the page, the page displays the items in the list or library that you selected. What view is displayed by default depends on the type of list.

If you want to change what information is displayed, you can do this by using the same method you use to edit a view in a list or library. To edit the view the web part is displaying, you hover over the web part with your mouse. Doing this exposes a check box that allows you to select the web part in the web part's title row. When you check the check box, you see the List Tools ribbon or Library Tools ribbon, with the List or Library tab available. To modify the view shown in the web part, you follow the same instructions as in "Modify a View" in Chapter 8, "Creating List Views."

NOTE The view you will be modifying does not exist in the list but instead is configured in the web part. So even if it looks like you are editing the default view of the list itself, you needn't worry: You are only modifying the view of the web part and not the view used in the list.

In addition to changing the view, you can configure additional settings for the web part, using the web part's settings pane. For more information about how to modify a web part and get to its settings pane, see "Modify a Web Part," later in this chapter.

When you're viewing the editing pane for a list view web part, you can select from the list of views that were created for the list or library different views for the web part. You can also create a view just for the web part by clicking the Edit the Current View link if you want the web part to display a view that was not created in the list or library.

You can also select the toolbar type for the web part. This setting defines whether the web part displays a summary toolbar (that is, a link at the bottom for adding a new item to the list or creating a new document in the library), no toolbar, or a full toolbar as shown in Figure 9.34. A full toolbar is used only for picture libraries and surveys because they do not have ribbons.

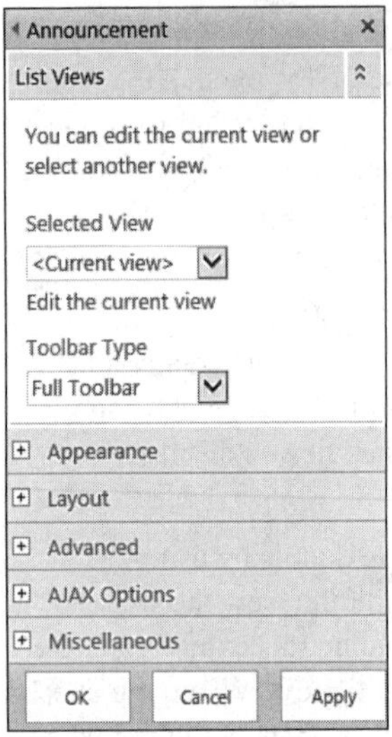

FIGURE 9.34   The List View web part's settings pane.

Use the Content Editor Web Part

You can type any kind of text in a Content Editor web part, including scripts. To add a Content Editor web part to a page, switch the web part selection pane to the Media and Content category and select the Content Editor web part from the list of web parts.

After you add the web part, it does not appear with any text. Instead, you see an instruction telling you that you need to add text (content) to the web part by opening the tool ribbons for the web part. To do so, click the link in the text. The web part switches into text editing mode, exposing the Editing Tools ribbon, with the Format Text and Insert tabs (see the section "Use the Text Editing Control in a Page," earlier in this chapter).

However, unlike the text editing control, the content editor web part does not support inserting some types of content, such as web parts and video and audio. If in the future you would like to change the text, you can. See "Modify a Web Part," later in this chapter, for details.

Use the Image Viewer Web Part

The Image Viewer web part enables you to display just an image. To add an Image web part, select it from the list of available web parts under the Media and Content category.

When you add the web part to the page, it doesn't have any image set. Instead, it offers instructions on how to specify the image: by clicking the Open the Tool Pane link. If you need to change the image later, you can, as described in the section "Modify a Web Part," later in this chapter.

When the tool pane is open, you can specify the link to the image that should be displayed, as well as some settings for how it will be displayed (see Figure 9.35).

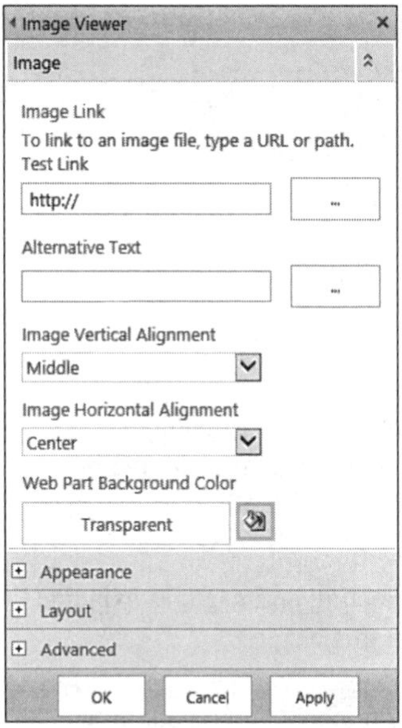

FIGURE 9.35   The tool pane for the Image Viewer web part.

The first setting is the link to the image. You just type (or paste) the link into the Image Link box, and then click the Test Link hyperlink above the box to make sure the link you typed is correct and points to the correct picture. If the link is fine, the picture opens in a new window, which you can then close.

In the Alternative Text box, type the text that you want to appear in the web part if the user who is browsing the site is using a browser that doesn't support images or has that option turned off. This text is also displayed when the user hovers the mouse cursor over the picture.

Use the Media Web Part in SharePoint Server

You use the Media web part to either display a video or play an audio file in a page. You can find the Media web part under the Media and Content category in the web part selection pane. After you add the Media web part to a page, the web part is shown with an empty space in it, as shown in Figure 9.36.

NOTE   This web part uses Silverlight to play the audio and video and also to configure itself. If you don't have Silverlight installed, the link to configure might not work.

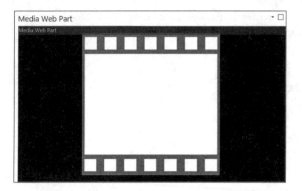

FIGURE 9.36   An empty media web part.

When you click on the web part the Media ribbon appears. On this ribbon, you can select the media file by opening the drop-down menu under the Change Media button and set different options for the media itself, such as whether it should start automatically and how it should look.

Selecting a media file (audio or video) is the same as selecting an image, as explained in "Use the Picture Editing Control in a Page," earlier in this chapter.

> **TIP**   Media files, especially video files, are often big. You should take note of the size of a file before uploading it. If it is bigger than the size allowed by the system administrator, SharePoint prevents you from uploading it. If you need to be able to upload a large file and are unable to, you should contact your site administrator and ask for a bigger size quota.

When a file is selected, the web part allows users to click Play. Or, if you chose the option to start the media automatically in the Options ribbon (see Figure 9.37), it starts playing the file each time the page opens.

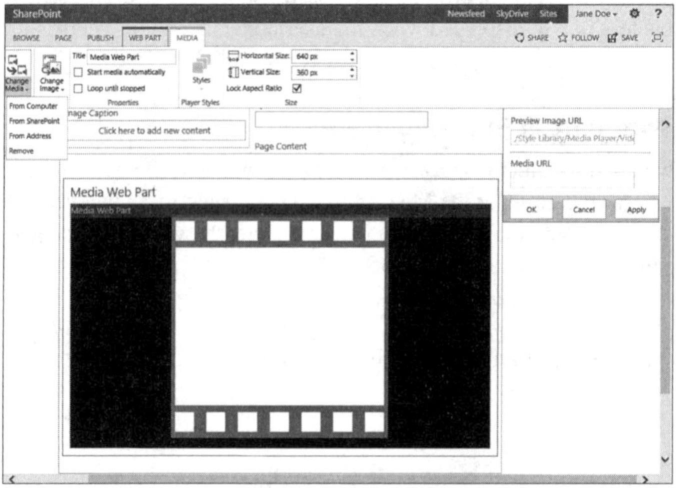

FIGURE 9.37   The Media web part's Media ribbon.

Use the Content Query Web Part in SharePoint Server

The Content Query web part is one of the most useful web parts. You use it to display information in the current site or in other sites in the current site collection, based on a query. For example, if you want to show an aggregation of all the announcements from all the sites, this web part does it. It is a quite complex web part with a lot of options (some of which a developer must configure), but most of them are easy to set up, as shown here. The Content Query web part is available only in publishing sites and is not available in sites that are not at least under a root publishing site.

You find the Content Query web part under the Content Rollup category in the web part selection pane. After it is added, this web part displays a link to open the web part's tool pane to configure the query it should perform.

To modify the query that the web part performs and display a different kind of content, click the link to open the tool pane for the web part (see Figure 9.38).

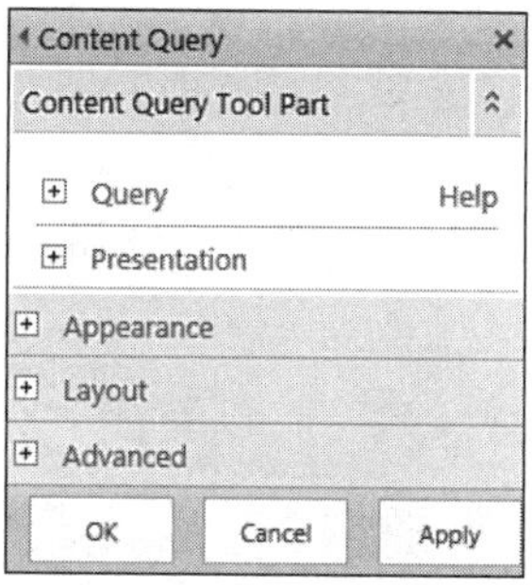

FIGURE 9.38   The tool pane for the Content Query web part.

In the tool pane, expand the Query section to see the options to specify what content should be displayed and from where (see Figure 9.39).

You can specify whether the query will be on all sites in the site collection, on a specific site and its subsites, or on just a specific list. For the last two options, use the Browse button to open a dialog that enables you to select the site or list in question (see Figure 9.40). Click OK to return to the Content Query web part tool pane.

In the List Type selection box, you can define what kind of list type the web part should look in for its content. This includes document libraries, pages libraries, picture libraries, and all other list templates.

The Content Type section enables you to select what content types the web part will limit its query to. If you don't want to specify a content type, you can leave it at the default All Content Types. Otherwise, you can limit it to a group of content types (for example, all the document content types) and to a specific content type. To do that, select the content type group (for example, document content types) and then either select All Content Types in the second drop-down menu or select the specific content type that you want.

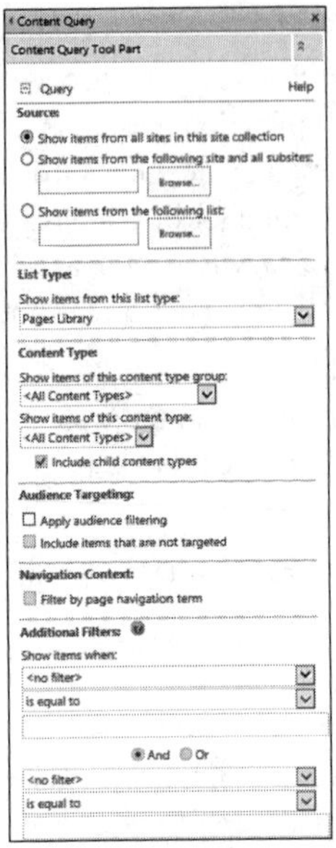

FIGURE 9.39   The Query section of the content query web part tool pane.

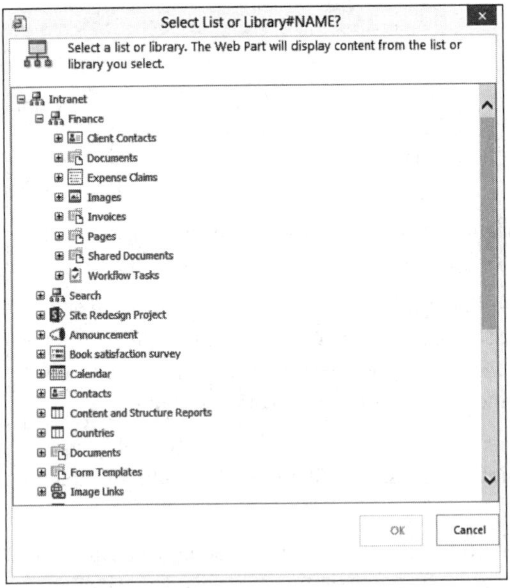

FIGURE 9.40   Selecting a list for the Content Query web part.

Next, you can set the filters (see Figure 9.41). You can specify that the web part will display only list items or documents that have specific values in specific columns by setting up to three filters on the web part. To do so, scroll down in the tool pane to the Filters section, and under Show Items When, you select the column you want, the kind of filter you want, and the value to filter on. For example, select Company Is Equal to AdventureWorks or Article Date Is Equal to Today.

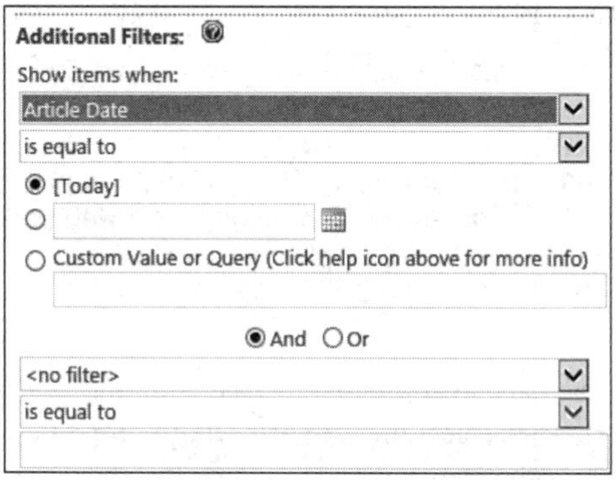

FIGURE 9.41   The Filter section in the Content Query web part, with a filter specified on Article Date Is Equal to Today.

In addition to configuring the query itself, you can modify how the items will be displayed by expanding the Presentation section of the pane. You can specify how many items should be displayed; how they should be sorted, grouped, or styled; and which columns to display (see Figure 9.42).

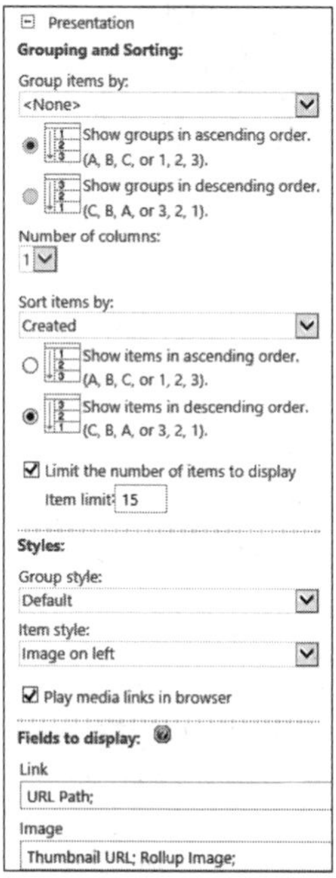

FIGURE 9.42   The Presentation section in the Content Query web part.

Modify a Web Part

Scenario/Problem: When editing a page, you want to change the settings for existing web parts on that page.

Solution: The following sections explain how to get a web part into editing mode. These sections discuss some of the common settings you can modify for a web part in each mode, such as modifying the web part's title, its display settings, and the web part's position on the page.

To modify a web part of any kind, switch the page to editing mode (see "Edit the Contents of a Page," earlier in this chapter). Then select the web part whose properties you want to edit by hovering your mouse over the web part and selecting the check box that appears at the top-right corner of the web part (on the title row). Doing so should reveal the Web Part ribbon, as shown in Figure 9.43.

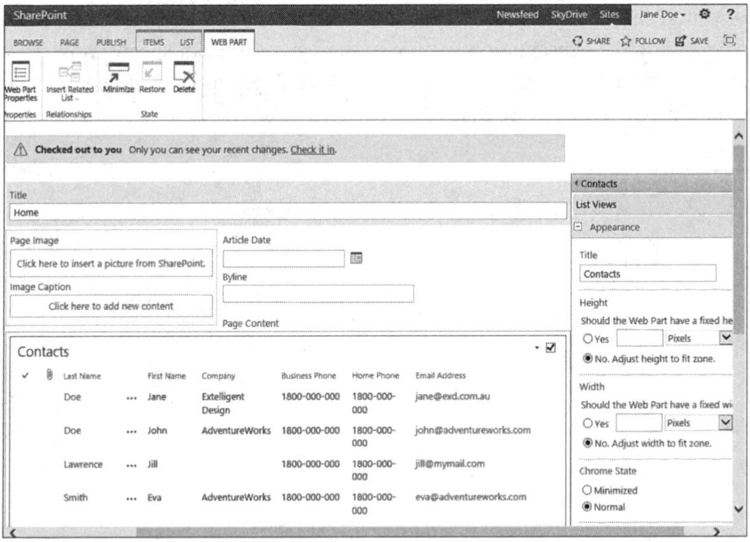

FIGURE 9.43   The Web Part ribbon and a web part's properties pane with the Appearance section expanded.

This tab has the Web Part Properties button at the top left. Clicking this button opens the tool pane for the web part. Different web parts have different tool panes with different settings, but all of them have some basic settings that you can modify.

TIP   Another way to get to the web part's properties pane is to open the web part's drop-down menu, as described in the section "Reuse a Web Part (Export/Import)," later in this chapter.

Modify a Web Part's Title

To modify a web part's title, expand the Appearance section in the web part's tool pane (refer to Figure 9.43). The first option in the Appearance section is the title of the web part. Simply type in the title you want and click OK to save it.

Modify a Web Part's Title Bar and Border Settings

To modify whether a web part displays the title bar and whether it displays a border line around its contents, expand the Appearance section in the web part's tool pane and scroll down to the Chrome Type selection (refer to Figure 9.43).

Chrome Type can be set to one of these options:

▶ **None**—The web part does not display a title bar or border. This is typical for Image Viewer web parts, where you want the picture to appear without a title bar above it and without a border around it, as if it is part of the page and not in a web part (see Figure 9.44).

FIGURE 9.44   The Image web part with the None chrome type.

▶ **Title and Border**—The web part displays the title bar and a border around the content (see Figure 9.45).

Dog in the grass

FIGURE 9.45   The Image web part with the Title and Border chrome type.

▶ **Title Only**—The web part displays the title bar without a border around the content (see Figure 9.46).

Dog in the grass

FIGURE 9.46   The Image web part with the Title Only chrome type.

▶ **Border Only**—The web part does not display the title bar but does display a
border around the content (see Figure 9.47).

FIGURE 9.47   The Image web part with the Border Only chrome type.

Modify or Remove the Link for the Web Part's Title

In some web parts, you want the title to be a link that the users can click. To set that
link or remove it (some web parts have a link by default), expand the Advanced section
in the web part's tool pane and scroll down to the Title URL box. In this box, type the
link that you want for the web part's title or clear the box to remove the link.

Move a Web Part in a Page

To move an existing web part in a page, switch the page to editing mode (see "Edit the
Content of a Page" earlier in this chapter), and then just drag and drop the title of the
web part to the location where you want it to appear. To do so, just hover the mouse
cursor over the web part's title; then hold down the left mouse button and, without
releasing it, move the mouse cursor to the place where you want the title—either in
the same web part zone or in another, or to a different location in the text (if you are
editing the contents of a publishing page or a wiki page).

The location of your mouse cursor is displayed by the title of the web part you are
moving. When you are hovering the mouse cursor over a web part zone, the place in
that zone where the web part will be added is signified by a bold line above, below, or
between the existing web parts already in that zone (see Figure 9.48). When you have
the mouse cursor where you want the web part to be, you release the mouse button.

TIP You cannot drag and drop a web part in a text area in a wiki page except to another location within the text in that area. To move a web part to another text area in the same page, you will need to export and import the web part (see "Reuse a Web Part (Export/Import)," later in this chapter).

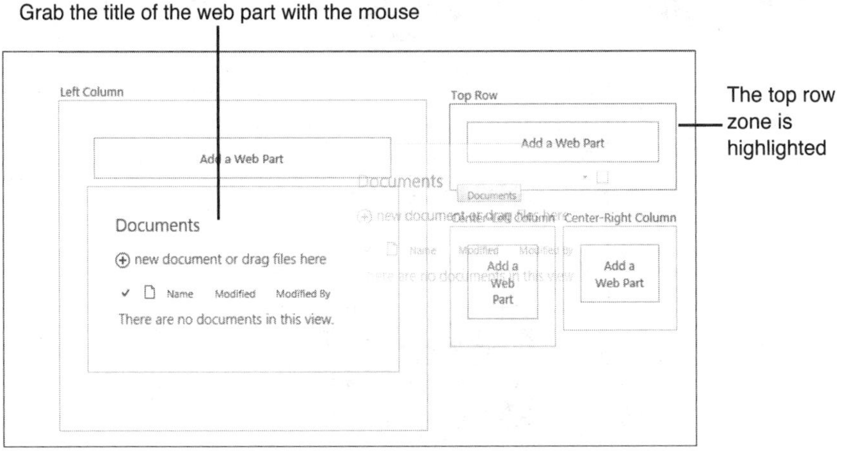

Grab the title of the web part with the mouse

FIGURE 9.48   Dragging and dropping the Documents web part to the Top Row zone.

Reuse a Web Part (Export/Import)

Scenario/Problem: After you have configured a web part to your liking, you want to save that web part and use it again in another page with similar settings.

Solution: To save the web part and use it again, you must export the web part and then import it to the other page. The following sections explain how to export a web part and then import it to another page.

Export a Web Part

Exporting a web part involves saving the web part's settings as a file to your computer. Not all web parts support this option, and in some web parts, the owner of the page might choose to disable this option. In those cases, you should look in the options in that web part's properties tool pane (see "Modify a Web Part," earlier in this chapter) to see whether the option to allow the web part to be exported is enabled. (Not all web parts have this option; some web parts cannot be exported.)

To export a web part that allows exporting, switch the page that has the web part to editing mode (see "Edit the Contents of a Page," earlier in this chapter) and then hover your mouse over the web part's title row. Doing so exposes a small black triangle on the right corner of the title row. Click this triangle and expose the web part's drop-down menu, shown in Figure 9.49. If the web part allows exporting, the Export option appears on the menu.

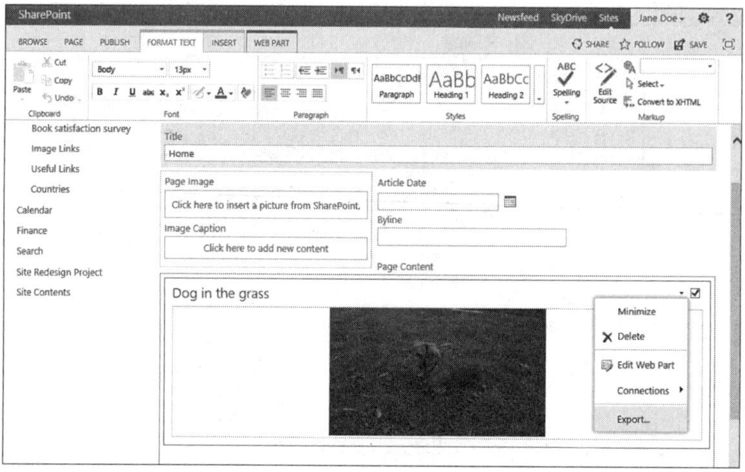

FIGURE 9.49   The web part's drop-down menu.

After you select the Export option, a File Download dialog appears, allowing you to save the web part to your computer. You can save the file anywhere on your computer so that you can import it later (see the following section).

Import a Web Part

To import a web part that you have previously saved to your computer, open the page in editing mode (see "Edit the Contents of a Page," earlier in this chapter) and click the web part zone where you want the web part to be added, as if you were adding a new web part. However, when the dialog with the list of web parts appears, instead of selecting a web part from the list, click the Upload a Web Part link shown under the Categories box (refer to Figure 9.33). When you click this link, you see a button to browse and a button to upload the file you have exported, as shown in Figure 9.50.

After the web part is uploaded, it is added to the Imported Web Parts category in the web part selection pane. To add it to the page, simply follow the instructions from the section "Add a Web Part or an App," earlier in this chapter, and select the Imported Web Parts category to find the web part you have uploaded.

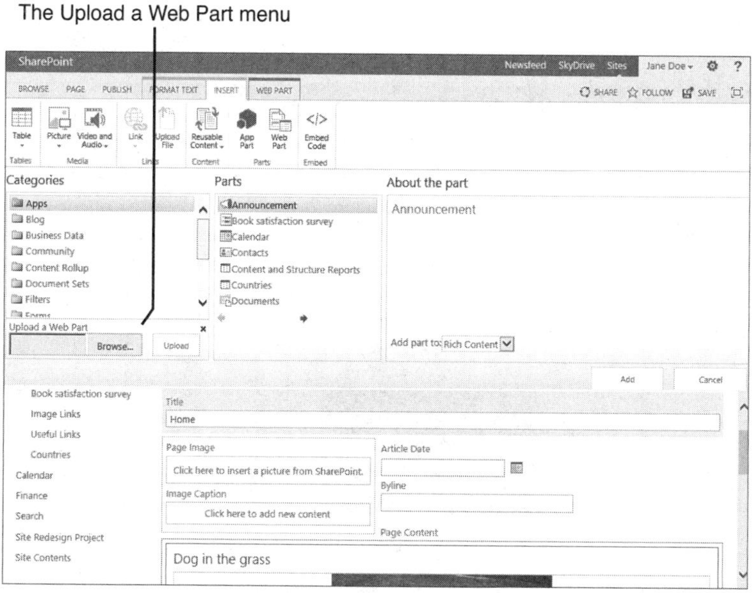

The Upload a Web Part menu

FIGURE 9.50   The Upload a Web Part menu appears under the list of categories.

Publish a Page

Scenario/Problem: When a page is located in a document library that requires publishing—something that is common when you're using the publishing features (where all pages in a site are in the Pages library)—you must publish the page in order for users to be able to see it.

Solution: Publishing can be accomplished from the document library itself, just like publishing any other file that is in a document library (see "Check In and Check Out a File or List Item" in Chapter 6). You check in the page and then publish it, going through any approval process that might be required. (Again, refer to Chapter 6 for more information about the publishing and approval process.)

However, publishing pages is different from publishing regular files in that you can publish pages directly from the pages themselves. When you are editing a page that requires publishing, a Publish ribbon appears, with buttons designed to assist you in publishing the page (see Figure 9.51). If the library where the page is located does not require approval, simply click the Publish button to publish the page for everyone to see.

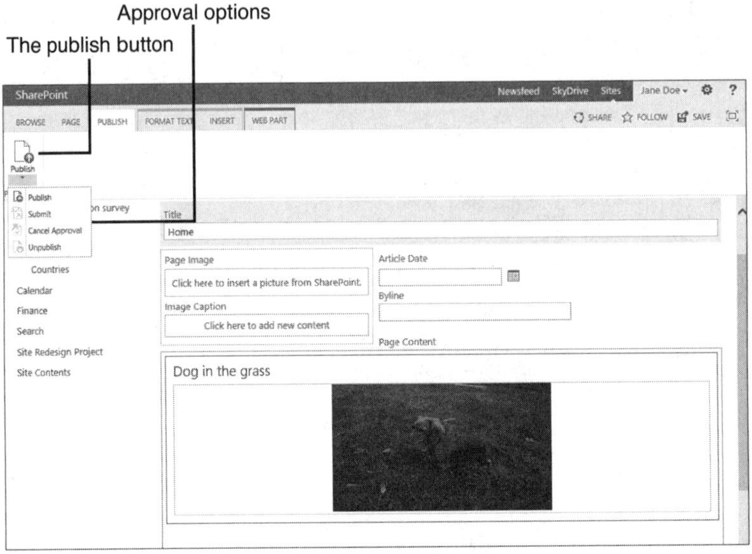

FIGURE 9.51 The Publish ribbon with only the Publish button available if approval is not required.

However, if the library requires approval before publishing, you see the Submit button instead, as shown in Figure 9.52.

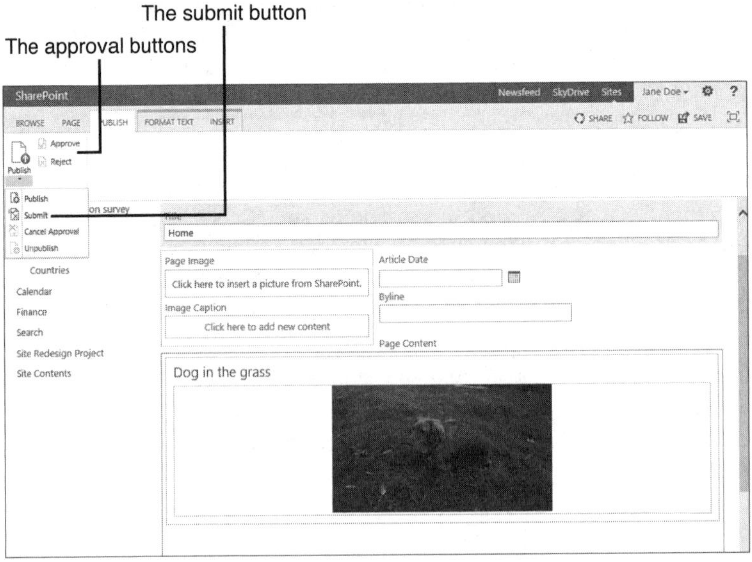

FIGURE 9.52 The Submit button is available if approval is required.

When you submit for approval, most users are not able to see your changes, but the people who have permissions to approve items in the document library can view your changes and approve or reject them. If an approver approves the page, it is published for other users to view. Approvers who navigate to the page can also use the Publish ribbon to approve or reject the page from the page itself, as shown in Figure 9.52.

Discard the Check-out of a Page

Scenario/Problem: Often you start editing a page and then either change your mind or regret a change and want to roll back and start again.

Solution: To start over, just discard the check-out of the page. This section explains how to accomplish that.

The option to discard a check-out is available only when the page is in a document library that tracks versions and requires a check-out, such as in publishing websites. Pages that are not in such document libraries do not give you the option, and any change you make is saved; therefore, you must manually roll it back.

To discard the check-out of a page, use the built-in Discard Check Out option for that page from the library view, exactly as you would discard a check-out of a file in a document library (see "Check In and Check Out a File or List Item" in Chapter 6). However, an easier and more accessible way to discard the check-out of the page is through the Page ribbon. In the Page ribbon, open the drop-down menu under the Check In button, and then select the Discard Check Out option, as shown in Figure 9.53.

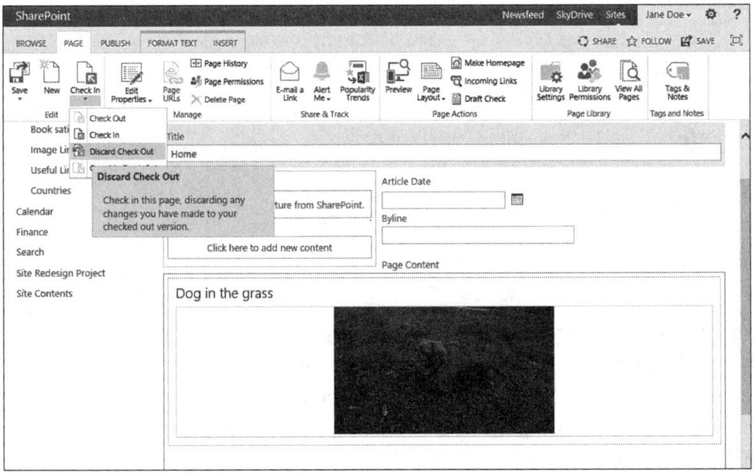

FIGURE 9.53   Use the Page menu to get to the Discard Check Out option.

Compare Versions of a Page

Scenario/Problem: Often you want to restore a page to a previous state (before some changes were made to the page), but you want to compare differences between the versions before making up your mind about which one to restore.

Solution: Pages that reside in a document library that supports versioning enable you to restore previous versions of the pages, just like any other files in document libraries that support versioning. However, with pages, you also get the option to view the changes that were made to them between each version and compare them.

NOTE   Page changes that are tracked by versioning include changes to add and remove web parts and edit content in the page's editing controls, such as the text editing control and image editing control. However, changes made to the contents in the web parts on the page do not count as part of the page's contents and are not restored when you restore a previous version. They are also not shown in the comparison of versions.

To compare the changes between versions of a page, switch to the page's Page ribbon and click the Page History button in the ribbon.

The page that opens shows the changes made in each version. The list of versions is in the left pane, and the current text with change tracking is in the right pane (see Figure 9.54).

FIGURE 9.54   The version comparison screen.

When a change is made to a piece of content in the page (for example, the text in a text editing control on the page), the section in the version comparison page shows the old value and the new value, indicating what editing was done (refer to Figure 9.54). Text that was deleted appears with strikethrough. If you wrote over a piece of text, the new text is shown after the old text as was shown in Figure 9.54.

You can browse the other versions of the page by clicking the version date and time on the left. You can delete or restore the version by using the toolbar in the page.

CHAPTER 10

Managing Security

If you are in charge of managing a list or library, you should learn how to manage the security on either the list or library or on the single items in them. This chapter covers some basic tasks related to security of lists, libraries, and list items.

See What Permissions Are Set

Scenario/Problem: You want to see what permissions are given to whom in a list or library or on a specific list item. For example, you want to know who can read, write, or delete files in a document library. Alternatively, you want to know who has permissions to read a specific document or to edit it.

Solution: The following sections explain how to check what permissions are defined for files, list items, document libraries, and lists.

Check Permissions on Files and List Items

To check what permissions are set on a file or list item, you must have the right to manage permissions on the file or item. If you don't have the appropriate permissions, the option to manage them is not available.

To view the permissions on a file in a document library or a list item in a list, select the file or item's row, switch to the Files ribbon or the Items ribbon, and then click the Shared With button, as shown in Figure 10.1.

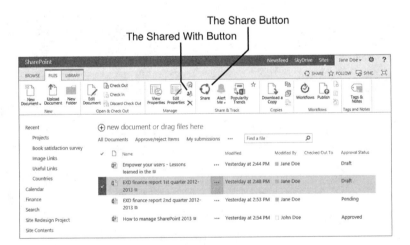

FIGURE 10.1   The Shared With button in the Files ribbon is available only when you have the required permissions on the file or item.

Clicking the Shared With button opens a page that shows the permissions for the file or item you're looking at (see Figure 10.2). On this page, you cannot see what type of permissions each user or group of users has on the file or item. To view this, click the Advanced link on the page to see the permissions page. This page is explained later in this chapter, in the section, "Read the Permissions Page."

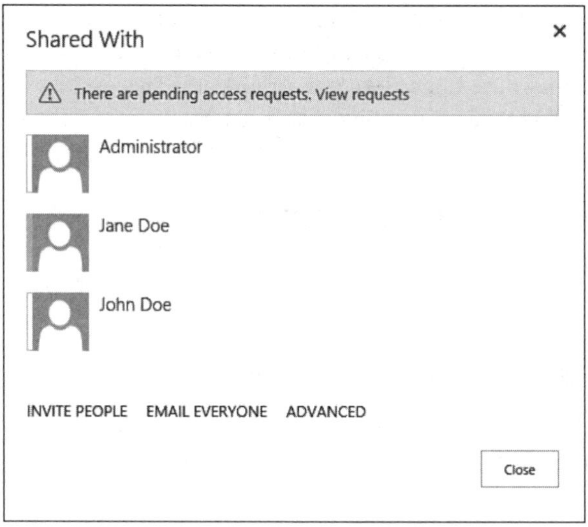

FIGURE 10.2   The Shared With dialog shows who has permissions to view the file or item.

Check Permissions on Lists and Libraries

To be able to check what permissions are set on a list or library, you must have the permissions to manage the list or library. If you do not have the appropriate permissions, the button to manage permissions is not available. To manage the permissions on a list, switch to the Library or List ribbon and click the Shared With button in the Settings section. The page that opens is the same as the one for a document or a list items (refer to Figure 10.2 and see the following section).

Read the Permissions Page

By clicking the Advanced link from the Shared With dialog, you get to the permissions page for either a file, item, list, or library. This page is used to administrate the permissions of the object in question.

In the Browse ribbon of the page, if you are managing the permissions of a list item or file; the name of the file or title for the item is shown before the word *Permissions*. This information helps you make sure you are viewing the permissions for the right file or item. If the permissions page is for a list or library, the Browse ribbon shows a link to the Settings page of that list or library instead.

In the main section of the page, the name of the user or group is in the first column, and the type (identifying whether it is a user or group) is in the second column. In the last column, you can see the permission set that the user or group has on the item, file, list, or library. Depending on the configuration of your server, other columns with more information about the user or group might also appear.

For example, in Figure 10.3, people in the SharePoint Team Site Visitors group can only read the file or item because they have only the Read permission, whereas SharePoint Team Site Owners can do everything to the file or item (including manage the permissions on it, delete it, and so on) because they have the Full Control permission set. Some accounts may have Limited Access permissions. This type of permission can mean different things in different sites but usually means read-only permission.

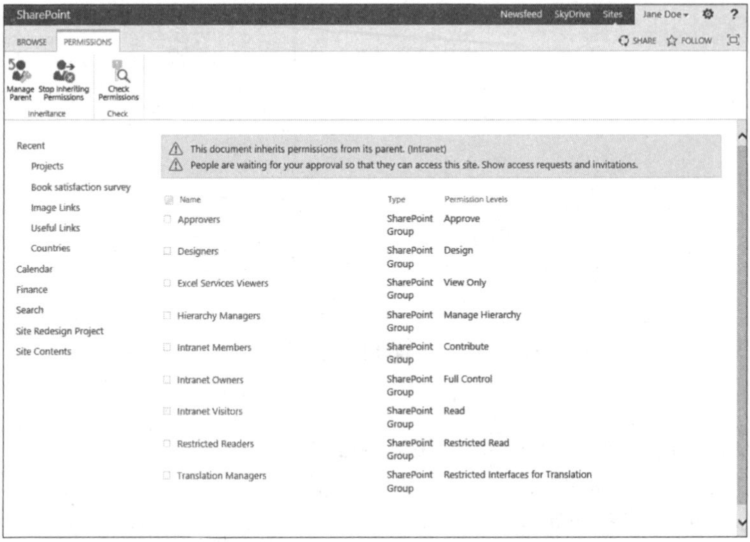

FIGURE 10.3   The advanced Permissions management page.

It is important to note that if permissions are given to a group and then separately to a user, if that user is a member of the group, the higher permission level wins. For example, suppose user A is a member of group B, and group B has Full Control permissions on an item. Although user A was given just Read access, because user A is a member of group B, that user also has full control of the item and not just Read access. The same would apply if the situation were reversed: If user A has Full Access and that user is a member of group B, which has Read-Only access, the user still has full access to the item.

Check the Permissions for a Specific User or Group

The Permissions ribbon, shown in Figure 10.3, has buttons for managing the permissions of the parent (if the file or item is inheriting from a parent), to stop inheriting permissions, and to check permissions. Clicking on the Check Permissions button opens a dialog that allows you to check what permission levels a certain user or group has on the file, item, list, or library, as shown in Figure 10.4.

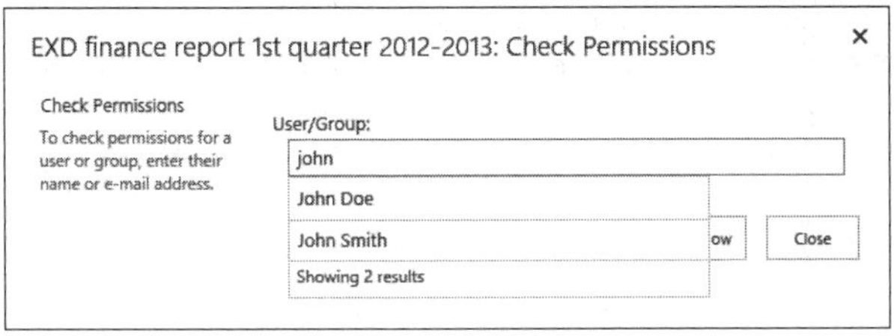

FIGURE 10.4   The Check Permissions dialog. Typing part of a name shows a list of possible users.

To use the dialog, simply type the user name or group name in the User/Group box and click the Check Now button. The dialog then shows you what permission levels that person or group has on the file, item, list, or library, as shown in Figure 10.5.

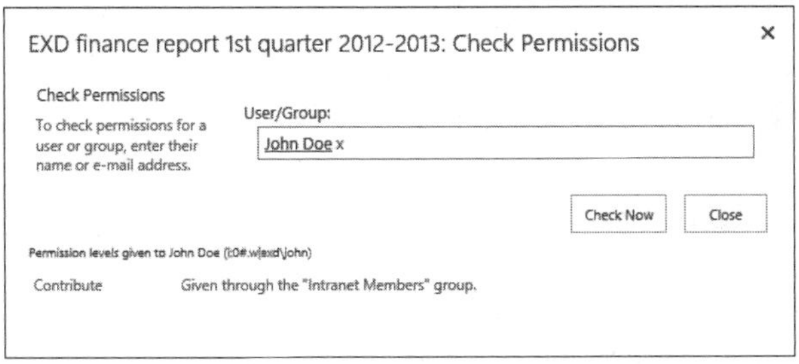

FIGURE 10.5   The Check Permissions dialog, showing what permissions John Doe has on a document.

NOTE   For more information about groups, see the section "See Who Is a Member of a SharePoint Group," later in this chapter.

Grant Permissions to a File or List Item

Scenario/Problem: You want to change the permissions a certain user or group of users has on a file or list item. Because permissions for items are inherited from the list or library they are in, the items or files have the same permissions as the list. Sometimes you want to set different permissions on documents or items than for the list. For example, say you want to upload a document to share with several colleagues but not with other people who have access to the document library.

Solution: To assign permissions on a file or list item, you can either use the Invite People button in the Shared With dialog (refer to Figure 10.2), the Share button in the Files or Items ribbon (refer to Figure 10.1), or the manage permissions page of that file or list item (refer to Figure 10.3). The first two methods use the Invite concept to invite people to the item or document. This mechanism is a quick way to grant permissions to files or items, but it is also limited in the fact that you can only grant permissions to view or edit, but no more. For more specific permissions levels, use the third option as described later in "Using the Permissions Page."

Using the Share Option

To grant permissions to a file or item using the Share button, choose the file or item and, in the Files or Items ribbon click the Share button. A Share dialog box opens, as shown in Figure 10.6.

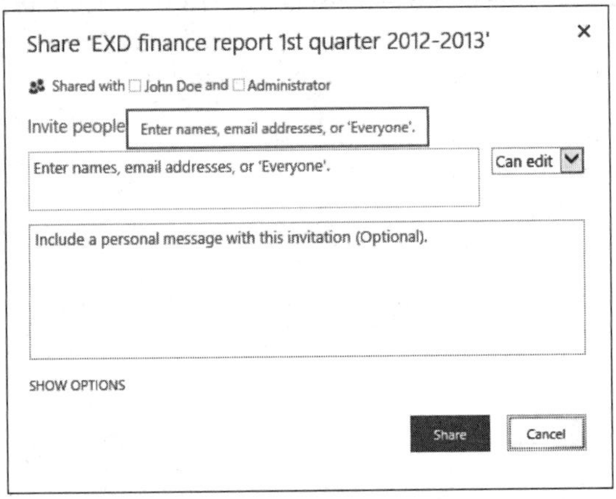

Share 'EXD finance report 1st quarter 2012-2013'   ×

Shared with ☐ John Doe and ☐ Administrator

Invite people   Enter names, email addresses, or 'Everyone'.

Enter names, email addresses, or 'Everyone'.   Can edit ☑

Include a personal message with this invitation (Optional).

SHOW OPTIONS

Share   Cancel

FIGURE 10.6   The Share document dialog box.

In this dialog you can specify one or more people in the text box titled Invite People, and choose what level of permissions they should have via the drop-down menu (either Can Edit or Can View). You can also include a message that would be sent as an email to the people you specified. If you don't want an email to be sent, click on the Show Options link at the bottom of the dialog and select or clear the option to send the email.

Using the Invite People Link

In the Shared With dialog, click the Invite People link at the bottom to redirect to the same Share dialog as described in the previous section (refer to Figure 10.6).

Using the Permissions Page

When you're on the manage permissions page for the file or item, you might be able to immediately change permissions, or you might have to first disconnect the permission inheritance for that file or item. Permission inheritance is on by default for all files or items in SharePoint. It means that the file or item inherits its permissions from the list or library in which it is located and has exactly the same permission sets. If the permissions for the list or library change, the permissions for the file or item are updated automatically.

NOTE   If a file or an item is inheriting permissions from its list or library, which in turn is inheriting permissions from the site (which in turn might be inheriting from its parent site), the permission management page (refer to Figure 10.3) shows a yellow bar above the list of permissions. This bar says that the file or item is inheriting from a parent and displays a link to where you can manage the permissions—at the level of the list, library, site, or parent site.

While inheritance is active, setting a different permission level on a file or an item is not possible (refer to Figure 10.3). To stop a file or an item from inheriting permissions, click the Stop Inheriting Permissions button in the Permission Tools ribbon.

If you want to change the permissions for the parent—whether it's a list, library, or site—you can click the Manage Parent button in the ribbon or click the link to the parent in the yellow bar shown in Figure 10.3.

For more information about managing permissions on lists and libraries, see "Change a User's Permissions on a List or Library," later in this chapter. For information about managing permissions for sites, see Chapter 14, "Managing Site Security."

After you click the Stop Inheriting Permissions button, a prompt appears, asking you to confirm that you want to disconnect the permissions inheritance from the list or library. The prompt also explains that after you do so, changes to the permissions of the list and library will not affect the file or item you are managing. This means, for example, that if a certain user is granted permissions to edit files or items in the list or library after you disconnect the inheritance of permissions, that user still can't edit the specific list item or file that you managed unless you (or someone else) explicitly give that user the permissions to edit that document.

If you are sure that you want to manage the permissions for a file separately from the permission of the list or library, click OK. The page changes and allows you to manage the permissions for the file or item.

If the file's or item's permission inheritance was already disconnected in the past, by you or by someone else, you see the screen shown in Figure 10.7 when you click Manage Permissions for the file or list item. You can change your mind and switch the file or item back to inherit permission using the Delete Unique Permissions button on the ribbon.

Now you can manage the permissions on the file or item. To add permission to a user or group that doesn't already have permissions, click the Grant Permissions button in the Permissions tools ribbon. This opens the Grant Permission dialog, which enables you to select either a user or group and select what permission levels should be given. Although this dialog is similar to the dialog used by the Invite mechanism (refer to Figure 10.6), the additional options under the More Options enable you to specify a more specific permission level, as shown in Figure 10.8.

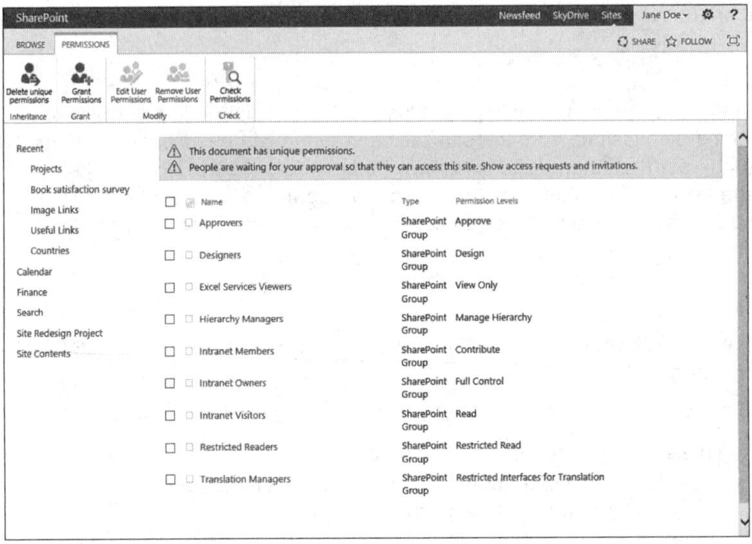

FIGURE 10.7   The edit permissions page for a list item or file when permission inheritance is disconnected.

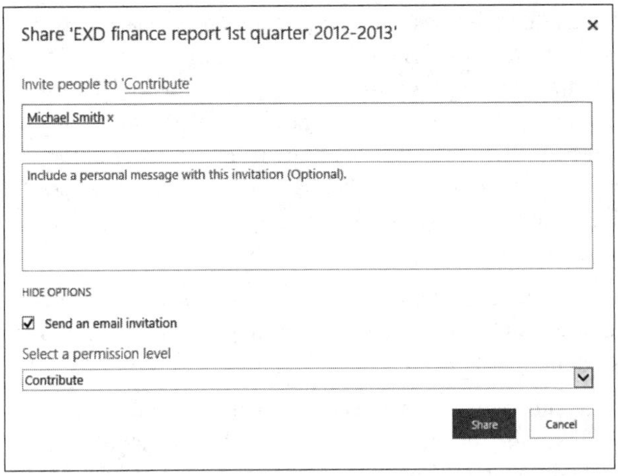

FIGURE 10.8   Granting permissions to a new user or group.

In the Select Users section, type the name (or part of a name) or e-mail address for the user or group that you want to add. Or click the address book icon to open the people search dialog, where you can search for people by typing a name or part of a name. You can add more than one user or group at a time by separating the names with semi-colons. This is similar to when you are writing an e-mail message in Microsoft Outlook and you choose who you want to send the e-mail to.

As you type the person's name or email address, SharePoint will show you a list of possible names to select from. If there is no exact match for the name you entered and you try to click the Share button, a red underline appears beneath the name (see Figure 10.9). You can then click the name to open a menu that shows users who are a close match to that name or select to remove the name. For example, typing "Joh" and clicking the Check Name icon causes a red line to appear under the name "Joh." When you click it, you see that there is a user called John Doe. If this is the user you're looking for, click the name. If not, you can click the "x" link next to the name to delete John from the text box.

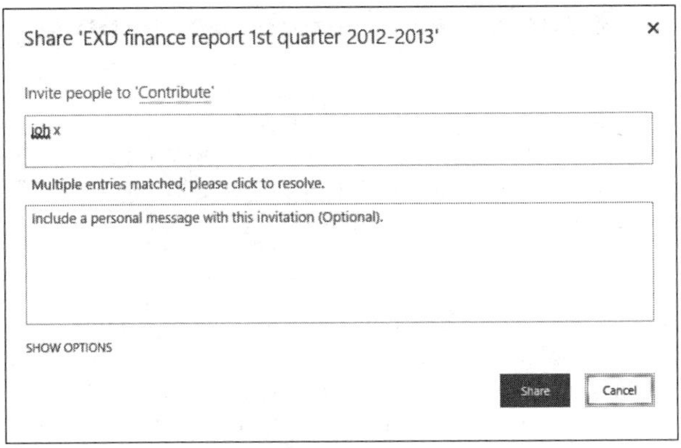

FIGURE 10.9   Typing part of a name in the text box.

To specify more than one person, simply continue typing after selecting the first one.

After you have selected all the users and/or groups that you want to add to the list, select the permissions they should have by clicking Show Options and selecting a permission level from the list of permissions, as shown in Figure 10.10. Selecting options here gives the users the permissions you selected.

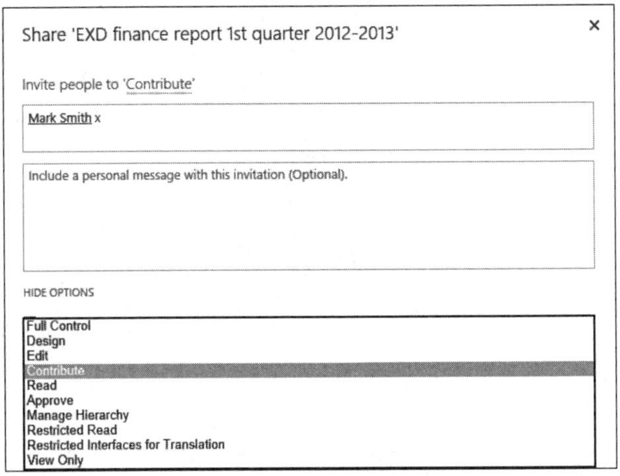

FIGURE 10.10   Selecting a specific permission level.

Similarly to the Invite dialog, if the server hosting the SharePoint site supports sending e-mail messages, another option appears, allowing you to send e-mail to the users to tell them that they have permissions on the file or item (refer to Figure 10.8). You have the option to select not to send the e-mail, or if you select to send it, you can change the title and body of the message.

When you are done selecting all the options, click OK to save the new permissions.

Change a User's or Group's Permissions on a File or List Item

Scenario/Problem: You want to change an existing permission that was granted to a user or group on a file or list item—perhaps to give that user more permissions or remove that user's permissions altogether.

Solution: To change permissions on a file or an item, open the manage permissions page for that file or item and select the name (or names) of the user or group for which you want to change the permissions. Then click the Edit User Permissions button in the Modify section of the Permissions tools ribbon. The Edit Permissions dialog appears, enabling you to select permissions for that user or group (see Figure 10.11).

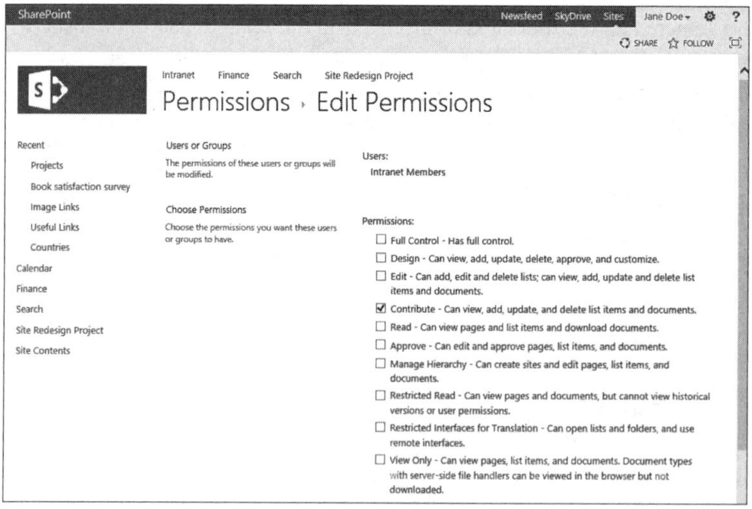

FIGURE 10.11   Changing a user's or group's permissions.

In the Edit Permissions dialog, you can select one or more permission levels. For example, if you select Contribute and Approve, the user will be able to both edit the document or list item and approve it but will not be able to set the permission on the file or item. When you are done selecting permissions, click OK.

Grant Permissions on a List or Library

Scenario/Problem: You want to change the permissions on a list or library. For example, you want to add a user to the list or library as a reader or as an author.

Solution: To assign permissions on a list or document library, you need to get to the manage permissions page of that list or document library (see "Check Permissions on Lists and Libraries," earlier in this chapter). This page is identical in functionality to the permission management page described in the section "Grant Permissions to a File or List Item," earlier in this chapter. Follow the instructions in that section to grant permissions to the list or library.

Change a User's Permissions on a List or Library

Scenario/Problem: You want to change the permissions that a user or group has on a list or library. For example, you might want to remove permissions altogether or grant more permissions.

Solution: To change permissions on a list or library, open the manage permissions page for that list or library (see "Check Permissions on Lists and Libraries," earlier in this chapter) and click the name of the user or group for which you want to change the permissions. This page is identical in functionality to the permission management page described in the section "Change a User's or Group's Permissions on a File or List Item," earlier in this chapter. You follow the instructions in that section to change permissions for a user on the list or library.

See Who Is a Member of a SharePoint Group

Scenario/Problem: SharePoint groups contain several users. You want to see who belongs to a group before you assign permissions to that group. (You might later want to add users to or remove them from a group; this task is explained in "Assign Users' Permissions on a Site" in Chapter 14.)

Solution: SharePoint groups are defined at a site level. To see who is a member of a SharePoint group, you need the right permissions on the site itself. If you have those rights, you can click on the cogwheel icon at the top of the page to open the menu and select Site Settings (see Figure 10.12).

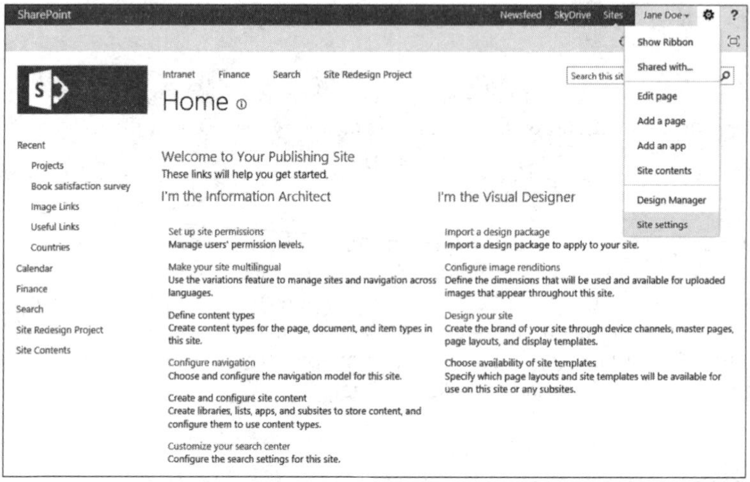

FIGURE 10.12   Selecting the Site Settings option.

Selecting this option opens the Site Settings page (see Figure 10.13). On this page, click the People and Groups link under the Users and Permissions header. The page that opens is the one used to manage security on a site (see Figure 10.14). The SharePoint groups are listed in the left navigation pane, under the Groups header.

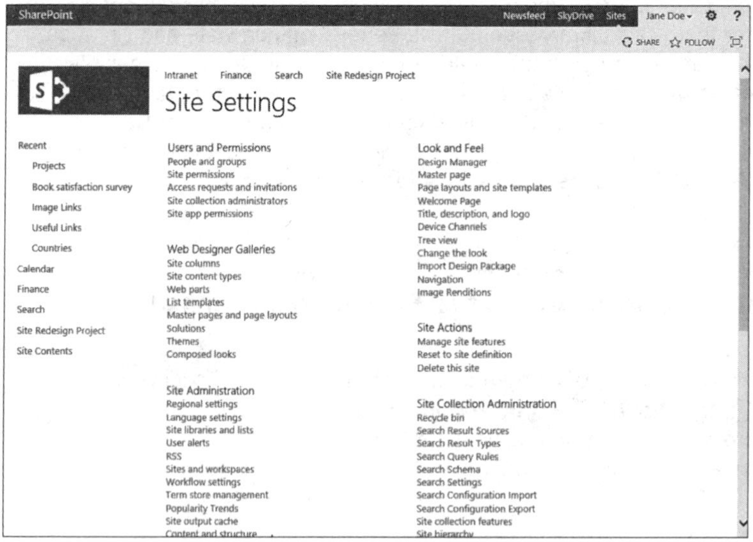

FIGURE 10.13   Clicking on the People and Groups link in the Site Settings page.

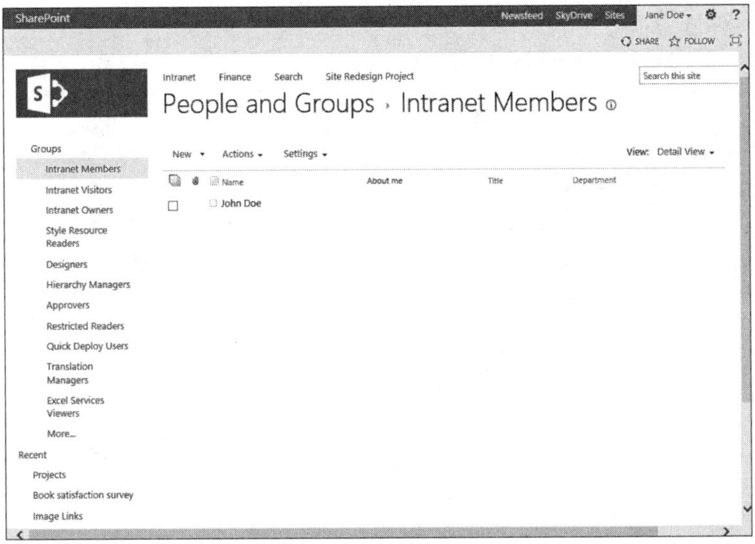

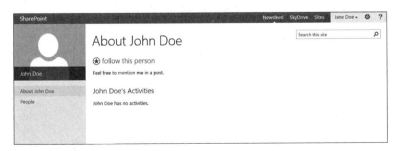

FIGURE 10.14   You can view the groups and who is in which group on this page.

TIP   The Site Actions menu might be hidden in some sites. To get to the manage site security page, you add **/_layouts/people.aspx** to the end of the site path. For example, if your site is at http://sharepoint/sample, type http://sharepoint/sample/_layouts/people.aspx in your browser to get to the page.

Click the link with the name of the group for which you want to see the members. Doing so shows a list of members—either users (such as John Doe) or security groups (such as Human Resources). Not all users have display names set, so some of them might not have anything under the Name column—leaving the column empty.

If you want to see the details of any user, just click that user's picture to open the user information page (see Figure 10.15).

FIGURE 10.15   The user information page for John Doe shows the user's details in the personal site for that user.

CHAPTER 11

Workflows

A developer can create a workflow to automate a process for files or list items. As an author or a contributor for a list or document library, you might be required to start a workflow or participate in one. This chapter covers basic workflow-related tasks, explaining how to start a workflow, track its progress, and attach a workflow to a document library or list that you are managing.

Start a Workflow

Scenario/Problem: When a workflow has been attached to a list or document library, it can be configured to start automatically when someone changes an item or file, or it can be configured to require the user to manually start the workflow. If it is configured to start manually, you might have to start it yourself.

Solution: To manually start a workflow on a list item or file, select the item's or file's row in the list or library view and switch to the Files ribbon or Items ribbon. If at least one workflow is associated with the document library that allows you to manually start it, the Workflows button is available in the ribbon (see Figure 11.1).

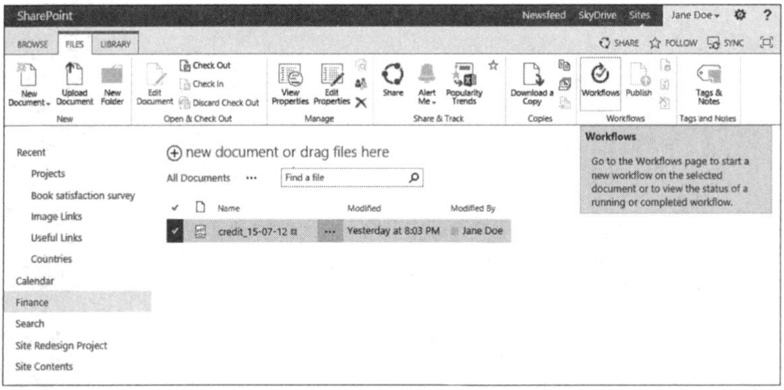

FIGURE 11.1   The Workflows button in the Files ribbon.

Clicking this button opens the Workflows screen, which has options for starting a workflow associated with the list or document library on the specific item (see Figure 11.2).

In the Start a New Workflow section of the Workflows screen, choose from the list of workflows that you can apply to the list item or file. Click the one you want to start to open the page that the workflow specifies as its initiation page (see Figure 11.3). This page appears every time you initiate a workflow on an item, and each different workflow might have a different page. Some workflows do not have an initiation form at all.

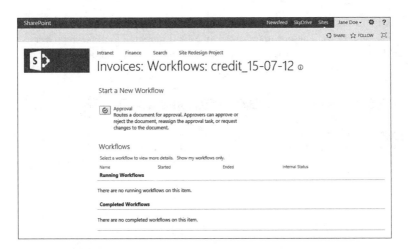

FIGURE 11.2   The Workflows screen.

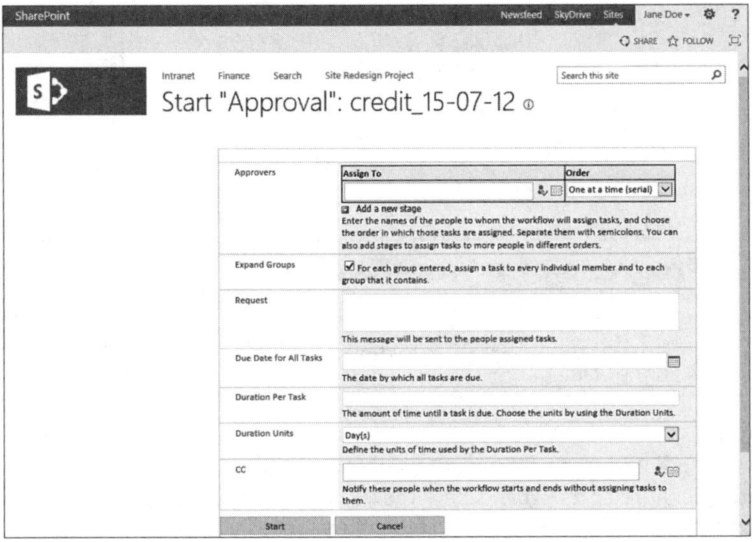

Start "Approval": credit_15-07-12

FIGURE 11.3   The Approval workflow's initiation page.

In the case of the Approval workflow, the initiation page asks for one or more approvers to assign the approval task to (this might be already filled in by the workflow's settings) and whether they should be approving in a serial sequence (one after another) or all at once. It also provides a place to write text describing your approval request and asks for a due date for the approval process and how long each person in the approvers list should have to complete the approval. Finally, it provides an option to notify other people on the approval process, in the CC section.

After you fill in the initiation form, click Start. The workflow might take a while to start, and then you are redirected to the list or library. The approval workflow then creates a task in the tasks list in the site and assigns it to the approvers you have selected (see Figure 11.4). The task then sends an e-mail message to those approvers, telling them of the task. The approver has options to approve, reject, request a change, cancel the task, or reassign it, as shown in Figure 11.4.

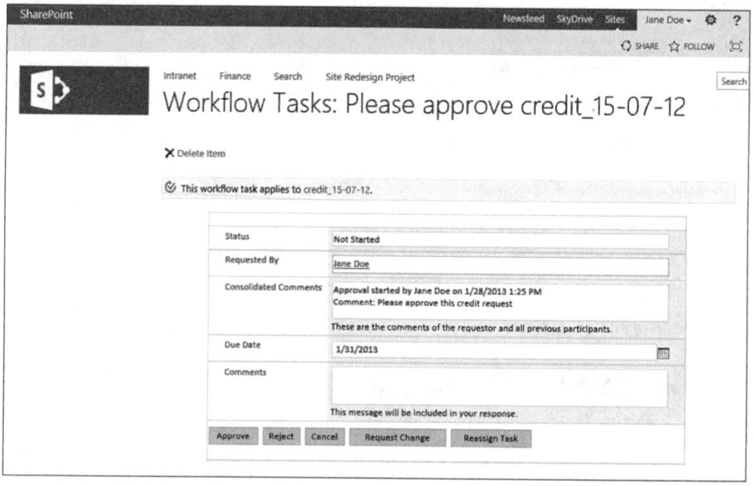

FIGURE 11.4   The Approval workflow creates tasks for approvers to approve.

Track the Progress of a Workflow

Scenario/Problem: You want to see the progress of a workflow that was started on a list item or file.

Solution: Select the item or file and click the Workflows button in the Items ribbon or Documents ribbon (refer to Figure 11.1). The workflows page that opens shows the running workflows as well as the completed ones (see Figure 11.5).

Click the name of a workflow or its status to get to the status summary page that is relevant to the workflow on the current item (see Figure 11.6).

The workflow's status summary page shows where the workflow is by displaying a graphic image of the workflow. It also shows a list of tasks that have been generated by the workflow and the history of the workflow progress below it. More complex workflows have more steps, so viewing the history can be useful when you want to know who did what during the workflow runtime. For example, if a workflow was canceled, the history screen shows that information, including who canceled the workflow. If any errors occurred in any of the workflow steps, you can use this information to see why the workflow was not completed.

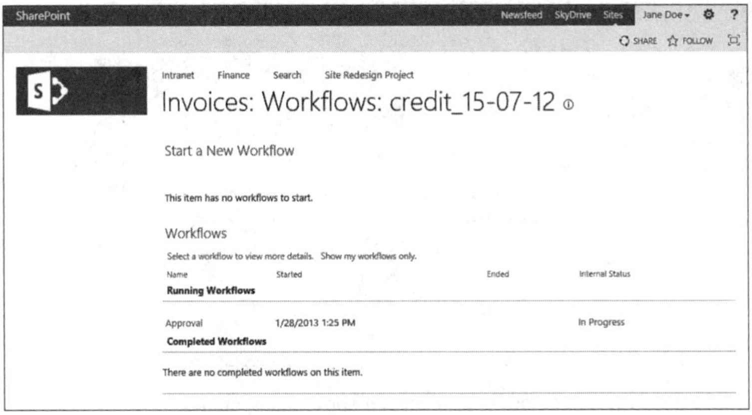

FIGURE 11.5   The Approval workflow creates tasks for approvers to approve.

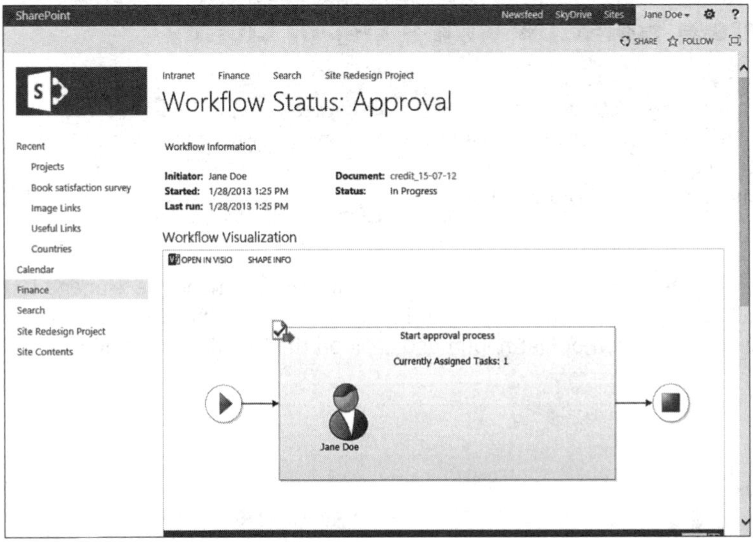

FIGURE 11.6   The status summary page for a workflow.

Some workflows offer quicker ways to get to the workflow status summary window. These workflows add a column to the list or library view that shows the status in that view. For example, the approval workflow adds an Approval column to the views of the list or library, showing you the status of the workflow and enabling you to click the status to get to the status summary page (see Figure 11.7).

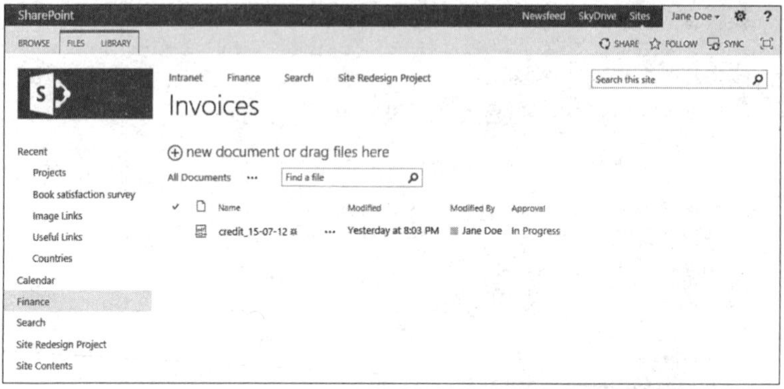

FIGURE 11.7   The Approval workflow adds a column showing the status.

Associate a Workflow with a List or Library

Scenario/Problem: You want to assign a workflow to a list or library so that users can select it from the list of available workflows, or you might want to define a workflow that starts automatically when a document or list item is added or modified in the library or list.

Solution: To attach different workflows to a list or library, you need the Manage List or Manage Library permission on that list or library. If you have those permissions, switch to the Library ribbon or List ribbon and click on the Workflows button (see Figure 11.8).

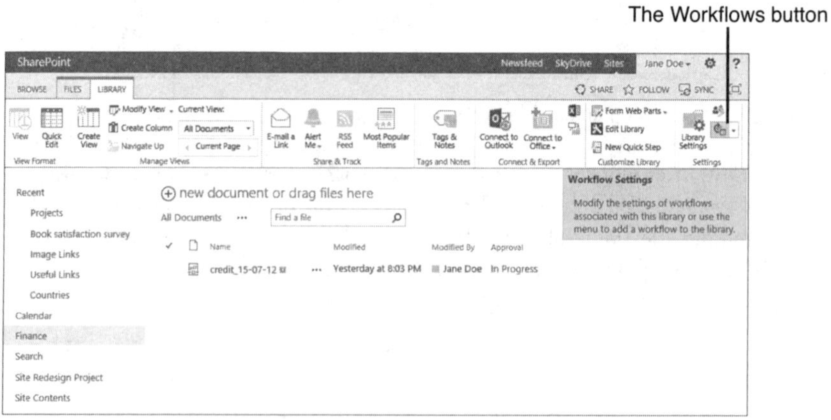

The Workflows button

FIGURE 11.8   The Workflows button in the Library ribbon.

Clicking the Workflows button opens the Workflow Settings page for the list or library. This page enables you to associate a workflow with the list or library (see Figure 11.9).

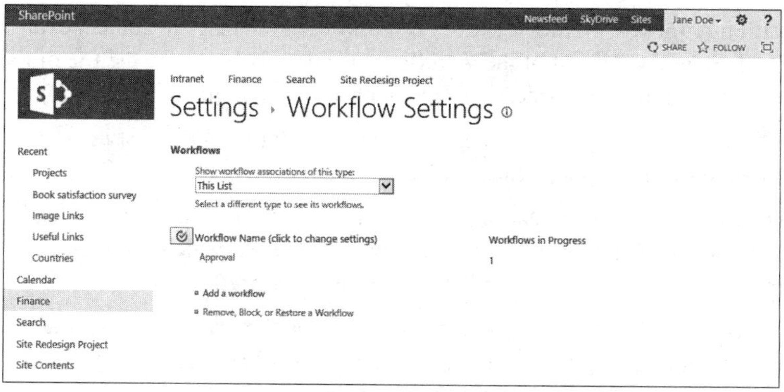

FIGURE 11.9   The Workflow Settings page for adding a workflow or managing the existing ones.

The list of workflows that were already added to the list or library appears at the top of the page (under the Workflows title). The option to add a workflow is shown as a link at the bottom of the page. Click this link to open the Add a Workflow page, shown in Figure 11.10.

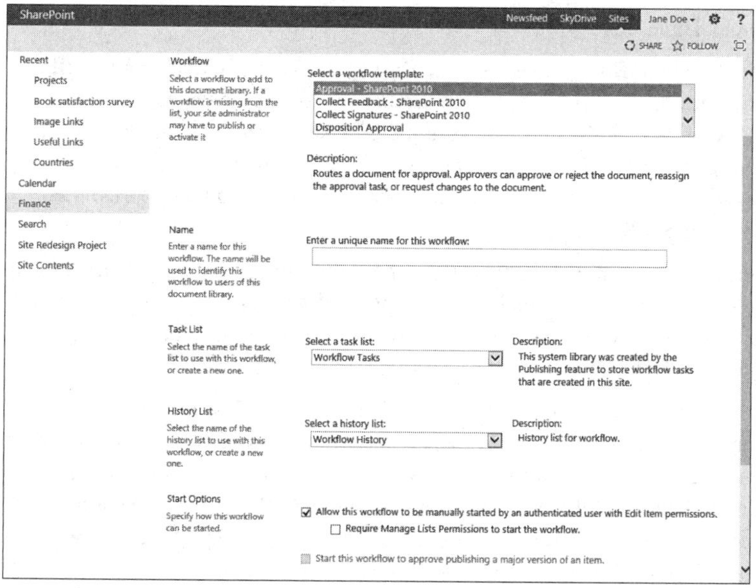

FIGURE 11.10   The Add a Workflow page.

In the Add a Workflow page, you can define what workflow you want to create on the list or library by selecting from the workflow box that lists the available workflows. By default, the only workflows available in SharePoint Server are the five built-in workflows:

▶ **Disposition Approval**—Allows starting a workflow to manage document expiration and retention. As part of the workflow, people involved with the file or list item are required to decide whether to retain or delete expired documents.

▶ **Three-State**—Tracks the progress of approval of a document or a list item through three states: Active, Ready for Review, and Complete.

▶ **Collect Feedback**—Allows starting a review workflow for a document or list item in the list or library. Reviewers can provide feedback, which is compiled and sent to the owner of the file or list item when the workflow has completed.

▶ **Approval**—Allows starting an approval workflow on the list's or library's items, where approvers can approve or reject the document or list item, reassign the approval task, or request changes to the document.

▶ **Collect Signatures**—Allows starting a workflow for collecting signatures that are required to complete a business process on a document. Note that this workflow can be started only from within a Microsoft Word 2007 or Microsoft Excel 2007 client (or later versions), and then only from certain versions of Microsoft Office 2007 (Ultimate, Professional Plus, and Enterprise). If you cannot start this workflow from your Microsoft Office client, you should check the version of your Microsoft Office and upgrade if necessary.

In SPF, only the Three-State workflow is available by default.

After you choose a workflow, choose a name for it. Because more than one workflow of any type can be attached to the document library or list, each must have a unique name so that the users can recognize it in the list of workflows. For example, a document library might require two approval workflows: one for expense claims and one for travel expenses. To create those two, you need to add them both as approval workflows—but each one with a different name.

The next choice is what task list the workflow should use to create tasks associated with it. As you saw earlier in this chapter, the Approval workflow creates tasks for approvers to approve the file or list item when the workflow starts. You can point each workflow to a specific task list or tell the workflow to create a new task list for itself.

The History List section enables you to define where the workflow reports its progress, for the purpose of storing the history. As you saw earlier in this chapter, when viewing a workflow's progress, you can see the history of steps taken in the workflow. Here, you can define in which list that history is kept. By default, the history is kept in a hidden list called Workflow History that the users do not ordinarily see. If you want to store the information in another list, you can define that here.

Finally, the last section of the page, Start Options, enables you to specify when the workflow starts (see Figure 11.11).

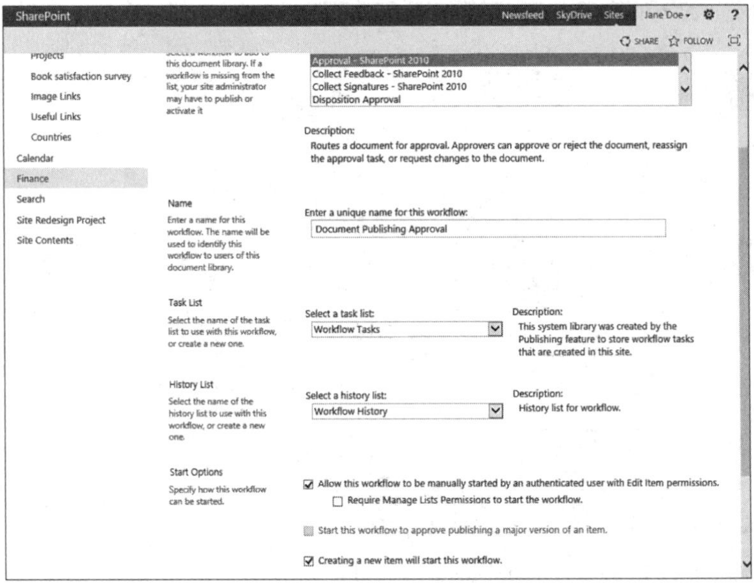

FIGURE 11.11   Creating a new approval workflow that starts automatically for new items.

With the first option, Allow This Workflow to Be Manually Started, users can start the workflow manually. The third option, Start This Workflow When a New Item Is Created, causes the list or library to start the workflow automatically when a new item or file is added to the list or library. As you can see in Figure 11.11, if you choose to let the users start the workflow manually, the users must have the Edit Items permission on the list or library; otherwise, they can't start the workflow on any item. Select the Require Manage Lists Permissions to Start the Workflow check box to allow only managers of the list to be able to start the workflow.

You can use the second option, Start This Workflow to Approve Publishing a Major Version of an Item, only if the list or library has versioning set to allow major and minor versions. If this option is selected, this workflow starts when a user submits a file or list item for approval to get published as a major version. The last option causes the workflow to start when an item or a file is changed in the list or library.

When you are finished configuring the workflow, click Next to open the workflow's association form (if the workflow has one). A workflow association form is different for each workflow type and is used to configure settings that are specific for that workflow type (see Figure 11.12). For example, the Approval workflow's association form enables you to set whether the approval is done in parallel or in a serial manner. Parallel approval means that all the approvers get an e-mail message at the same time, whereas serial approval means the first approver on the list must approve before the second one gets the request to approve, and so on.

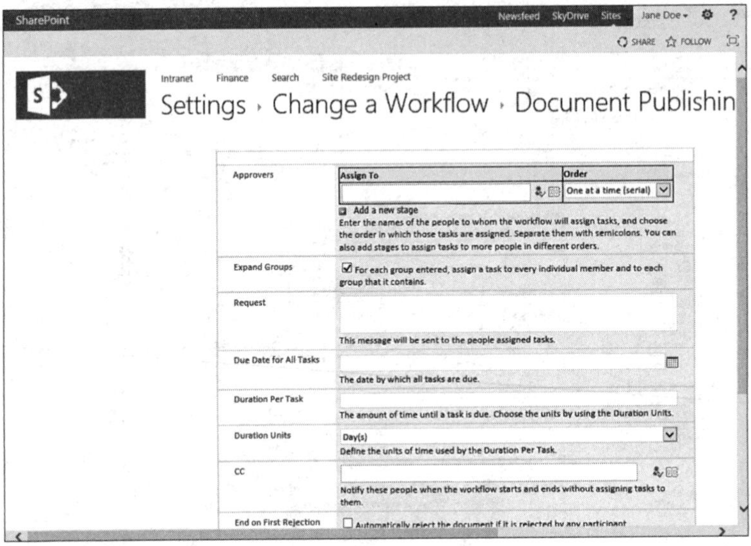

FIGURE 11.12   The Approval workflow's association form.

When you are done setting the configuration for the workflow, or if there are no additional configuration settings, click OK. If you selected that users can start the workflow automatically, your new workflow is added to the list of workflows the user can start.

CHAPTER 12

Creating Subsites

If you are a site manager, you might want to create subsites under the site you are managing. For example, you might have a site called Projects, under which you will create a subsite for each project to hold the project's files and details. This chapter explains how to create subsites, including the different templates for subsites that come with SharePoint.

Create a Subsite

Scenario/Problem: You want to create a subsite under an existing site. For example, you want to create a site for a team, or a blog site for a certain person, or a wiki site for a specific topic.

Solution: The following section explains how to create a site in general and then gives examples of creating three types of sites.

To create a subsite under an existing Microsoft SharePoint 2013 site, open the Site Contents page (refer to "See What Lists and Document Libraries Are in a Site" in Chapter 3, "Solutions Regarding Files, Documents, List Items, and Forms"). At the bottom of that page you will find a list of the existing subsites of the current site, and a New Subsite button. Clicking on that button opens the New SharePoint Site page shown in Figure 12.1.

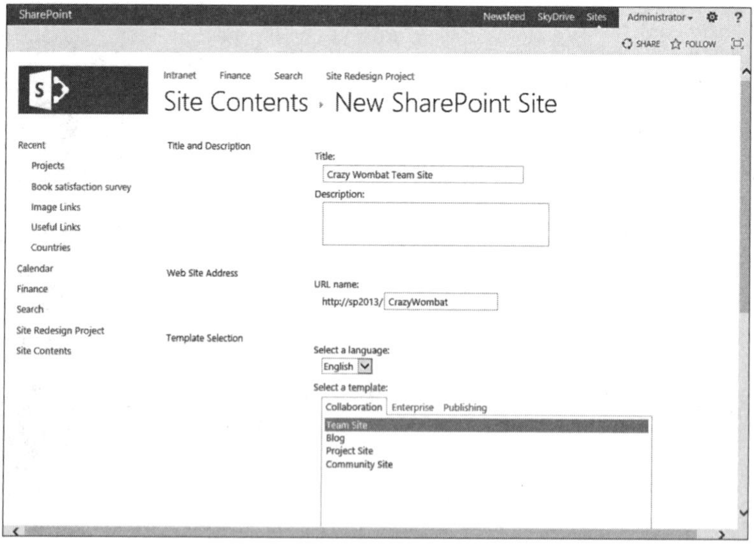

FIGURE 12.1   The New SharePoint Site page.

At the top of the page, type the title for the new site. The title is displayed on the top of the site and in the navigation links pointing to the site. You can change this title at any time from the site settings.

Next, choose and type the URL name for the site. This name determines how the link to the site will look. Considering this name carefully is recommended because, although you can change it after the site is created, if it changes, shortcuts that your users have created and links that point to that site break (without considerable work by the SharePoint administrator). Keep this text as short as possible, and you shouldn't use spaces and special characters in the URL name of a site.

You can also set a description for the site. This information is usually displayed as a pop-up dialog next to the site's title in most site templates, where users can click a small button next to the site's title to see the description.

In the Template Selection section of this page you can choose the kind of site you want to create from the list of available templates (this list might be different from site to site). To choose the template, click on the tabs for the template categories, and then choose a template from the list of available templates shown here. For example, under the Collaboration tab shown in Figure 12.1, you can choose the Team Site template to create a team site, or switch to the Publishing tab to choose the Publishing Site template or the Enterprise Wiki template.

> **NOTE** To change any of the first three settings in the Create dialog, see "Change the Name, Description, Icon, or URL of a Site" in Chapter 13, "Customizing a SharePoint Site."

Next, in the dialog, choose options in the Permissions section shown in Figure 12.2. You can define whether the site will have the same permission set as its parent site (the site you are currently on) or unique permissions. If you are happy with the new site having the same permissions as the current site, you can leave the default setting, Use Same Permissions as Parent Site. If you choose Use Unique Permissions, you must set permissions on the site after it has been created. You can modify the permissions of the site at any time. See Chapter 14, "Managing Site Security," for more information about changing the site's permissions.

Finally, choose in the Navigation Inheritance section whether the site should have the same top navigation bar as the parent site or whether it should have a navigation bar of its own. This section lets you create subsites that look either like part of the top site or like separate sites altogether. You can change these settings later (see "Modify the Top or Left Navigation Bar" in Chapter 13).

> **TIP** For consistency, usually it is recommended that subsites inherit the navigation from their parent site, which allows the users of the site to orient themselves quickly. Usually, the left navigation shows navigation that is unique to the current site. Chapter 13 has more information about configuring navigation in a site.

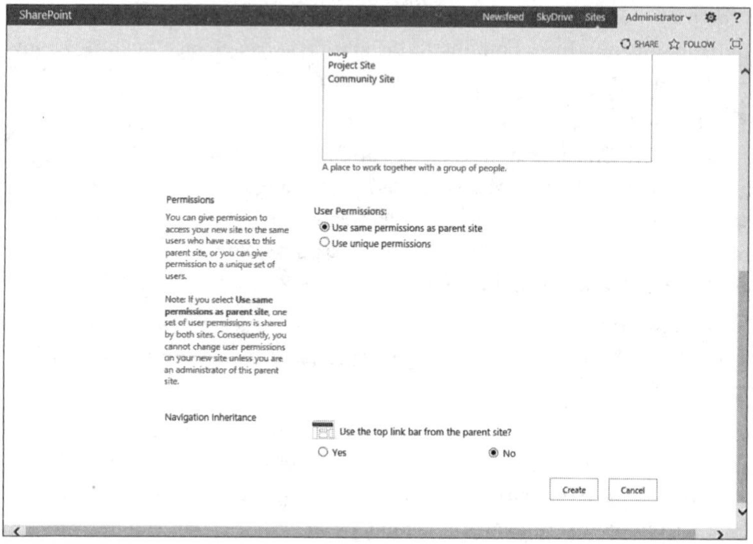

FIGURE 12.2 The Permissions and Navigation sections of the New SharePoint Site page.

When you are finished setting the options for the new site, click the Create button to create the site. The new site opens unless you have chosen to have unique permissions for the site. In that case, the permissions setting page for the site opens first (see Figure 12.3). For more information about setting these permissions, see Chapter 14.

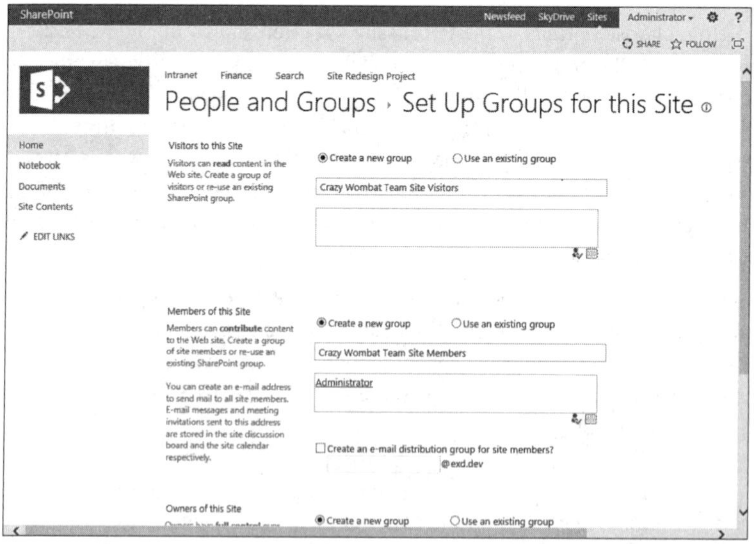

FIGURE 12.3 Setting up groups and permissions for a new site with unique permissions.

Create a Team Site

A team site is a simple site with a document library, an announcements list, a calendar list, a links list, a tasks list, and a team discussion board. To create a team site, select the Team Site template in the site creation page (refer to Figure 12.1) and fill in the site's title and URL name (and, if you want, other parameters [such as the description], using the More Options button, as shown in Figure 12.2). Click Create. The new team site opens, ready for the team to start collaborating.

Create an Enterprise Wiki Site in SharePoint Server

A wiki site is for managing and sharing information. This type of site is used mostly to share ideas and knowledge among many people. The Enterprise Wiki Site template enables users who use the site to easily change the pages and create new pages. It also comes with a ratings system that allows users to rate each wiki article and a categories system that enables grouping of articles by categories.

> **NOTE** The Enterprise Wiki Site template might or might not be available to you, because some templates are available only if certain features have been installed and activated on the site.

To create a wiki site, in the New SharePoint Site page select the Enterprise Wiki Site template under the Publishing tab (refer to Figure 12.1), fill in the parameters for the site as explained earlier in this chapter, and click Create. When the site is created, it has only one page, the home page for the site. The page has some default text explaining what a wiki is. It also has an Edit This Page button on the top that allows users to edit the content of the page (see Figure 12.4).

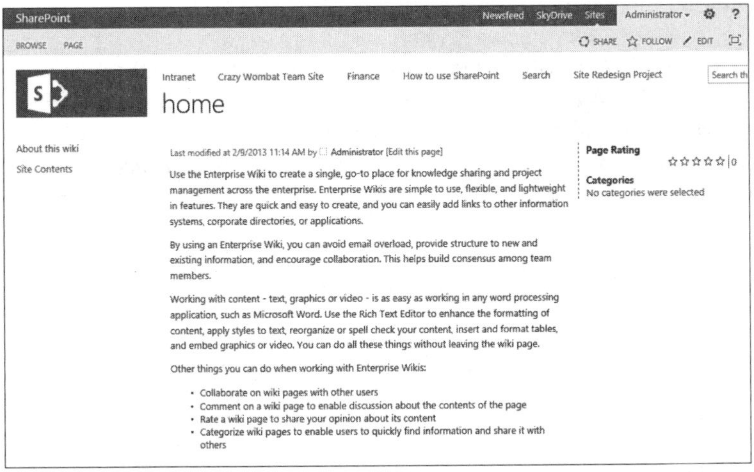

FIGURE 12.4   A new Enterprise Wiki site.

Create a Blog Site

A blog site is another type of site for sharing information, usually articles or blog posts. Each article or post is much like an announcement, with a title and some text containing the information to be shared. However, blog posts also offer readers the option to comment on them, and the posts can be grouped into categories that can be managed in the blog site itself as a separate list. The layout of a blog site is customized to show blog tools (such as Manage Posts and Manage Comments), as shown in Figure 12.5. A blog site also offers integration with Microsoft Word to easily create posts in that application using the Launch Blogging App link.

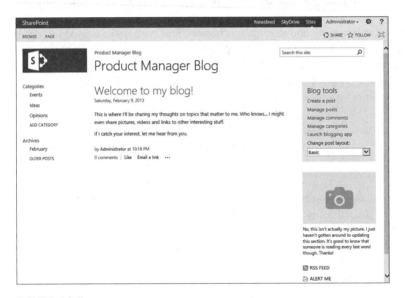

FIGURE 12.5   A new blog site.

To create a blog site, select the Blog option (refer to Figure 12.1), fill in the details, and click Create. After you create the site, the home page of the blog shows a sample post that explains what a blog is and displays a list of actions you can perform on the blog, including creating a new post and managing the posts and comments (refer to Figure 12.5).

CHAPTER 13

Customizing a SharePoint Site

When you are in charge of a SharePoint site, you will want to customize it to fit your view of how it should look and behave. Such customization includes changing the site's title, the way the site looks (using themes), the page used as the home page for the site, the site's navigation, the site's search settings, and more.

This chapter covers these topics and explains how to accomplish some of the most common site customization tasks.

Open the Site Settings Page

Scenario/Problem: You want to change a site's settings.

Solution: To change a site's settings, access the Site Settings page by opening the Site Actions menu and choosing Site Settings, as shown in Figure 13.1.

FIGURE 13.1   Opening the Site Settings page.

Some types of sites have more settings than others (see Figures 13.2 and 13.3).

A root-level site has more settings than a subsite, and publishing sites have additional settings. The settings available on a page vary based on the permissions you have on the site. For example, in a root-level site, the link to the settings for the site collection (see Figure 13.3) is displayed only if you have site collection administrator privileges.

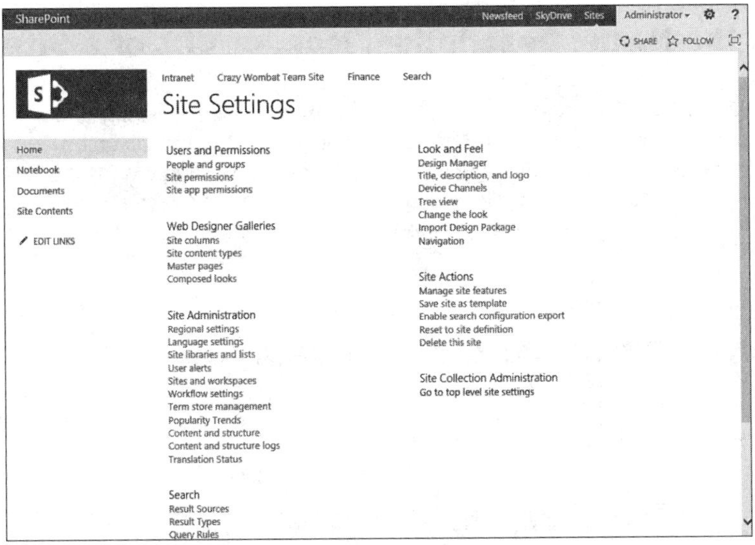

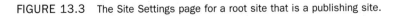

FIGURE 13.2   The Site Settings page for a subsite.

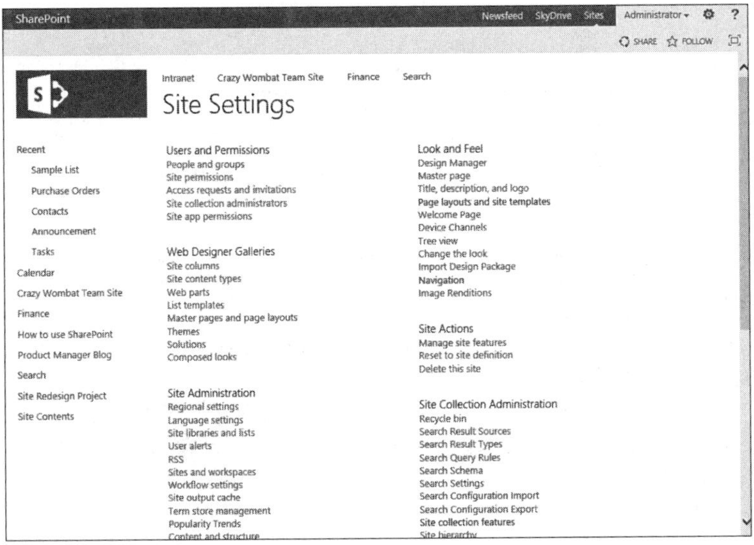

FIGURE 13.3   The Site Settings page for a root site that is a publishing site.

Change the Name, Description, Icon, or URL of a Site

Scenario/Problem: Every site has a name or title that is usually displayed on all the pages, generally above the top navigation bar and in the breadcrumbs. The description of a site sometimes appears under the breadcrumbs or at the top of some of the pages, and the icon usually appears next to the title (see Figure 13.4). You might want to change the title, description, or icon for a site.

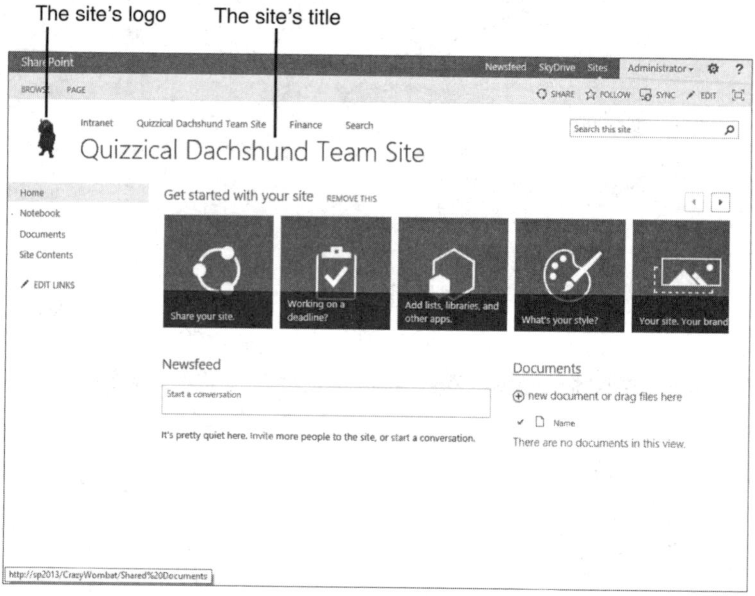

The site's logo   The site's title

FIGURE 13.4   The site's title and icon. The description isn't normally shown.

Solution: To change these settings, open the Site Settings page, as explained in the preceding section. In the Site Settings page, click the Title, Description, and Logo link in the Look and Feel section of the page (refer to Figure 13.2).

The Title, Description, and Logo settings page opens, as shown in Figure 13.5, allowing you to change the settings.

TIP   Although you can change the URL name of the site from the Title, Description, and Logo page, it is not recommended that you do so after users have begun using your site. If you change the URL name, any link or bookmark that users have created pointing to the site is broken.

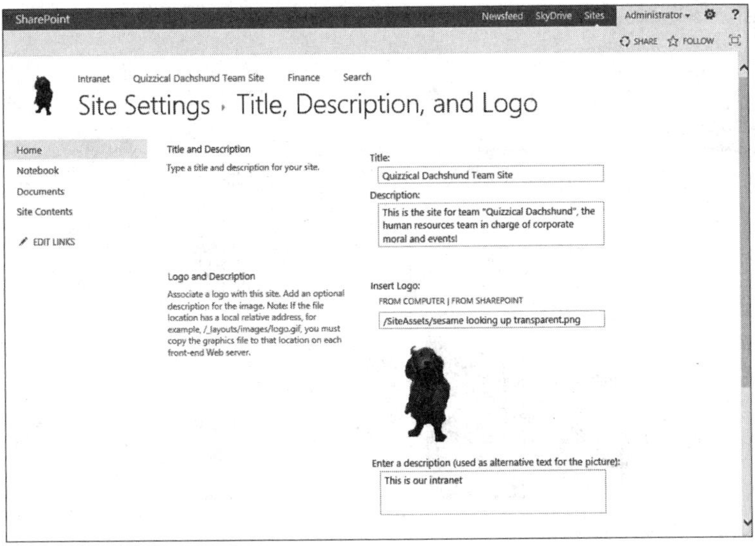

FIGURE 13.5   The Title, Description, and Logo settings page.

Change the Look of a Site

Scenario/Problem: You can change how a site looks by applying different designs to the site. Designs feature different color schemes and different fonts. You might want to change how a site looks by switching the site to use a different design.

Solution: To apply a different design to a site, open the Site Settings page, as explained earlier. In the Look and Feel section of the page, click the Change the Look link. This selection opens a page that enables you to pick a new look for the site (see Figure 13.6). Graphic designers can create new styles for you to pick from, so your list of available designs might vary.

When you click the preview image for a specific design, a page opens that allows you to customize the design by specifying different color schemes, different page layouts, and fonts. A link at the top of the page allows you to "Try it out." Clicking this link generates a preview image of the home page of the site with the new design as shown in Figure 13.7. You can then choose to keep it, or go back to choose different colors, fonts, or a different design altogether.

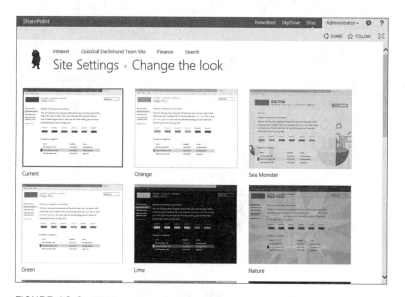

FIGURE 13.6 Picking a new site design.

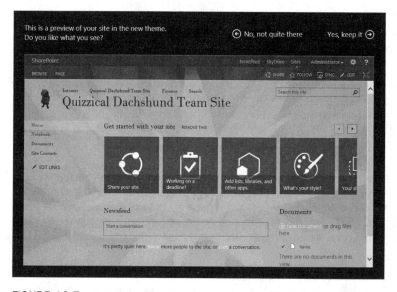

FIGURE 13.7 A preview of the home page of a site with the new design.

TIP By default, SharePoint sites use the Orbit design. If you ever want to go back to the default look, just locate Orbit in the list of designs.

Change the Home Page of a Site

Scenario/Problem: You want to change which page is opened when a user types in the address of the site or clicks the site's link in the navigation bar.

Solution: If the site you are working on has multiple pages, you can choose which page in the site is the home page (also known as the welcome page) for the site. For information about creating pages, see Chapter 9, "Authoring Pages."

To select a page to be the home page, navigate to that page and switch to the Page ribbon. If you have sufficient permissions on the site, you see the Make Homepage button in the Page Actions section of the ribbon. To make the page the home page, click the Make Homepage button and confirm the action in the pop-up prompt that shows up.

Alternatively, in publishing sites, click the Welcome Page link in the Look and Feel section of the site. (Again, this option appears only in publishing sites.) This selection opens the Site Welcome Page setting page, which enables you to specify which page should be opened (see Figure 13.8). Simply type in the link or use the Browse button to browse to the page in the site that you want to be the home page.

FIGURE 13.8   The Site Welcome Page settings page.

NOTE The browsing function allows you to select a list or library in the site. However, if you select a list or library and try to save it as a new welcome page, SharePoint will not allow it and will tell you that the selection is not valid. You can only select pages or list items as the welcome page for a site.

Modify the Top or Left Navigation Bar

Scenario/Problem: You want to modify the links shown on the top or left navigation bar. For example, you might want to add a tab to the top navigation bar or remove a link from the left navigation bar.

Solution: How you modify the links shown on the top or left navigation bar depends on the type of site you are using. The following sections provide the details.

Modify the Top or Left Navigation Bar in a Non-Publishing Site

In a non-publishing site, you can edit the links for the top and left navigation bars from a page such as the home page. The two navigation bars have an Edit Links button next to each of them, as shown in Figure 13.9.

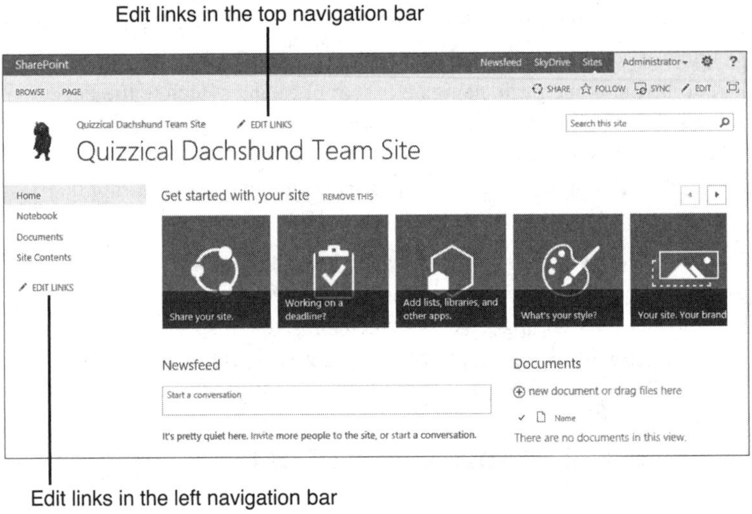

Edit links in the top navigation bar

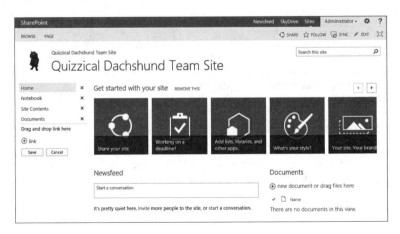

Edit links in the left navigation bar

FIGURE 13.9   The Site Welcome page.

After you click on either button, the existing links appear as buttons, allowing you to rearrange them by dragging and dropping them. You can also delete them, or add new ones by using the +link button as shown in Figure 13.10.

FIGURE 13.10   Editing the left navigation bar's links.

Modify the Top or Left Navigation Bar in a Publishing Site

In a publishing site, the navigation settings for both navigation bars are in the same page. To get to the navigation management page, open the Site Settings page and click the Navigation link in the Look and Feel section of the page. The Site Navigation Settings page opens, as shown in Figure 13.11.

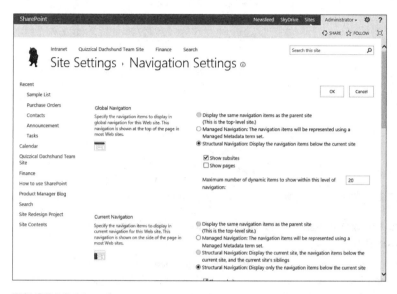

FIGURE 13.11   The Site Navigation Settings page.

On the Site Navigation Settings page, you can define what links and headings each navigation bar will have—and you can add, remove, or change the order of those links. The top navigation bar is referenced on this page as Global Navigation, and the left navigation bar is called Current Navigation.

In a subsite, this page has more options, as you can see in Figure 13.12. On it, you can set whether the site should display the same top or left navigation options as its parent site or whether it should have its own set of navigation bar links. A third option is to use Managed Navigation, which is covered later in this chapter, in the "Use Managed Metadata Navigation in a Publishing Site" section.

If you choose either Display the Same Navigation Items as the Parent Site (available only if you are in a subsite) or Structural Navigation, the options to choose whether the navigation bars should show subsites under the current site and whether the navigation bars should show pages appear (refer to Figure 13.12). If you choose to use structural navigation or managed navigation, you will be able to modify the navigation for the site. Inheriting the navigation from the parent site means that to edit the navigation you have to go to the parent site's navigation settings page.

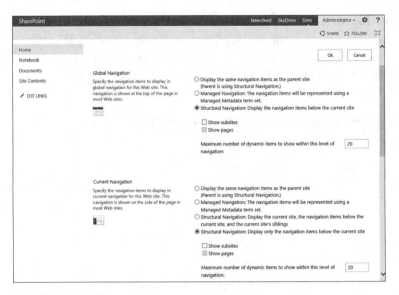

FIGURE 13.12   The Site Navigation Settings page for a subsite.

Use Structural Navigation to Add a Link to the Top or Left Navigation Bar

To add a link to either navigation bar, after selecting to use Structural Navigation, scroll down and locate the Structural Navigation: Editing and Sorting section of the page, and click the Global Navigation node (for the top navigation bar) or Current Navigation node (for the left navigation bar) in the Navigation Editing and Sorting box. Click the Add Link option in the menu. This selection opens a dialog where you can specify the link to be added (see Figure 13.13).

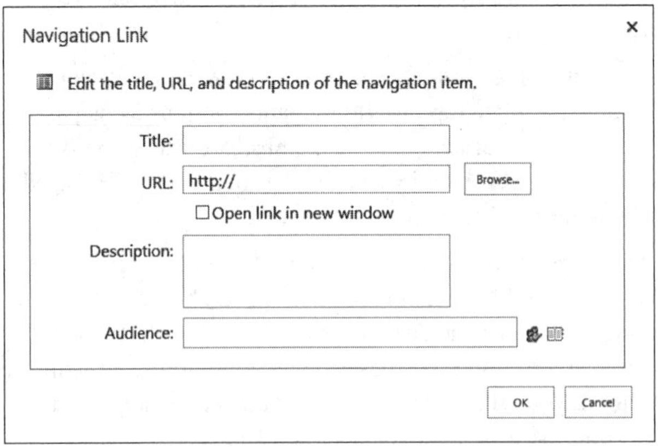

FIGURE 13.13   Adding a link to a navigation bar.

In the Title box, you can specify what text the link displays to the user. Also, you can either type in a link or browse to a page in the site by using the Browse button. You can also specify whether the link is opened in a new window when clicked. In sites where it is enabled, you can choose an audience for the link, specifying who should see the link.

Add a Heading to the Top or Left Navigation Bar

In a publishing site, you can add headings to both the top and left navigation bars. A heading in a publishing site can be a link or just text that can have other links under it.

> **NOTE** In a publishing site the heading doesn't have to be a link. Instead, a heading can just be a container for links, without allowing users to click it in the navigation bar.

To add a heading, simply click the Global Navigation node (for the top navigation bar) or Current Navigation node in the Navigation Editing and Sorting box, and then click the Add Heading button in the menu. The dialog that pops up is the same as the one for adding a link (refer to Figure 13.13), but unlike with adding a link, in this case you can keep the URL setting empty if you don't want the heading to be a link.

Edit a Link or a Heading in the Top or Left Navigation Bar

To edit a link or heading from either navigation bar, click the link or heading in the Navigation Editing and Sorting box, and then click the Edit button on the toolbar. The dialog for the link's setting opens, allowing you to specify how this link should behave (refer to Figure 13.13).

Remove a Link from the Top or Left Navigation Bar

To remove a link from either navigation bar, click the link in the Navigation Editing and Sorting box, and then click the Delete button on the toolbar.

Change Which Heading a Link Is Under

To select the heading for a link in a publishing site, move the link up or down in the Navigation Editing and Sorting box until it is under the heading you want. Select the link, and then use the Move Up and Move Down buttons to move the link in or out of headings.

> **NOTE** You can have a link exist in the root (not under a heading). Simply move the link to be under either Current Navigation or Global Navigation.

Use Managed Metadata Navigation in a Publishing Site

Scenario/Problem: You want to modify the links shown on the top or left navigation bar by using a Managed Metadata term set.

Solution: In SharePoint 2013 using Managed Metadata term sets as navigation controls is possible, which allows you to create a term set, configure terms in it, and assign links to the terms. SharePoint can then use the terms to build either the top navigation and or the left navigation. This feature allows for more flexibility in editing the navigation items, allowing you to create a deeper navigation hierarchy than the other options (in the other navigation configurations you can create links under headers, but not headers under headers; with managed metadata, you can create a virtually unlimited number of levels of links). It also allows you to configure friendly URLs for a site, whereby the link shown to the users is simple and short; for example, "http://intranet/home" instead of the full link to the actual page at "http://intranet/pages/home.aspx."

Choosing a Term Set for Navigation in a Site

To configure SharePoint to use a managed navigation term set, simply choose Managed Navigation in either the global navigation or the current navigation. When you do that, a box appears that allows you to select from the list of existing term sets, and a button to create a new term set, as shown in Figure 13.14.

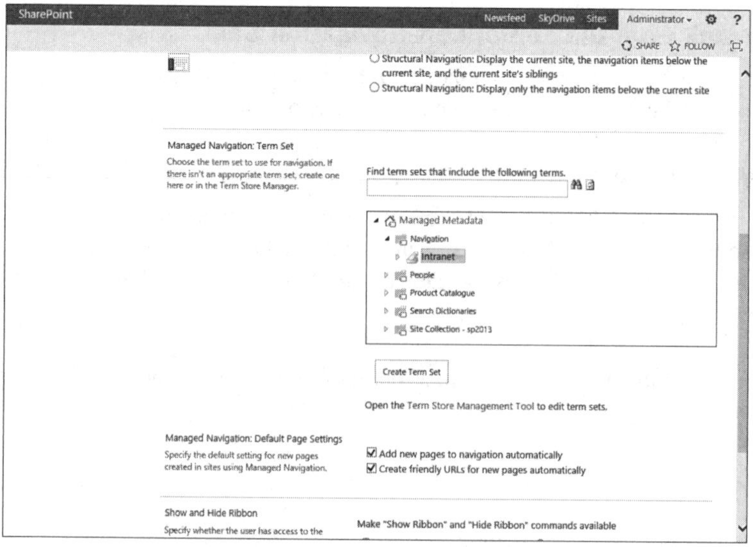

FIGURE 13.14   Choosing a managed navigation term set.

If you cannot find the term set that you want, click the Create Term Set button. This creates a new, empty term set with the name of the site.

Editing a Term Set for Navigation in a Site

To add, remove, or edit terms in the term set, select the term set and click the Term Store Management Tool link (refer to Figure 13.14). This opens the site's term store management tool that allows you to find the term set you want to edit. If you created a new term set, you should find it under the Site Collection group as shown in Figure 13.15; otherwise, find your term set from the list of term sets on the right.

> **TIP** You can also get to the term store management page directly from the Site Settings page by clicking the Term Store Management link under the Site Administration section.

After you find your term set, you can click it to open a drop-down menu that lets you create new terms in the term set, as shown in Figure 13.15.

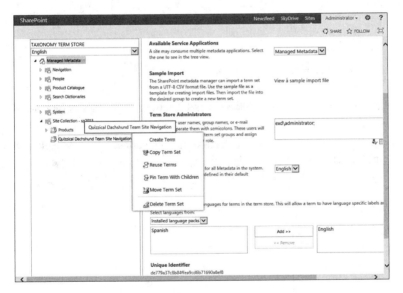

FIGURE 13.15   Creating a new term in an empty navigation term set.

Clicking the Create Term option creates a new term, allowing you to type the name for that term. This is what will be displayed to the users in the navigation. Type the name, and press Enter, which will automatically create another term. If you don't want another term, just click elsewhere.

When you have created a terms, click on the term's name. The page then shows on the right the settings for that term, including a Navigation tab with navigation settings for the term, as shown in Figure 13.16. Switch to that tab to specify whether the link should show in top navigation bars and/or left navigation bars, as well as the target link for the term.

To set a target, you first need to select the navigation node type, either a simple link or header, in which case you can specify a link to a page, or keep the link empty (making it a header without a link). Configuring a term-driven page with a friendly URL is covered in the next section.

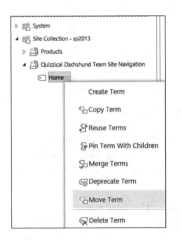

FIGURE 13.16   A term's navigation settings page.

After setting the settings on the term, click Save at the bottom of the page before going on to edit other terms.

To add terms under an existing term, move the term (to another term set or to be under a different term), or delete a term, hover the mouse cursor over the term's name in the left bar, and open the drop-down menu for the term as shown in Figure 13.17.

FIGURE 13.17   The drop-down menu for a term allows you to create terms under it, move the term, or delete the term.

Configuring a Friendly URL

If you select Term-Driven Page with Friendly URL in the term's navigation node type, you need to configure more options for this term. First, click the Save button, and then switch to the Term-Driven Pages tab as shown in Figure 13.18.

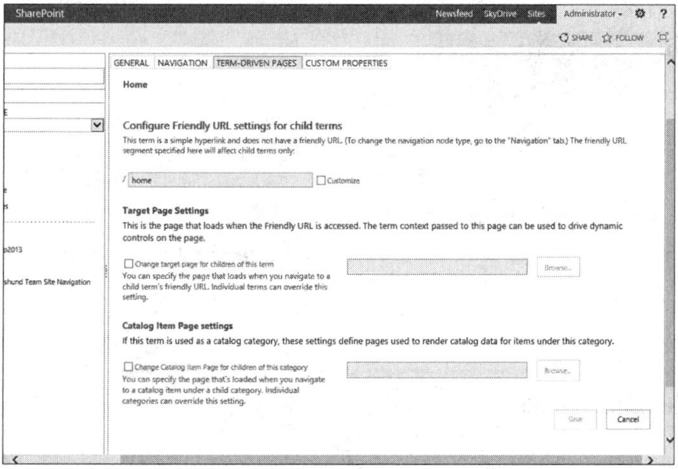

FIGURE 13.18   Term-Driven Pages configuration tab.

In this tab, you can customize the link that will be shown to the users in the address bar (for example "/home" as shown in Figure 13.18, or "/contacts" if you want a friendly link to the contacts list). You can then choose the target page that the users will be taken to when they click the link (for example, the default view of the contacts list) as shown in Figure 13.19. When you are finished, click Save.

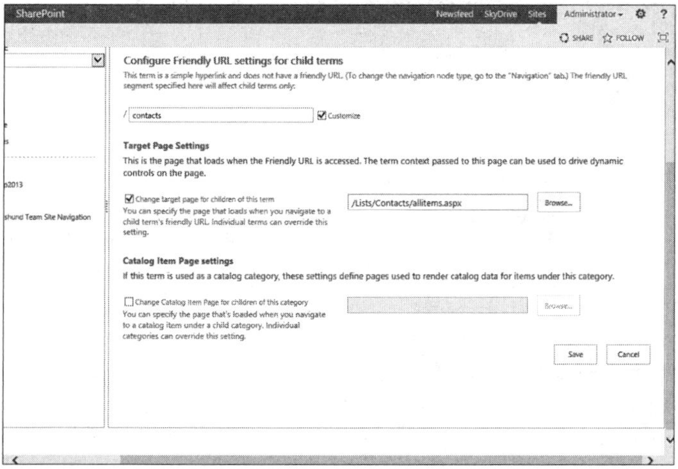

FIGURE 13.19   Adding a friendly URL to the contacts list.

After configuring a friendly URL, users who click the link in the navigation will be redirected to the page you selected, but the address bar will show only the simple, friendly link you specified as shown in Figure 13.20.

FIGURE 13.20   A friendly URL in the address bar opens the contacts list from the top navigation.

Create a Site Column

Scenario/Problem: You want to create a site column.

Solution: To create a site column, open the Site Settings page, as explained at the beginning of this chapter, and then click Site Columns in the Galleries section of the page. This selection opens the Site Columns gallery page, where you can create new site columns or edit or remove existing ones (see Figure 13.21).

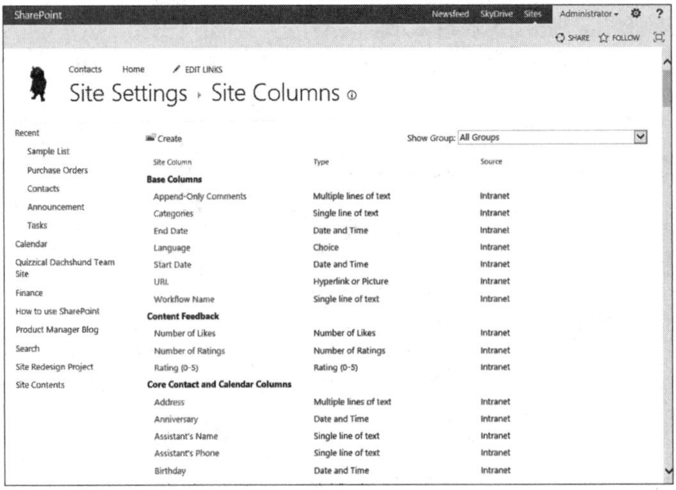

FIGURE 13.21   The Site Columns gallery page.

To create a new column, click the Create button on the toolbar. This selection opens a page where you can define the column's name and type, as well as additional settings—just like creating a list column (see Chapter 7, "Creating Lists and Document Libraries"). The one difference from creating a list or library column in this page is that site columns can be added to a group to make finding the columns from the list of site columns easier, as shown in Figure 13.22.

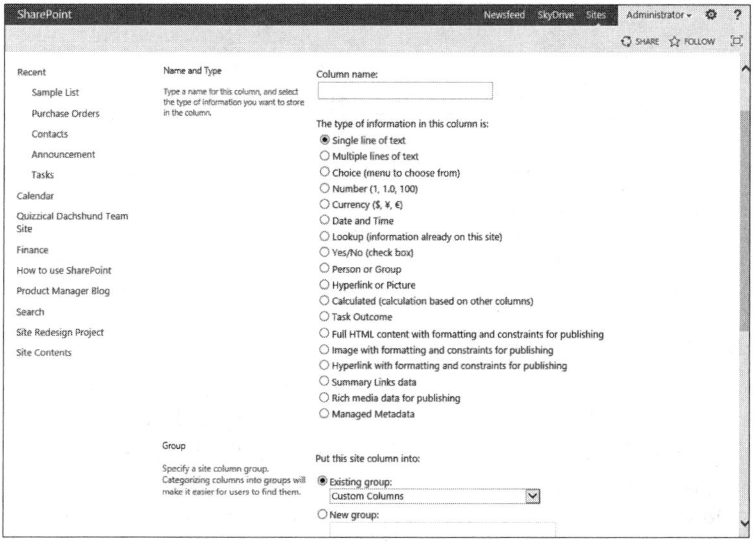

FIGURE 13.22   When adding a site column, you can specify which group it should belong to.

The Group option enables you to either add the column to an existing group or create a new group by typing that group's name. By default, the columns you create are added to the Custom Columns group.

Create a Content Type

> **Scenario/Problem:** You want to create a content type and define what columns are included in the content type.

Solution: As explained in Chapter 1, "About Microsoft SharePoint 2013," a content type is a collection of site columns and additional settings that can be created for a site. To create a new content type in a site, open the Site Settings page, as explained at the beginning of this chapter, and click Content Types in the Galleries section of the page. This selection opens a page where you can create or modify content types (see Figure 13.23).

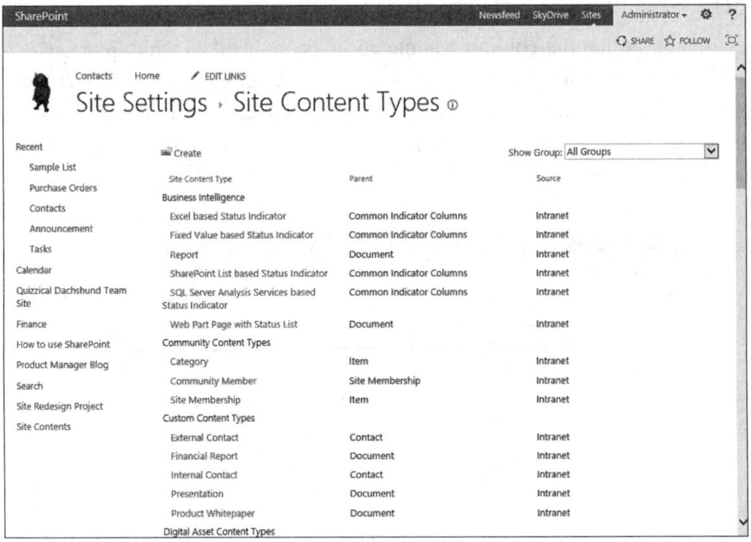

FIGURE 13.23 The Site Content Types gallery page.

Click the Create button on the toolbar to create a new content type. The page shown in Figure 13.24 opens. The first setting you need to set for a content type is the name for the content type, followed by its description. The name and description appear in the New drop-down in the document library or site when the user opens it to select a content type.

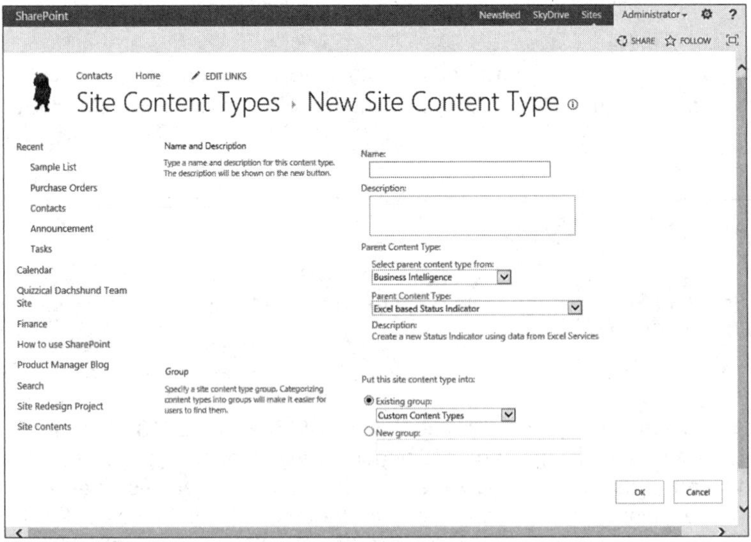

FIGURE 13.24 Creating a new content type.

TIP   Naming a content type in singular form (for example, Corporate Financial Report, Board Meeting Presentation) is recommended. This name appears under the New button for document libraries and lists when you are creating a new item and signifies to the user that clicking the option will create a single document.

Next, select the parent content type. This step is important because most of the time, you do not want to start the content type from scratch but instead want to rely on an existing content type. Selecting the parent content type is also important because changing it can (but does not necessarily) affect the child content type. For example, suppose you want to create a content type named External Contact that has exactly the same settings as the built-in Contact content type, but with additional columns to capture the contact's company address and company description (see Figure 13.25).

If you specify that the new content type is the child of the existing Contact content type, you must specify only the columns you want to add on top of the default Contact columns. Also, if in the future you decide that all contacts should have an additional column—for example, Birthday—adding it to the parent content type Contact can also add it automatically to the child External Contact, as shown later in this chapter in the section "Modify a Content Type."

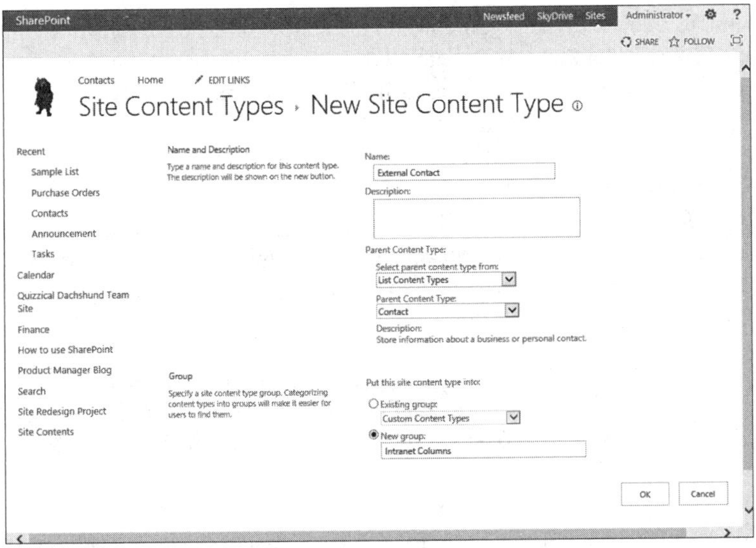

FIGURE 13.25   Creating a new content type named External Contact that inherits from the Contact content type.

After you select the content type main settings, click OK to create the content type. This selection opens the page where you can define the additional settings for the content type. For example, you can add, edit, or remove columns; set workflow settings; and perform other advanced settings (see Figure 13.26).

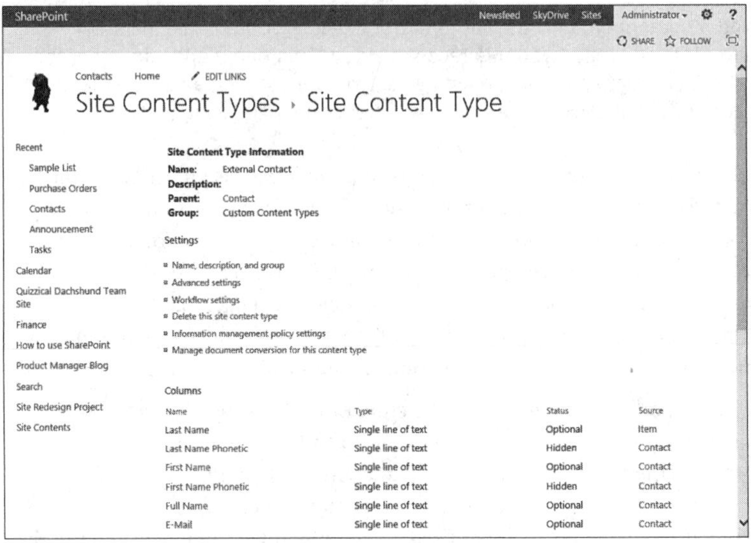

FIGURE 13.26   The settings page for a content type.

To add a column to a content type, scroll down to the bottom of the page shown in Figure 13.19, where you can find links to either create a new site column for the content type or add a column from the list of available site columns.

Modify a Content Type

Scenario/Problem: You want to modify an existing content type by changing its name or perhaps adding or removing a column and other settings.

Solution: To modify an existing content type, open the Site Settings page, as explained at the beginning of this chapter, and click Content Types in the Galleries section of the page. This selection opens a page where you can modify content types (refer to Figure 13.26).

Click the name of the content type you want to change to open the content type's setting page (refer to Figure 13.23). To edit the content type, change any setting available on this page, including the content type's name, description, and group; its workflow settings; its columns; and more advanced settings.

With every setting you change, you have an option to also update all content types inheriting from the content type. Updating them ensures that a change you make is also made to other content types created with the current content type as their parent. For example, if you add a Birthday column to the Contact content type and you want the change to also affect any other content types that inherit from Contact, such as External

Contact, select Yes under Update All Content Types Inheriting from This Type? when adding the site column (see Figure 13.27).

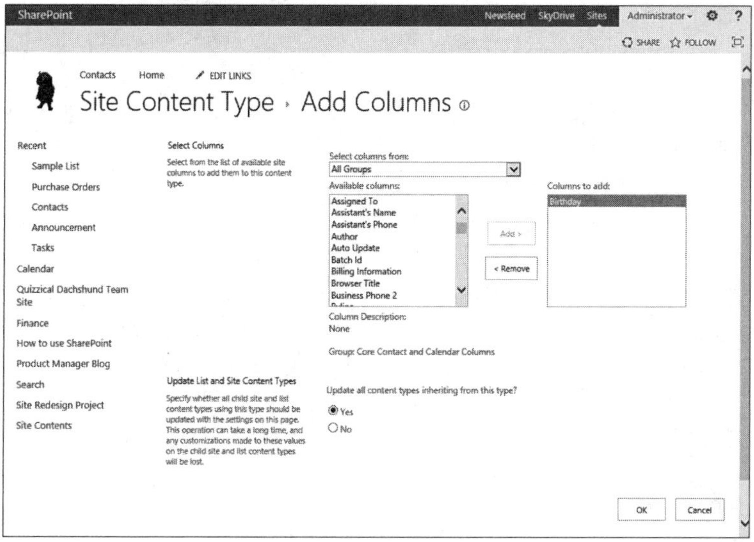

FIGURE 13.27   Adding a site column to a content type and updating the child content types.

CHAPTER 14

Managing Site Security

When you own or help administrate a SharePoint site, you might want to restrict or allow different users to do different tasks. For example, you might want certain users to be able to add items to lists and upload files to document libraries, while allowing other users to only read those items. You might want to give permission to approve items and files to a group of people, and you might want to allow another group to create new lists and libraries or even manage the site together with you.

When you are managing SharePoint security, it is important to remember that you can set the permissions for either a specific user or group of users from the corporate directory or from other forms of external user databases (depending on the configuration on the server). The corporate directory groups or groups in other external databases are defined by the administrators of those directories or databases and not as part of SharePoint. You can give them access to your SharePoint site (or restrict them) without having to manage the members of the group. For example, most organizations have a group for each division or team.

Furthermore, for security reasons, you might want to create groups that you manage on a site-by-site basis. These are called SharePoint groups, and SharePoint sites usually have several such groups set up—for example, the group of "visitors" who are allowed only to read content in the site and the group of "members" who are allowed to add content to the site. Most of the time, you should add users and groups to SharePoint groups to simplify changing the permissions later.

This chapter explains how to manage the security aspects of SharePoint sites. All these tasks assume that you have the required permission to manage the security of the site you are browsing.

Get to a Site's Permission Management Page

Scenario/Problem: You want to manage the security in a site.

Solution: To get to a site's security settings page, open the site's Site Actions menu and click the Site Settings option to open the site's settings page, then click the Site Permissions link under the Users and Permissions heading (see Figure 14.1).

Either method opens the site permission management page, where you can manage the permissions for the site (see Figure 14.2).

NOTE A list, library, or list item in a site might have unique permissions—that is, someone might have changed the permissions on it and broken its inheritance from the site. In this case, a yellow bar warns you that changes made in the site level will not impact those items, as shown in Figure 14.2.

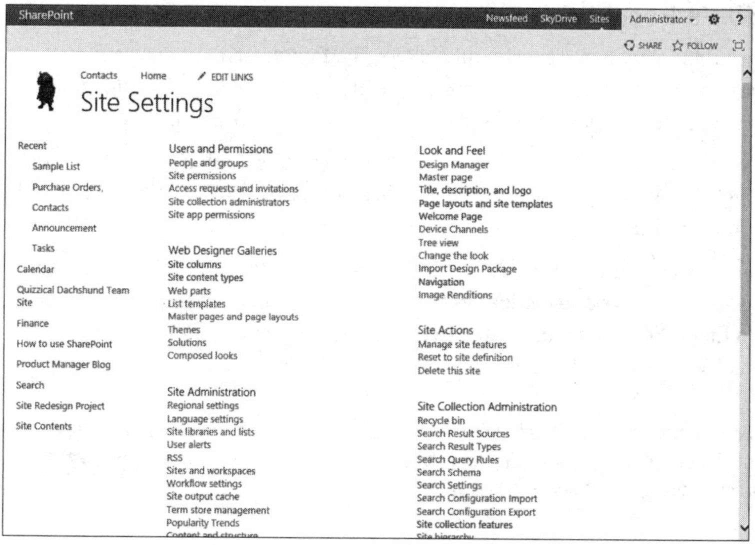

FIGURE 14.1   Opening a site's permission management page from the Site Settings page.

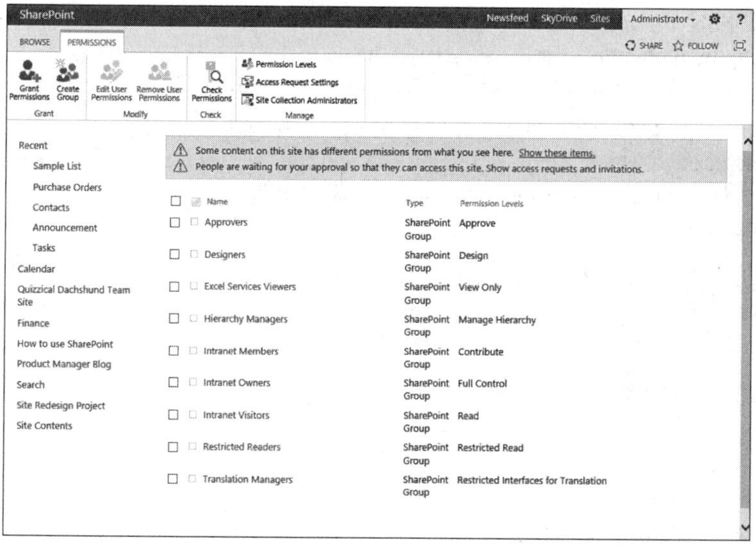

FIGURE 14.2   A site's security management page with a yellow bar alerting you that some content in the site isn't using the permissions on the page.

Get to a Site's People and Groups Settings Page

A useful page when managing security on a site is the People and Groups settings page. This page allows you to browse through the groups available in the site and see which users and security groups are assigned to each SharePoint group.

To get to a site's People and Groups page, open the site's Site Actions menu and click the Site Settings option in the menu. In the Site Settings page, click on the People and Groups link (refer to Figure 14.1).

The People and Groups page shows the names of the available SharePoint groups in the left navigation pane. You can click on them to see the users and security groups that belong in them. For example, Figure 14.6 later in this chapter shows John Doe in the SharePoint Team Site Visitors group.

> **TIP**   If your site has a lot of SharePoint groups, the left navigation pane will show only the first dozen or so. To see all the groups, click the More button at the bottom of the list of groups. This opens a page with all the groups in the site.

Check What Permissions a User or a Group Has on a Site

To check what permission a specific user or a group has on a site, open the site's Permissions Management page and click the Check Permissions button in the Check section of the ribbon (refer to Figure 14.2). The dialog that appears allows you to select a user or group by typing the user name or group name in the User/Group box. You then perform a check by using the Check Now button (see Figure 14.3).

When you click Check Now, the dialog displays the permission levels the user or group has and through which group. In Figure 14.4 you can see that the user Jane Doe has been given some permissions directly, and she has other permissions because she belongs to a group.

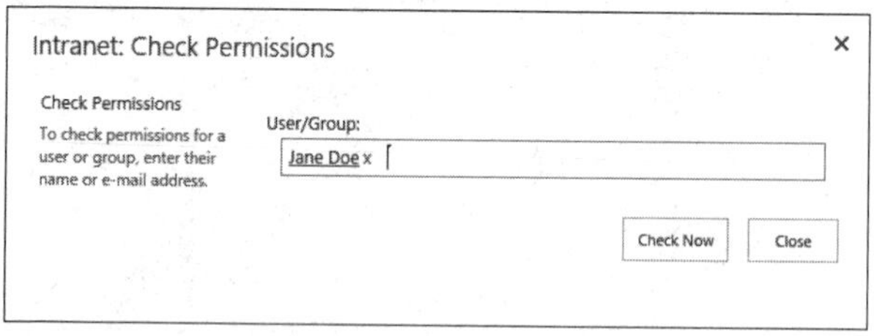

FIGURE 14.3   The Check Permissions dialog.

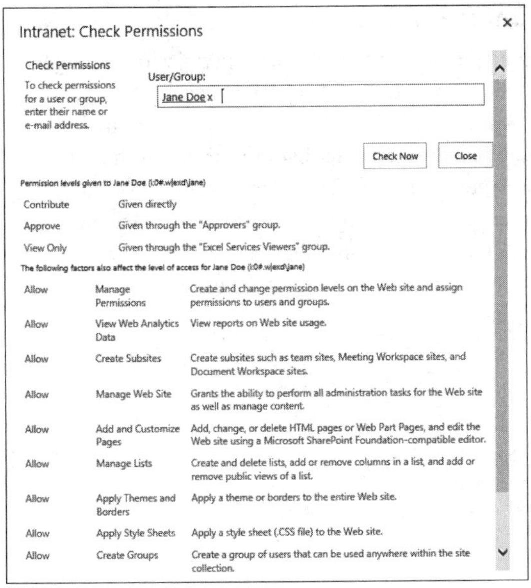

FIGURE 14.4   The Check Permissions dialog, showing the results of a check.

Assign Users' Permissions on a Site

Scenario/Problem: You want to assign a user or a group permissions to a site or add a user to an existing group.

Solution: To allow users to view a site to which they previously didn't have access, you can either add them to one of the SharePoint groups or add them to the site directly, without adding them to a specific group. The following sections explain how to perform these options.

TIP   As mentioned earlier in this chapter, always adding users to SharePoint groups is recommended because doing so makes the permissions easier to manage in the future.

NOTE   A site normally inherits permissions from its parent site (unless the site is a root site and doesn't have a parent). Therefore, you might not be able to edit a site's permissions unless you break the site's inheritance, using the Stop Inheriting Permissions option in the Permission Tools ribbon in the site's security page. You might want to manage the security of the parent site and not the current site, so you should make sure you want to break the inheritance.

Add or Remove Users in a SharePoint Group

To add a user to a security group in a site, navigate to the site's permission management page, as explained earlier in this chapter. In the Permission Tools ribbon, click the Grant Permissions button. The Grant Permissions dialog appears, allowing you to select the user or group and to which SharePoint group that user or group should be added (see Figure 14.5). By default, when you click Grant Permissions, this dialog defaults to adding the user or group to the Members group—with the Contribute permission set. If you want to change that, click on the Show Options link at the bottom of the dialog to see the drop-down menu of groups and permission sets you can choose from instead as shown in Figure 14.5.

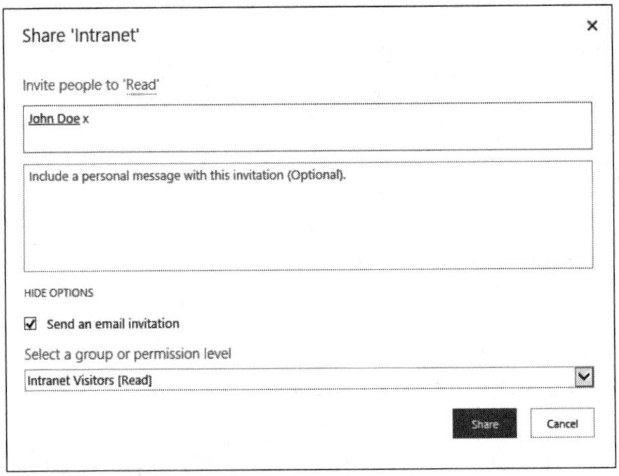

FIGURE 14.5 The Grant Permissions dialog allows you to add users to a site group.

On the Grant Permissions page use the Add Users box to type the names of the people you want to add (separated with semicolons—for example, John doe;Jane smith). For example, to add a person as a visitor to the site, type that person's user name in the Users/Groups box and select the site's visitors group from the permissions level drop-down (refer to Figure 14.5). When you are finished selecting the users and the group to which they should belong, click the Share button.

The page showing the people in the group is updated to show the people you added (see Figure 14.6). For instruction on how to see who is in a SharePoint group, see "Get to a Site's People and Groups Settings Page," earlier in this chapter.

To remove people from the group, navigate to the page for that group (see "Get to a Site's People and Groups Settings Page," earlier in this chapter) and select the check boxes next to their names. Open the Site Actions menu on the toolbar and then select Remove Users from Group (see Figure 14.7).

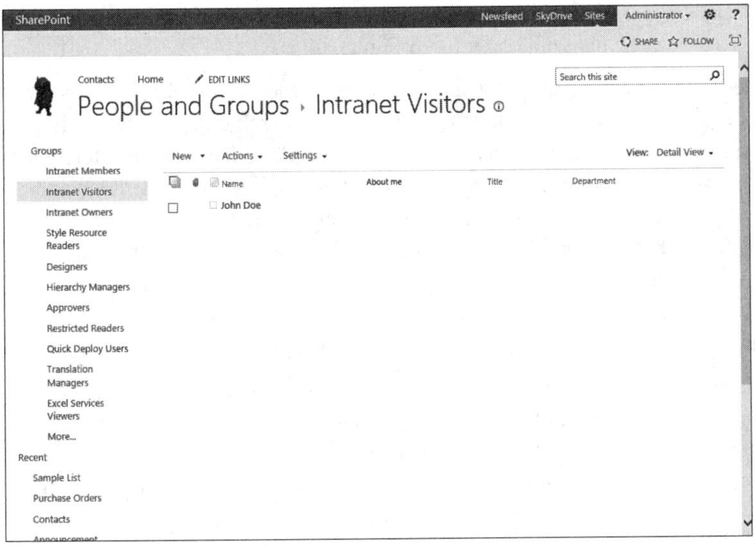

FIGURE 14.6   The user John Doe has been added to the Intranet Visitors group.

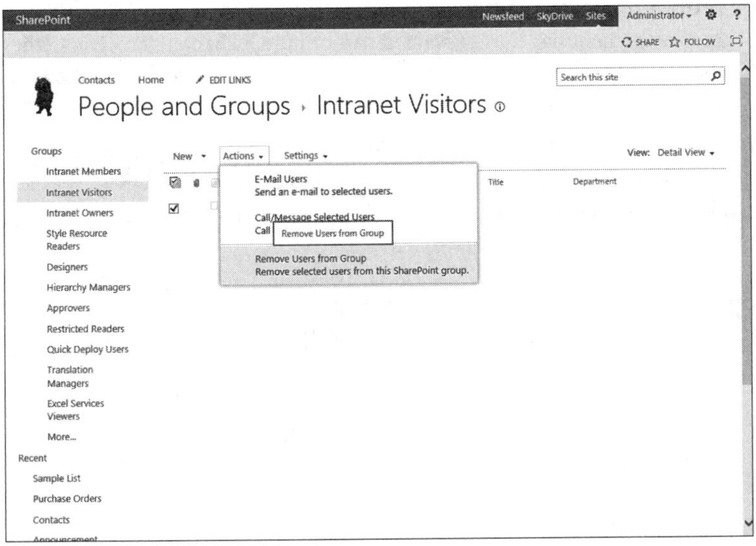

FIGURE 14.7   Removing a user from a group.

Add Users' Permissions Directly to or Remove Them from a Site

You might not want to add a user to a SharePoint group in a site but instead might want to give a user a specific set of permissions unrelated to a specific group. In this case, navigate to the site's security page and click the Grant Permissions button in the Permission Tools ribbon (refer to Figure 14.2). In the dialog that appears, select the users and select what permissions they have on the site by choosing a permission level instead of a group in the Share dialog (refer to Figure 14.5).

You can either type the names of the people you want to add in the Users/Groups box at the top or click the Address Book icon to use a people search dialog to select the users. Then select the permission levels you want the people to have on the site. You can select more than one permission level; for example, if you select Contribute and Approve, you allow the users you selected to add list items and files to the site and approve documents that they or other people have added. Remember that the higher permission always wins, so the user or security group has all the permissions from all the permission levels. To learn how to create a customized permission level, see "Create Permission Levels for a Site," later in this chapter.

To remove users from a site, open the site's permission management page (see "Get to a Site's Permission Management Page," earlier in this chapter), select the users in the page, and then click the Remove User Permissions button in the Modify section of the ribbon. This removes the users from the site, including any SharePoint groups the users belonged to.

Change Permissions of Users or SharePoint Groups in a Site

To change the permissions that are allocated to a user or group in a site, navigate to the site's permission management page, as explained earlier in this chapter. To change the permission levels, select the users or groups that you want to change and click the Edit User Permissions button in the Modify section of the ribbon.

The Edit Permissions dialog that opens allows you to set what permissions those users or groups will have (see Figure 14.8). After you select them, click OK to set the permission levels. To learn how to create a customized permission level, see "Create Permission Levels for a Site," later in this chapter.

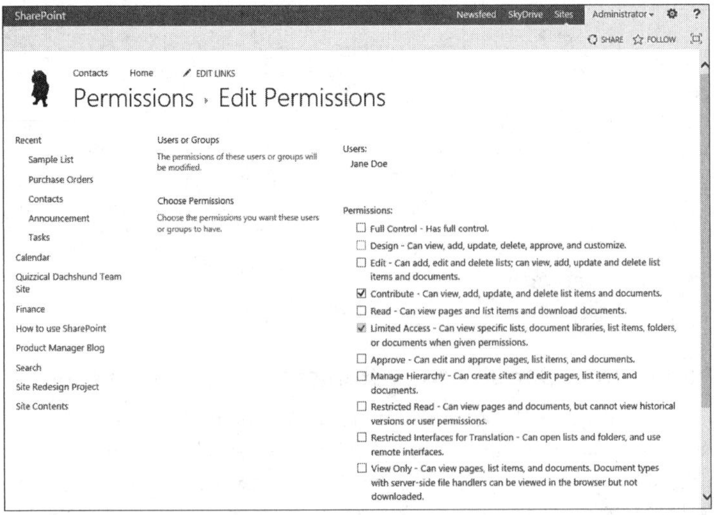

FIGURE 14.8   Selecting the permissions users and/or groups should have.

Create a SharePoint Group for a Site

Scenario/Problem: You want to create a SharePoint group so that you can manage who is in the group. You then want to assign permission to everyone in the group to sites, lists, libraries, and list items.

Solution: By default, when you create a site, SharePoint automatically creates some groups for you to use in that site. To create a new SharePoint group, open the site permissions settings page, as shown earlier in this chapter, and then click the Create Group button in the Grant section of the ribbon (refer to Figure 14.2).

The page for creating a new SharePoint group has several options you can set for the group (see Figure 14.9). You can modify all these settings later by editing the group's settings.

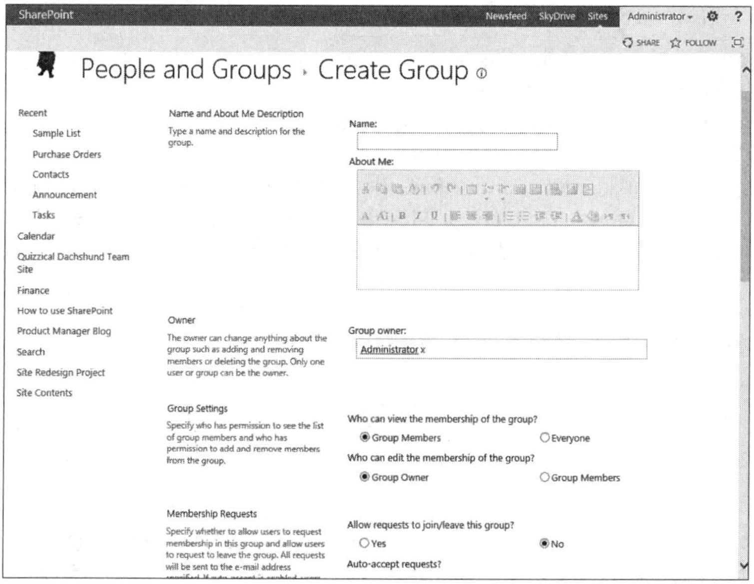

FIGURE 14.9   The SharePoint group creation page.

The first options are the name for the group and its description. The next option is the owner of the group. This setting defaults to you, but you can choose any other user. You just need to make sure the user you choose has permissions to access the site. The owner can add and remove users from the group, as well as change the group's settings, even if the owner doesn't have permissions to manage the site itself. This means you can make anyone an owner of a group without giving that user permissions to manage other aspects of the site.

> **TIP**   If you want more than one user to be the group's owner, you can specify a different SharePoint group as the owner of your group.

In the Group Settings section, you can define who can see the list of people who have been added to the group; the options are everyone or just the people who are members of the group. Also, you can define whether only the owner can add and remove members or whether anyone who is a member can do so (effectively making the group self-managing).

The next section on this page, Membership Requests, enables you to define whether people can send requests to join or be removed from the group. If you want to enable this option, you must specify an e-mail address to which the requests will be sent. Users then have the option of sending requests to join the group when viewing it. You can also choose that if a user requests to join the group, the request should be automatically accepted.

In the next section of the page, you can define what permission levels the group will have on the site. To learn how to create a customized permission level, see "Create Permission Levels for a Site," later in this chapter.

Finally, the last two sections of the page allow you to configure the group as an e-mail distribution list, and to create an archive list that will hold e-mails sent to the e-mail list. This is an advanced feature that requires the SharePoint administrator to configure and allow it. When allowed, you can specify an e-mail address for the group—and sending an e-mail to that address will distribute the e-mail to all members of the group. The archive list option allows you to create a list, or use an existing one, and then all e-mails sent to the group's e-mail address will appear in that list automatically.

Edit a SharePoint Group's Settings

> **Scenario/Problem:** You want to change the settings for an existing SharePoint group.

Solution: To change a SharePoint group's settings, navigate to the site's People and Groups settings page, as shown earlier in this chapter, and then click the name of the group in the left navigation bar. Open the Settings drop-down menu and click the Group Settings option (see Figure 14.10). The page that opens enables you to modify the settings for the group (see Figure 14.11).

> **NOTE**   Although the group's settings page allows you to modify the settings for the group, it does not provide an option to change the group's security settings. To do that, use the method described in "Change Permissions of Users or SharePoint Groups in a Site," earlier in this chapter.

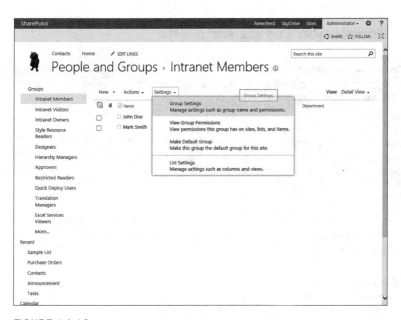

FIGURE 14.10   Getting to a SharePoint group's settings page.

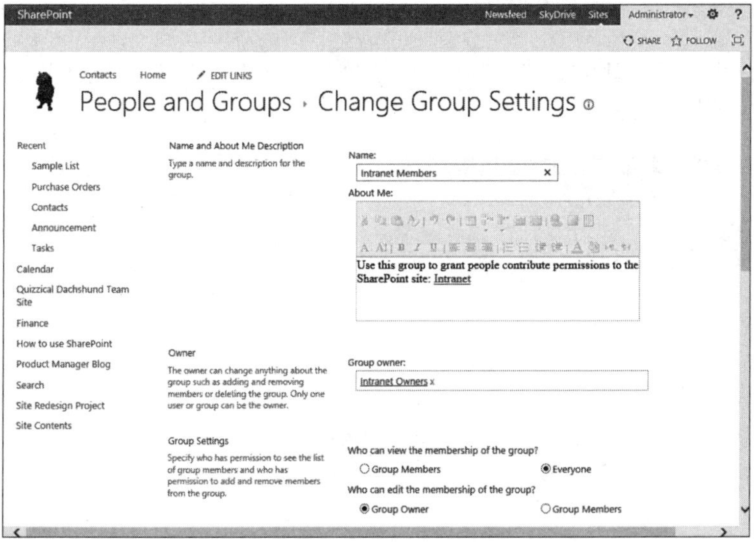

FIGURE 14.11   The Intranet Members group's settings page.

Create Permission Levels for a Site

Scenario/Problem: Earlier in this chapter, you saw that to assign permissions to users or groups, you can choose from a predefined list of permission levels, such as Readers, Contributors, and Approvers. If you want to create a permission level that differs from the existing permission levels, you can create a custom permission level. For example, you might want to create a permission level that enables users to view and delete items or files but not edit them, or maybe you want to create a permission level that allows users to view the site and be able to create subsites but not edit items in the site.

Solution: To create permission levels, open the site's permissions management page and click the Permission Levels button in the Manage section of the ribbon (refer to Figure 14.2).

NOTE   If you are working on a subsite, by default the permission levels are inherited from the parent site. Although you can still edit them (an action that breaks the inheritance), you should make sure this is what you actually want to do. If you want to make sure you are editing the permission levels in the top site, use the Manage Parent option in the Inheritance section of the Edit ribbon of the permission management page to get to the parent site's permissions management page.

On the Permission Levels page, you can see and manage all the existing permission levels (see Figure 14.12).

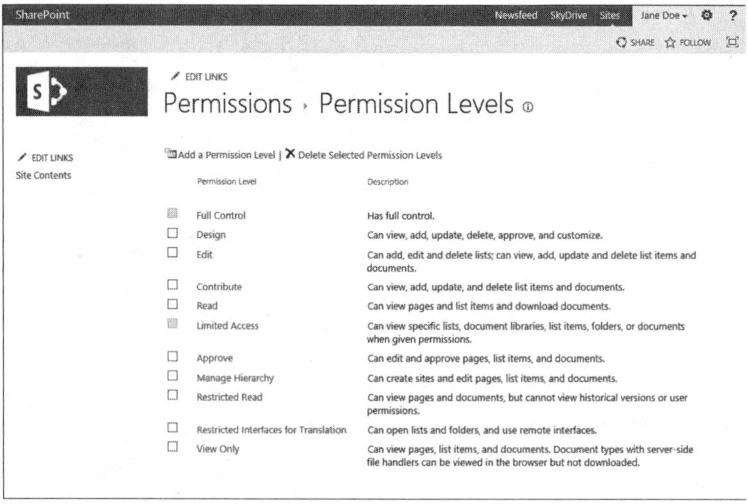

FIGURE 14.12   The Permission Levels page.

To create a new permission level, click the Add a Permission Level button on the toolbar. The Add a Permission Level page opens (see Figure 14.13). On this page, you can define the name for the new permission level and what permissions set it should include. Simply select the permissions you want the permission level to include and click the Create button at the bottom of the screen.

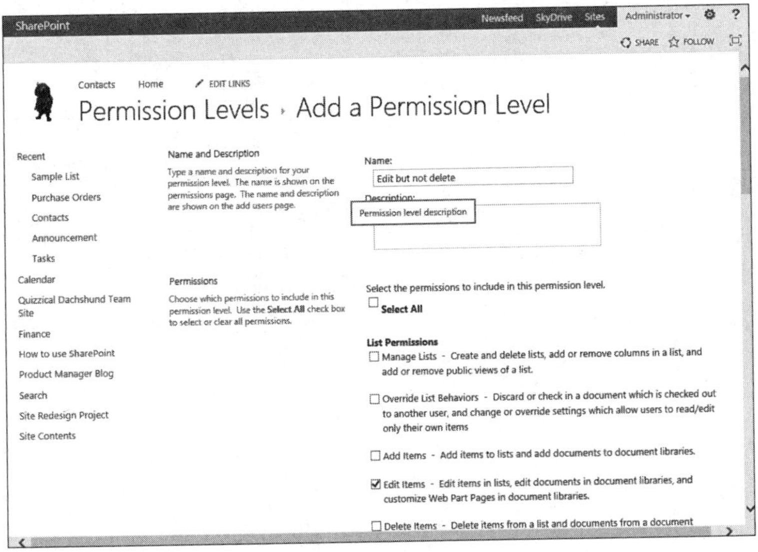

FIGURE 14.13   Creating a new permission level that allows users to edit but not delete.

CHAPTER 15

Managing an Office 365 SharePoint Site

IN THIS CHAPTER

When you own or help administrate an Office 365 SharePoint site, you might want to create new sites and manage settings for all sites. You might want to create a private site, available only to people who work with you and that requires logging on, or you might want to create an open Internet site, available to whomever navigates to your site.

> **NOTE**   At the time of writing this book, the 2013 version of Office 365 was still in "Preview" mode, and so the figures and instructions might be slightly different from the final release version. Also, Microsoft keeps updating Office 365, and options might move around, or new ones might be added.

Sign In to Office 365 SharePoint Administrator Console

> **Scenario/Problem:** You want to manage your Office 365 SharePoint environment.

Solution: To get to the administrator console, use the link provided to you by the Office 365 provider (which differs in each country). Normally, the link should be https://portal.microsoftonline.com/admin/default.aspx, but different providers might require you to log in using a different link.

When you open this link, the site requires you to sign in. Use the user name and password either given to you, or that you selected when you created the Office 365 account, as shown in Figure 15.1.

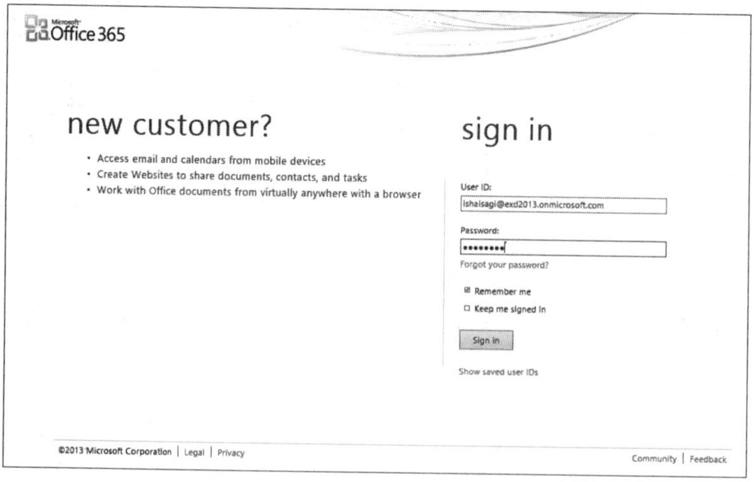

FIGURE 15.1   Signing in to the Office 365 Administrator Console.

The screen that opens next depends on the Office 365 plan you have purchased. This is the administrator center for all Office 365 features (not just SharePoint) as shown in Figure 15.2.

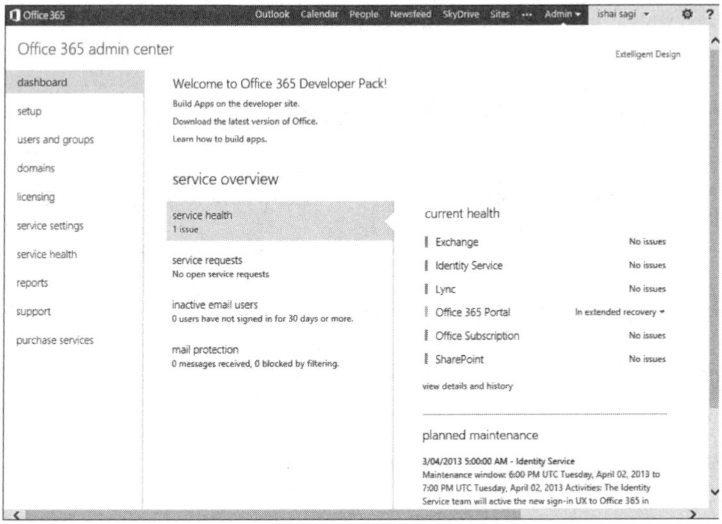

FIGURE 15.2   The Admin Center for Office 365 Enterprise.

In the Admin Center, click the Admin link in the top-right side of the page to open the administration options drop-down menu, and then click SharePoint from the menu to open the SharePoint Admin Center as shown in Figure 15.3.

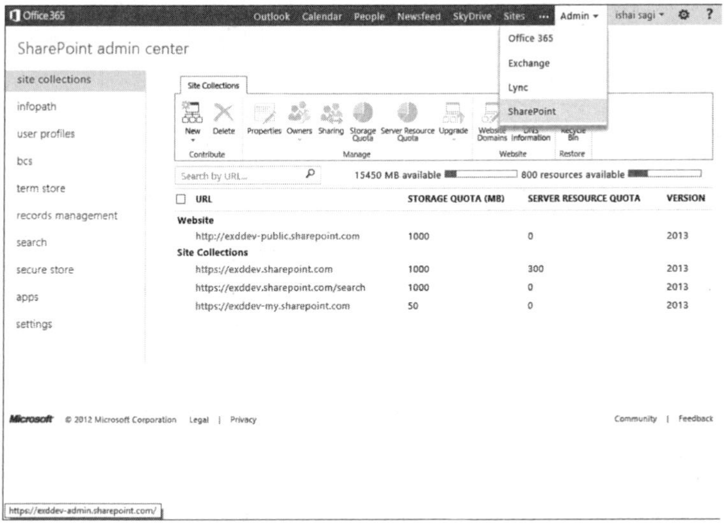

FIGURE 15.3   The Admin drop-down menu with the SharePoint option, and the SharePoint Admin Center page.

The Admin Center shows you a variety of options on the left, which changes based on the plan you have purchased (for example, you might or might not have the user profiles and InfoPath options shown in Figure 15.3 with cheaper plans).

In the main section of the page you see a list of existing site collections, which you can then manage, and a ribbon with actions for those site collections.

Create a New Private Site Collection

Scenario/Problem: You want to create a site only accessible to people in your company.

Solution: To create a private site, navigate to the SharePoint Admin Center page (refer to Figure 15.3) and click the New button in the ribbon to open the drop-down menu shown in Figure 15.4. In this menu, choose Private Site Collection.

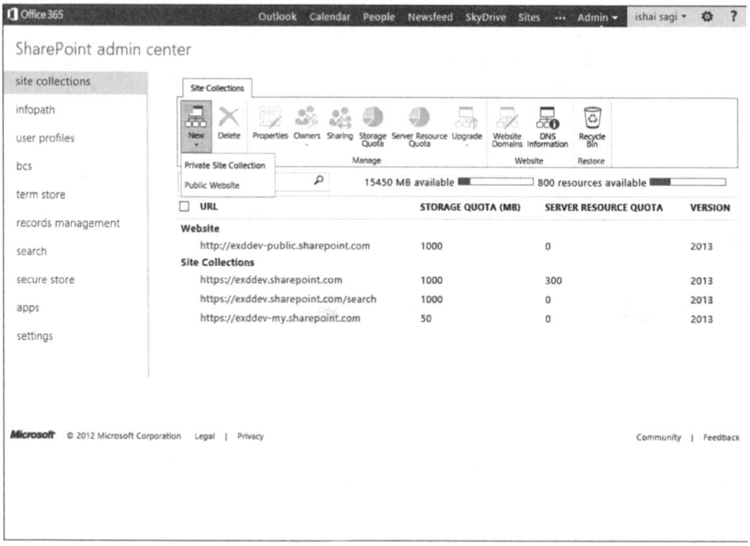

FIGURE 15.4   The New button drop-down menu with Private Site Collection and Public Site options.

This opens the New Site Collection dialog, which is similar to the new subsite dialog described in "Create a Subsite" in Chapter 12, "Creating Subsites." You have to specify the site's title (which can be changed later), the website address, and the template for the site. However, when creating a site collection you also have to specify an administrator for that site collection (this person will have full access to everything in the site) and storage quota—restricting how much space the site can take in the system, as well as the amount of documents users can upload to the site or its subsites.

> **TIP** You should consider the quota carefully, as in Office 365 you will have to pay extra if you go over the limit of what your contract offers. Consider the amount of information people will need from any particular site, and spread the quotas across the different sites as you see fit.

Additionally, in Office 365, you might have several domains for site collections, and so, unlike the dialog shown in Chapter 12, this dialog allows you to first choose which domain the site will be under. If you only have one domain, only that domain will be shown in the drop-down list under Web Site Address. Finally, because Office 365 is a global solution, and you might be sharing the site with people from different time zones, you have to specify the default time zone for the site, as shown in Figure 15.5.

> **NOTE** A site administrator (also known as site collection administrator) can do everything and see everything in the entire site collection (the site, and all the sites under it). Restricting access from the person you specify in this option within the site (for example, not allowing them to read a document or edit a list) is not possible.

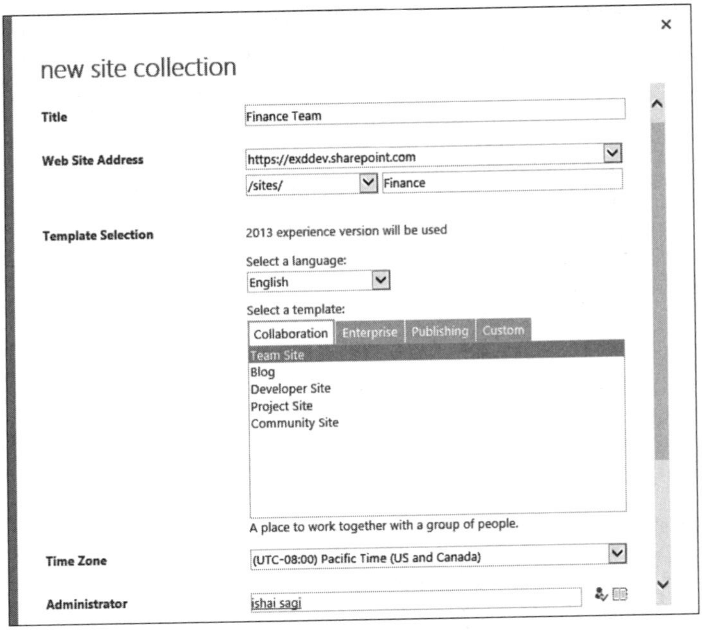

FIGURE 15.5 Creating a new site collection, and specifying an administrator, a time zone, and a domain.

To create the site collection, click OK. This takes you back to the SharePoint Admin Center page, and shows the site with a process animation next to it while the site is still being created, as shown in Figure 15.6. Wait for the site collection to finish provisioning. When the process is done, the animation disappears and the link to the site becomes available for you to click on.

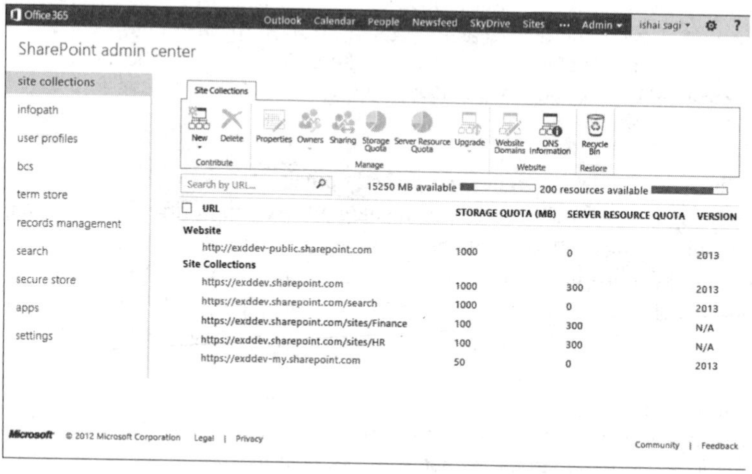

FIGURE 15.6   The site collection list with two sites in the process of provisioning.

When you click on the link for a site collection, a dialog appears with the properties of the site collection and a link that will open the actual site in a new window, as shown in Figure 15.7.

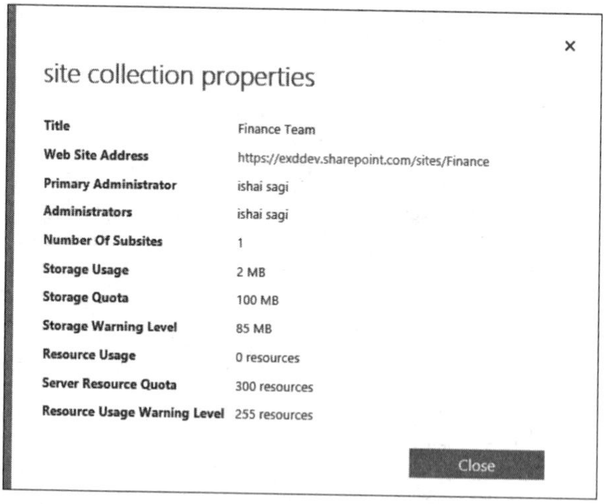

FIGURE 15.7   The Site Collection Properties dialog.

Create a New Public Site Collection

Scenario/Problem: You want to create an Internet site with Office 365.

Solution: To create an Internet site, navigate to the SharePoint Admin Center page (refer to Figure 15.3) and click the New button in the ribbon to open the drop-down menu shown in Figure 15.4. In this menu, choose Public Site. The dialog that opens asks you for a site title, an address (in which you can select from the list of domains you have registered with your Office 365 account), a language, a time zone, the site's administrator and quota—similarly to the dialog shown in Figure 15.5, but in this dialog you can only pick from the list of domains, and not specify any other URL addresses, as shown in Figure 15.8.

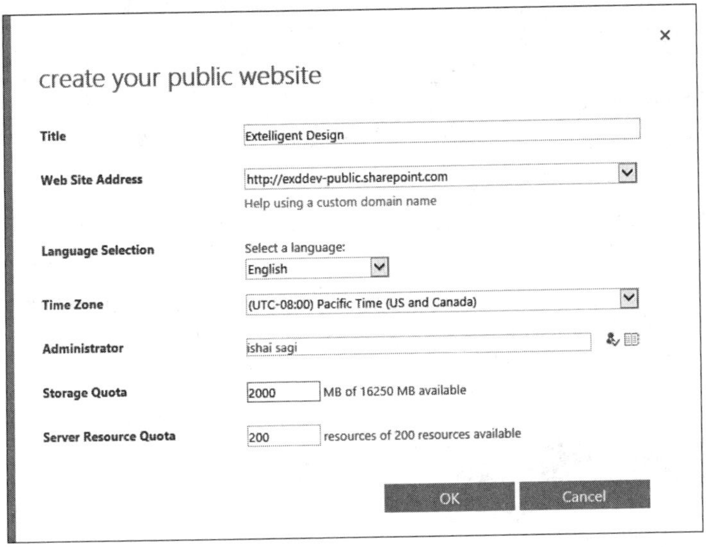

	✕
create your public website	

Title	Extelligent Design
Web Site Address	http://exddev-public.sharepoint.com ▾
	Help using a custom domain name
Language Selection	Select a language: English ▾
Time Zone	(UTC-08:00) Pacific Time (US and Canada) ▾
Administrator	ishai sagi
Storage Quota	2000 MB of 16250 MB available
Server Resource Quota	200 resources of 200 resources available

OK   Cancel

FIGURE 15.8   Creating a new public site collection.

After clicking OK, you are redirected back to the SharePoint Admin Center, where you see an animation next to the link to the site, signifying that the site is being provisioned. Wait for the animation to stop, and click the link of the site collection to open the dialog for the site collection properties. This dialog will have two links to the actual site—one for you as a site owner (who will need to edit the site) and another—the public website address for the visitors to the site. Clicking either of these opens a new window. When you have just created a site, it is not yet available to visitors from the Internet, until you decide to do so by clicking on the Make Website Online button in the new site, as shown in Figure 15.9.

> **NOTE**   To have your site accessible to people over the Internet you must set up DNS for it. To do that, click the DNS Information button in the ribbon, and follow the instructions provided in that dialog.

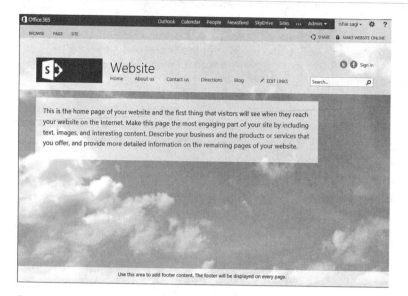

FIGURE 15.9   A new public site, with the Make Website Online button at the top.

When you click the Make Website Online button, a dialog appears explaining that the website is currently only available to users who are logged on (and to whom you have to grant permissions—refer to Chapter 14, "Managing Site Security"), and a button to make the website online, as shown in Figure 15.10.

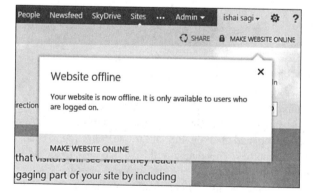

FIGURE 15.10   The Make Website Online dialog.

Clicking the button opens another confirmation dialog, in which you confirm again that you are ready to make the site online. After you approve that dialog, a final dialog appears telling you the site is now available to anyone on the Internet. Open it from another computer, or from another browser to see it as visitors will see it—without the editing controls, as shown in Figure 15.11.

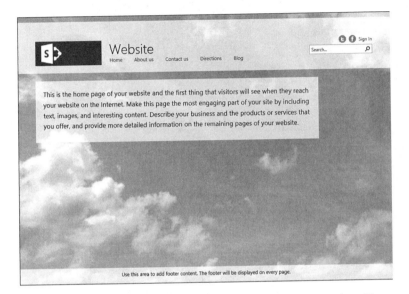

FIGURE 15.11   The new Internet site is shown to visitors without the editing controls.

APPENDIX A

Common Keyboard Shortcuts

Sometimes using the keyboard is more effective than using the mouse, especially if the graphical designer of the page moved things around and you are not certain where on the page they are. Knowing the keyboard shortcuts can help you quickly get where you want to go.

Like the rest of this book, this appendix is useful both to anyone using a SharePoint site and to those who are adding or editing content in a SharePoint site. Also, some of these shortcut combinations work in all pages, whereas others are unique to certain types of pages. Each section lists where the shortcuts can be used.

Using Keyboard Shortcuts

The keyboard shortcut combinations are described in this book as a series of keys that you need to press. If you must press several keys at the same time, this is expressed with the + sign. If after pressing a certain key combination you must release the keys before pressing another, this is expressed with "and then." For example, if you want to switch a calendar view to the daily view (instead of the monthly view), use the shortcut Alt+period and then Enter, which should be read as instructions to hold down the Alt key and the period key (.) at the same time, and then release them and press Enter.

Keyboard Shortcuts for Anyone Using a SharePoint Site

General Shortcuts

To get to the:	Press this:
First link in the top navigation bar	Alt+1 and then Enter
Help	Alt+6 and then Enter
Search box	Alt+S and then Enter

Site Personal Settings menu	Alt+/ and then Enter
All Site Content	Alt+3 and then Enter
Next web part	Alt+W

Top Navigation

To get to the:	Press this:
Top navigation tab	Alt+1 (Enter to select)
Next navigation tab	Tab (Enter to select)
Previous navigation tab	Shift+Tab (Enter to select)

List or Library Views

To get to the:	Press this:
(Calendar view) Previous day, week, or month	Alt+Shift+< and then Enter
(Calendar view) Next day, week, or month	Alt+Shift+> and then Enter

Ribbon Shortcuts

To:	Press this:
Skip ribbon commands	Alt+Y and then Enter

Keyboard Shortcuts for Authors and Editors

Editing List Items or File Properties

To get to the:	Press this:
Cancel button	Alt+C
Save button (or OK button)	Alt+O
Save and Close (in a survey response)	Alt+S
(Date picker control) Previous month	Alt+Shift+< and then Enter
(Date picker control) Next month	Alt+Shift+> and then Enter

Editing Pages in a Web Part Tool Pane

To get to the:	Press this:
OK button	Alt+O
Apply button	Alt+Y
Cancel button	Alt+C

All Site Content Page

To get to the:	Press this:
Site Workflows button	Alt+W and then Enter

Using the Rich Text Editor

To get to the:	Press this:
Right-to-Left text direction button	Ctrl+Shift+<
Left-to-Right text direction button	Ctrl+Shift+>
Bold button	Ctrl+B
Copy button	Ctrl+C
Center button	Ctrl+E
Italics button	Ctrl+I
Align Left button	Ctrl+L
Increase Indent button	Ctrl+M
Decrease Indent button	Ctrl+Shift+M
Font Size menu	Ctrl+Shift+P
Align Right button	Ctrl+R
Underline button	Ctrl+U
Paste button	Ctrl+V
Cut button	Ctrl+X

APPENDIX B

Useful Links

This appendix contains a collection of useful links that you might want to use to quickly get to a certain place in a SharePoint site. In this appendix, the placeholder {Site} is used for the site path. For example, if you want to get to the View All Site Content page of a site, the link would be written as {Site}/_layouts/viewlsts.aspx. To get to that page for a site with the path http://sharepoint, you replace the {Site} placeholder with the path http://sharepoint and add the rest of the text to complete the link: http://sharepoint/_layouts/viewlsts.aspx.

Similarly, some links include the path to a specific page, in which case the placeholder {Page} is used. You simply replace the placeholder with the full path to that page.

Useful Links for Anyone Using a SharePoint Site

The View All Site Content page	{Site}/15/_layouts/ viewlsts.aspx
My Memberships page	{Site}/_layouts/15/mymember- ships.aspx
My Links page	{Site}/15/_layouts/myquick- links.aspx
Add a Link to My Links page	{Site}/15/_layouts/ quicklinks.aspx
My Site page	{Site}/_layouts/mysite.aspx
My Alerts page	{Site}/15/_layouts/ MySubs.aspx
Site Content and Structure page	{Site}/15/_layouts/SiteManager. aspx
Search Current Site and Below page	{Site}/15/_layouts/ OSSSearchResults.aspx

Useful Links for Authors and Editors

Manage Content page	`{Site}/15/_layouts/mcontent.aspx`
List of last content you edited	`{Site}/15/_layouts/myinfo.aspx`
Create a new page	`{Site}/_layouts/CreatePage.aspx` (in a publishing site)
Web part page maintenance	`{Page}?contents=1`

Useful Links for Site Managers

Manage Site Settings	`{Site}/_layouts/settings.aspx`
Manage Sub Webs Page	`{Site}/_layouts/mngsubwebs.aspx`
Manage Navigation Options	`{Site}/_layouts/navoptions.aspx`
Modify Top Navigation aspx	`{Site}/_layouts/AreaNavigationSettings.`
Manage People and Groups	`{Site}/_layouts/people.aspx`
Create New Subsite	`{Site}/_layouts/newsbweb.aspx`
Manage Alerts	`{Site}/_layouts/ SiteSubs.aspx`
Delete Current Site	`{Site}/_layouts/deleteweb.aspx`

INDEX

A

M

publishing sites
managed metadata
choosing term sets for navigation, 310-311
configuring a friendly URL, 313-314
editing term sets for navigation, 311-312
managed metadata navigation, 310
modifying navigation bars, 307

Q

Quick Edit view, 127
adding
list items, 129
multiple list items from Excel, 129-130
creating, 204
switching to, 70, 128

R

Range Text setting, Rating Scale columns, 174
Rating Scale columns, 172-174
reading
opening documents for, 54-55
permissions page, 271-272
recovering deleted files/list items, 122-123
regional settings, changing, 40-43
rejecting files/list items, 134-135
relationship behavior, Lookup columns, 168
removing
alerts, 75
columns, lists/document libraries, 181-182
content types from lists/document libraries, 191-192
links
from navigation bars, 309
web parts, 262
notes, from notes board, 97-98
permissions from sites, 327-328

synchronized folders, SkyDrive Pro, 140
users in SharePoint groups, 326
renaming
document libraries, 185
lists, 185
restoring earlier versions of files/list items, 134
reusing web parts, 263
ribbons, 12, 36-40
Calendar ribbon, 37
Show Ribbon, 36-37
switching between, 37

S

Search Center, 83-84
search results, alerts, 82
searching, 80
advanced searches, SharePoint Server, 85-88
for files/list items within a specific list or library, 80
for people, SharePoint Server, 88
Search Center, 83-84
searching for files/list items in the entire SharePoint environment, 80-83
security
People and Groups settings page, 324
permission levels, creating for sites, 332-333
permission management page, 322
permissions. See permissions
assigning users' permissions on a site, 325
checking, 324
SharePoint groups, adding/removing users, 326
Security Notice dialog, 76
selecting multiple items in views, 222-221
sending links to files/libraries by email, 58
Share options, granting permissions, 274
SharePoint 365, 7
determining what a site is based on, 8-9

ISHAI SAGI

SharePoint® 2013
HOW-TO

SAMS

Safari
Books Online

FREE
Online Edition

Your purchase of *SharePoint 2013 How-To* includes access to a free online edition for 45 days through the **Safari Books Online** subscription service. Nearly every Sams book is available online through **Safari Books Online**, along with thousands of books and videos from publishers such as Addison-Wesley Professional, Cisco Press, Exam Cram, IBM Press, O'Reilly Media, Prentice Hall, Que, and VMware Press.

Safari Books Online is a digital library providing searchable, on-demand access to thousands of technology, digital media, and professional development books and videos from leading publishers. With one monthly or yearly subscription price, you get unlimited access to learning tools and information on topics including mobile app and software development, tips and tricks on using your favorite gadgets, networking, project management, graphic design, and much more.

Addison Wesley · AdobePress · ALPHA · Cisco Press · FT Press · IBM Press · Microsoft Press · New Riders · O'REILLY · Peachpit Press · PRENTICE HALL · QUE · Redbooks · SAMS · SAS Publishing · vmware PRESS · WILEY · wrox